Windows NT Server 4 Enterprise, Second Edition

201 West 103rd Street, Indianapolis, Indiana 46290

MCSE TestPrep: Windows NT Server 4 Enterprise, Second Edition

Copyright © 1999 by New Riders Publishing

All rights reserved. No part of this book shall be reproduced, stored in a retrieval system, or transmitted by any means, electronic, mechanical, photocopying, recording, or otherwise, without written permission from the publisher. No patent liability is assumed with respect to the use of the information contained herein. Although every precaution has been taken in the preparation of this book, the publisher and author assume no responsibility for errors or omissions. Neither is any liability assumed for damages resulting from the use of the information contained herein.

International Standard Book Number: 0-7357-0009-5

Library of Congress Catalog Card Number: 98-88512

Printed in the United States of America

First Printing: November, 1998

00 99 98   4 3 2 1

Trademarks

All terms mentioned in this book that are known to be trademarks or service marks have been appropriately capitalized. New Riders Publishing cannot attest to the accuracy of this information. Use of a term in this book should not be regarded as affecting the validity of any trademark or service mark.

Warning and Disclaimer

Every effort has been made to make this book as complete and as accurate as possible, but no warranty or fitness is implied. The information provided is on an "as is" basis. The authors and the publisher shall have neither liability nor responsibility to any person or entity with respect to any loss or damages arising from the information contained in this book.

EXECUTIVE EDITOR
Mary Foote

ACQUISITIONS EDITOR
Steve Weiss

DEVELOPMENT EDITOR
Ami Frank

MANAGING EDITOR
Sarah Kearns

PROJECT EDITOR
Jennifer Chisholm

COPY EDITOR
Daryl Kessler

COVER DESIGNER
Ruth Lewis

BOOK DESIGNER
Barbara Kordesh

INDEXERS
Chris Barrick
Lisa Stumpf

TECHNICAL EDITORS
Bruce Ford
Walter Glenn

PRODUCTION
Cheryl Lynch

PROOFREADING
Mary Ellen Stephenson
Tricia Sterling

Contents at a Glance

Introduction	*xiii*
1 Planning	1
2 Installation and Configuration	49
3 Managing Resources	107
4 Connectivity	165
5 Monitoring and Optimization	219
6 Troubleshooting	275
Practice Exam 1	381
Practice Exam 2	399
Appendix A: Exam Strategies	*415*
Appendix B: Glossary	*433*
Appendix C: Fast Facts	*449*
Index	*473*

Table of Contents

1 Planning — 1

Practice Questions: Selecting the Appropriate Directory Services Architecture — 3

Answers & Explanations: Selecting the Appropriate Directory Services Architecture — 6

Further Review: Selecting the Appropriate Directory Services Architecture — 18
- Key Words — 18
- One-way Versus Two-way Trusts — 18
- Built-in NT Groups — 18
- Windows NT Domain Models — 19

Practice Questions: Planning the Fault-Tolerance Configurations for Windows NT Server 4.0 — 21

Answers & Explanations: Planning the Fault-Tolerance Configurations for Windows NT Server 4.0 — 25

Further Review: Planning the Fault-Tolerance Configurations for Windows NT Server 4.0 — 32
- Key Words — 32
- Supported Windows NT RAID Levels — 32

Practice Questions: Selecting the Proper Protocol — 34

Answers & Explanations: Selecting the Proper Protocol — 39

Further Review: Selecting the Proper Protocol — 47
- Key Words — 47
- Windows NT Server Protocols — 47

Summary — 48

2 Installation and Configuration — 49

Practice Questions: Installing Windows NT in Various Server Roles — 51

Answers & Explanations: Installing Windows NT in Various Server Roles — 54

Further Review: Installing Windows NT in Various Server Roles — 58
- Key Words — 58
- Server Roles in Windows NT Server — 58

Practice Questions: Configuring Network Protocols and Bindings 60
Answers & Explanations: Configuring Network Protocols and Bindings 62
Further Review: Configuring Network Protocols and Bindings 66
    Key Words 66
    Additional Protocol Configuration 66
Practice Questions: Configuring Windows NT Server Core Services 67
Answers & Explanations: Configuring Windows NT Server Core Services 70
Further Review: Configuring Windows NT Server Core Services 79
    Key Words 79
    More on Directory Replication 79
Practice Questions: Configuring Hard Disks to Improve Performance 80
Answers & Explanations: Configuring Hard Disks to Improve Performance 83
Further Review: Configuring Hard Disks to Improve Performance 89
    Key Words 89
Practice Questions: Configuring Printers 90
Answers & Explanations: Configuring Printers 92
Further Review: Configuring Printers 95
    Key Words 95
    Adding a Printer 95
    Connecting to an Existing Network Printer 96
Practice Questions: Configuring Windows NT Server for Various Types of Clients 97
Answers & Explanations: Configuring Windows NT Server for Various Types of Clients 100
Further Review: Configuring Windows NT Server for Various Types of Clients 105
    Key Words 105
    Windows NT Clients 105
Summary 106

3 Managing Resources   107

Practice Questions: Managing User and Group Accounts 109
Answers & Explanations: Managing User and Group Accounts 112
Further Review: Managing User and Group Accounts 121
    Key Words 121
    Managing Windows NT User Rights 121
    Auditing Changes to the User Account Database 124

Practice Questions: Creating and Managing System Policies and User Profiles 125
Answers & Explanations: Creating and Managing System Policies and User Profiles 128
Further Review: Creating and Managing System Policies and User Profiles 138
 Key Words 138
 Additional System Policies Information 138
Practice Questions: Administering Remote Servers from Various Client Computers 140
Answers & Explanations: Administering Remote Servers from Various Client Computers 142
Further Review: Administering Remote Servers from Various Client Computers 148
 Key Words 148
Practice Questions: Managing Disk Resources 149
Answers & Explanations: Managing Disk Resources 152
Further Review: Managing Disk Resources 161
 Key Words 161
 The Windows NT Security Model 161
 Implementing File-level Auditing 162
 Auditing Logons and Logoffs 163
Summary 163

4 Connectivity   165

Practice Questions: Interoperability with NetWare 167
Answers & Explanations: Interoperability with NetWare 170
Further Review: Interoperability with NetWare 177
 Key Words 177
 Steps for Migrating from NetWare 177
Practice Questions: Installing and Configuring Multiprotocol Routing 178
Answers & Explanations: Installing and Configuring Multiprotocol Routing 181
Further Review: Installing and Configuring Multiprotocol Routing 187
 Key Words 187
Practice Questions: Installing and Configuring Internet Information Server 188
Answers & Explanations: Installing and Configuring Internet Information Server 190
Further Review: Installing and Configuring Internet Information Server 195
 Key Words 195

Practice Questions: Installing and Configuring Internet Services 196
Answers & Explanations: Installing and Configuring Internet Services 198
Further Review: Installing and Configuring Internet Services 202
   Key Words 202
Practice Questions: Remote Access Service (RAS) 203
Answers & Explanations: Remote Access Service (RAS) 206
Further Review: Remote Access Service (RAS) 217
   Key Words 217
Summary 218

5 Monitoring and Optimization 219

Practice Questions: Establishing a Baseline for Measuring System Performance 222
Answers & Explanations: Establishing a Baseline for Measuring System Performance 225
Further Review: Establishing a Baseline for Measuring System Performance 230
   Key Words 230
Practice Questions: Performance Monitoring 231
Answers & Explanations: Performance Monitoring 233
Further Review: Performance Monitoring 242
   Key Words 242
   An Overview of Performance Monitor 242
   What Resources Should You Monitor? 242
   Performance Analysis 244
Practice Questions: Analysis Using Network Monitor 245
Answers & Explanations: Analysis Using Network Monitor 247
   File Session Traffic 251
Further Review: Analysis Using Network Monitor 255
   Key Words 255
   Client-to-Server Browser Traffic 255
   Server-to-Server Traffic 255
Practice Questions: Identifying and Resolving Performance Bottlenecks 257
Answers & Explanations: Identifying and Resolving Performance Bottlenecks 260
Further Review: Identifying and Resolving Performance Bottlenecks 266
   Key Words 266
   Bottleneck Indicators 266

Practice Questions: Performance Optimization 267
Answers & Explanations: Performance Optimization 269
Further Review: Performance Optimization 274
    Key Words 274
Summary 274

6 Troubleshooting   275

Practice Questions: Solving Installation Failures 279
Answers & Explanations: Solving Installation Failures 282
Further Review: Solving Installation Failures 290
    Key Words 290
Practice Questions: Solving Boot Failures 291
Answers & Explanations: Solving Boot Failures 293
Further Review: Solving Boot Failures 303
    Key Words 303
Practice Questions: Solving Configuration and Registry Failures 304
Answers & Explanations: Solving Configuration and Registry Failures 306
Further Review: Solving Configuration and Registry Failures 312
    Key Words 312
Practice Questions: Solving Printer Problems 313
Answers & Explanations: Solving Printer Problems 316
Further Review: Solving Printer Problems 322
    Key Words 322
    Files Involved in the Windows NT Print Process 322
Practice Questions: Troubleshooting Remote Access Service 323
Answers & Explanations: Troubleshooting Remote Access Service 326
Further Review: Troubleshooting Remote Access Service 332
    Key Words 332
    Troubleshooting Other Issues with the Client 332
    Other Issues That Affect RAS Connections 332
Practice Questions: Solving Connectivity Problems 334
Answers & Explanations: Solving Connectivity Problems 337
Further Review: Solving Connectivity Problems 343
    Key Words 343
    Tools for Troubleshooting Connectivity Problems 343

Practice Questions: Solving Resource Access and Permissions Problems ... 345
Answers & Explanations: Solving Resource Access and Permissions Problems ... 348
Further Review: Solving Resource Access and Permissions Problems ... 353
   Key Words ... 353
   Combining Permissions ... 353
   Implementing Permissions in a Multidomain Environment ... 353
Practice Questions: Solving Fault-Tolerance Failures ... 355
Answers & Explanations: Solving Fault-Tolerance Failures ... 358
Further Review: Solving Fault-Tolerance Failures ... 366
   Key Words ... 366
   Backup Strategies ... 366
Practice Questions: Advanced Problem Resolution ... 367
Answers & Explanations: Advanced Problem Resolution ... 369
Further Review: Advanced Problem Resolution ... 379
   Key Words ... 379
   Analyzing Memory Dump Files ... 379
   Finding More Information ... 380
Summary ... 380

Practice Exam 1   381

Exam Answers ... 395

Practice Exam 2   399

Exam Answers ... 395

Appendix A: Exam Strategies   415

Types of cerification ... 415
Certification Requirements ... 416
   How to Become a Microsoft Certified Professional ... 416
   How to Become a Microsoft Certified Professional+Internet ... 416
   How to Become a Microsoft Certified Professional+Site Building ... 416
   How to Become a Microsoft Certified Systems Engineer ... 417
   How to Become a Microsoft Certified Systems Engineer+Internet ... 418
   How to Become a Microsoft Certified Solution Developer ... 419
   Becoming a Microsoft Certified Trainer ... 421

Study and Exam Preparation Tips	422
Study Tips	422
Exam Prep Tips	424
Putting It All Together	428
Final Considerations	430

Appendix B: Glossary — 433

Appendix C: Fast Facts — 449

Breaking a mirror set.	470
Regenerating a stripe set with parity	471

Index — 473

Publisher's Acknowledgment

New Riders would like to thank Mr. James Cooper for his feedback and advice. Jim's desire to see all certification resources meet the highest standards of excellence is appreciated and shared by the publisher.

Tell Us What You Think!

As the reader of this book, you are our most important critic and commentator. We value your opinion and want to know what we're doing right, what we could do better, what areas you'd like to see us publish in, and any other words of wisdom you're willing to pass our way.

As the Executive Editor for the Certification team at Macmillan Computer Publishing, I welcome your comments. You can fax, email, or write me directly to let me know what you did or didn't like about this book—as well as what we can do to make our books stronger.

Please note that I cannot help you with technical problems related to the topic of this book, and that due to the high volume of mail I receive, I might not be able to reply to every message.

When you write, please be sure to include this book's title, as well as your name and phone or fax number. I will carefully review your comments and share them with the editors who worked on the book.

Fax: 317-581-4663

Email: certification@mcp.com

Mail: Mary Foote
Executive Editor
Certification Team
Macmillan Computer Publishing
201 West 103rd Street
Indianapolis, IN 46290 USA

Introduction

The MCSE TestPrep series serves as a study aid for people preparing for Microsoft Certification exams. The series is intended to help reinforce and clarify information with which you are already familiar by providing sample questions and tests, as well as summary information relevant to each of the exam objectives. Note that this series is not intended to be the only source for your preparation, but rather a review of information with a set of practice tests that can be used to increase your familiarity with the exam questions. Using books in this series in conjunction with MCSE Training Guides can increase the likelihood of your success when taking the exam.

Who Should Read This Book

The Windows NT Server 4 Enterprise book in the MCSE TestPrep series is intended specifically for students who are in the final stages of preparation for Microsoft's Windows NT Server 4 Enterprise (70-068) exam, which is one of the core exams in the MCSE Microsoft Windows NT 4.0 Track program.

How This Book Helps You

This book provides a wealth of review questions similar to those you will encounter in the actual exam, categorized by the objectives published by Microsoft for the exam. Each answer is explained in detail in the "Answers and Explanations" section for each objective. The "Further Review" section provides additional information that is crucial for passing the exam. The two full-length practice exams at the end of the book will help you determine whether you have mastered the skills necessary to successfully complete the Microsoft exam. The practice exams will also identify which areas you need to study further before taking the actual exam.

How to Use This Book

This book series is designed to be used during the final stages of exam preparation. When you feel as though you're fairly well prepared for the exam, use this book as a test of your knowledge. Each objective is covered by a minimum of 10 questions. Start by using the practice questions as a self-quiz. Circle what you think is the correct answer (or answers), and then check your answers against the "Answer Key." Identify the questions you missed, and look them up in the "Answers and Explanations" section. Here you will find the question repeated, the correct answer(s) identified, and a thorough explanation of the answer. You can hit the "Further Review" section if you missed several questions for one objective. After following this process for each objectives, you will know on which topics your comprehension is sufficient and which objective require continued study. This is the best study tool available to help you reinforce what you already know, and identify areas that require more work.

After you have taken the practice tests and feel confident in the material on which you were tested, you should be ready to schedule your exam. Use this book for a final quick review just before taking the test to make sure that all the important concepts are set in your mind. Appendix C, "Fast Facts," summarizes key information you need to know about each objective. This feature is excellent for the last minute review before you take the exam.

Hardware/Software Recommendations

MCSE TestPrep: Windows NT Server 4 Enterprise, Second Edition is meant to help you review concepts with which you already have training and experience. In order to make the most of the review, you should have as much background and experience as possible. The best way to do this is to combine studying with working on real networks using the products on which you will be tested. The following list provides a description of the minimum computer requirements you need to build a good practice environment.

- Any computer on the Microsoft Hardware Compatibility List
- 486DX 33 MHz or better (Pentium recommended)
- A minimum of 16 MB of RAM (32 MB recommended)
- 125 MB (or more) of free disk space (160 MB for RISC-based systems)
- 3.5-inch 1.44 MB floppy drive
- VGA (or Super VGA) video adapter
- VGA (or Super VGA) monitor
- Mouse or equivalent pointing device
- Two-speed (or faster) CD-ROM drive
- Presence on an NT Network
- Windows NT Server software

What Exam 70-068 Covers

Just as other Microsoft exams are, the Windows NT Server 4 Enterprise exam is organized by categories, with objectives and subobjectives in each. The following sections address the Microsoft objectives for the exam that were current at the time of printing of this book. Be aware that the objectives may change at any time. It is wise to check out the preparation guide for the exam on the Microsoft Web site.

Planning

Plan the implementation of a directory services architecture. Considerations include the following:

- Selecting the appropriate domain model
- Supporting a single logon account
- Allowing users to access resources in different domains

Plan the disk drive configuration for various requirements. Requirements include choosing a fault-tolerance method.

Choose a protocol for various situations. Protocols include the following:

- TCP/IP
- TCP/IP with DHCP and WINS

- NWLink IPX/SPX-Compatible Transport
- Data Link Control (DLC)
- AppleTalk

Installation and Configuration

Install Windows NT Server to perform various server roles. Server roles include the following:

- Primary Domain Controller
- Backup Domain Controller
- Member server

Configure protocols and protocol bindings. Protocols include the following:

- TCP/IP
- TCP/IP with DHCP and WINS
- NWLink IPX/SPX-Compatible Transport
- DLC
- AppleTalk

Configure Windows NT Server core services. Services include the following:

- Directory Replicator
- Computer Browser

Configure hard disks to meet various requirements. Requirements include the following:

- Providing redundancy
- Improving performance

Configure printers. Tasks include the following:

- Adding and configuring a printer
- Implementing a printer pool
- Setting print priorities

Configure a Windows NT Server computer for various types of client computers. Client computer types include the following:

- Windows NT Workstation
- Windows 95
- Macintosh

Managing Resources

Manage user and group accounts. Considerations include the following:

- Managing Windows NT user accounts
- Managing Windows NT user rights
- Managing Windows NT groups
- Administering account policies
- Auditing changes to the user account database

Create and manage policies and profiles for various situations. Policies and profiles include the following:

- Local user profiles
- Roaming user profiles
- System policies

Administer remote servers from various types of client computers. Client computer types include the following:

- Windows 95
- Windows NT Workstation

Manage disk resources. Tasks include the following:

- Creating and sharing resources
- Implementing permissions and security
- Establishing file auditing

Connectivity

Configure Windows NT Server for interoperability with NetWare servers by using various tools. Tools include the following:

- Gateway Service for NetWare
- Migration Tool for NetWare

Install and configure multiprotocol routing to serve various functions. Functions include the following:

- Internet router
- BOOTP/DHCP Relay Agent
- IPX router

Install and configure Internet Information Server.

Install and configure Internet services. Services include the following:

- World Wide Web
- DNS
- Intranet

Install and configure Remote Access Services (RAS). Configuration options include the following:

- Configuring RAS communications
- Configuring RAS protocols
- Configuring RAS security

Monitoring and Optimization

Establish a baseline for measuring system performance. Tasks include creating a database of measurement data.

Monitor performance of various functions by using Performance Monitor. Functions include the following:

- Processor
- Memory
- Disk
- Network

Monitor network traffic by using Network Monitor. Tasks include the following:

- Collecting data
- Presenting data
- Filtering data

Identify performance bottlenecks.

Optimize performance for various results. Results include the following:

- Controlling network traffic
- Controlling server load

Troubleshooting

Choose the appropriate course of action to take to resolve installation failures.

Choose the appropriate course of action to take to resolve boot failures.

Choose the appropriate course of action to take to resolve configuration errors. Tasks include the following:

- Backing up and restoring the Registry
- Editing the Registry

Choose the appropriate course of action to take to resolve printer problems.

Choose the appropriate course of action to take to resolve RAS problems.

Choose the appropriate course of action to take to resolve connectivity problems.

Choose the appropriate course of action to take to resolve resource access and permission problems.

Choose the appropriate course of action to take to resolve fault-tolerance failures. Fault-tolerance methods include the following:

- Tape backup
- Mirroring
- Stripe set with parity

Perform advanced problem resolution. Tasks include the following:

- Diagnosing and interpreting a blue screen
- Configuring a memory dump
- Using the event log service

Good Luck!

As you approach the final stages of your exam preparation, New Riders wishes you the best of luck. If you should find after using this TestPrep tool that you need further study in a particular area, look into purchasing a New Riders Training Guide, Second Edition, a complete, thorough, and accurate study guide. If you would like to try computerized testing, check out New Riders' Top Score software simulation suite in the software or computer book section of your neighborhood bookstore. It includes an exclusive test engine that simulates the Microsoft exam and also includes a new Windows NT Simulator.

Keep us posted on your success. There is a registration card in the back of the book. Fill it out and fax or send it in. We'd love to hear from you. Good luck on your exam!

CHAPTER 1

Planning

The "Implementing and Supporting Windows NT 4.0 in the Enterprise" exam focuses primarily on planning an enterprise installation. This chapter covers the planning process as Microsoft has laid out in the exam goals.

OBJECTIVES

This chapter helps you prepare for the exam by covering the following Planning objectives:

Select the appropriate directory services architecture for given scenarios (considerations include selecting the appropriate domain model, supporting a single logon account, and allowing users to access different resources in different domains).

▶ To prepare for this part of the exam, you need to recognize which domain model is appropriate for a given network environment. You need to know how to set up the trusts for each of these models and how to assign groups to give permissions across the trust relationship.

▶ Windows NT domains can be organized into one of four different domain models. Each of these models supports the goal of directory services. Although there are other ways to combine domains, these four domain models (single domain, single master, multiple master, and complete trust) are the ones Microsoft expects you to know for the exam.

continues

OBJECTIVES (continued)

Plan the disk drive configurations for various requirements. Requirements include fault tolerance, stripe sets, and volume sets.

▶ To prepare for this section of the exam, you must understand each of the fault-tolerant disk arrays supported by Windows NT Server and know which method should be used for a given scenario.

Select the proper protocol for various situations. Protocols include the following:

- **TCP/IP**
- **TCP/IP with WINS and DHCP**
- **NWLink IPX/SPX-compatible Transport Protocol**
- **Data Link Control (DLC)**
- **AppleTalk**

▶ The interconnectivity of Windows NT with other operating systems and other Windows NT systems is critical to the proper functioning of your enterprise system. The protocols installed on a server determine the type of systems with which Windows NT can communicate. They include the following:

- NetBEUI
- TCP/IP
- NWLINK IPX/SPX-compatible
- DataLink Control (DLC)
- AppleTalk Protocol

The types of questions you will see on the Enterprise exam will be both scenario-based and standard multiple-choice questions. The passing score for the Microsoft exam is 784 (78.4 percent).

PRACTICE QUESTIONS

SELECTING THE APPROPRIATE DIRECTORY SERVICES ARCHITECTURE

1. How are the trusts configured in a single master domain model?

    A. The master domain trusts all the resource domains in a one-way trust.

    B. The resource domains trust the master domain with a one-way trust and trusts the other resource domains with two-way trusts.

    C. The master domain is trusted by all the resource domains.

    D. All the domains trust each other with two-way trusts.

2. What can be added to a local group in a resource domain in a multiple master domain model?

    A. Members of the resource domain

    B. Members of the resource domain and any master domain

    C. Members of resource domain and global groups from the resource domain

    D. Members of the resource domain and any master domain and global groups from any of these domains

3. An administrator in a resource domain is administering a local group on a server in his domain. The administrator adds members to the group by selecting a trusted domain. What can the administrator add to the local group from the trusted domain?

    A. Local groups from the trusted domain

    B. Global groups from the trusted domain

    C. Global and local groups from the trusted domain

    D. Users and global groups from the trusted domain

4. Which utility is used to create trust relationships?

    A. Server Manager

    B. User Manager for Domains

    C. Trust Manager

    D. DNS Manager

5. The Sales domain trusts the HR domain. The HR domain trusts the Accounting domain. How can users in the Accounting domain access resources in the Sales domain?

    A. Add a global group from the Accounting domain to a local group in the Sales domain.

    B. Add a global group from the Accounting domain to a global group in the HR domain, and then add the global group from the HR domain to a local group in the Sales domain.

C. Add a global group from the Sales domain to a local group in the Accounting domain.

D. Users in the Accounting domain cannot access resources in the Sales domain.

6. **What best describes the trust relationships in a complete trust domain model?**

    A. Each domain trusts every other domain.

    B. Each domain trusts the complete domain.

    C. All the resource domains and the master domain share a one-way trust.

    D. All the resource domains and the master domain share a two-way trust.

7. **You have established a trust relationship between two domains. Users in the trusted domain cannot log on to the trusting domain. What is the problem?**

    A. Users in the trusted domain do not have access to accounts in the trusting domain.

    B. The trust is broken.

    C. The Domain Users group from the trusting domain has not been assigned to the Users group of the trusted domain.

    D. The pass-through authentication service must be started.

8. **A trust is established between a master domain and two resource domains. Which of the following can be added to local groups in each of the resource domains? Select all that apply.**

    A. Global groups from the other resource domain

    B. Global groups from the master domain

    C. Users from the master domain

    D. Global groups from the same resource domain

9. **How should trust relationships be established?**

    A. The trusting domain should specify the name of the trusted domain, and then the trusted domain should specify the name of the trusting domain.

    B. The trusting domain should specify the name of the trusted domain and the trusting domain along with a password; the trusted domain then enters the password.

    C. The trusted domain should specify the name of the trusting domain and the trusted domain along with a password; the trusting domain then enters the password.

    D. The trusted domain should specify the name of the trusting domain, and then the trusting domain should specify the name of the trusted domain.

10. **What happens if the trust relationship is initiated by the trusting domain?**

    A. A dialog box appears indicating that the trust relationship is established.

    B. The trust relationship is established without a dialog box confirming the trust.

    C. The trust relationship cannot be established.

    D. A two-way trust is established.

11. JPS Printing has a single location with 1,000 users spread across the LAN. JPS has special printers and applications installed on the servers in its environment and needs to be able to centrally manage the user accounts and the resources. Which domain model would best fit its needs? Choose the best answer.

    A. Single domain model

    B. Single master domain model

    C. Multiple master domain model

    D. Complete trust model

12. Worldwide Training has locations spread around the world. The North American headquarters are located in Seattle; the European headquarters in London, England. Smaller locations are distributed throughout the world. All the user accounts would be maintained from the two corporate headquarters, but each location needs to manage its own resources. Which domain model would best fit this scenario?

    A. Single domain model

    B. Single master domain model

    C. Multiple master domain model

    D. Complete trust model

13. Riverton City wants to install an NT network. It has 600 employees located in five divisions. The network administrator wants to manage all the user accounts, but will allow administrators in each division to control access to its resources. Which domain model is best for this situation?

    A. Single domain model

    B. Single master domain model

    C. Multiple master domain model

    D. Complete trust model

14. You are planning a complete trust domain model with four domains. How many trust relationships are required for this model?

    A. 4

    B. 6

    C. 10

    D. 12

15. Your domain has 5,000 Windows 95 clients and 1,000 Windows NT Workstation clients. How much space in the SAM database is required for these clients?

    A. 500 KB

    B. 1 MB

    C. 3 MB

    D. 6 MB

ANSWER KEY

1. C	4. B	7. A	10. B	13. B
2. D	5. D	8. B-C-D	11. A	14. D
3. D	6. A	9. D	12. C	15. A

> **ANSWERS & EXPLANATIONS**

SELECTING THE APPROPRIATE DIRECTORY SERVICES ARCHITECTURE

1. How are the trusts configured in a single master domain model?

    C. The master domain is trusted by all the resource domains.

1. CORRECT ANSWER: C

All the domains with resources trust the single domain with user accounts.

Answer A is incorrect—the trust relationship is in the wrong direction. Answer B is incorrect—the single master domain model is a hub spoke configuration; that is, the resource domains all trust the master domain, but do not have trust relationships with each other. Answer D is incorrect—this describes the Complete Trust domain model.

The trust relationships in a single master domain model are relatively easy to implement. In this model, the master domain holds all the user accounts and global groups, and may also have resources. The other domains in the organization become resource domains. The master domain is the *trusted* domain, whereas the resource domains are the *trusting* domains. All resource domains trust the master domain

2. What can be added to a local group in a resource domain in a multiple master domain model?

    D. Members of the resource domain and any master domain and global groups from any of these domains

2. CORRECT ANSWER: D

Individual users and global groups from the local domain as well as any trusted domain can be added to local groups.

Answer A is incorrect—members of any trusted domain can also be added. Answer B is incorrect because groups can also be added. Answer C is incorrect because members and groups from the master domain can also be added.

The accounts in the multiple master are distributed across multiple master domains. Each user still has only one account; however, global groups may have to be duplicated in all the master domains. If, for example, an organization has members of the marketing department spread across both master domains, a marketing global group must be created in each master domain because users can only be assigned to global groups in their own domains. To give these marketing users access to a resource, the marketing global group from each master domain must be added to the local group for that resource.

The key points to remember regarding accounts in a multiple master domain are the following:

- User accounts are located in one of the master domains.
- Global groups are defined in all the master domains.
- Local groups are defined in resource domains, and contain global groups from all the master domains.

3. An administrator in a resource domain is administering a local group on a server in his domain. The administrator adds members to the group by selecting a trusted domain. What can the administrator add to the local group from the trusted domain?

D. Users and global groups from the trusted domain

3. CORRECT ANSWER: D

Both users and global groups can be added.

Answer A is incorrect because local groups cannot be added to other local groups. Answer B is also incorrect—users can also be added from the trusted domain. Lastly, Answer C is incorrect because local groups cannot be added and users can.

Assigning permissions across a trust uses Microsoft's strategy to give users rights; global groups with users are added to local groups with permissions. When trusts are involved, a global group from a trusted domain is added to a local group in a trusting domain. Adding global groups from another domain to a local group is done in much the same way as adding global groups from the same domain. Create or edit the local group in User Manager, and then choose the Add button to add members to the group. Then, select the trusted domain from the List Names pull-down menu. The global groups and users from the trusted domain are listed and can be added to the local group.

Local groups and local accounts cannot be seen from this view because local accounts and local groups cannot be used across trusts.

4. **Which utility is used to create trust relationships?**

   B. User Manager for Domains

FIGURE 1.1
Trust Relationships dialog box.

5. **The Sales domain trusts the HR domain. The HR domain trusts the Accounting domain. How can users in the Accounting domain access resources in the Sales domain?**

   D. Users in the Accounting domain cannot access resources in the Sales domain.

4. CORRECT ANSWER: B

The Policies menu within User Manager for Domains is used to create trusts.

Answer A is incorrect—Server Manager displays all machines in a domain. Answer C is incorrect—there isn't any utility called Trust Manager. Answer D is incorrect because the DNS Manager controls the Domain Name Service.

Establishing a trust relationship must be completed by an administrator from each domain in the trust relationship by using the Trust Relationships dialog box. This dialog box is accessed from User Manager for Domains by selecting Trust Relationships from the Policies menu.

This dialog box (see Figure 1.1) has two different sections. The administrator specifies in the dialog box the relationship of the other domain in the trust relationship. The name of the administrator's own domain never appears in the Trust Relationships dialog box; only the name of the trust partner appears.

5. CORRECT ANSWER: D

No trust relationship exists between the Sales and Accounting domains. Users from one domain cannot access resources in another domain unless a trust relationship is explicitly created between them.

Answer A is incorrect—the Sales domain does not trust the Accounting domain. Answer B is incorrect—trusts cannot be transferred from one domain to another. Answer C is incorrect because the Accounting domain does not trust the sales domain.

Trust relationships are nontransitive—in other words, you cannot pass through one trust into another. A trust relationship involves only two domains. The domain with user accounts must be explicitly trusted by the domain with the resources the users need to access.

ANSWERS & EXPLANATIONS

Assume an environment in which Domain A trusts Domain B and Domain B trusts Domain C. Because trusts are not transitive, a user from Domain C can access resources in Domain B, but cannot access any resources in Domain A, even though Domain B and Domain A also have a trust relationship. There isn't a trust relationship between Domain A and Domain C, which are the two domains in question. Domain A must trust Domain C if a user in Domain C wants to access resources in Domain A.

6. What best describes the trust relationships in a complete trust domain model?

   A. Each domain trusts every other domain.

6. CORRECT ANSWER: A

Each domain has accounts and resources; therefore, every domain must trust every other domain.

Answer B is incorrect—the term *complete domain* doesn't exist. Answer C is incorrect—this describes a single master domain model. Answer D is incorrect because all domains are equal in a complete trust domain model.

The complete trust model enables each domain to maintain its own control of users and resources with the opportunity to assign permissions to users of any other domain in the model. The complete trust model implements two-way trust relationships between every domain in the environment. Each domain is both an account domain and a resource domain.

This model is scalable and flexible because domains can easily be added and removed from the model. However, the model does not allow for centralized administration of user accounts or resources.

7. You have established a trust relationship between two domains. Users in the trusted domain cannot log on to the trusting domain. What is the problem?

   A. Users in the trusted domain do not have access to accounts in the trust-

7. CORRECT ANSWER: A

A trust allows accounts in the trusted domain to be visible to the trusting domain. Users in the trusted domain don't see anything from the trusting domain.

Answer B is incorrect—the trust can only be broken manually. Answer C is incorrect—you cannot assign users from a trusting domain, only from the trusted domain. Answer D is incorrect because there is no pass-through authentication service.

Every trust relationship has a trusted and a trusting domain. The *trusted* domain, also referred to as the *account* domain, is the domain that contains the user accounts. The *trusting* domain uses the accounts from the trusted domain. Located in the trusting domain are the resources that you need to share. The trusting domain assigns security permissions to any user in its SAM and any user in a trusted domain's SAM. By creating a trusting domain, departments can maintain control of their resources while still allowing the users to be administered centrally. A trusting domain is also referred to as a *resource* domain.

8. **A trust is established between a master domain and two resource domains. Which of the following can be added to local groups in each of the resource domains? Select all that apply.**

   B. Global groups from the master domain
   C. Users from the master domain
   D. Global groups from the same resource domain

8. CORRECT ANSWERS: B-C-D

You can always add users and global groups from the local domain. You also can add users and global groups from any trusted domain.

Answer A is incorrect because there isn't a trust relationship between the resource domains.

In Windows NT Server, the two types of groups are local and global. *Local* groups are restricted to being used where they are created, such as within a domain for local groups created on a domain controller. On the other hand, *global* groups are designed to contain users used across trusts.

The recommended strategy is to collect users together in global groups and to assign permission to local groups. Users get permission to use resources when the global groups they belong to are added to local groups for resources they want to access.

9. **How should trust relationships be established?**

   D. The trusted domain should specify the name of the trusting domain, and then the trusting domain should specify the name of the trusted domain.

9. CORRECT ANSWER: D

The trusted domain starts the process by naming its partner. The trusting domain then finishes the process by naming its partner.

Answer A is incorrect—the trusted domain should establish the trust first. Answer B is incorrect—a password is not necessary because NT will automatically change the password. Answer C is incorrect because, again, no password is needed to establish the trust.

You can configure the trust in either order; however, Microsoft recommends the trusted domain initiate the trust by entering the name of the trusting domain. When the trusting domain completes the trust by entering the name of the trusted domain, the message `Trust Successfully Established` is displayed.

▼ **NOTE**

When a trust is established, Windows NT changes the password that was used to establish the trust. The domain controllers in both domains know the new password; however it is not visible to the users. Frequently, this password is changed by Windows NT for added security. If one of the domains in the trust relationship were to break the trust, the trust could not be reestablished without breaking both sides and starting the trust relationship from the beginning. This is because the administrators do not know the current correct password.

10. What happens if the trust relationship is initiated by the trusting domain?

   B. The trust relationship is established without a dialog box confirming the trust.

10. CORRECT ANSWER: B

Although this is not the preferred method for creating a trust, the trust is still established. However, the user does not receive a dialog box with a positive confirmation that the trust has been created.

Answer A is incorrect—a dialog box does not appear. Answer C is incorrect—the trust relationship is eventually established. Answer D is incorrect because a two-way trust must be established from both domains; it is essentially two one-way trusts.

If the trust relationship were established in the opposite order (trusting domain initiates the trust), it can still be completed; however, you receive a dialog box warning that the trust could not be verified. In this case, the trust is not immediately established (it can take up to 15 minutes), and you need to manually verify the trust later.

11. JPS Printing has a single location with 1,000 users spread across the LAN. JPS has special printers and applications installed on the servers in its environment and needs to be able to centrally manage the user accounts and the resources. Which domain model would best fit its needs? Choose the best answer.

   A. Single domain model

11. CORRECT ANSWER: A

The single domain model would best fit the needs of a small network environment requiring centralized user and resource administration.

Answers B and C are incorrect because there is no need for resource or multiple master domains. Answer D is incorrect because only one domain is needed.

The single domain model is the easiest to implement. It places all users, groups, and resources into a single domain. The single domain is the starting point of all the domain models; in any implementation, you must ensure that each domain can function as a single domain before you should consider any of the other models.

The single domain model is ideal for smaller organizations. The benefits of a single domain model are as follows:

- Simple installation; just install the first server as a Primary Domain Controller and you have a single domain model.

- Centralized administration of accounts because there is only one domain database.

- Centralized administration of resources because all the resources are in one domain.

- No trust relationships to establish.

The limitations of the single domain model affect larger organizations that have a distributed WAN environment. The limitations of the single domain model are as follows:

- Can support a SAM database of only 40 MB, which is the maximum size Microsoft recommends for a single domain.

- No departmental administrative controls (decentralized administration) can be assigned because there is only one domain database for assigning security permissions.

- Browsing is slow if the domain contains a large number of servers and resources.

12. Worldwide Training has locations spread around the world. The North American headquarters are located in Seattle; the European headquarters in London, England. Smaller locations are distributed throughout the world. All the user accounts would be maintained from the two corporate headquarters, but each location needs to manage its own resources. Which domain model would best fit this scenario?

   C. Multiple master domain model

12. CORRECT ANSWER: C

The multiple master domain model best suits large organizations that require multiple account or master domains for user administration with distributed resource management.

Answers A and B are incorrect—because each headquarters is to manage its own users, multiple master domains are required. Answer D is incorrect because a complete trust model would be very complicated and is not necessary for this environment—all the user accounts would be maintained from the two corporate headquarters.

The multiple master domain model is designed for very large organizations that have users distributed across multiple domains. In this model, there is more than one master domain. Each master domain contains user and global group accounts to be used by all other domains in the environment. In this model, account administration can still be centralized. For all administrators to manage accounts, the Domain Admins global group from each master domain must be added to the local administrators group in each master domain.

The multiple master domain model is the most scalable of the domain models. Each master domain can be the maximum recommended size of 40 MB. Additional master domains can be added to this model to enable the network to expand to include an unlimited number of users. The number of master domains available in this model is not limited.

The advantages of the multiple master domain model are the following:

- Scalable to networks with a large number of users.

- Resources are grouped into resource domains to enable distributed resource management.

- Each master domain can have a domain administrator, or can be grouped to achieve centralized administration.

- User accounts and global groups are maintained in the master domains.

The limitations of the multiple master domain model are the following:

- Complex trust relationships have to be configured to maintain this domain model.

- User accounts are distributed across multiple master domains.

- Global groups may have to be defined multiple times, one in each master domain.

The multiple master domain model requires more planning than the single domain or the single master domain models. Domain planners must decide how the master domains are divided. Master domains can be based on geographical areas or different parts of an organization, such as unique business units. Centralized account administration can still be achieved in this model by adding the global Domain Admins group from each master domain into the local administrators group in all the other master domains. The trust relationships are more complex in this model.

13. Riverton City wants to install an NT network. It has 600 employees located in five divisions. The network administrator wants to manage all the user accounts, but will allow administrators in each division to control access to its resources. Which domain model is best for this situation?

   B. Single master domain model

13. CORRECT ANSWER: B

A small number of users with centralized account administration means a single accounts domain. With the demand for decentralized resource administration, separate resource domains must be created, thus necessitating the single master domain model.

Answer A is incorrect—a single domain model does not provide decentralized resource management. Answers C and D are incorrect because the number of users and management requirements do not support the need for the multiple master or complete trust model.

The single master domain model has one domain with user accounts and other domains to control access to resources. This model maintains the centralized administration of user accounts while allowing decentralized management of resources.

These resource domains can maintain their own resources and permissions, with all user accounts residing in the master domain. From a user's perspective, the domain appears to be one large system—every user logs on to the master. The users can connect to other domains in the environment without requiring additional user accounts or passwords.

The benefits of a single master domain model are as follows:

- This domain model has centralized administration of user accounts.

- Resources can be distributed and administered throughout resource domains.

- Each resource domain can have a domain administrator to maintain its resources, without giving access to the master domain.

- The trust relationships are fairly easy to implement.

- The single master domain model maintains one user and one account goal of directory services.

- Global groups can be maintained from the master domain.

The limitations of a single master domain model are similar to those of the single domain model. The single master domain model still uses one domain database for all the users, so the number of user accounts this model supports is limited. The limitations of the single master domain model are as follows:

- Local groups must be defined in each domain, both master and resource domains.

- Maximum number of users is limited by the 40 MB maximum size of the SAM database.

- Resource domains have no control over group memberships of global groups from the master domain.

- Trust relationships must be established in the proper direction to maintain the directory services structure.

The single master domain model is best suited for organizations with fewer than 20,000 users that require some departmental resource administration. This model is excellent for companies with locations spread across a WAN because the trust relationships allow for the centralized administration of user accounts.

14. You are planning a complete trust domain model with four domains. How many trust relationships are required for this model?

    D. 12

14. CORRECT ANSWER: D

All four domains must trust the other three domains: 4×3 = 12.

The complete trust domain model requires more trust relationships than any other domain model. Every domain has a two-way trust with every other domain.

You can use the following formula to determine the number of trusts required in a complete trust model:

```
N*(N-1)
```

N is the total number of domains in the model.

15. Your domain has 5,000 Windows 95 clients and 1,000 Windows NT Workstation clients. How much space in the SAM database is required for these clients?

    A. 500 KB

15. CORRECT ANSWER: A

Windows 95 computers do not require computer accounts. Each Windows NT computer account uses 0.5 KB of space; therefore, 1,000 computers would require 500 KB of disk space.

A single domain maintains all the directory database information in the Security Account Manager (SAM). The SAM contains all user accounts, Windows NT computer accounts, group accounts, and any account settings assigned in the domain, all of which contribute to the SAM's size. Microsoft recommends that the SAM not exceed 40 MB. Table 1.1 shows the size of each account or group included in the SAM database.

TABLE 1.1 SAM DATABASE LIMITATIONS

SAM Database Item	Size Per Item
User accounts	1.0 KB
Local groups	512 bytes per group plus 36 bytes per user
Global groups	512 bytes per group plus 12 bytes per user
Computer accounts	0.5 KB

The maximum size of the SAM is a physical limitation of the domain. Domains are also often broken down into logical units, such as departments within a company. The organizational chart and political influences usually need to be addressed in the design. Individual departments may require control of their own resources.

FURTHER REVIEW

SELECTING THE APPROPRIATE DIRECTORY SERVICES ARCHITECTURE

The following key words are important terms that were covered in this section. You should make sure you understand what each one is and what it does.

Key Words

- Complete trust domain model
- Directory services
- Directory synchronization
- Domain
- Multiple master domain model
- Nontransitive trusts
- One-way trust
- Security Account Manager (SAM)
- Single domain model
- Single master domain model
- Trust relationships
- Two-way trust
- Universal resource access

One-way Versus Two-way Trusts

The following sections describe the differences between one-way and two-way trusts in more detail. Knowing the difference between types of trusts is an important part of understanding how Windows NT domain models work.

One-way Trusts

A one-way trust is a trust relationship with a single trusted domain and a single trusting domain.

The accounts exist in the trusted domain, and the trusting domain has resources that are assigned permissions to users in the trusted domain.

Two-way Trusts

A two-way trust is nothing more than two one-way trusts. In a two-way trust, both domains are trusted domains and trusting domains. This type of trust is necessary when each domain has user accounts and also has resources that users in the other domain need to access.

Built-in NT Groups

Built-in groups are automatically created in a Windows NT domain. Table 1.2 shows the built-in local groups and Table 1.3 shows the built-in global groups.

TABLE 1.2   BUILT-IN LOCAL GROUPS

Local Group	Initially Contains	Rights
Administrators	Domain Admins	Administrator group, to manage Administrator and maintain the entire system.
Users	Domain Users	Access resources, day-to-day operation of computer system.
Guests	Domain Guests	Guest account disabled by default.
Server Operators	None	Share and Stop sharing resources. Shut down/Lock servers. Stop and Start services. Server Maintenance. Backup and restore server.
Print Operators	None	Share and Stop sharing printers. Manage printers.
Backup Operators	None	Back up and restore server.
Account Operators	None	Create and manage user and group accounts.
Replicators	None	Used for the Directory Replicator service.

TABLE 1.3   BUILT-IN GLOBAL GROUPS

Global Group	Initial Accounts	Member of:
Domain Admins	Administrator	Administrators
Domain Users	AdministratorUsers	All accounts created in domain.
Domain Guests	Guests	Guests

Remember that only global groups and user accounts can be used across trust relationships.

Windows NT Domain Models

The following sections describe the four different types of domain models that are used in a Windows NT network.

Single Domain Model

The single domain model is the easiest to implement. It places all users, groups, and resources into a single domain. The single domain is the starting point of all the domain models; in any implementation, you must ensure that each domain can function as a single domain before you should consider any of the other models.

Single Master Domain Model

The single master domain model has one domain with user accounts and other domains to control access to resources. This model maintains the centralized administration of user accounts while allowing decentralized management of resources.

These resource domains can maintain their own resources and permissions, with all user accounts residing in the master domain. From a user's perspective, the domain appears to be one large system; every user logs on to the master. The users can connect to other domains in the environment without requiring additional user accounts or passwords.

Multiple Master Domain Model

The multiple master domain model is designed for very large organizations that have users distributed across multiple domains. In this model, there is more than one master domain. Each master domain contains user and global group accounts to be used by all other domains in the environment. In this model, account administration can still be centralized. For all administrators to manage accounts, the Domain Admins global group from each master domain must be added to the local administrators group in each master domain.

The multiple master domain model is the most scalable of the domain models. Each master domain can be the maximum recommended size of 40 MB. Additional master domains can be added to this model to enable the network to expand to include an unlimited number of users. The number of master domains available in this model is not limited.

Complete Trust Model

The complete trust model enables each domain to maintain its own control of users and resources with the opportunity to assign permissions to users of any other domain in the model. The complete trust model implements two-way trust relationships between every domain in the environment. Each domain is both an account domain and a resource domain.

This model is scalable and flexible because domains can easily be added and removed from the model. However, the model does not allow for centralized administration of user accounts or resources.

PRACTICE QUESTIONS

PLANNING THE FAULT-TOLERANCE CONFIGURATIONS FOR WINDOWS NT SERVER 4.0

1. On which disk-partitioning scheme can you place a system partition?

    A. Volume set

    B. Stripe set without parity

    C. Stripe set with parity

    D. Disk mirror

2. Which fault-tolerant disk scheme requires the least overhead in disk storage?

    A. Striping with parity

    B. Disk mirroring

    C. Disk duplexing

    D. Striping without parity

3. How many physical disks are required for a RAID 5 array?

    A. 2

    B. 3

    C. 4

    D. 32

4. How many physical disks can be included in a RAID 5 array?

    A. 2

    B. 3

    C. 4

    D. 32

5. Which file system can be used for a stripe set with parity? Select all that apply.

    A. HPFS

    B. FAT

    C. CDFS

    D. NTFS

6. Which file system supports sector sparing?

    A. HPFS

    B. FAT

    C. CDFS

    D. NTFS

7. What happens to data on a bad sector when sector sparing occurs?

    A. The data is copied to a good sector.

    B. The data is copied to a file called FILExxxx.chk.

    C. The data is copied to the sparing partition.

    D. The data can be recovered with the SECTCHK command.

8. This is a scenario question. First, you must review the scenario, then review the required and optional results. Following that is a proposed solution.

Scenario:
Your SQL Server has four physical disks. The first disk is where the Windows NT files are located. SQL data is stored on the other three disks. You are asked to implement a fault-tolerant disk scheme for this SQL server.

Required Result:
The boot partition must be protected from a single disk failure.

Optional Results:
The SQL data must have the fastest read and write access possible.

The SQL data must be protected from a single disk failure.

Proposed Solution:
Mirror the first physical drive to the second physical drive. Make a stripe set without parity with the remaining two disks. Store the SQL data on the stripe set without parity.

Evaluation of Proposed Solution:
(Choose the most correct answer.)

A. The proposed solution produces the required result and produces both optional results.

B. The proposed solution produces the required result and produces only one optional result.

C. The proposed solution produces the required result but does not produce any optional results.

D. The proposed solution does not produce the required result.

9. What best describes a volume set?

A. It allows a system partition to be duplicated.

B. It combines disk space from several disks into one logical drive.

C. It requires equal disk space from each drive included in the volume set.

D. It provides faster read access to data.

10. What type of information can be put on a stripe set? Select all that apply.

A. The boot sector

B. Spool directory

C. Data files

D. Registry hives

11. What type of drives can be used to create a RAID 5 array? Select all that apply.

A. Removable drives

B. SCSI drives

C. IDE drives

D. EIDE drives

12. A server is currently used to store data on its single disk drive. How many disks must be added to protect the operating system from disk failure and also to protect the data?

A. 0

B. 1

C. 2

D. 3

13. A server currently has two EIDE controllers with a physical drive attached to each controller. What must be added to the server to enable sector sparing?

A. Two SCSI hard drives with controllers

B. A tape device

C. A PCI controller for the EIDE drives

D. A Y-cable connecting the two EIDE drives

14. Which of the following best describes striping with parity?

    A. Provides fastest write access to the disk for any disk array

    B. Enables addition of new disks to an existing partition

    C. Can be used only with NTFS

    D. Requires at least three disks to implement

15. A Windows NT Server has four physical disks. The first disk, which contains the WINNT directory on a 400 MB FAT partition, has 200 MB of free space. The second disk has a 400 MB NTFS partition and 100 MB of free space. The third and fourth disks are unformatted with 500 MB of free space on each disk. Which fault-tolerant scheme would allow a 300 MB application to be installed on the disks? Select all that apply.

    A. Make a stripe set with parity using all the free space on disks 1, 3, and 4.

    B. Make a volume set using the remaining disk space on disk 2.

    C. Make a mirror using all the free space on disks 3 and 4.

    D. Make a mirror with the boot partition using free space on disk 4. Make a stripe set with parity using the remaining disk space on all four disks.

16. Which tool is used to create a RAID 5 array in Windows NT?

    A. RAID Configuration Wizard

    B. DNS Manager

    C. Disk Administrator

    D. Server Manager

17. You have created a stripe set with parity that uses five physical disks with 200 MB used on each disk. How much storage is available for data?

    A. 500 MB

    B. 600 MB

    C. 800 MB

    D. 1 GB

18. You have created a stripe set with parity that uses three physical disks. The stripe set is now filled and you want to expand it. How can you do this?

    A. Add a new volume to the stripe set.

    B. Regenerate the stripe set.

    C. Back up the data, create a new stripe set, and restore the data.

    D. Install the new drive and configure the stripe set to recognize the new drive.

19. Which disk arrays are supported by Windows NT Workstation?

    A. Striping

    B. Striping with parity

    C. Disk mirroring

    D. Volume sets

20. You are creating a stripe set with parity from five physical drives. One drive has 300 MB of free space left, another drive has 500 MB left, and the other three drives have 700 MB left. What is the maximum size of a stripe set with parity that can be created by using a combination of these disks, including both usable space and parity space?

   A. 1.5 GB

   B. 2.0 GB

   C. 2.1 GB

   D. 2.9 GB

ANSWER KEY

1. D
2. A
3. B
4. D
5. B-D
6. D
7. A
8. B
9. B
10. B-C
11. B-C-D
12. B
13. A
14. D
15. A-C-D
16. C
17. C
18. C
19. A-D
20. C

ANSWERS & EXPLANATIONS

PLANNING THE FAULT-TOLERANCE CONFIGURATIONS FOR WINDOWS NT SERVER 4.0

1. On which disk-partitioning scheme can you place a system partition?

    D. Disk mirror

1. CORRECT ANSWER: D

Only a disk mirror allows a system partition.

Answers A, B, and C are incorrect—a volume set or a stripe set cannot contain the system partition.

Disk Mirroring is the only disk partitioning scheme that can contain the system partition. Neither volume sets, stripe sets with parity, nor stripe sets without parity are allowed to contain the system partition because the data is written across multiple partitions and/or drives.

2. Which fault-tolerant disk scheme requires the least overhead in disk storage?

    A. Striping with parity

2. CORRECT ANSWER: A

Although striping without parity requires no overhead, it's not a fault-tolerant scheme.

Answers B and C are incorrect because disk mirroring or duplexing requires more system overhead. Answer D is incorrect—it's not fault-tolerant.

A stripe set with parity disk partitioning scheme requires less overhead than disk mirroring because the data is only being written once with a parity bit, as opposed to the data being written twice with mirroring or duplexing.

3. How many physical disks are required for a RAID 5 array?

    B. 3

3. CORRECT ANSWER: B

At least three disks are required for a RAID 5 array; the equivalent space of two disks is for data and the equivalent space of one disk is for parity.

Answer A is incorrect—at least three disks are required.
Answers C and D are incorrect—only three disks are required.

A RAID 5 array uses two data stripes itself, and one more data stripe is used to provide fault tolerance. The parity information that can be used to re-create lost data is written in 64 KB blocks, and the disk it is being written to is changed after each block is written (block 1 on disk 1, block 2 on disk 2, and so on). This provides the capability to re-create the data by using the parity bits to reconstruct the information.

4. How many physical disks can be included in a RAID 5 array?

D. 32

4. CORRECT ANSWER: D

Up to 32 disks can be part of a RAID 5 array.

To implement the disk striping with parity (RAID 5), a minimum of three physical disks is required and a maximum of 32 disks can be used. Note that an extra disk is required over striping without parity. The equivalent of one disk is devoted to parity information. If any one of the disks in the stripe set with parity fails, the data can be regenerated from the remaining disks. Striping with parity is supported only on Windows NT Server.

5. Which file system can be used for a stripe set with parity? Select all that apply.

B. FAT
D. NTFS

5. CORRECT ANSWERS: B-D

Any supported file system can be used for any of the disk arrays.

Answer A is incorrect—HPFS is not supported for Windows NT 4.0. Answer C is incorrect—CDFS is the file system used to read data from CD-ROMs.

All Windows NT disk-partitioning schemes will work with all supported file systems. The file systems supported under Windows NT Server v4.0 are FAT and NTFS.

6. Which file system supports sector sparing?

D. NTFS

6. CORRECT ANSWER: D

Only NTFS supports sector sparing.

Answer A is incorrect—HPFS is not supported under NT v4.0. Answer B is incorrect—FAT does not support sector sparing. Answer C is incorrect—CDFS is the Windows NT CD-ROM file system.

ANSWERS & EXPLANATIONS

Sector sparing is described in question 7's explanation.

7. What happens to data on a bad sector when sector sparing occurs?

   A. The data is copied to a good sector.

7. CORRECT ANSWER: A

The data is automatically copied to a new sector and the process is transparent to the user.

Answer B is incorrect—the data is not copied to a file. Answer C is incorrect—there is no sparing partition. Answer D is incorrect—there is no SECTCHK command.

Sector sparing automatically fixes data on bad sectors of a hard drive. This is also known as *hot fixing*. Sector sparing is supported only on SCSI drives in RAID 1 or RAID 5 arrays that are formatted as NTFS partitions. Sector sparing is supported only on Windows NT Server. Sector sparing verifies each write of data onto the disk and, if it does not reread the data successfully, it moves the data to another sector of the drive. The operating system never receives a message about the bad write because the sector sparing automatically corrects the error. After a sector of the disk has been marked bad, the system does not use the bad sector until a disk defragmentation utility, or a disk tool utility, has been executed.

8. Proposed solution:
   Mirror the first physical drive to the second physical drive. Make a stripe set without parity with the remaining two disks. Store the SQL data on the stripe set without parity.

   B. The proposed solution produces the required result and produces only one optional result.

8. CORRECT ANSWER: B

Mirroring the first disk protects the boot partition. The stripe set without parity provides the fastest read and write access, but it isn't a fault-tolerant disk array.

Answer A is incorrect because fault-tolerance is not provided. Answer C is incorrect—the solution provides the fastest data access. Answer D is incorrect—the solution does produce the required result.

9. What best describes a volume set?

   B. It combines disk space from several disks into one logical drive.

9. CORRECT ANSWER: B

A volume set joins dissimilar disk space together in a single drive letter, but it does not improve access times, nor is it fault tolerant.

Answer A is incorrect—the system partition cannot be on a volume set. Answer C is incorrect—a volume set does not require equal disk space. Answer D is incorrect—a volume set does not provide faster data read access.

10. **What type of information can be put on a stripe set? Select all that apply.**
    - B. Spool directory
    - C. Data files

10. CORRECT ANSWERS: B-C

Data can be placed on any partition. Although the spool directory is part of the boot partition by default, it can be moved to any partition.

Answer A is incorrect—the boot sector cannot be on a stripe set. Answer D is incorrect—the Registry is on the system partition, which cannot be on a stripe set.

A stripe set can contain any data, including the spool directory. It cannot contain the boot sector or system partition.

11. **What type of drives can be used to create a RAID 5 array? Select all that apply.**
    - B. SCSI drives
    - C. IDE drives
    - D. EIDE drives

11. CORRECT ANSWERS: B-C-D

Any fixed type of hard drive can be used in a RAID 5 array.

Answer A is incorrect because NT does not support removable drives in a RAID configuration.

Windows NT Server can use any fixed disk drive for a stripe set with parity (RAID 5). To use hot-pluggable disk drives, a hardware-based RAID implementation must be used.

12. **A server is currently used to store data on its single disk drive. How many disks must be added to protect the operating system from disk failure and also to protect the data?**
    - B. 1

12. CORRECT ANSWER: B

An additional drive would allow mirroring of both the operating system and data.

Answer A is incorrect—multiple drives must be used to provide fault-tolerance. Answers C and D indicate more drives than are required.

Disk mirroring duplicates writes to the hard drive onto two physical disks. If each disk has a separate hard drive controller, a mirror is called disk duplexing, which provides redundancy for both hard drive failure and controller failure.

ANSWERS & EXPLANATIONS

This method of fault tolerance is considered to be more expensive per megabyte of data due to the complete duplication of data. Every disk mirror requires two physical disks. Disk mirroring (and disk duplexing) are supported only on Windows NT Server.

13. A server currently has two EIDE controllers with a physical drive attached to each controller. What must be added to the server to enable sector sparing?

    A. Two SCSI hard drives with controllers

13. CORRECT ANSWER: A

Sector sparing is supported only on SCSI drives.

14. Which of the following best describes striping with parity?

    D. Requires at least three disks to implement

14. CORRECT ANSWER: D

Striping without parity is faster, and a stripe set cannot be modified after it's created. A stripe set can be formatted as FAT or NTFS.

Answer A is incorrect—striping with parity does not provide the fastest write access. Answer B is incorrect—you cannot add new disks to an existing partition in a stripe set. Answer C is incorrect—a stripe set can be used with the FAT file system.

Disk striping with parity is the most common of the fault-tolerant methods available through Windows NT Server 4.0. Disk striping with parity uses the same basic process of disk striping; it writes the data in 64 KB blocks across multiple physical disks.

A stripe set uses the stripes on disk to store redundant information, known as parity. The parity is basically a checksum that can be used to restore the rest of the data if a disk is lost. For example, consider a stripe set with parity with three disks.

If the data values 1 and 2 were written to the stripe set, the parity 3 (which is the sum of 1 and 2) would be written to the third disk. If one of the disks were lost, the data could still be recovered because an algebraic statement would exist. If disk 2 were lost, the equation 1 + ? = 3 would exist. The value 2 could be computed as the missing data and Windows NT could recover the missing drive.

Chapter 1 PLANNING

15. A Windows NT Server has four physical disks. The first disk, which contains the WINNT directory on a 400 MB FAT partition, has 200 MB of free space. The second disk has a 400 MB NTFS partition and 100 MB of free space. The third and fourth disks are unformatted with 500 MB of free space on each disk. Which fault-tolerant scheme would allow a 300 MB application to be installed on the disks? Select all that apply.

   A. Make a stripe set with parity using all the free space on disks 1, 3, and 4.

   C. Make a mirror using all the free space on disks 3 and 4.

   D. Make a mirror with the boot partition using free space on disk 4. Make a stripe set with parity using the remaining disk space on all four disks.

15. CORRECT ANSWERS: A-C-D

The mirror would be 1 GB, with 500 MB of usable space. A stripe set on three disks would yield 600 MB total, with 400 MB of usable space. A stripe set on four disks would yield 400 MB total, with 300 MB of usable space.

Answer B is incorrect—a volume set is not fault-tolerant.

16. Which tool is used to create a RAID 5 array in Windows NT?

   C. Disk Administrator

16. CORRECT ANSWER: C

Disk Administrator is the tool used to create any disk scheme.

Answer A is incorrect—there is no RAID Configuration Wizard. Answer B is incorrect—DNS Manager is used with the Domain Name Service. Answer D is incorrect—Server manager is used to control machine accounts in a domain.

17. You have created a stripe set with parity that uses five physical disks with 200 MB used on each disk. How much storage is available for data?

   C. 800 MB

17. CORRECT ANSWER: C

The equivalent of one disk is used for overhead; only 800 MB of the stripe set is usable space.

Answers A, B, and D are incorrect—the total storage available is incorrect.

The cost for the fault tolerance is one disk in the array. For the smallest array (3 disks), the cost is the largest (1/3, or one disk of the three). For the largest array (32 disks), the cost is relatively small (1/32, or one disk of the 32).

ANSWERS & EXPLANATIONS

18. You have created a stripe set with parity that uses three physical disks. The stripe set is now filled and you want to expand it. How can you do this?

C. Back up the data, create a new stripe set, and restore the data.

18. CORRECT ANSWER: C

You cannot expand a stripe set. You must remove it and create a larger one. To protect data, you should back it up first and then restore it to the larger stripe set.

Answers A, B, and D are incorrect—you cannot expand a stripe set in any way.

After a stripe set is created, no disks can be added to or removed from the array. When a stripe set is created, equal portions of disk space from each physical drive are used.

19. Which disk arrays are supported by Windows NT Workstation?

A. Striping

D. Volume sets

19. CORRECT ANSWERS: A-D

Fault-tolerant arrays are supported only on Windows NT Server.

Windows NT Server supports fault-tolerant disk arrays that provide data recovery if a single physical disk fails. These fault-tolerant arrays are not supported on Windows NT Workstation. However, the disk arrays supported by Windows NT Workstation (striping and volume sets) are also supported by Windows NT Server.

Windows NT Server 4.0 supports RAID (Redundant Array of Inexpensive Disks) Level 0 (Disk Striping), Level 1 (Disk Mirroring), and Level 5 (Disk Striping with parity). Disk duplexing is also supported, which is an extension to disk mirroring. RAID 0 is not a fault-tolerant disk array, but RAID 1 and RAID 5 are fault tolerant (the data is protected from the failure of a single disk).

20. You are creating a stripe set with parity from five physical drives. One drive has 300 MB of free space left, another drive has 500 MB left, and the other three drives have 700 MB left. What is the maximum size of a stripe set with parity that can be created by using a combination of these disks, including both usable space and parity space?

C. 2.1 GB

20. CORRECT ANSWER: C

Stripe sets must use an equal amount of space from each disk. The largest possible combination is to use the three 700 MB disks, for a stripe set of 2.1 GB. Using four disks with 500 MB yields 2.0 GB while using all five disks with 300 MB results in a 1.5 GB stripe set.

> **FURTHER REVIEW**

PLANNING THE FAULT-TOLERANCE CONFIGURATIONS FOR WINDOWS NT SERVER 4.0

The following key words are important terms that were covered in this section. You should make sure you understand what each one is and what it does.

Key Words

Disk duplexing

Disk mirroring

Disk striping

Disk striping with parity

Fault tolerance

Parity

RAID (Redundant Array of Inexpensive Disks)

Sector sparing

Striping

Volume sets

Supported Windows NT RAID Levels

The following section discusses the different RAID levels supported by Windows NT in more detail.

RAID Level 0: Stripe Sets

Stripe sets are not a fault-tolerant disk array. You can combine several disks into a single partition with a stripe set. The stripe set is similar to a RAID 5 array (striping with parity). RAID 0 is supported on both Windows NT Workstation and Server.

Disk striping divides the data into 64 KB blocks and writes the data across multiple physical disk drives. This process writes data to all the disks in the array at the same time, increasing write performance. Read performance is also improved because data can be read simultaneously from several disks at once. If one disk in the array fails, all the data on the stripe set is lost because the disks work together as a unit. A disk stripe set consists of multiple physical disks. A minimum of two disks is required to create a stripe set; a stripe set can include as many as 32 disks.

RAID Level 1: Disk Mirroring

Disk mirroring duplicates writes to the hard drive onto two physical disks. If each disk has a separate hard drive controller, a mirror is called *disk duplexing*, which provides redundancy for both hard drive failure and controller failure.

This method of fault tolerance is considered to be more expensive per megabyte of data due to the complete duplication of data. Every disk mirror requires two physical disks. Disk mirroring (and disk duplexing) are supported only on Windows NT Server.

RAID Level 5: Stripe Sets with Parity

Disk striping with parity is the more common of the fault-tolerant methods available through Windows NT Server 4.0. Disk striping with parity uses the same basic process of disk striping; it writes the data in 64 KB blocks across multiple physical disks.

A stripe set uses the stripes on disk to store redundant information, known as *parity*. The parity is basically a checksum that can be used to restore the rest of the data if a disk is lost. For example, consider a stripe set with parity with three disks.

If the data values 1 and 2 were written to the stripe set, the parity 3 (which is the sum of 1 and 2) would be written to the third disk. If one of the disks were lost, the data could still be recovered because an algebraic statement would exist. If disk 2 were lost, the equation 1 + ? = 3 would exist. The value 2 could be computed as the missing data and Windows NT could recover the missing drive.

To implement the disk striping with parity, a minimum of three physical disks is required and a maximum of 32 disks can be used. Note that an extra disk is required over striping without parity. This extra disk is devoted to parity information. If any one of the disks in the stripe set with parity fail, the data can be regenerated from the remaining disks. Striping with parity is supported only on Windows NT Server.

Table 1.4 includes a summary of the RAID levels supported by Windows NT.

TABLE 1.4 SUMMARY OF FAULT-TOLERANCE OPTIONS IN WINDOWS NT SERVER 4.0

Disk Striping	*Disk Mirroring/Disk Duplexing*	*Disk Striping w/Parity*
No fault-tolerance	Complete disk duplication	Data regeneration from stored parity information
Minimum of two physical disks; maximum of 32 disks	Two physical disks	Minimum of three physical disks; maximum of 32 disks
100 percent available disk utilization	50 percent available disk utilization	Dedicates the equivalent of one disk's space in the set for parity information; the more disks, the higher the utilization
Cannot include system/boot partition	Includes all partition types	Cannot include system/boot partition
Excellent read/write performance	Moderate read/write performance	Excellent read; moderate write performance

PRACTICE QUESTIONS

SELECTING THE PROPER PROTOCOL

1. The production department needs to access a software product that can be installed only on a NetWare Server. They currently connect to the Windows NT system and would like to be able to connect to both systems with one common protocol. Which of the following protocols can access both a NetWare system and a Windows NT system?

    A. NetWare Connect Protocol
    B. NetBEUI
    C. NWLink IPX/SPX-compatible
    D. GSNW

2. Users from your Windows NT system want to access your NetWare server, but you do not want to set up each one with the NetWare client. Which of the following is required to enable your Windows NT system to share a NetWare connection for the Windows NT users? Select all that apply.

    A. NWLink IPX/SPX-compatible
    B. NetBEUI
    C. GSNW
    D. Services for the Macintosh

3. You are installing Windows NT on a departmental LAN that will support 20 users. The network is wired on a single segment. Which of the following is the most efficient networking protocol you can use for this LAN configuration?

    A. NetBEUI
    B. NWLink
    C. TCP/IP
    D. AppleTalk

4. You are installing a Windows NT Server to support connections for Macintosh clients. This server will also have IIS installed to publish the company employee handbook. Which of the following protocols need to be installed on this server to support these functions? Select all that apply.

    A. NetBEUI
    B. NWLink
    C. TCP/IP
    D. AppleTalk

5. Your network includes Windows NT Servers and NetWare Servers running the IPX/SPX protocol. Which of the following protocols must be installed on the Windows NT Servers so that NetWare clients can connect to these servers? Select the best response.

    A. NetBEUI
    B. NWLink
    C. TCP/IP
    D. AppleTalk

6. You have several IBM AS400 servers in your environment that will communicate with a Windows NT Server using SNA.

You also have several HP network printers that will be managed by a Windows NT print server. Which of the following protocols must be installed on the Windows NT Server to support connections to peripherals? Select the best response.

   A. NWLink
   B. NetBEUI
   C. PrintTalk
   D. DLC

7. A Windows NT Server will be a RAS Server for incoming client calls. This server will provide file access to a NetWare Server and print support for a TCP/IP printer. Which of the following protocols must be installed on the RAS Server to provide client access to these resources and to enable the clients to connect over RAS using the most efficient protocol? Select all that apply.

   A. NetBEUI
   B. NWLink
   C. TCP/IP
   D. DLC

8. Which protocol uses broadcasts in attempts to communicate with other computers on the network?

   A. NetBEUI
   B. NWLink
   C. TCP/IP
   D. DLC

9. You want to configure a Windows NT Server to provide DHCP and WINS services. Which of the following protocols needs to be installed on the server to support these services?

   A. NetBEUI
   B. NWLink
   C. TCP/IP
   D. DLC

10. A Windows NT Primary Domain controller will be used to migrate accounts from several NetWare servers. This PDC will also provide domain-name resolution for web servers to the rest of the domain. Which of the following protocols need to be installed on this server? Select all that apply.

    A. NetBEUI
    B. NWLink
    C. TCP/IP
    D. DLC

11. Which of the following protocols can be used to support network printers? Select all that apply.

    A. NetBEUI
    B. NWLink
    C. TCP/IP
    D. DLC

12. This is a scenario question. First, you must review the scenario, then review the required and optional results. Following that is a solution. You must pick the best evaluation of that solution. Note that questions 13, 14, and 15 also deal with the same scenario.

Scenario:
Your company is adding two new servers to its network for applications, file serving, and print serving. The applications will be used by clients in the domain and also by NetWare clients.

Required Result:
Allow both NetWare and Microsoft clients access to the file and print services.

Optional Results:
Minimize the number of protocols used on the network.

Allow UNIX hosts to access printers on the Windows NT network.

Proposed Solution:
Install File and Print Services for NetWare on the Windows NT servers. Install JetDirect cards into the network printers. Install the NetBEUI protocol on the servers.

Evaluation of Proposed Solution:
(Choose the most correct answer.)

A. The proposed solution produces the required result and both optional results.

B. The proposed solution produces the required result and only one optional result.

C. The proposed solution produces the required result but does not produce any optional results.

D. The proposed solution does not produce the required result.

13. **This applies to the same scenario as number 12.**

Scenario:
Your company is adding two new servers to its network for applications, file serving, and print serving. The applications will be used by clients in the domain and also by NetWare clients.

Required Result:
Allow Microsoft clients to access all the services on the new servers.

Optional Results:
Allow the NetWare clients to access file and print services on the new servers.

Allow Macintosh clients to access files on the new servers.

Proposed Solution:
Install NWLink on the servers.

Evaluation of Proposed Solution:
(Choose the most correct answer.)

A. The proposed solution produces the required result and both optional results.

B. The proposed solution produces the required result and only one optional result.

C. The proposed solution produces the required result but does not produce any optional result.

D. The proposed solution does not produce the required result.

14. **This applies to the same scenario as number 12.**

Scenario:
Your company is adding two new servers to its network for applications, file serving, and print serving. The applications will be used by clients in the domain and also by NetWare clients.

Required Result:
Allow both NetWare and Microsoft clients to access the client/server application on the new servers.

Optional Results:
Minimize the protocols used on the network.

Allow NetWare clients to access the file and print services of the new servers.

Proposed Solution:
Install the client software needed for the application on the Microsoft and NetWare clients. Install NWLink on the servers.

Evaluation of Proposed Solution:
(Choose the most correct answer.)

A. The proposed solution produces the required result and both optional results.

B. The proposed solution produces the required result and only one optional result.

C. The proposed solution produces the required result but does not produce any optional results.

D. The proposed solution does not produce the required result.

15. **This applies to the same scenario as number 12.**

    Scenario:
    Your company is adding two new servers to its network for applications, file serving, and print serving. The applications will be used by clients in the domain and also by NetWare clients.

    Required Result:
    Allow access to the application for both Microsoft and NetWare clients.

    Optional Results:
    Minimize broadcast traffic on the network.

    Minimize the number of protocols used on the network.

    Proposed Solution:
    Install TCP/IP and the client software on the NetWare and Microsoft clients. Install TCP/IP on the new servers. Install a WINS Server and configure the Microsoft clients as WINS clients. Install WINS proxy agents on the network segments where the NetWare clients reside.

    Evaluation of Proposed Solution:
    (Choose the most correct answer.)

    A. The proposed solution produces the required result and both optional results.

    B. The proposed solution produces the required result and only one optional result.

    C. The proposed solution produces the required result but does not produce any optional results.

    D. The proposed solution does not produce the required result.

16. **Which protocols can be used in a segmented network with routers separating the segments? Select all that apply.**

    A. NetBEUI

    B. NWLink

    C. NDIS

    D. TCP/IP

17. **Which of the following protocols must be installed before File and Print Services for NetWare can be installed? Select the best response.**

A. NetBEUI
B. NWLink
C. DLC
D. TCP/IP

18. Which of the following protocols must be installed so that a server can be used as a DNS server? Select the best response.

    A. NetBEUI
    B. NWLink
    C. DLC
    D. TCP/IP

19. Windows NT supports printing to network printers that have a specific address assigned to the printer. Which of the following protocols supports this type of printing?

A. NetBEUI
B. NWLink
C. NDIS
D. TCP/IP

20. Which protocol allows the greatest variety of non-Microsoft clients to connect to a Windows NT Server?

    A. NetBEUI
    B. NWLink
    C. DLC
    D. TCP/IP

ANSWER KEY

1. C	6. D	11. C-D	16. B-D
2. A-C	7. A-B-C	12. C	17. B
3. A	8. A	13. C	18. D
4. C-D	9. C	14. B	19. D
5. B	10. B-C	15. A	20. D

ANSWERS & EXPLANATIONS

SELECTING THE PROPER PROTOCOL

1. The production department needs to access a software product that can be installed only on a NetWare Server. They currently connect to the Windows NT system and would like be able to connect to both systems with one common protocol. Which of the following protocols can access both a NetWare system and a Windows NT system?

    C. NWLink IPX/SPX-compatible

1. CORRECT ANSWER: C

NWLink is the protocol that Microsoft provides to work with NetWare.

Answer A is incorrect—this is not a valid protocol. Answer B is incorrect—NetBEUI is not supported on NetWare. Answer D is incorrect—GSNW is a service that allows Microsoft clients to access NetWare servers through a Windows NT Server without having NetWare client software installed.

NWLink is Microsoft's version of IPX/SPX, the protocol suite that has been used within the NetWare environment for years. NWLINK is best suited for networks requiring communication with Windows NT and NetWare servers, and for existing NetWare clients.

2. Users from your Windows NT system want to access your NetWare server, but you do not want to set up each one with the NetWare client. Which of the following is required to enable your Windows NT system to share a NetWare connection for the Windows NT users? Select all that apply.

    A. NWLink IPX/SPX-compatible
    C. GSNW

2. CORRECT ANSWERS: A-C

You need the protocol to let the Windows NT Server talk to NetWare (NWLink) and the service to let the Windows NT Server function as a gateway for Microsoft clients (Gateway Service for NetWare or GSNW).

Answer B is incorrect—NetBEUI is not supported on NetWare. Answer D is incorrect because Service for Macintosh is used for a Windows NT server to communicate with Macintosh clients.

A Windows NT Server running NWLink can serve as an application server for NetWare clients. However, the NetWare clients also need client software to communicate with the application; NWLink provides the common protocol. Other services can be installed on a Windows NT Server to enable additional NetWare connectivity. All these services depend on NWLink.

The NetWare clients also can use the Windows NT Server for file and print access if an additional service is installed (File and Print Services for NetWare [FPNW]). If the Gateway Service for NetWare (GSNW) is installed on the Windows NT Server, clients on the Windows NT network can communicate with NetWare servers without having NetWare client software installed.

If GSNW and NWLink are installed on a Windows NT Server, the Migration Tool for NetWare can be used to migrate NetWare users and files to the Windows NT Server. Microsoft also provides Client Services for NetWare (CSNW) to allow Windows NT Workstation computers to connect to NetWare servers.

3. You are installing Windows NT on a departmental LAN that will support 20 users. The network is wired on a single segment. Which of the following is the most efficient networking protocol you can use for this LAN configuration?

A. NetBEUI

3. CORRECT ANSWER: A

NetBEUI is the most efficient protocol for this small, single-segment LAN.

Answers B and C are incorrect because NWLink and TCP/IP are less efficient then NetBEUI. Answer D is incorrect because AppleTalk cannot be used by Windows-based machines as a LAN protocol—only by an NT server for communication with Macintosh clients.

The NetBEUI protocol is the easiest to implement. The NetBEUI protocol uses NetBIOS broadcasts to locate other computers on the network. This broadcasting generates extra traffic on the network, which increases to excessive amounts on larger networks. Also, the broadcasts that NetBEUI uses are not routable; in other words, you cannot access computers that are not on your physical network segment. For these reasons, NetBEUI is recommended only for small- to medium-sized networks that are on a single segment. NetBEUI does not provide connectivity to many other network types. This protocol is supported by most Microsoft clients as well as IBM OS/2 clients.

ANSWERS & EXPLANATIONS

4. You are installing a Windows NT Server to support connections for Macintosh clients. This server will also have IIS installed to publish the company employee handbook. Which of the following protocols need to be installed on this server to support these functions? Select all that apply.

    C. TCP/IP
    D. AppleTalk

4. CORRECT ANSWERS: C-D

AppleTalk is needed for the Mac clients and IIS requires TCP/IP.

Answers A and B are incorrect because neither NetBEUI nor NWLink is needed for IIS or Macintosh communications.

IIS (Internet Information Server) is Microsoft's Windows NT web server. The Internet uses the TCP/IP protocol stack for all communications.

Apple Macintosh clients can connect to Windows NT servers running the AppleTalk protocol. This protocol is installed when Services for Macintosh is installed. This service (and the underlying AppleTalk protocol) allows Macintosh computers on your network to be able to access files and printers on the Windows NT Server. It also enables Windows NT clients to print to AppleTalk printers.

5. Your network includes Windows NT Servers and NetWare Servers running the IPX/SPX protocol. Which of the following protocols must be installed on the Windows NT Servers so that NetWare clients can connect to these servers? Select the best response.

    B. NWLink

5. CORRECT ANSWER: B

NWLink is Microsoft's implementation of IPX/SPX.

Answers A, C, D are incorrect because the NetBEUI, TCP/IP, and AppleTalk protocols are not used by NetWare clients

NWLink was developed by Microsoft to provide Windows clients and Windows NT servers with an IPX/SPX-compatible protocol to use in environments that include NetWare servers and clients.

6. You have several IBM AS400 servers in your environment that will communicate with a Windows NT Server using SNA. You also have several HP network printers that will be managed by a Windows NT print server. Which of the following protocols must be installed on the Windows NT Server to support connections to peripherals? Select the best response.

    D. DLC

6. CORRECT ANSWER: D

The DLC (Data-Link Control) protocol provides support for IBM mainframes and AS400s in addition to HP network printer support.

Answers A and B are incorrect—the NetBEUI and NWLink protocols are not used for communication with an IBM AS/400. Answer C is incorrect—PrintTalk is not a valid protocol.

DLC is used to provide connectivity to IBM mainframes and AS400 servers. The BackOffice product SNA is used to connect to these IBM servers and requires DLC as its underlying protocol. DLC also can be used for HP network printers. However, if an HP printer has a JetDirect card installed, it can be assigned a TCP/IP address and thus use TCP/IP rather than DLC for its printing protocol. DLC is not used by any Microsoft clients; it is only used on a Windows NT Server to support IBM and HP connections.

7. A Windows NT Server will be a RAS Server for incoming client calls. This server will provide file access to a NetWare Server and print support for a TCP/IP printer. Which of the following protocols must be installed on the RAS Server to provide client access to these resources and to enable the clients to connect over RAS using the most efficient protocol? Select all that apply.

   A. NetBEUI
   B. NWLink
   C. TCP/IP

7. CORRECT ANSWERS: A-B-C

NWLink and TCP/IP must be installed so that the server can connect to these resources. NetBEUI is the most efficient protocol to use over a RAS link. The RAS Server functions as a NetBIOS gateway, converting the NetBEUI protocol to the protocols used by the servers with which the RAS client is trying to communicate.

Answer D is incorrect—the DLC protocol is not required to access these resources.

The NetBEUI protocol is the most efficient RAS protocol. NWLink is required to access the NetWare servers and the TCP/IP protocol is needed to access the TCP/IP-based printers.

8. Which protocol uses broadcasts in attempts to communicate with other computers on the network?

   A. NetBEUI

8. CORRECT ANSWER: A

NetBEUI is broadcast based.

Answers B and C are incorrect—TCP/IP and NWLink are not broadcast based. Answer D is incorrect because DLC is used to communicate with mainframes and printers, not as a LAN protocol.

The NetBEUI protocol uses NetBIOS broadcasts to locate other computers on the network. This broadcasting generates extra traffic on the network, which increases to excessive amounts on larger networks. Also, the broadcasts that NetBEUI uses are not routable; in other words, you cannot access computers that are not on your physical network segment.

9. You want to configure a Windows NT Server to provide DHCP and WINS services. Which of the following protocols needs to be installed on the server to support these services?

C. TCP/IP

9. CORRECT ANSWER: C

TCP/IP is needed for DHCP and WINS.

TCP/IP is required for several Windows NT services. Because these services depend on TCP/IP, they cannot be installed if TCP/IP is not installed on the server. WINS, DHCP, DNS, and IIS all require TCP/IP.

DHCP (Dynamic Host Configuration Protocol) is a service that allocates TCP/IP addresses automatically to all the clients configured for DHCP. When clients use DHCP to obtain IP addresses and configuration information, the administrator does not have to manually configure these clients.

WINS (Windows Internet Name Service) Server is a dynamic database to resolve NetBIOS names to IP addresses. It is often used in conjunction with DHCP because an administrator does not know which client will receive a particular IP address. WINS automatically registers a client's current IP address in the WINS database. In addition to the computer name, any networking services a computer provides are also registered with WINS.

10. A Windows NT Primary Domain controller will be used to migrate accounts from several NetWare servers. This PDC will also provide domain-name resolution for web servers to the rest of the domain. Which of the following protocols need to be installed on this server? Select all that apply.

B. NWLink
C. TCP/IP

10. CORRECT ANSWERS: B-C

NWLink supports the NetWare migration and TCP/IP supports DNS for domain-name resolution.

Answers A and D are incorrect—NetBEUI and DLC are not used for NetWare or Web connectivity.

NWLink is Microsoft's version of IPX/SPX, the protocol suite that has been used within the NetWare environment for years. NWLINK is best suited for networks requiring communication with existing NetWare servers, and for existing NetWare clients.

DNS (Domain Name System) is used to resolve domain names, such as www.microsoft.com, to IP addresses. DNS is often used to resolve Internet names or to resolve names on a local intranet.

11. Which of the following protocols can be used to support network printers? Select all that apply.

  C. TCP/IP
  D. DLC

11. CORRECT ANSWERS: C-D

DLC supports HP network printers and TCP/IP supports network printers, including HP network printers with JetDirect cards that can be assigned an IP address.

Answers A and B are incorrect because NetBEUI and NWLink do not support network printers.

12. Proposed Solution:
Install File and Print Services for NetWare on the Windows NT servers. Install JetDirect cards into the network printers. Install the NetBEUI protocol on the servers.

  C. The proposed solution produces the required result but does not produce any optional results.

12. CORRECT ANSWER: C

Installing File and Print Services for NetWare forces the installation of NWLink. This allows both Microsoft and NetWare clients file and print access.

Answers A and B are incorrect because adding NetBEUI is not necessary and TCP/IP was not installed to allow UNIX printing support. Answer D is incorrect because the required result was produced.

13. Proposed Solution:
Install NWLink on the servers.

  C. The proposed solution produces the required result but does not produce any optional results.

13. CORRECT ANSWER: C

NWLink allows Microsoft clients to connect to the server, but without additional services (FPNW).

Answers A and B are incorrect because NetWare clients cannot access the file and print server without FPNW, and Macintosh clients require the AppleTalk protocol on the server. Answer D is incorrect because the required result was produced.

14. Proposed Solution:
Install the client software needed for the application on the Microsoft and NetWare clients. Install NWLink on the servers.

  B. The proposed solution produces the required result and only one optional result.

14. CORRECT ANSWER: B

The client software combined with the NWLink protocol allows both Microsoft and NetWare clients to access the application.

Answer A is incorrect because the NetWare clients require FPNW on the server before they can connect for file and print access. Answer C and D are incorrect because one of the optional results and the required result were produced.

ANSWERS & EXPLANATIONS 45

15. Proposed Solution:
Install TCP/IP and the client software on the NetWare and Microsoft clients. Install TCP/IP on the new servers. Install a WINS Server and configure the Microsoft clients as WINS clients. Install WINS proxy agents on the network segments where the NetWare clients reside.

   A. The proposed solution produces the required result and both optional results.

15. CORRECT ANSWER: A

NetWare clients can connect by using TCP/IP if they have the protocol installed. TCP/IP uses few broadcasts, and a single protocol can be used for these requirements.

Windows NT also can communicate with NetWare using TCP/IP if the NetWare servers have TCP/IP installed. However, NWLink (IPX/SPX) is usually thought of as the protocol used to connect to NetWare.

Answers B, C, and D are incorrect because both the optional results and the required result were produced.

16. Which protocols can be used in a segmented network with routers separating the segments? Select all that apply.

   B. NWLink
   D. TCP/IP

16. CORRECT ANSWERS: B-D

Both NWLink and TCP/IP can be used in this environment. NetBEUI is the only protocol limited to a single segment.

Answer A is incorrect—NetBEUI cannot be segmented. Answer C is incorrect because NDIS is the communicating layer between the protocol and the network card, not a protocol.

17. Which of the following protocols must be installed before File and Print Services for NetWare can be installed? Select the best response.

   B. NWLink

17. CORRECT ANSWER: B

FPNW depends on NWLink.

Answers A, C, and D are incorrect because FPNW requires only NWLink to function.

NetWare clients also can use the Windows NT Server for file and print access if an additional service is installed (File and Print Services for NetWare [FPNW]).

18. Which of the following protocols must be installed so that a server can be used as a DNS server? Select the best response.

   D. TCP/IP

18. CORRECT ANSWER: D

DNS depends on TCP/IP.

Answers A, B, and C are incorrect because DNS (Domain Name Service) requires the TCP/IP protocol stack.

DNS (Domain Name System) is used to resolve domain names, such as www.microsoft.com, to IP addresses. DNS is often used to resolve Internet names or to resolve names on a local intranet.

Chapter 1 PLANNING

19. Windows NT supports printing to network printers that have a specific address assigned to the printer. Which of the following protocols supports this type of printing?

    D. TCP/IP

19. CORRECT ANSWER: D

TCP/IP fits this description.

Answers A and B are incorrect—NetBEUI and NWLink do support network printers. Answer C is incorrect because NDIS is the communicating layer between the protocol and the network card, not a protocol.

If an HP printer has a JetDirect card installed, it can be assigned a TCP/IP address and thus use TCP/IP rather than DLC for its printing protocol.

20. Which protocol allows the greatest variety of non-Microsoft clients to connect to a Windows NT Server?

    D. TCP/IP

20. CORRECT ANSWER: D

TCP/IP is the most common protocol.

Answers A, B, and C are incorrect because these protocols are not widely supported outside their specific system functions.

TCP/IP allows Windows NT to connect with many non-Microsoft systems. Some of the systems with which it can communicate include the following:

- Any Internet-connected system
- UNIX systems
- IBM Mainframe systems
- DEC Pathworks
- TCP/IP printers directly connected to the network

TCP/IP has increased in popularity and is now supported by virtually all the new operating systems being released today. Using TCP/IP gives you the widest possible choice of connectivity options.

FURTHER REVIEW

SELECTING THE PROPER PROTOCOL

The following key words are important terms that were covered in this section. You should make sure you understand what each one is and what it does.

Key Words

DHCP (Dynamic Host Configuration Protocol)
DLC (Data Link Control)
DNS (Domain Name System)
IIS (Internet Information Server)
TCP/IP
WINS (Windows Internet Name Service)

Windows NT Server Protocols

The following sections discuss the network protocols supported by Windows NT in greater detail.

NetBEUI

The NetBEUI protocol is the easiest to implement. The NetBEUI protocol uses NetBIOS broadcasts to locate other computers on the network. This broadcasting generates extra traffic on the network, which increases to excessive amounts on larger networks. Also, the broadcasts that NetBEUI uses are not routable; in other words, you cannot access computers that are not on your physical network segment. For these reasons, NetBEUI is recommended only for small- to medium-sized networks that are on a single segment. NetBEUI does not provide connectivity to many other network types. This protocol is supported by most Microsoft clients as well as IBM OS/2 clients.

TCP/IP

Transmission Control Protocol/Internet Protocol, or TCP/IP, is the most common protocol. TCP/IP is an industry-standard protocol that is supported under most network operating systems. Because of this acceptance throughout the industry, TCP/IP allows a Windows NT system to connect to other systems running TCP/IP.

TCP/IP is a routable protocol that lends itself directly to enterprise or WAN communication. You can communicate with any number of physical network segments with TCP/IP.

NWLink IPX/SPX-compatible Protocol

NWLink is Microsoft's version of IPX/SPX, the protocol suite that has been used within the NetWare environment for years. NWLINK is best suited for networks requiring communication with existing NetWare servers, and for existing NetWare clients.

Data Link Control (DLC)

DLC is used to provide connectivity to IBM mainframes and AS400 servers. The BackOffice product SNA is used to connect to these IBM servers and requires DLC as its underlying protocol. DLC also can be used for HP network printers. However, if an HP printer has a JetDirect card installed, it can be assigned a TCP/IP address and thus use TCP/IP rather than DLC for its printing protocol. DLC is not used by any Microsoft clients; it is only used on a Windows NT Server to support IBM and HP connections.

AppleTalk Protocol (Services for Macintosh)

Apple Macintosh clients can connect to Windows NT servers running the AppleTalk protocol. This protocol is installed when Services for Macintosh is installed. This service (and the underlying AppleTalk protocol) allows Macintosh computers on your network to be able to access files and printers on the Windows NT Server. It also enables Windows NT clients to print to AppleTalk printers.

SUMMARY

Planning a Windows NT 4.0 installation in an enterprise environment requires a solid knowledge of the software and implementation requirements that must be achieved. This includes choosing a domain model and network protocol to fit the network infrastructure.

CHAPTER 2

Installation and Configuration

This chapter focuses on the installation and configuration of your Windows NT Server computer in an enterprise environment. It also covers the additional components and services that can be used in an enterprise environment.

The Enterprise exam does not place a great deal of emphasis on the installation process. You need to have a strong knowledge of the configuration options, and an understanding of the reasons for selecting a specific configuration. As you go through the sections of this chapter, you are introduced to the configuration options and the steps required to install and configure each component.

OBJECTIVES

This chapter prepares you for the exam by covering the following objectives:

Install Windows NT Server in the various server roles of Primary Domain Controller, Backup Domain Controller, and Member Server.

▶ This chapter begins with a quick overview of the entire installation process to provide you with a solid understanding of the steps involved in installing a Windows NT Server system for various roles.

Configure network protocols and protocol bindings (including TCP/IP with DHCP and WINS, NWLink IPX/SPX-compatible Transport Protocol, DLC, and AppleTalk).

▶ Installing and configuring network protocols is controlled in the network properties of your Windows NT system. The installation of all the protocols is identical. The configuration of each protocol is different, however, so you must understand the process required for configuring each of the supported protocols.

continues

OBJECTIVES (continued)

Configure Windows NT Server core services, including Directory Replication and Computer Browser.

▶ Windows NT takes full advantage of its multi-threaded, multitasking capabilities by running services in the background. In this section, you look at configuring some of the core services in Windows NT Server. These services are the following:

- Server service
- Workstation service
- Computer Browser service
- Directory Replication service

Configure hard disks to provide redundancy and to improve performance.

▶ In Windows NT Server, various hard disk options and fault tolerance options are available to help you improve disk performance. In this section, you look at configuring your system to use the disk options available in Windows NT Server. All hard disk configuring can be done using the Disk Administrator tool. The different disk configurations you need to understand for the enterprise exam are as follows:

- Stripe set
- Volume set
- Disk mirroring
- Stripe set with parity

Configure printer tasks, such as adding and configuring a printer, implementing a printer pool, and setting print priorities.

▶ In this section, you examine the options available for configuring a printer. You also go through the installation steps required to configure a network printer.

All the settings for installing and configuring printers are found by clicking the Printer icon in My Computer or by selecting Start, Settings, Printers. The Printers dialog box contains all of your installed printers as well as an icon used for installing new printers.

Configure NT Server for various types of clients, including Windows NT Workstation, Windows 95, and Macintosh.

▶ Your Windows NT Server is the selected server for various client operating systems. In this section, you look at the configuration requirements for Windows NT Workstation clients, Windows 95 clients, and Macintosh clients.

▶ Windows NT Server handles all the requests from each of these clients automatically. The Windows NT Workstation and Windows 95 clients use Windows NT logon security and provide complete functionality as a Windows NT client right out of the box. To enable connectivity with Apple Macintosh computers, the services for the Macintosh must be installed. The Network Client Administrator can be used to simplify the installation of your client computers.

The Network Client Administrator is found in the Administrative Tools group. You can use the Network Client Administrator program to do the following:

- Make a network installation startup disk.
- Make an installation disk set.
- Copy client-based Network Administration Tools.
- View remoteboot client information.

PRACTICE QUESTIONS

INSTALLING WINDOWS NT IN VARIOUS SERVER ROLES

1. You need to install a new Member Server in the Pittsburgh Domain, but you are in St. Louis. What is the best method to install and configure a Member Server when it is not physically attached to the Domain?

    A. Install the new server as a PDC; then, convert it to a Member Server when it can be attached physically.

    B. Install it as a BDC of the St. Louis Domain and change its domain when in the correct location.

    C. Install the machine as a computer in the workgroup. When it is in the correct location, add the computer to the Pittsburgh Domain.

    D. None of the above.

2. You have correctly installed your NT server, but it has developed a problem that requires the Emergency Repair Disks. You do not have the three disks created during the original installation. Which program should you use to create them?

    A. SETUP32.EXE /B

    B. WINNT32.EXE /OX

    C. WINNT32.EXE /B

    D. WINNT32.EXE /UDF

3. Your company has one server running Windows NT and has no plans to add additional servers. With 40 employees and 30 workstations, what kind of licensing do you choose?

    A. Purchase 30 CALs and configure them as Per Seat.

    B. Purchase 40 CALs and configure them as Per Seat.

    C. Purchase 30 CALs and configure them as Per Server.

    D. Purchase 40 CALs and configure them as Per Server.

4. This is a scenario question. First you must review the scenario, then review the required and optional results. Following that is a solution. You must pick the best evaluation of that solution.

    Scenario:
    You have installed four NT Server machines in one domain (one PDC and three BDCs). Your company has grown and the following objectives have been set for the changing company network.

    Required Result:
    You want to add another domain to the network, but must use only the existing domain controllers.

    Optional Result:
    When the new domain has been created, you want to move several users and their machines to the new domain.

Proposed Solution:
To accomplish this, you want to promote one BDC to a PDC and rename it. You then plan to change another BDC to belong to the new domain by changing the domain name from the Network option in Control Panel.

In addition, you want to migrate several NT Workstation computers by changing the domain name and by creating the computer account from the system option in the Control Panel.

Evaluation of Proposed Solution:
(Choose the most correct answer.)

  A. This solution fulfills the required result and the optional results.

  B. This solution fulfills the required result but not the optional result.

  C. This solution does not fulfill the required result but does fill the optional result.

  D. This solution does not fulfills the required result or the optional result.

5. **If a Windows NT Workstation machine needs to migrate to another domain, what needs to happen? Select all that apply.**

  A. From the Server Manager, use Add to Domain; then, from the workstation machine, change the workstation name from My Computer properties.

  B. From the Server Manager, use Add to Domain; then, from the workstation machine, change the domain name from Network Neighborhood properties.

  C. Reinstall and create the computer account during the installation.

  D. On the local computer, add the computer account from the network applet in the Control Panel.

6. **You already have created NT setup boot disks and do not want to create them again. How can you avoid creating the disks and use your original set?**

  A. Start the installation with WINNT /X.

  B. Start the installation with WINNT /OX.

  C. Start the installation with WINNT /B.

  D. Start the installation with WINNT /disks:0.

7. **You want to upgrade a Windows NT Workstation 3.51 to a Windows NT Server 4 domain controller. How do you do this?**

  A. Run WINNT and respond Yes to the upgrade question.

  B. Run WINNT32 and respond Yes to the upgrade question.

  C. There is no direct upgrade path from Windows NT Workstation 3.51 to a Windows NT Server 4 domain controller.

  D. Run UPGRADE.EXE.

8. **You want to upgrade a Windows NT Server 3.51 Member Server to a Windows NT Server 4 domain controller. How do you do this?**

  A. Run WINNT and respond Yes to the upgrade question.

  B. Run WINNT32 and respond Yes to the upgrade question.

  C. There is no direct upgrade path from a Windows NT Server 3.51 Member Server to a Windows NT Server 4 domain controller.

  D. Run UPGRADE.EXE.

9. **You want to upgrade a Windows NT Server 3.51 Member Server to a Windows NT Server 4 Member Server. How do you do this?**

    A. Run WINNT and respond Yes to the upgrade question.

    B. Run WINNT32 and respond Yes to the upgrade question.

    C. There is no direct upgrade path from Windows NT 3.51 member server to a Windows NT Server 4 member server.

    D. Run UPGRADE.EXE.

10. **You want to upgrade a Windows NT Server 3.51 domain controller to a Windows NT Server 4 domain controller. How do you do this?**

    A. Run WINNT and respond Yes to the upgrade question.

    B. Run WINNT32 and respond Yes to the upgrade question.

    C. There is no direct upgrade path from a Windows NT 3.51 domain controller to a Windows NT Server 4 domain controller.

    D. Run UPGRADE.EXE.

ANSWER KEY

1. C	5. B-D	9. B
2. B	6. A	10. B
3. C	7. B	
4. D	8. C	

ANSWERS & EXPLANATIONS

INSTALLING WINDOWS NT IN VARIOUS SERVER ROLES

1. You need to install a new Member Server in the Pittsburgh Domain, but you are in St. Louis. What is the best method to install and configure a Member Server when it is not physically attached to the Domain?

    C. Install the machine as a computer in the workgroup. When it is in the correct location, add the computer to the Pittsburgh Domain.

1. CORRECT ANSWER: C

It is not possible to change a domain controller to a Member Server without reinstalling.

Answer A is incorrect—you cannot convert a PDC to a Member Server for another domain. Answer B is incorrect—you cannot install a BDC without connectivity to the parent domain, and also a BDC cannot be demoted to a Member Server either. Answer D is incorrect because Answer C is correct.

You can install a member server as a member of a workgroup and then when connectivity is established to the parent domain, the server can join the domain.

2. You have correctly installed your NT server, but it has developed a problem that requires the Emergency Repair Disks. You do not have the three disks created during the original installation. Which program should you use to create them?

    B. WINNT32.EXE /OX

2. CORRECT ANSWER: B

Use WINNT32 /OX to create the three disks without performing a complete repair.

Answer A is incorrect—there isn't a setup32.exe program. Answers C and D are incorrect—these are the wrong switches to create the boot disks.

The /OX switch works with both the WINNT.EXE and WINNT32.EXE programs. This option creates the three boot disks for a CD-ROM installation without actually starting a Windows NT installation.

3. Your company has one server running Windows NT and has no plans to add additional servers. With 40 employees and 30 workstations, what kind of licensing do you choose?

    C. Purchase 30 CALs and configure them as Per Server.

3. CORRECT ANSWER: C

Because there are only 30 workstations, only 30 connections would be used.

Answer A is incorrect because there will be no additional servers used; Per Seat licensing is not required. Answers B and D are incorrect because only 30 licenses will be needed.

Per Server licensing can be used in situations in which there is a set number of servers that will not change. In this situation, Per Seat licensing would limit the number of people that can log on, whereas Per Server licensing limits only the number of workstations that can access the server. In this case 50 people could use the 30 workstations and only require 30 licenses, whereas Per Seat would require 50 licenses.

4. Proposed Solution:
To accomplish this, you want to promote one BDC to a PDC and rename it. You then plan to change another BDC to belong to the new domain by changing the domain name from the Network option in Control Panel.

In addition, you want to migrate several NT Workstation computers by changing the domain name and by creating the computer account from the system option in the Control Panel.

D. This solution does not fulfill the required result or the optional result.

4. CORRECT ANSWER: D

It is not possible to migrate domain controllers, and although computer accounts can be made from an NT Workstation, they are created through the Network icon in the Control Panel.

The only way to accomplish this would be to reinstall one of the BDC computers as a new PDC. You could then create new computer accounts in the new domain for the workstations to be moved and delete the existing machine accounts in the original domain.

5. If a Windows NT Workstation machine needs to migrate to another domain, what needs to happen? Select all that apply.

B. From the Server Manager, use Add to Domain; then, from the workstation machine, change the domain name from Network Neighborhood properties.

D. On the local computer, add the computer account from the network applet in the Control Panel.

5. CORRECT ANSWERS: B-D

You can create the account from either the server or the workstation.

Answer A is incorrect—you cannot change domains from the My Computer properties. Answer C is incorrect—reinstalling is not necessary.

Machine accounts can be created either from the Server Manager applet or from the workstation that is being moved. If you create the account in Server Manager, you still must change the domain name on the workstation. To create the account from the workstation, you must have Domain Admin permissions.

56 Chapter 2 INSTALLATION AND CONFIGURATION

6. You already have created NT setup boot disks and do not want to create them again. How can you avoid creating the disks and use your original set?

   A. Start the installation with WINNT /X.

> **6. CORRECT ANSWER: A**
>
> /OX will create the startup disks. /X will start an installation and use previously created disks.
>
> Answers B, C, and D are incorrect because the switches are incorrect.
>
> You can use the /X parameter with both the WINNT.EXE and the WINNT32.EXE.

7. You want to upgrade a Windows NT Workstation 3.51 to a Windows NT Server 4 domain controller. How do you do this?

   B. Run WINNT32 and respond Yes to the upgrade question.

> **7. CORRECT ANSWER: B**
>
> When upgrading NT, use WINNT32.
>
> Answer A is incorrect—you must use the 32-bit setup program (WINNT32.EXE). Answer C is incorrect—you can upgrade to v4.0 from 3.51. Answer D is incorrect—there isn't a UPGRADE.EXE program. It is not possible to upgrade Windows NT Workstation to a domain controller without creating a dual-boot machine or installing Windows NT Server over Windows NT Workstation.
>
> Upgrading to Windows NT 4.0 from an earlier version is pretty straightforward. You simply start the installation, and when prompted, choose the Upgrade from the existing version option.

8. You want to upgrade a Windows NT Server 3.51 Member Server to a Windows NT Server 4 domain controller. How do you do this?

   C. There is no direct upgrade path from a Windows NT Server 3.51 Member Server to a Windows NT Server 4 domain controller.

> **8. CORRECT ANSWER: C**
>
> Although 3.51 Member Servers are upgradable, they can be upgraded only to Member Servers.
>
> Answers A, B, and D are incorrect because you must reinstall to change a Member Server to a domain controller.

ANSWERS & EXPLANATIONS

9. You want to upgrade a Windows NT Server 3.51 Member Server to a Windows NT Server 4 Member Server. How do you do this?

  B. Run WINNT32 and respond Yes to the upgrade question.

9. CORRECT ANSWER: B

Version 3.51 Member Servers are upgradable to 4.0 Member Servers.

Answer A is incorrect—you must use the 32-bit setup program (WINNT32.EXE). Answer C is incorrect—there is a direct upgrade path. Answer D is incorrect—there isn't an UPGRADE.EXE program.

When you upgrade a 3.51 member server to 4.0, the server's role stays the same.

10. You want to upgrade a Windows NT Server 3.51 domain controller to a Windows NT Server 4 domain controller. How do you do this?

  B. Run WINNT32 and respond Yes to the upgrade question.

10. CORRECT ANSWER: B

3.51 domain controllers are upgradable to 4.0 domain controllers.

Answer A is incorrect—you must use the 32-bit setup program (WINNT32.EXE). Answer C is incorrect—there is a direct upgrade path. Answer D is incorrect—there isn't an UPGRADE.EXE program.

When you upgrade a 3.51 domain controller to 4.0, the server's role stays the same.

FURTHER REVIEW

INSTALLING WINDOWS NT IN VARIOUS SERVER ROLES

The following key words are important terms that were covered in this section. You should make sure you understand what each one is and what it does.

Key Words

Backup Domain Controller
Primary Domain Controller
Member Server
WINNT.EXE
WINNT32.EXE

Server Roles in Windows NT Server

The different server roles in which Windows NT Server can be installed are as follows:

- Primary Domain Controller
- Backup Domain Controller
- Member Servers

Each server role provides a specific function in your Windows NT system. The next three sections address each of the roles. You gain an understanding of both the function each role performs and the reasons for selecting a particular server role for your Windows NT Server system.

Primary Domain Controllers

The Primary Domain Controller (PDC) is the first domain controller installed into a domain. As the first computer in the domain, the PDC creates the domain. Each domain can contain only one PDC. All other domain controllers in the domain are installed as Backup Domain Controllers (BDCs). In addition to standard Windows NT Server functionality, the PDC contains the original copy of the Security Accounts Manager (SAM) database, which contains all user accounts and security permissions for your domain and handles user requests and logon validation. The PDC runs the Net Logon service.

▼ **NOTE**

The three main functions of the Net Logon service are covered in different sections of this chapter. The three main functions are as follows:

- To handle logon requests from users
- To control database synchronization between PDCs and all BDCs
- To enable pass-through authentication of users across trust relationships

Backup Domain Controllers

The Backup Domain Controller (BDC) is an additional domain controller used to handle logon requests by users in the network. To handle the logon requests, the BDC must have a complete copy of the domain database, or SAM. The BDC also runs the Net Logon service.

A PDC will announce when there have been changes to one of the three SAM databases. The BDCs then connect to the PDC and request the changes that they do not have in their copy of the database. The entire database is not transferred, only the changes to the database are. The BDC helps the PDC handle user requests and logon validation. It also acts as a Windows NT Server, offering all the available options and functionality.

Member Servers

A computer that handles the server functionality you require without the overhead of handling logon validation is called a Member Server. A Member Server either is a part of the domain or is simply a participant in the Workgroup environment, but it does not need a copy of the SAM database nor does it handle logon requests. The main function of a Member Server is to share resources.

PRACTICE QUESTIONS

CONFIGURING NETWORK PROTOCOLS AND BINDINGS

1. **What is a subnet mask used for?**

    A. It is the address of the router.

    B. It is used to determine whether a target host is on the same subnet or on a remote subnet.

    C. It is a unique 32-bit address that identifies your machine across a TCP/IP network.

    D. It passes addressing information to the Internet.

2. **Your company is using TCP/IP as the primary network protocol. Users on the network randomly complain that they get messages about IP address conflicts. What could be a potential solution to this?**

    A. Implement IIS

    B. Implement DNS

    C. Implement WINS

    D. Implement DHCP

3. **Which service can be used to reduce the number of NetBIOS broadcast messages sent across the network to locate a computer?**

    A. TCP/IP

    B. HOSTS files

    C. WINS

    D. DNS

4. **By default, how are DHCP servers used to allocate an IP address to a client?**

    A. Each client is configured to request an IP address from a specific DHCP server.

    B. Each client sends out a broadcast requesting a number from any DHCP server that can respond.

    C. Each client is configured to look for an LMHOSTS file with the IP address of the DHCP server.

    D. A DHCP server sends out broadcasts announcing itself across the network. Any client needing an address will respond to the broadcast.

5. **Your multihomed system is connected to multiple TCP/IP subnets. What must be enabled to transfer packets between subnets?**

    A. IP repeating

    B. IP forwarding

    C. Default Gateway

    D. DNS

6. **What is the default frame type setting for Windows NT?**

    A. 802.2

    B. 802.3

    C. Auto Frame

    D. SNAP

7. **What needs to be installed to configure AppleTalk?**

    A. Gateway Services for Macintosh

    B. NWLink

    C. Services for Macintosh

    D. LocalTalk

8. **To optimize your binding order, the protocols should be placed in what order?**

    A. The protocols used most often should be at the top of the binding order.

    B. The least-used protocols should be at the top of the binding order.

    C. Binding order will not affect speed.

    D. Stagger the protocols to keep a balanced load.

9. **What configuration options are mandatory when installing TCP/IP?**

    A. DNS and IP address

    B. Default gateway and subnet mask

    C. IP address and subnet mask

    D. IP address and default gateway

ANSWER KEY

1. B
2. D
3. C
4. B
5. B
6. A
7. C
8. A
9. C

ANSWERS & EXPLANATIONS
CONFIGURING NETWORK PROTOCOLS AND BINDINGS

1. What is a subnet mask used for?

    B. It is used to determine whether a target host is on the same subnet or on a remote subnet.

1. CORRECT ANSWER: B

A subnet mask number identifies whether an address is local or needs to be passed on the default gateway.

Answer A is incorrect—the router address is the IP address of the default gateway on the network. Answer C is incorrect—the IP address identifies the machine, the subnet mask is used to identify the segment of the network, or subnet, that you are on. Answer D is incorrect—a subnet mask does not pass any information.

A subnet mask is used to identify the computers local to your network. Any address outside your subnet is accessed through the default gateway. The default gateway is the address of the router that passes your TCP/IP information to computers, or hosts, outside your subnet.

2. Your company is using TCP/IP as the primary network protocol. Users on the network randomly complain that they get messages about IP address conflicts. What could be a potential solution to this?

    D. Implement DHCP

2. CORRECT ANSWER: D

DHCP assigns IP addresses as needed. This provides users with unique addresses and minimizes the possibility of conflicts.

Answer A is incorrect—IIS (Internet Information Server) is Microsoft's web server. Answer B is incorrect—DNS (Domain Name Service) is used for host name resolution. Answer C is incorrect—WINS (Windows Internet Naming Service) is used to resolve NetBIOS name to IP addresses.

A DHCP server can provide either dynamic or static IP address assignments for a network.

3. Which service can be used to reduce the number of NetBIOS broadcast messages sent across the network to locate a computer?

    C. WINS

3. CORRECT ANSWER: C

WINS keeps a list of all NetBIOS names for machines.

Answer A is incorrect—TCP/IP does not affect NetBIOS broadcasts because it is a network protocol suite. Answer B is incorrect—HOSTS files are used in place of a DNS server for

ANSWERS & EXPLANATIONS 63

host name resolution. Answer D is incorrect—DNS is used for host name resolution.

WINS is used to reduce the number of NetBIOS broadcast messages sent across the network to locate a computer. By using a WINS server, the names of computers on your network are kept in a WINS database. Each computer or NetBIOS service registers its name into the database, enabling immediate lookup of computer names. WINS also enables name resolution across routers, which would not forward NetBIOS broadcasts otherwise.

4. By default, how are DHCP servers used to allocate an IP address to a client?

   B. Each client sends out a broadcast requesting a number from any DHCP server that can respond.

4. CORRECT ANSWER: B

Machines broadcast requests for addresses and accept addresses from any servers that respond unless configured otherwise.

Answer A is incorrect—you cannot specify which DHCP server to request an address from. Answer C is incorrect—an LMHOSTS file is used in place of a WINS server to resolve NetBIOS names. Answer D is incorrect—a DHCP server does not send out broadcasts, but rather responds to client address request broadcasts.

A DHCP server uses a user-defined set of addresses to dynamically or statically (by machine MAC address) assign IP addresses and other TCP/IP parameters, such as subnet mask, default gateway, WINS server, DNS server and domain name.

5. Your multihomed system is connected to multiple TCP/IP subnets. What must be enabled to transfer packets between subnets?

   B. IP forwarding

5. CORRECT ANSWER: B

A router works at the network layer of the OSI model and can filter protocol information.

Answer A is incorrect—IP repeating is not a valid term. Answer C is incorrect—the default gateway is the router port used to access the network outside of the local subnet. Answer D is incorrect—DNS is used to resolve host names.

In an environment in which multiple subnets are used, you can configure your Windows NT Server as a multihomed system. By installing multiple network adapters, each connecting to a different subnet, you can enable the Enable IP Forwarding option: Your computer acts as a router, forwarding the packets through the network cards in the multihomed system to the other subnet.

6. What is the default frame type setting for Windows NT?

   A. 802.2

6. CORRECT ANSWER: A

802.2 is used in Windows NT as the preferred frame type.

Answers B and D indicate the incorrect frame type. Answer C is incorrect because NT uses the Auto Frame Type Detection as a default setting, but if a frame type is not detected, NT will revert to 802.2.

By default, Windows NT Server uses the Auto Frame Type Detection setting, which scans the network and loads the first frame type it encounters. If no frame types or multiple frame types are detected, NT will default to using the 802.2 frame type. The topologies and frame types are listed in Table 2.1:

TABLE 2.1 SUPPORTED FRAME TYPES

Topology	Supported Frame Types
Ethernet	802.2, 802.3, Ethernet II, SNAP
Token ring	802.5, SNAP
FDDI	802.2, SNAP

The default frame type is 802.2 in NetWare 3.12 and later. Earlier versions of NetWare used 802.3 as a default frame type.

7. What needs to be installed to configure AppleTalk?

   C. Services for Macintosh

7. CORRECT ANSWER: C

Services for Macintosh must be installed from the Service tab of the Network icon.

Answer A is incorrect—there is not a service called Gateway Services for Macintosh. Answer B is incorrect—NWLink is the Microsoft version of IPX/SPX. Answer D is incorrect—LocalTalk is the protocol used by an Apple-only local network.

To install the AppleTalk protocol, you must install Services for Macintosh. You examine the requirements for that later in this chapter. Select the AppleTalk protocol, then click Properties. The Microsoft AppleTalk Protocol Properties dialog box appears.

8. To optimize your binding order, the protocols should be placed in what order?

   A. The protocols used most often should be at the top of the binding order.

8. CORRECT ANSWER: A

To optimize the protocols, place the most-used protocol at the top of the list.

Answer B is incorrect—the least used protocols should be at the bottom of the binding order. Answer C is incorrect—the binding order can affect the system's network performance. Answer D is incorrect—you should arrange the protocols in a most-used to least-used order.

The binding order is the sequence your computer uses to select which protocol to use for network communication. Each protocol is listed for each network-based service, protocol, and adapter available. Setting the binding order of your network services and protocols can optimize your network configuration. To modify the binding order, go to the Bindings tab in the Network dialog box.

The Bindings tab in the Network properties contains the option Show Bindings For, which can be used to select the service, adapter, or protocol that you want to modify in the binding order. By clicking the appropriate option, each binding can be enabled or disabled, or it can be moved up or down in the binding order.

9. What configuration options are mandatory when installing TCP/IP?

  C. IP address and subnet mask

9. CORRECT ANSWER: C

Every network device on a TCP/IP network must include an IP address and subnet mask.

Answer A is incorrect—a DNS address is not required but a subnet mask is. Answer B is incorrect—a default gateway is not required but an IP address is. Answer D is incorrect—a default gateway is not required but a subnet mask is.

An IP address is a 32-bit address that is broken into four octets and is used to identify your network adapter card as a TCP/IP host. Each IP address must be unique. If users have IP address conflicts on the network, they cannot use the TCP/IP protocol until the conflict is resolved.

Your IP addresses then are grouped into a subnet. To subnet your network, assign a subnet mask.

> **FURTHER REVIEW**

CONFIGURING NETWORK PROTOCOLS AND BINDINGS

The following key words are important terms that were covered in this section. You should make sure you understand what each one is and what it does.

Key Words

- Default Gateway
- DHCP relay
- DNS
- IP address
- Subnet mask
- WINS

Additional Protocol Configuration

The following sections provide further information regarding advanced protocol configurations, such as DHCP relay agents and further NWLink parameters.

Using a DHCP Relay Agent with TCP/IP

The DHCP relay agent is used to find your DHCP servers across routers. IP addresses are handed out by the DHCP servers. The client request, however, is made with local subnet broadcast messages. Broadcast messages do not normally cross routers. The solution is to use a DHCP relay agent to assist the clients in finding the DHCP server across a router.

After the DHCP Relay Agent Service is installed, you can configure your DHCP relay agent. Settings include the Seconds Threshold, the Maximum Number of Hops to use in searching for the DHCP servers, and the IP addresses of the DHCP servers you want to use.

NWLink IPX/SPX-compatible

The NWLink IPX/SPX-compatible protocol was designed for NetWare connectivity, but it can be used for network connectivity between any systems running IPX-compatible protocols. The configuration of the NWLink protocol is simple in comparison to the TCP/IP protocol. To configure your NWLink protocol, highlight NWLink IPX/SPX Compatible Transport in the Network dialog box; then click Properties. The NWLink IPX/SPX Properties dialog box appears. The NWLink IPX/SPX Properties dialog box has two tabs: General and Routing.

On the General tab, you have the option to assign an internal network number. This eight-digit, hexadecimal number format is used by some programs with services that can be accessed by NetWare clients.

You also have the option to select a frame type for your NWLink protocol. The frame type you select must match the frame type of the remote computer with which you need to communicate.

The Routing tab of the NWLink IPX/SPX Properties dialog box is used to enable or disable the Routing Information Protocol (RIP). If you enable RIP routing over IPX, your Windows NT Server can act as an IPX router. This also requires the installation of the RIP for NWLink IPX/SPX-compatible Transport Service.

PRACTICE QUESTIONS

CONFIGURING WINDOWS NT SERVER CORE SERVICES

1. Where do you go to configure your Server service?

    A. Double-click the System icon in Control Panel and select the Services tab.

    B. Double-click the Network icon in Control Panel and select the Services tab.

    C. Double-click the Services icon in Control Panel and select the Services tab.

    D. From the Run line, type **Net Start server/config**.

2. When an NT server is utilized as a desktop machine, which server configuration is appropriate?

    A. Minimize Memory Used

    B. Balance

    C. Maximize Throughput for File Sharing

    D. Maximize Throughput for Network Applications

3. If a server needs to run distributed applications, which server configuration is appropriate?

    A. Minimize Memory Used

    B. Balance

    C. Maximize Throughput for File Sharing

    D. Maximize Throughput for Network Applications

4. Which server configuration is appropriate if a server needs the most amount of memory available for network connections?

    A. Minimize Memory Used

    B. Balance

    C. Maximize Throughput for File Sharing

    D. Maximize Throughput for Network Applications

5. Which server configuration is appropriate when a machine will never have more than 64 network connections?

    A. Minimize Memory Used

    B. Balance

    C. Maximize Throughput for File Sharing

    D. Maximize Throughput for Network Applications

6. Where do you go to use a graphical interface to configure your workstation service?

    A. Double-click the System icon in Control Panel and select the Services tab.

    B. Double-click the Network icon in Control Panel and select the Services tab.

    C. There are no GUI interface configuration options for the Workstation service.

    D. From Run, type **Net service /workstation**.

7. **What does the Workstation service provide?**
   A. It maintains a list of computer resources available to the current user.
   B. When requests are made that are not local, the Workstation service forwards the request to the network.
   C. When requests are made to a computer, the Workstation service provides the information to the requesting client.
   D. It enables replication information broadcasts to be made.

8. **Which service maintains the dynamic list of computers on the network?**
   A. DHCP
   B. Computer Browser service
   C. DNS
   D. Messenger service

9. **How is a computer registered with the browser?**
   A. Every computer with file and print sharing enabled sends a broadcast across the network with domain and computer name information that is picked up by the browser.
   B. Browsers send out broadcast requests across the network asking for domain and computer names.
   C. A machine is configured during installation to be the browser. All machines automatically send an identity packet to this machine upon startup.
   D. The network administrator manually logs NetBIOS names into a file on the browser computer.

10. **How is the Windows NT Server browsing role configured?**
    A. Right-click Network Neighborhood and choose Properties.
    B. Run the Registry Editor and open the HKEY_Local_Machine hive.
    C. Browsing roles are automatic. Configuration is not possible.
    D. Open Control Panel Services and edit the Computer Browser Startup tab.

11. **Which operating system is going to take precedence in a browser election?**
    A. NT Server 3.51.
    B. NT Server 4.
    C. NT Workstation 4.
    D. Either of the Server versions have equal criteria.

12. **When directory replication occurs, how much information is copied over to import servers?**
    A. Initially, the whole directory structure is copied; subsequent imports copy only changes.
    B. The whole directory structure is copied each time.
    C. The directory structure is copied in stages. This prevents excessive traffic on the network.

D. The entire directory structure is copied once a week. In between, full transfers of changed information are replicated.

13. **Where must information be placed for replication to occur?**

    A. Folders are placed in `Systemroot\system32\repl\import`.

    B. Folders are placed in `Systemroot\system32\repl\import\scripts`.

    C. Folders are placed in `Systemroot\system32\repl\export\scripts`.

    D. Folders are placed in `Systemroot\system32\repl\export`.

14. **What can you use Directory Replication to maintain? Select all that apply.**

    A. Directory database information

    B. System Policies

    C. Logon scripts

    D. User profiles

15. **What groups should the Directory Replication service account be a member of? Select all that apply.**

    A. Administrators

    B. Backup Operators

    C. Power Users

    D. Replicators

16. **How do you change the properties of the Directory Replication service?**

    A. Make sure it is selected in the Service list, then click Startup.

    B. Use the Policy menu in User Manager for Domains.

    C. Run `replication /configure`.

    D. Replication is automatically configured when NT is first installed.

ANSWER KEY

1. B	5. B	9. A	13. D
2. A	6. C	10. B	14. B-C-D
3. D	7. B	11. B	15. B-D
4. C	8. B	12. A	16. A

ANSWERS & EXPLANATIONS

CONFIGURING WINDOWS NT SERVER CORE SERVICES

1. Where do you go to configure your Server service?

   B. Double-click the Network icon in Control Panel and select the Services tab.

1. CORRECT ANSWER: B

Services are configured through the Network icon in Control Panel, or by right-clicking Network Neighborhood.

Answer A is incorrect—you cannot change the Server service properties from the System icon. Answer C is incorrect—the Services icon is used to change the startup and logon parameters of each service and to start and stop services. Answer D is incorrect—this is not a valid command.

The Server service answers network requests. By configuring Server service, you can change the way your server responds and, in a sense, the role it plays in your network environment. Servers in a network environment can be grouped into three different classes or roles:

- Logon server (domain controller)
- Application server
- File/print server

When configuring the Server service, the first step is to select the role your computer will play in your network environment. To configure Server service, you must open the Network dialog box. To do this, double-click the Network icon in Control Panel and select the Services tab.

To configure Server service, highlight Server and click Properties. You are then able to view the properties of your Server service. In the Server dialog box, you have four optimization settings. Each of these settings modifies memory management based on the role the server plays. These options are described in the following sections.

ANSWERS & EXPLANATIONS

> **EXAM TIP**
>
> For the Enterprise exam, you need to know when each optimization setting should be used and the differences between the four settings.

2. When an NT server is utilized as a desktop machine, which server configuration is appropriate?

    A. Minimize Memory Used

2. CORRECT ANSWER: A

Enable Minimize Memory Used if no more than 10 users are going to connect to the machine.

Answer B is incorrect—the balance configuration would not be used. Answer C is incorrect—this setting is used for a machine that is being used in a true server role. Answer D is incorrect—this setting is used on a server supporting network applications.

The Minimize Memory Used setting is used when your Windows NT Server system is accessed by a small number of users (fewer than 10). This setting is used when the Windows NT Server computer is used as a user's desktop computer, rather than in a true server role. This setting allocates memory so that a maximum of 10 network connections can be properly maintained. By restricting the memory for network connections, more memory is available at the local or desktop level.

3. If a server needs to run distributed applications, which server configuration is appropriate?

    D. Maximize Throughput for Network Applications

3. CORRECT ANSWER: D

Applications running across the network are going to benefit from this if they do not perform memory management themselves.

Answer A is incorrect—this setting is for a machine being accessed by a small number of users. Answer B is incorrect—balance is used on a machine that is accessed with fewer than 64 network connections. Answer C is incorrect—this setting is used for a machine that is being used in a true server role.

72 Chapter 2 INSTALLATION AND CONFIGURATION

If you are running distributed applications, such as SQL Server or Exchange Server, the network applications do their own memory caching. Therefore, you want your system to enable the applications to manage the memory. This is accomplished by using the Maximize Throughput for Network Applications setting. This setting also is used for very large networks and is suggested for domain controllers.

4. Which server configuration is appropriate if a server needs the most amount of memory available for network connections?

   C. Maximize Throughput for File Sharing

4. CORRECT ANSWER: C

Maximize Throughput for File Sharing is the default selection.

Answer A is incorrect—this setting is for a machine being accessed by a small number of users. Answer B is incorrect—balance is used on a machine that is accessed with fewer than 64 network connections. Answer D is incorrect—this setting is used on a server supporting network applications.

The Maximize Throughput for File Sharing setting allocates the maximum amount of memory available for network connections. It is the default on any Windows NT Member Server computer. This setting is excellent for large networks in which the server is accessed for file and print sharing.

5. Which server configuration is appropriate when a machine will never have more than 64 network connections?

   B. Balance

5. CORRECT ANSWER: B

The Balance setting is not recommended for more than 64 connections.

Answer A is incorrect—this setting is for a machine being accessed by a small number of users. Answer C is incorrect—this setting is used for a machine that is being used in a true server role. Answer D is incorrect—this setting is used on a server supporting network applications.

The Balance setting can be used for a maximum of 64 network connections. This setting is the default when using the NetBEUI protocol. As with the Minimize setting, Balance is best used for a relatively low number of users connecting to a server that also can be used as a desktop computer.

ANSWERS & EXPLANATIONS

6. Where do you go to use a graphical interface to configure your workstation service?

C. There are no GUI interface configuration options for the Workstation service.

6. CORRECT ANSWER: C

Workstation is a service not generally configured. If needed, there are some settings in the Registry that can be modified.

Answers A and B are incorrect—there aren't any parameters associated with the Workstation service. Answer D is incorrect—this is an invalid command.

The Workstation service has no configuration options through the Control Panel, unlike the other services discussed. You can make some Registry changes. Registry modification is not recommended unless you have a strong understanding of the Registry and its entries.

▼ **NOTE**

To make Registry changes, run the REGEDT32.exe program. The Registry in Windows NT is a complex database of configuration settings for your computer. If you want to configure the Workstation service, open the `HKEY_LOCAL_MACHINE` hive. The exact location to configure your Workstation service is:

```
HKEY_Local_Machine\System\CurrentControlSet\
Services\LanmanWorkstation\Parameters
```

7. What does the Workstation service provide?

B. When requests are made that are not local, the Workstation service forwards the request to the network.

7. CORRECT ANSWER: B

This service enables a client to request information from a server.

Answer A is incorrect—this is done by the browser service.
Answer C is incorrect—this is done by the Server service.
Answer D is incorrect—this is done by Directory Replication.

The Workstation service is your redirector in Windows NT Server. The Workstation service handles all outgoing network communication.

8. Which service maintains the dynamic list of computers on the network?

B. Computer Browser service

8. CORRECT ANSWER: B

Browse lists contain machines on the network.

Answer A is incorrect—DHCP provides IP address assignments.
Answer C is incorrect—DNS provides host name resolution.

74 Chapter 2 INSTALLATION AND CONFIGURATION

Answer D is incorrect—this service provides the capability to send and receive messages between clients.

The Computer Browser service is responsible for maintaining the list of computers on the network that are running the Server service or that have file and print sharing enabled. The browse list contains all the computers located on the physical network. As a Windows NT Server, your system plays a big role in the browsing of a network. The Windows NT Server acts as a master browser or backup browser.

9. How is a computer registered with the browser?

   A. Every computer with file and print sharing enabled sends a broadcast across the network with domain and computer name information that is picked up by the browser.

9. CORRECT ANSWER: A

Browse lists are gathered through broadcasts.

Answer B is incorrect—browsers do not send out broadcast requests. Answer C is incorrect—a machine does not need to be configured to be a browser. Answer D is incorrect—there isn't a manual browser file.

The functions of a master or backup browser are to hold the list of computers in the domain and to share that list with other computers. In the Microsoft networking environment, all computers send broadcast messages across the network containing the domain/workgroup to which they belong as well as their computer names.

A master browser gathers all of these broadcasts for its subnets. The domain master browser collects the lists from all master browsers to build a total domain browse list. Periodically, the master browser copies the browse list to backup browsers. When clients request a browse list, they receive it from a backup browser on their subnet.

10. How is the Windows NT Server browsing role configured?

    B. Run the Registry Editor and open the HKEY_Local_Machine hive.

10. CORRECT ANSWER: B

Browse roles are configured in the Registry.

Answer A is incorrect—you cannot modify the browser settings in the Network properties. Answer C is incorrect—you can configure browsing roles. Answer D is incorrect—there isn't a Computer Browser startup tab in Control Panel.

Browsing happens automatically, so no configuration is required. You can, however, configure whether you want your server to be a master or backup browser. The configuration is done in the Registry. The settings are found in the following location:

```
HKEY_Local_Machine\System\CurrentControlSet\Services
\Browser\Parameters
```

Two entries can be modified to select whether your server is a preferred master. The first entry is `IsDomainMaster=True/False`. You select `True` if you want your computer to be the master browser; select `False` if you do not want it to be the master browser.

The other entry is `MaintainServerList=Auto`. If this entry is set to `Auto`, your server is able to act in a browser role on the network.

11. Which operating system is going to take precedence in a browser election?

B. NT Server 4

11. CORRECT ANSWER: B

Election criteria includes OS versions, time available, and others.

Answer A is incorrect—this is an older OS version. Answer C is incorrect—Server is considered above Workstation. Answer D is incorrect—the newer version will win the election.

The selection of browsers is made through an election. The election is called by any client computer when it cannot connect to a master browser or when a preferred master browser computer starts up. The election is based on broadcast messages. Every computer has the opportunity to nominate itself, and the computer with the highest settings wins the election. The election criteria are based on three things:

- The operating system (Windows NT Server, Windows NT Workstation, Windows 95, Windows for Workgroups)

- The version of the operating system (NT 4, NT 3.51, NT 3.5)

- The current role of the computer (master browser, backup browser, potential browser)

Chapter 2 INSTALLATION AND CONFIGURATION

This is a simplified breakdown of the election criteria. Look in the Windows NT Resource Kit for detailed information about the election criteria.

12. When directory replication occurs, how much information is copied over to import servers?

    A. Initially, the whole directory structure is copied; subsequent imports copy only changes.

12. CORRECT ANSWER: A

When replication first occurs, the entire structure is copied only after the changed files are replicated out.

Answer B is incorrect—the entire directory structure is only copied the first time. Answer C is incorrect—the structure is copied all at once, not in stages. Answer D is incorrect—there is not a schedule for copying the structure, and the entire structure is only copied once.

In configuring the directory replication service, you must select the export server and all the import servers. The export server is the computer with the original copy of the directory structure and files. Each import server receives a complete copy of the export server's directory structure, which is monitored by the Directory Replication service. If the contents of the directory change, the changes are copied to all the import servers. A special service account you create is needed by the service. You configure the Directory Replication service to use this service account.

13. Where must information be placed for replication to occur?

    D. Folders are placed in `Systemroot\system32\repl\export`.

13. CORRECT ANSWER: D

Files must be placed in Folders under the export folder to replicate.

Answer A is incorrect—the import directory is for incoming files. Answers B and C are incorrect—the scripts directory is not used to export files.

To configure the export server, start Server Manager and double-click the export server. Click Replication in the Server Properties dialog box. When configuring the export server, you have the option to specify the export directory. The default export directory is as follows:

`%SystemRoot%\system32\repl\export\`

All subdirectories and corresponding files are sent to all the computers listed as import computers in the Export Directories section of the Directory Replication dialog box. It is critical that you include all systems requiring the files. It is possible for your own computer to act as both an export and import computer.

14. What can you use Directory Replication to maintain? Select all that apply.
    B. System Policies
    C. Logon scripts
    D. User profiles

14. CORRECT ANSWERS: B-C-D

Only information that will be applied to a number of users is practical to replicate. Policies and profiles typically apply to many users on a network.

Answer A is incorrect—there isn't any directory database information.

In any network environment, it is a challenge to maintain consistent logon scripts and system policies across multiple servers. In Windows NT Server, this is handled through the use of the Directory Replication service. The Directory Replication service can be configured to synchronize an entire directory structure across multiple servers.

The Directory Replication service can be used to maintain consistent logon scripts, system policies, or data files across the distributed network environment.

15. What groups should the Directory Replication service account be a member of? Select all that apply.
    B. Backup Operators
    D. Replicators

15. CORRECT ANSWERS: B-D

The account must be a member of both.

Answer A is incorrect— the Directory Replication account does not need Administrator permissions. Answer C is incorrect— Power User permission is not required.

The Directory Replication service account must have proper access on all the servers participating in the directory replication process. The following access is required for your Directory Replication service account:

- The account should be a member of the Backup Operators and Replicator groups.
- There should be no time or logon restrictions for the account.

78 Chapter 2 INSTALLATION AND CONFIGURATION

- The Password Never Expires option should be selected.
- The User Must Change Password at Next Logon option should be turned off.
- This account also must be assigned the user right to logon as a service. This happens when replication is configured through the Services icon in Control Panel.

▼ **NOTE**

If you are not running the service packs for Windows NT Server, this replication account does not work properly. To fix this problem, apply the Windows NT service packs or assign the Administrators group membership to the service account. Another solution is to edit the Registry in the following area:

`HKEY_LOCAL_MACHINE\System\CurrentControlSet\Control\SecurePipeServers\WinReg\AllowedPaths`

You can modify the `Machine` value to include the entry `System\CurrentControlSet\Services\Replicator`.

16. How do you change the properties of the Directory Replication service?

   A. Make sure it is selected in the Service list; then click Startup.

16. CORRECT ANSWER: A

Replication is also configured in Server Manager.

Answer B is incorrect—you cannot configure the service from the User manager for Domains program. Answer C is incorrect—this is not a valid command. Answer D is incorrect—Replication is not automatically configured.

The Directory Replication services Start up option is set to Manual. The service is not started at this time, and you should not start the system until all configuration has been completed. To change the properties for the Directory Replication service, make sure it is selected in the Service list and then click Startup.

FURTHER REVIEW

CONFIGURING WINDOWS NT SERVER CORE SERVICES

The following key words are important terms that were covered in this section. You should make sure you understand what each one is and what it does.

Key Words

Browser election

Directory Replication service

Export server

Import server

Server service

More on Directory Replication

The following sections discuss the configuration of the Directory Replication service in more detail. This includes configuring the import server, as well as managing the service.

Configuring the Import Server

The import computer is configured in the Server Manager, Properties dialog box. To configure the import computer, click Replication to open the Directory Replication dialog box. The import computer can be the same computer as the export server.

In the Import Directories section of the Directory Replication dialog box, you can select the import directory. The default import directory is as follows:

`%SystemRoot%\system32\repl\import`.

Remember that the default directory for executing logon scripts in a Windows NT system is as follows:

`%SystemRoot%\system32\repl\import\scripts`

The net logon share points to the same directory. You must also select the export server from which the import computer should receive the information. Make sure your import computer does not receive updates from multiple export servers, or you might have difficulty maintaining consistency across your servers.

Managing Directory Replication

You can control directory replication from both the export and import servers. You can place locks on certain directories to exclude them from the replication process. You also can designate a stabilization time to ensure that the files in your directories are not modified during a replication.

The import server has similar options. Directory locking can be managed from either the export server or the import server.

PRACTICE QUESTIONS

CONFIGURING HARD DISKS TO IMPROVE PERFORMANCE

1. You have several areas of free space on multiple hard disks. What is the best way to collect this area for use?

    A. Create a stripe set.

    B. Create a volume set.

    C. Create a new logical drive.

    D. Create a new primary partition.

2. You want to create a volume set. What is the minimum number of disks required to do so?

    A. 1

    B. 2

    C. 3

    D. 4

3. You are running out of space on your NT boot partition and want to make it bigger. How do you do so?

    A. Select an empty section of the disk and extend the NT partition as a volume set.

    B. Select an empty section on another disk and create a stripe set.

    C. Choose a separate disk and mirror the NT partition.

    D. Back up the NT partition, create a larger partition, and restore the data.

4. You want to create a stripe set. What is the minimum number of disks required?

    A. 1

    B. 2

    C. 3

    D. 4

5. Disk striping is considered to be which RAID level?

    A. 0

    B. 1

    C. 2

    D. 5

6. How many disks can be combined into one stripe set?

    A. 12

    B. 22

    C. 32

    D. 42

7. What type(s) of hard disks can be used in a stripe set?

    A. SCSI only

    B. IDE only

    C. ESDI or SCSI or IDE

    D. A combination of disk types can be used.

8. You want to create a stripe set with parity. What is the minimum number of disks required?

    A. 1

    B. 2

    C. 3

    D. 4

9. What type of fault tolerance can contain a system or boot partition?

    A. RAID 0

    B. RAID 1

    C. RAID 5

    D. RAID cannot be used on a system or boot partition

10. How many partitions can removable media contain?

    A. 2

    B. 3

    C. 4

    D. 1

11. What does an administrator need to do to add another hard disk to the system?

    A. Run WINNT and choose to update.

    B. Nothing; NT automatically detects the new disk.

    C. Run the Disk Administrator and choose Update from the Disk menu.

    D. In the Control Panel, go to the System icon and then to the Hardware Profiles tab.

12. You have formatted your D: drive with NTFS and need it to be FAT without losing data. What is the best method to do this?

    A. From a command prompt, type `Convert d: /fs:NTFS`.

    B. From a command prompt, type `Format d: /fs:NTFS`.

    C. Back up the D: drive to tape. Format the drive with FAT and restore the data.

    D. You cannot restore a drive to FAT after it is NTFS.

13. Your computer has two hard disks installed in a master/slave combination. On the first disk you have two primary partitions and one extended partition with three logical drives. On the second disk you have one primary partition and one extended partition with two logical drives. What ARC name would appear in the `BOOT.INI` file if Windows NT were installed in the default directory on the primary partition of the second disk?

    A. `multi(0)disk(0)rdisk(0)partition(0)\ WINNT`

    B. `multi(1)disk(0)rdisk(0)partition(0)\ WINNT`

    C. `multi(0)disk(0)rdisk(1)partition(1)\ WINNT`

    D. `multi(1)disk(0)rdisk(1)partition(1)\ WINNT`

14. After you add a new partition, NT will no longer boot. What needs to be done to correct the problem?

    A. Edit the BOOT.INI file to reflect the new partition numbering.

    B. Run WINNT and change the partition information.

    C. Select MS-DOS from the Boot menu. At the C:\ prompt, copy the NTOSKRNL file to the boot partition.

    D. You must reinstall NT.

15. You have installed NT on a FAT partition (D:) and want the partition to be NTFS. How do you change it?

    A. From the command prompt, type **Convert D: /FS:ntfs**. This will immediately start the conversion.

    B. From the command prompt, type **Convert D: /FS:ntfs**. This will start the conversion the next time NT is started.

    C. From the command prompt, type **Format D: /FS:ntfs**. This will immediately start the conversion.

    D. Back up the data, and then reformat the drive to NTFS and restore the data.

ANSWER KEY

1. B	6. C	11. B
2. A	7. D	12. C
3. D	8. C	13. C
4. B	9. B	14. A
5. A	10. D	15. B

ANSWERS & EXPLANATIONS

CONFIGURING HARD DISKS TO IMPROVE PERFORMANCE

1. You have several areas of free space on multiple hard disks. What is the best way to collect this area for use?

    B. Create a volume set.

1. CORRECT ANSWER: B

Volume sets can take areas on the same disk or multiple disks and collect them into a larger logical drive.

Answer A is incorrect because a stripe set requires partitions of the same size, which is not the most efficient use of drive space. Answer C is incorrect—you cannot create a logical drive using multiple drives. Answer D is incorrect—you cannot create a primary partition covering multiple drives.

2. You want to create a volume set. What is the minimum number of disks required to do so?

    A. 1

2. CORRECT ANSWER: A

Because areas on the same disk can be used in a volume, only one disk is required.

A volume set enables you to extend a drive. The partitions can be on multiple physical disks or on the same physical disk. When setting up a volume set, select the free space from all the drives you want to include and then select Partition, Create Volume Set.

After the volume set has been created, you then must format the volume set. To format the drive, select Tools, Format in the Disk Administrator. If formatted with NTFS, you can extend the volume set if more space is required.

To extend a volume set, select the volume set and the free space to be added to it. Then select Partition, Extend Volume Set. The volume set can be extended across the entire disk space, or it can be spread across multiple physical disks and treated as one partition.

84 Chapter 2 INSTALLATION AND CONFIGURATION

▼ **NOTE**

Volume sets are discussed on the Windows NT Server exam. They also might be mentioned on the Enterprise exam, especially in a question about extending a volume set. Only an NTFS partition can be extended in a volume set. If the file system is FAT, the partition cannot be extended.

3. You are running out of space on your NT boot partition and want to make it bigger. How do you do so?

    D. Back up the NT partition, create a larger partition, and restore the data.

3. CORRECT ANSWER: D

Volume sets and stripe sets are not supported on system or boot partitions.

Answer A is incorrect—you cannot have a volume set on the boot partition. Answer B is incorrect—you cannot have a stripe set on the boot partition. Answer C is incorrect—mirroring does not increase available space.

Boot and system partitions are supported only on fault tolerant partitions by using Disk Mirroring.

4. You want to create a stripe set. What is the minimum number of disks required?

    B. 2

4. CORRECT ANSWER: B

A stripe set requires a minimum of two disks.

Implementing a stripe set improves disk performance. Information is written across multiple physical disks and can increase the speed of disk reads and writes.

To create a stripe set, start the Disk Administrator and select the free space from each of the disks to be used in the stripe set. To select multiple disks, hold down Ctrl and click with the mouse on each section. When all the sections have been selected, select Partition, Create Stripe Set. The stripe set is created, and the space is treated as one drive letter.

5. Disk striping is considered to be which RAID level?

    A. 0

5. CORRECT ANSWER: A

Disk striping does not provide any fault tolerance and is considered to be RAID 0.

If any single drive is lost in a stripe set, all data will be lost. Stripe sets are, therefore, not considered fault-tolerant.

ANSWERS & EXPLANATIONS   85

6. How many disks can be combined into one stripe set?

C. 32

6. CORRECT ANSWER: C

A maximum of 32 disks can be combined.

A stripe set is created from free space on a non-boot or system partition of your hard disks. A stripe set is created using free disk space across multiple physical disks. A stripe set must use equal amounts of disk space on each physical disk. A stripe set requires a minimum of two disks and is limited to a maximum of 32 disks.

7. What type(s) of hard disks can be used in a stripe set?

D. A combination of disk types can be used.

7. CORRECT ANSWER: D

Windows NT stripe sets can be created using any combination of hard drive types, such as SCSI, IDE, EIDE, and ESDI.

Answers A, B, and C are incorrect—any combination of types can be used.

8. You want to create a stripe set with parity. What is the minimum number of disks required?

C. 3

8. CORRECT ANSWER: C

Because parity information is written across all disks, a minimum of three disks is needed.

A stripe set with parity writes data and parity information across a minimum of three and a maximum of 32 physical disks. If any one of the disks fails, the data can be regenerated from the remaining data and the parity. As with a stripe set, you cannot create a stripe set with parity from an existing partition. By holding down the Ctrl key, you can select multiple sections of free space. Only after the three sections have been selected can you select Create Stripe Set with Parity in the Fault Tolerance menu.

After you select Create Stripe Set with Parity, you are prompted to enter the size of the stripe set with parity. By default, the value shown is the maximum size available. The minimum size also is listed for your information. The stripe set is then configured. In the Disk Administrator, you can see that the stripe set is written across multiple physical disks. The legend across the bottom of the Disk Administrator shows which partitions belong to the stripe set with parity.

9. What type of fault tolerance can contain a system or boot partition?

   B. RAID 1

After the creation of any new partition, you also must format your drive. To format the drive, select the stripe set with parity and then select Format from the Tools menu.

9. CORRECT ANSWER: B

Only Disk Mirroring can be used on a system or boot partition.

To establish a disk mirror, you are required to have two physical disks in your NT system. With disk mirroring, you are able to use an existing disk partition, including the system or boot partition. Disk mirroring provides a duplicate set of your data on a spare disk. To establish a disk mirror, select the drive to mirror, and then select the free space to use on a second physical disk. Select Establish Mirror from the Fault Tolerance menu. The mirror set begins to duplicate all existing information from the first drive onto the mirror copy. Any new data is written to both drives by FTDISK.SYS.

After the disk mirror has been created, you might need to break the mirror. As part of configuration, however, you should know how to break a mirror set. The mirror set is split across two physical disks. Both partitions, however, are labeled E:. To remove or break a mirror set, select the mirror set and then select Break Mirror from the Fault Tolerance menu.

Adding a second controller to the machine provides extra redundancy, as well as a significant boost in drive access speed. By placing each disk in a mirror set on a separate controller, there is a lesser chance of both disks being made unavailable. This is commonly referred to as *disk duplexing*.

ANSWERS & EXPLANATIONS

10. How many partitions can removable media contain?

   D. 1

10. CORRECT ANSWER: D

Only one partition on removable media is supported.

Windows NT 4.0 supports only one partition on removable media, such as Iomega Jaz or Zip drives.

11. What does an administrator need to do to add another hard disk to the system?

   B. Nothing; NT will automatically detect the new disk.

11. CORRECT ANSWER: B

NT recognizes the new drive when the computer is restarted.

Answer A is incorrect—you would not do an OS reinstall just to add a drive. Answer C is incorrect—this is not a valid option in Disk Administrator. Answer D is incorrect—you do not add a drive in the system properties.

There is no configuration necessary to add a drive to a Windows NT system.

12. You have formatted your D: drive with NTFS and need it to be FAT without losing data. What is the best method to do this?

   C. Back up the D: drive to tape. Format the drive with FAT and restore the data.

12. CORRECT ANSWER: C

FAT can be converted to NTFS but not the other way around.

Answer A is incorrect—this command is used to convert from FAT to NTFS. Answer B is incorrect—this would reformat the drive with the NTFS file system. Answer D is incorrect—you can restore a backup of a drive that was formatted with NTFS to a drive formatted with FAT.

Windows NT contains a conversion program, CONVERT.EXE, to convert FAT to NTFS, but the only way to change a drive or partition that is formatted NTFS to FAT is to reformat the hard drive or partition.

88 Chapter 2 INSTALLATION AND CONFIGURATION

13. Your computer has two hard disks installed in a master/slave combination. On the first disk you have two primary partitions and one extended partition with three logical drives. On the second disk you have one primary partition and one extended partition with two logical drives. What ARC name would appear in the BOOT.INI file if Windows NT were installed in the default directory on the primary partition of the second disk?

    C. multi(0)disk(0)rdisk(1)partition(1)\ WINNT

13. CORRECT ANSWER: C

Remember that the second disk is a slave disk on the first controller.

Answer A lists the first, rather than the second, drive. Answers B and D indicate the wrong controller numbers.

See the explanation for question 14 for further information regarding ARC paths.

14. After adding a new partition, NT will no longer boot. What needs to be done to correct the problem?

    A. Edit the BOOT.INI file to reflect the new partition numbering.

14. CORRECT ANSWER: A

The BOOT.INI file uses ARC paths to locate NT.

Answer B is incorrect—you would not run setup to change partition information. Answer C is incorrect—this would not work because you can't do what the steps tell you to do. Answer D is incorrect—you do not need to reinstall NT.

An example of an ARC Name would be multi(0)disk(0)rdisk(1)partition(1)\WINNT. The multi parameter denotes which controller the drive resides on, the rdisk parameter denotes what number the drive is on the controller (first, second, and so on), and partition denotes which partition the system is installed on.

15. You have installed NT on a FAT partition (D:) and want the partition to be NTFS. How do you change it?

    B. From the command prompt, type Convert D: /FS:ntfs. This will start the conversion the next time NT is started.

15. CORRECT ANSWER: B

Because the Boot partition is in use, it can't be converted until the machine is restarted.

Answer A is incorrect—the conversion cannot immediately start because the partition is in use. Answer C is incorrect—this command would attempt to format the drive. Answer D is incorrect—you cannot do this with the system partition.

The CONVERT.EXE utility requires an update if the partition is in use because it cannot obtain an exclusive lock on that partition.

FURTHER REVIEW

CONFIGURING HARD DISKS TO IMPROVE PERFORMANCE

The following key words are important terms that were covered in this section. You should make sure you understand what each one is and what it does.

Key Words

Disk Administrator
Disk Mirroring RAID level 1
Stripe Set
Stripe Set with Parity RAID level 5
Volume Set

PRACTICE QUESTIONS

CONFIGURING PRINTERS

1. What is the default permission granted to the Everyone group with Printer Permissions?

    A. Manage documents

    B. Print

    C. Full Control

    D. Creator Owner

2. Who can install a printer on a Domain Controller?

    A. Administrators, Power Users, and Print Operators

    B. Administrators, Power Users, and Server Operators

    C. Administrators, Server Operators, and Print Operators

    D. Administrators

3. After sharing a network printer for Windows NT and 95 clients, what else needs to be done to allow NT Workstation clients to use the printer?

    A. Users just connect to the printer.

    B. Users must right-click the printer under network neighborhood and choose to configure it to the appropriate port.

    C. Users must install a printer driver locally.

    D. Nothing else needs to be done. The printer will automatically be available for use.

4. For DOS-based clients using LAN Manager, what is the syntax to point LPT1 to the correct network location?

    A. `Capture quename`

    B. `lpr -Sserver_name -Pshare_name`

    C. `net use LPT1 = \\server_name\share_name`

    D. `net use LPT \\server_name\share_name`

5. When Joe prints, he needs his documents to be processed as soon as possible. Where should you set a printer priority and what should it be?

    A. In User Manager for Domains, edit Joe's account and set the priority to 99.

    B. In User Manager for Domains, edit Joe's account and set the priority to 1.

    C. Go to the Printer properties for each of the printers using the Print device and, on the Security tab, set Joe's account to use priority 99.

    D. Go to the Scheduling tab on the properties of the printer that Joe is using and set the priority to 99.

6. By default, who on a Windows NT Server can take ownership of a printer?

    A. Only the Administrator

    B. Everyone

C. Administrators, Print Operators, and Server Operators

D. Creator Owner

7. **What clients can access an NT printer? Select all that apply.**

    A. Macintosh

    B. NetWare

    C. OS/2 (with LAN Manager 2.2C)

    D. Windows 3.1

8. **When should you create a printer pool?**

    A. When all of your print devices are identical and are located in the same general area. Some printers are used more heavily and you want to balance the load.

    B. When print devices are dissimilar and need to be grouped together.

    C. When employees are in different buildings, but all use the same kind of print devices.

    D. When identical print devices are located in each wing of a building.

9. **What permission is necessary for users to delete their own documents?**

    A. Assign each user the Print permission, and then they can delete their own documents.

    B. Only Administrators with Full Control can delete a document.

    C. Creator Owner with the Manage Document permission.

    D. Creator Owner with Print permission.

10. **To connect to a shared network printer, a user can do which of the following? Select all that apply.**

    A. Browse Network Neighborhood and right-click a printer to install it.

    B. Use the Add Printer Wizard and choose Local Printer and install the printer.

    C. Use the Add Printer Wizard and choose Network Printer and install the printer.

    D. The administrator will need to install printers on workstations.

ANSWER KEY

1. B
2. C
3. A
4. D
5. D
6. C
7. A-B-C-D
8. A
9. C
10. A-C

ANSWERS & EXPLANATIONS

CONFIGURING PRINTERS

1. What is the default permission granted to the Everyone group with Printer Permissions?

    B. Print

1. CORRECT ANSWER: B

Unlike shared folder permissions, which give everyone Full Control, printer permissions allow Print.

Answers A and C are incorrect—these are not the default NT print permissions. Answer D is incorrect—this is not a valid print permission.

The four NT print permissions are No Access, Print, Manage Documents, and Full Control. By default, Windows NT will assign the print permission to the Everyone group.

2. Who can install a printer on a Domain Controller?

    C. Administrators, Server Operators, and Print Operators

2. CORRECT ANSWER: C

Only the Administrators, Server Operators, and Print Operators Windows NT groups have permission to install printers on a Windows NT system.

3. After sharing a network printer for Windows NT and 95 clients, what else needs to be done to allow NT Workstation clients to use the printer?

    A. Users just connect to the printer.

3. CORRECT ANSWER: A

A user may connect to a printer to install the driver.

Answer B is incorrect—configuring the port does not relate to installing the driver. Answer C is incorrect—the user does not need to install a local driver. Answer D is incorrect—the user still must connect to the printer.

When a user connects to a Windows NT printer using a Windows NT computer, the printer is immediately available for use. The user does not need to install a driver or configure the printer.

ANSWERS & EXPLANATIONS

4. For DOS-based clients using LAN Manager, what is the syntax to point LPT1 to the correct network location?

   D. `net use LPT \\server_name\share_name`

4. CORRECT ANSWER: D

You must map the printer share to a specific LPT port for DOS-based clients.

Answer A is incorrect—`capture` is not a valid command. Answer B is incorrect—`lpr` is used for TCP/IP-based printers. Answer C indicates the incorrect syntax for the `net use` command.

A DOS client running the LAN Manager redirector can connect to a network printer simply by mapping an LPT port with the `net use` command.

5. When Joe prints, he needs his documents to be processed as soon as possible. Where should you set a printer priority and what should it be?

   D. Go to the Scheduling tab on the properties of the printer that Joe is using and set the priority to 99.

5. CORRECT ANSWER: D

Priorities are set on the Print Properties.

Answers A and B are incorrect—User Manager for Domains does not have any relation to the printing process. Answer C is incorrect—you do not set priority in the Security tab.

Windows NT allows the prioritizing of print jobs and printers. This is done in the print properties of each specific printer.

6. By default, who on a Windows NT Server can take ownership of a printer?

   C. Administrators, Print Operators, and Server Operators

6. CORRECT ANSWER: C

Anyone with Full Control can take ownership.

Answer A is incorrect—not only Administrators can take ownership of a printer. Answer B is incorrect—by default, the Everyone group has only Print permissions. Answer D is incorrect—the Creator Owner group cannot take ownership of a printer.

The Full Control print permission allows a user to take ownership of a printer.

7. What clients can access an NT printer? Select all that apply.

   A. Macintosh
   B. NetWare
   C. OS/2 (with LAN Manager 2.2C)
   D. Windows 3.1

7. CORRECT ANSWERS: A-B-C-D

Windows NT can support printers for a wide range of clients.

8. When should you create a printer pool?

   A. When all of your print devices are identical and are located in the same general area. Some printers are used more heavily and you want to balance the load.

8. CORRECT ANSWER: A

Printer pools are most effective with similar printers in close proximity.

Answer B is incorrect—the print devices must be the same. Answer C is incorrect—the devices and employees should be located in the same area. Answer D is incorrect—the print devices should be grouped together.

A printer pool enables one print driver to send documents to multiple print devices. Up to eight print devices can be combined to use the same printer driver and print spooler. This method can help to meet your organization's printing needs and speed up the printing process.

9. What permission is necessary for users to delete their own documents?

   C. Creator Owner with the Manage Document permission.

9. CORRECT ANSWER: C

By default, the Creator Owners can delete their own documents.

Answer A is incorrect—the Print permission does not allow documents to be deleted. Answer B is incorrect—deleting documents does not require Administrator or Full Control permissions. Answer D is incorrect—the Print permission does not allow documents to be deleted.

By default, Windows NT assigns the Creator Owner group the Manage Documents permission. This allows users to delete their own documents.

10. To connect to a shared network printer, a user can do which of the following? Select all that apply.

    A. Browse Network Neighborhood and right-click a printer to install it.
    C. Use the Add Printer Wizard and choose Network Printer and install the printer.

10. CORRECT ANSWERS: A-C

If users have permissions to use a printer, they just need to browse to it to gain access.

Answer B is incorrect—it describes how to install a locally attached printer. Answer D is incorrect—it does not require an Administrator to install a printer.

A user can connect to a Windows NT printer simply by browsing the Network Neighborhood and right-clicking on the printer, then choosing Connect. The user can also use the Add Printer Wizard to install a network printer.

FURTHER REVIEW

CONFIGURING PRINTERS

The following key words are important terms that were covered in this section. You should make sure you understand what each one is and what it does.

Key Words

Local printer
Network printer
Print device
Printer
Printer pool

Adding a Printer

Add printers in Windows NT by accessing the Add Printer Wizard. When adding a printer, you must follow these steps:

1. Make sure the print device is on the Hardware Compatibility List (HCL) or have the driver for your printer available.

2. Log on to the system as a user with Print Operator, Administrator, or Server Operator access privileges.

3. Run the Add Printer Wizard and follow all prompts.

When installing a printer in a Windows NT system, you can connect to an existing network printer, or install your own printer and share it with other computers. To add a new printer to your computer, follow these steps:

1. Double-click the Add Printer icon to start the Add Printer Wizard.

2. Select whether you are installing a printer on your computer or connecting to a network printer server. For example, select the My Computer option and click Next.

3. Select the port on which you're installing your printer and click Next.

4. You are then prompted to select the manufacturer and model of your print device from the list boxes. You can click Have Disk if your print device is not listed and you have the printer driver for the computer. After your printer has been selected, click Next to continue.

5. Assign a name for your printer. The default is the printer model name, but you can assign any name to the actual printer. Then specify whether you want your Windows programs to use this printer as the default printer.

6. If you want to share your printer with other users on the network, assign a share name and select which client operating systems can access your shared printer. If you are not sharing the printer, select Not Shared. After the screen has been completed, click Next to continue.

7. Finally, you get the option to print a test page to verify that your printer is communicating properly. Select the appropriate test option and click Finish.

The printer driver is now installed. If you are prompted for the location of the NT source files, enter the directory that contains the printer driver.

Connecting to an Existing Network Printer

If you are adding an existing network printer to your system, you can use the Add Printer Wizard to configure the printer with the following steps:

1. Start the Add Printer Wizard by double-clicking the Add Printer icon.
2. Select the Network Printer Server option and click Next.
3. Enter the network path to the network printer or select it from the Shared Printers list. When you have located the network printer, click OK to continue.
4. Select whether to use this printer as your default Windows printer, then click Next.
5. Click Finish and the printer driver is installed. You also can assign a name to this printer.

PRACTICE QUESTIONS

CONFIGURING WINDOWS NT SERVER FOR VARIOUS TYPES OF CLIENTS

1. The client Network Administration Tools are available for which operating systems on the Windows NT 4 Server CD-ROM? Select all that apply.

    A. Windows for Workgroups

    B. Windows 95

    C. Windows NT Workstation

    D. DOS

2. Which tools are available for network administration when the Network Administration Tools are installed on a Windows 95 client system? Select all that apply.

    A. Event Viewer

    B. DHCP Manager

    C. User Manager for Domains

    D. Server Manager

3. Which tools are installed when the Network Administration Tools are added to a Windows NT Workstation computer? Select all that apply.

    A. Event Viewer

    B. DHCP Manager

    C. User Manager for Domains

    D. Server Manager

4. How do you install the Windows 95 Network Administration Tools?

    A. Run SETUP.EXE from the CD:\clients\srvtools\win95 directory.

    B. Right-click the SRVTOOLS.INF file in the CD:\clients\srvtools\win95 directory and choose install.

    C. Use the Add/Remove programs applet in Control Panel and run SETUP.EXE from there.

    D. Use the Add/Remove programs applet in Control Panel and use the Have Disk option to point to the CD:\clients\srvtools\win95 directory.

5. How do you install the Windows NT Workstation Network Administration Tools?

    A. Run SETUP.BAT from the CD:\clients\srvtools\winnt directory.

    B. Right-click the SRVTOOLS.INF file in the CD:\clients\srvtools\winnt directory and choose install.

    C. Use the Add/Remove programs applet in Control Panel and run SETUP.BAT from there.

    D. Use the Add/Remove programs applet in Control Panel and use the Have Disk option to point to the CD:\clients\srvtools\winnt directory.

98 Chapter 2 INSTALLATION AND CONFIGURATION

6. What manual configuration step must be performed on a Windows 95 client when the Network Administration Tools are installed?

    A. All icons must be created for the Network Administration Tools.

    B. Security must be set to use User level security on the Windows 95 system.

    C. `c:\srvtools` must be added to the path.

    D. No manual configuration must be performed.

7. Which Network Client Administrator program option is used to install TCP/IP support for a Windows for Workgroups client?

    A. Make a Network Installation Startup Disk

    B. Make an Installation Disk Set

    C. Copy Client-based Network Administration Tools

    D. View remoteboot Client Information

8. Which protocols can be used by an MS-DOS v3.0 network client? Select all that apply.

    A. NetBEUI

    B. IPX/SPX

    C. TCP/IP

    D. DLC

9. What file format(s) is/are supported for Macintosh Accessible Volumes?

    A. FAT

    B. NTFS

    C. HPFS

    D. FAT and NTFS

10. This is a scenario question. First you must review the scenario, then review the required and optional results. Following that is a solution. You must pick the best evaluation of that solution.

    Scenario:
    Sprockets, Inc., is installing a Windows NT Server domain controller for its network. Currently, there are 50 Windows 95, 20 Macintosh Workstation, and 10 Windows NT Workstation computers on the network.

    Required Result:
    Allow Macintosh clients to access file folders on the NT server.

    Optional Results:
    Allow the NT Server to be administered from the NT Workstations.

    Allow the Windows 95 computers to administer the NT Server.

    Proposed Solution:
    Format a partition with NTFS Install Services for Macintosh on the Windows NT Server.

    Install the Network Administration Tools in a shared directory on the server to be used by both the Windows NT Workstation and Windows 95 computers.

    Evaluation of Proposed Solution:
    (Choose the most correct answer.)

    A. Both the required result and both optional results were met.

    B. The required result and only one of the optional results were met.

    C. Only the required result was met.

    D. The required result was not met.

ANSWER KEY

1. B-C
2. A-C-D
3. B-C-D
4. D
5. A
6. C
7. B
8. A-B-C
9. B
10. C

ANSWERS & EXPLANATIONS

CONFIGURING WINDOWS NT SERVER FOR VARIOUS TYPES OF CLIENTS

1. The client Network Administration Tools are available for which operating systems on the Windows NT 4 Server CD-ROM? Select all that apply.

   B. Windows 95
   C. Windows NT Workstation

1. CORRECT ANSWERS: B-C

Answer A is incorrect—NT 4.0 does not include administration tools for WfW. Answer D is incorrect—there is not a version for the administration tools available for DOS clients.

The Windows NT Server 4 CD-ROM ships with Network Administration Tools for Windows 95 and Windows NT Workstation. You also can administer Windows NT using Windows for Workgroups. The client software is available on the Windows NT Server 3.51 CD-ROM.

2. Which tools are available for network administration when the Network Administration Tools are installed on a Windows 95 client system? Select all that apply.

   A. Event Viewer
   C. User Manager for Domains
   D. Server Manager

2. CORRECT ANSWERS: A-C-D

You cannot perform DHCP administration from a Windows 95 system running the Network Administration Tools.

Answer B is incorrect—the DHCP Manager applet is not supported on Windows 95.

The Network Administration Tools for Windows 95 clients include User Manager for Domains, Server Manager, and Event Viewer.

3. Which tools are installed when the Network Administration Tools are added to a Windows NT Workstation computer? Select all that apply.

   B. DHCP Manager
   C. User Manager for Domains
   D. Server Manager

3. CORRECT ANSWERS: B-C-D

The Event Viewer is already included with Windows NT Workstation administrative tools.

Answer A is incorrect—the Event Viewer is not part of the NT Workstation Server Tools. See Table 2.2 for a list of the tools.

ANSWERS & EXPLANATIONS

TABLE 2.2 WINDOWS NT WORKSTATION SERVER TOOLS

Tools	Use this Tool to:
Server Manager	Manage Windows NT-based computers and domain controllers.
User Manager for Domains	Manage users, groups, and user rights for Windows NT domains.
WINS Manager	Administer the WINS servers.
DHCP Manager	Administer the DHCP servers.
Remote Access Admin	Administer the Remote Access Service on a computer running Windows NT.
Service for Macintosh	Share Windows NT resources with Macintosh clients.
System Policy Editor	Modify and maintain user and system policies.

4. How do you install the Windows 95 Network Administration Tools?

   D. Use the Add/Remove programs applet in Control Panel and use the Have Disk option to point to the CD:\clients\srvtools\win95 directory.

4. CORRECT ANSWER: D

The Network Administration Tools are added using the Add/Remove Programs applet in Windows 95.

Answer A is incorrect—you do not run a setup program to install the tools. Answer B is incorrect—this will not install the tools. Answer C is incorrect—you do not run a setup program from the Add/Remove Programs applet.

Windows 95 also has server tools available to enable Windows 95 computers to administer a Windows NT system. These tools are installed from the Windows NT Server CD-ROM.

The recommended procedure for installing the tools is as follows:

1. In Control Panel, double-click Add/Remove Programs.

2. Click the Windows Setup tab, and then click Have Disk.

3. Specify the \clients\srvtools\win95 folder on the NT Server CD-ROM. This folder contains the Srvtools.inf file.

4. Click Install.

Chapter 2 INSTALLATION AND CONFIGURATION

5. How do you install the Windows NT Workstation Network Administration Tools?

   A. Run SETUP.BAT from the `CD:\clients\srvtools\winnt` directory.

5. CORRECT ANSWER: A

Answer B is incorrect—this will not install the tools. Answer C is incorrect—the NT tools are installed using a setup program. Answer D is incorrect—you do not use the Add/Remove Programs applet to install the NT tools.

The Network Administration Tools are installed using SETUP.BAT on Windows NT Workstation. The batch file determines the platform that Windows NT Workstation is running on and then installs the correct version of the files.

6. What manual configuration step must be performed on a Windows 95 client when the Network Administration Tools are installed?

   C. `C:\srvtools` must be added to the path.

6. CORRECT ANSWER: C

The directory where the Network Administration Tools are installed (`C:\srvtools`) must be added to the path to use the Explorer extensions.

Answer A is incorrect—the icons are installed during setup. Answer B is incorrect—security does not need to be set. Answer D is incorrect—the path must be added manually.

The Windows 95 Network Administration Tools do not automatically register the directory path during installation. This must be done manually. The default directory for the Network Administration Tools is `C:\srvtools`. If the installation directory is changed, the new directory path must be entered.

7. Which Network Client Administrator program option is used to install TCP/IP support for a Windows for Workgroups client?

   B. Make an Installation Disk Set

7. CORRECT ANSWER: B

Using the Make an Installation Disk Set option, you can create the TCP/IP 32B for Windows for Workgroups installation disks.

Answer A is incorrect—this is not a valid option. Answer C is incorrect—you do not need to copy the tools. Answer D is incorrect—this will not create the installation disks.

The Windows NT Network Client Administrator has the capability to create installation disks for many different clients.

ANSWERS & EXPLANATIONS   103

8. Which protocols can be used by an MS-DOS v3.0 network client? Select all that apply.

   A. NetBEUI
   B. IPX/SPX
   C. TCP/IP

8. CORRECT ANSWERS: A-B-C

All of the standard protocols can be used with the MS-DOS client software.

Answer D is incorrect—DLC is not used as a Microsoft network protocol.

The DOS network client can support NetBEUI, NWLink, and TCP/IP to connect to a Windows NT network.

9. What file format(s) is/are supported for Macintosh Accessible Volumes?

   B. NTFS

9. CORRECT ANSWER: B

MAC-accessible volumes must be formatted using NTFS.

Answer A is incorrect—FAT is not supported on Macintosh-accessible volumes. Answer C is incorrect—HPFS is not supported by NT 4.0. Answer D is incorrect—only NTFS is supported.

For Windows NT to integrate with Apple Macintosh clients, you must first install Services for Macintosh on your Windows NT Server. Services for Macintosh enable file and print sharing between the Macintosh clients and the Windows NT Server. The Windows NT Server also is able to share Macintosh printers with the other clients of Windows NT Server. When Services for Macintosh is installed, the AppleTalk protocol is installed as well.

The requirements for the Windows NT Server computer are as follows:

- 2 MB of free disk space
- NTFS partition to be used as the Macintosh volume

Requirements for the Macintosh computer are as follows:

- Version 6.0.8 or later of the Macintosh operating system
- Version 2.0 of the AppleTalk Filing Protocol
- Network cards that enable connectivity into the same network as the Windows NT Server system

10. **Proposed Solution:**
    Format a partition with NTFS Install Services for Macintosh on the Windows NT Server.

    Install the Network Administration Tools in a shared directory on the server to be used by both the Windows NT Workstation and Windows 95 computers.

    C. Only the required result was met.

10. CORRECT ANSWER: C

The Network Administration Tools must be installed on each system.

For Macintosh clients to access file volumes on Windows NT Server, you must format the data partition with NTFS and install Services for Macintosh on the server. This allows the creation of Mac Volumes on the NT Server that the Macintosh clients can access.

The Network Administration Tools are unique to each platform (Windows NT Workstation, Windows 95) and cannot be installed in a shared directory. They must be installed on each system individually.

FURTHER REVIEW

CONFIGURING WINDOWS NT SERVER FOR VARIOUS TYPES OF CLIENTS

The following key words are important terms that were covered in this section. You should make sure you understand what each one is and what it does.

Key Words

Network Administration Tools
Network Client Administrator
Services for Macintosh

Windows NT Clients

The following sections briefly describe the administration capabilities for the NT clients that fall into one of three categories: Workstation clients, Windows 95 clients, or Macintosh clients.

Windows NT Workstation Clients

Windows NT Workstation computers require a computer account to be created in order to join a domain. The computer account is then used by the Remote Procedure Call (RPC) service to make a secured communication. This verifies when the computer is started and can be used for monitoring services on your NT Workstation computer. Windows NT Workstation can be installed as a standalone system and then, in the Network dialog box, joined to the domain. You must, however, have Account Operator or Administrator access, or be assigned the User Right Add Workstations to the Domain to create this computer account. If you want to create the computer account in the Windows NT Server computer, you can use Server Manager.

After you have a Windows NT Workstation client configured, the users and the client computer can use the Windows NT security. You also can install the client-based Network Administration Tools. These tools enable you to manage your Windows NT Server from your Windows NT Workstation client computer.

Windows 95 Clients

Using the Network Client Administrator program, you can create an automated installation from a floppy disk. Any installation of Windows 95 with a Microsoft Network client loaded, however, can be configured to log on to a Windows NT domain. This can be configured in the Network properties of a Windows 95 computer.

Windows 95 also has server tools available to enable Windows 95 computers to administer a Windows NT system.

Macintosh Clients

For Windows NT to integrate with Apple Macintosh clients, you must first install Services for Macintosh on your Windows NT Server. Services for Macintosh enables file and print sharing between the Macintosh clients and the Windows NT Server. The Windows NT Server also can share Macintosh printers with the other clients of Windows NT Server. When Services for Macintosh is installed, the AppleTalk protocol is installed as well.

SUMMARY

Although the Enterprise exam does not focus on installing Windows NT, it is recommended that you have a thorough knowledge of the services available in Windows NT and what is needed to configure them. For further information regarding the specific services, it is recommended that you refer to New Riders' *MCSE Training Guide: Windows NT Server 4, Second Edition* for a more in-depth look at the services.

CHAPTER 3

Managing Resources

One of the primary tasks of Windows NT administrators is managing resources. It is important to have a good network design and implementation because this leads to ease of administration and management. This chapter covers the different facets of Windows NT administration and management, including users, groups, remote administration tools, profiles and policies.

OBJECTIVES

This chapter helps you prepare for the exam by covering the following objectives:

Manage user accounts and rights.

▶ The explanation for the following objective also provides details for this objective.

Manage group accounts and rights.

▶ The Windows NT security model is based on assigning rights to users and groups. The first two objectives are focused on you knowing how to assign these rights, such as when to assign permission to a specific user, and when to assign permission to an entire group. It also covers creating new users and groups.

▶ Managing user and group accounts is best understood when divided into the following topics:

- Managing Windows NT user accounts
- Managing Windows NT user rights
- Managing Windows NT groups

continues

OBJECTIVES (continued)

- Administering account policies
- Auditing changes to the user account database

Create and manage policies and profiles for various situations. Policies and profiles include local user profiles, roaming user profiles, and system policies.

▶ System policies and user profiles assist in the centralization of management in a Windows NT Enterprise network. System policies help an administrator implement common Registry settings across the enterprise. User profiles store the user portion of the Registry, and you can implement the user profiles as either local profiles or roaming profiles. A roaming profile enables users to have the user portion of their configuration follow them wherever they log in on the Windows NT network.

Administer remote servers from various types of client computers, including Windows 95 and Windows NT Workstation.

▶ A common initial misconception is that you must be located at a Windows NT domain controller to manage a Windows NT Domain. On the contrary, you can choose from several versions of the Remote Administration Tools for Windows NT that enable you to administer Windows NT Domains from Windows 95 and from Windows NT Workstation.

Manage disk resources. Tasks include creating and sharing resources, implementing permissions and security, and establishing file auditing.

▶ After you create your groups in Windows NT, the next step in securing your system is to protect your disk resources. Windows NT has two levels of security for protecting disk resources:

- Share permissions
- NTFS permissions

▶ The management of both sets of permissions protects your Window NT system from inappropriate access.

▶ The Managing disk resources objective also covers creating shares, assigning permissions to both shares and files and auditing share and file access.

PRACTICE QUESTIONS

MANAGING USER AND GROUP ACCOUNTS

1. Which feature enables Windows NT users to access accounts and log on to a network?

    A. Unique identifiers

    B. Bindery entries

    C. NDS entries

    D. Policies

2. Accessing resources and identifying yourself to a network require which two items?

    A. Policies

    B. User ID

    C. Password

    D. Group accounts

3. Where are Windows NT user accounts created?

    A. User Manager

    B. Server Manager

    C. Network Administrator

    D. User Manager for Domains

4. To create a new account, the user running the utility must be a member of either of which two groups?

    A. Administrators

    B. Account Operators

    C. Domain Users

    D. Guest

5. Which portion of account policy determines your rules for password security?

    A. User

    B. Group

    C. Logon

    D. Password

6. Which of the following is *not* an option within the account policy?

    A. Maximum Password Age

    B. Minimum Password Age

    C. Maximum Password Length

    D. Minimum Password Length

7. Template accounts work best when you make use of which environment variable for both the User Profile Path and the Home Directory?

    A. %root%

    B. %Winnt%

    C. %username%

    D. %path%

8. The password for each username must be no longer than how many characters?

    A. 14

    B. 20

    C. 26

    D. 256

9. Which setting does not normally appear in the User Properties dialog box unless there is a problem?

    A. User Must Change Password at Next Logon

    B. User Cannot Change Password

    C. Password Never Expires

    D. Account Locked Out

10. Which two statements are true of the Password Never Expires setting in the User Properties dialog box?

    A. This setting overrides the account policy of password expiration.

    B. This setting forces users to change their password when they next log on to the network.

    C. This setting is used in higher security networks in which the users are assigned passwords for their accounts.

    D. This setting should be used only for service accounts in Windows NT.

11. The `%username%` variable must be unique in the domain, and no longer than how many characters?

    A. 14

    B. 20

    C. 26

    D. 256

12. Which feature enables an administrator to configure common drive mappings, run central batch files, and configure the system?

    A. User Manager for Domains

    B. Server Manager

    C. Login scripts

    D. User Manager

13. When configuring a login script, what are the recommended extensions? Select two.

    A. *.bat

    B. *.cmd

    C. file

    D. *.txt

14. The logon scripts are stored by default in which directory?

    A. \%systemroot%

    B. \%systemroot%\system32

    C. \%systemroot%\system32\scripts

    D. \%systemroot%\system32\repl\import\scripts

15. The `netlogon` directory is which directory?

    A. \%systemroot%

    B. \%systemroot%\system32

    C. \%systemroot%\system32\scripts

    D. \%systemroot%\system32\repl\import\scripts

16. Which Properties page enables the administrator to determine whether callback security is to be implemented?

    A. RAS

    B. Dial-In Properties

C. System

D. Modem

17. Which of the following is a call-back option commonly used in low-security networks and for users working out of hotel rooms?

    A. No Call Back

    B. Set by User

    C. Preset to

    D. Permanent Connection

18. Which key should you press in User Manager for Domains to create a copy of the template account?

    A. F3

    B. F5

C. F8

D. F10

19. Global groups can contain what? Select the best answer.

    A. Local groups

    B. Global groups from the same domain

    C. Users from the same domain

    D. Users from a trusted domain

20. Local groups can contain what? Select all that apply.

    A. Local groups

    B. Global groups from the same domain

    C. Global groups from a trusted domain

    D. Users from the same domain

    E. Users from a trusted domain

ANSWER KEY

1. A	6. C	11. B	16. B
2. B-C	7. C	12. C	17. A
3. D	8. A	13. A-B	18. C
4. A-B	9. D	14. D	19. C
5. D	10. A-D	15. D	20. B-C-D-E

ANSWERS & EXPLANATIONS

MANAGING USER AND GROUP ACCOUNTS

1. Which feature enables Windows NT users to access accounts and log on to a network?

    A. Unique identifiers

1. CORRECT ANSWER: A

Unique identifiers enable a user to log on to the Windows NT network.

Answer B is incorrect—bindery entries do not exist in Windows NT. Answer C is incorrect—NDS entries do not exist in Windows NT. Answer D is incorrect—policies do not enable a user to log onto Windows NT. Policies are discussed later in the chapter.

Windows NT user accounts, with their unique identifiers, enable users to log on to the Windows NT network. Their user account/password combinations are their tickets to all the resources on the NT network.

2. Accessing resources and identifying yourself to a network require which two items?

    B. User ID
    C. Password

2. CORRECT ANSWERS: B-C

User ID and password combinations are the access tickets to all resources on the NT network.

Answer A is incorrect—policies are not required to access resources. Answer D is incorrect—group accounts are not required.

3. Windows NT user accounts are created in:

    D. User Manager for Domains

3. CORRECT ANSWER: D

You create Windows NT Server user accounts in User Manager for Domains. Windows NT Workstation uses a more limited version called User Manager to create local workstation accounts.

Answer A is incorrect—User Manager is used on Windows NT Workstation to create local users. Answer B is incorrect—Server Manager is used to manage computer accounts. Answer C is incorrect—there isn't a Network Administrator application.

ANSWERS & EXPLANATIONS

4. To create a new account, the user running the utility must be a member of either of which two groups?

   A. Administrators
   B. Account Operators

4. CORRECT ANSWER: A-B

To create a new account, the user running User Manager for Domains by default must be a member of either the Administrators local group or the Account Operators local group. Any user can be assigned the permission to create accounts through the account rights property page in User manager for Domains.

Answer C is incorrect—the Domain Users group cannot create new accounts. Answer D is incorrect—the Guest account has the least permissions of any account and is by default disabled.

5. Which portion of account policy determines your rules for password security?

   D. Password

5. CORRECT ANSWER: D

The password portion of account policy determines your rules for password security.

Answer A is incorrect—the User portion defines the user's information. Answer B is incorrect—the Group portion defines what groups the account is a member of. Answer C is incorrect—there isn't a specific logon portion.

Before you start implementing user accounts, you should set your account policies. These policies affect every account in the domain—you cannot pick and choose which ones are affected. The account policies define how password changes and improper passwords are handled.

6. Which of the following is *not* an option within the account policy?

   C. Maximum Password Length

6. CORRECT ANSWER: C

Options within the account policy include Maximum Password Age, Minimum Password Age, and Minimum Password Length.

Answers A, B, and D are incorrect—these *are* included in the account policy page.

Options within the account policy include the following:

- Maximum password age
- Minimum password age

Chapter 3 MANAGING RESOURCES

- Minimum password length
- Password uniqueness
- Account lockout
- Account lockout duration
- Handling remote users whose logon hours have expired
- Changing passwords

7. Template accounts work best when you make use of which environment variable for both the User Profile Path and the Home Directory?

   C. %username%

7. CORRECT ANSWER: C

Template accounts work best when you make use of the %username% environment variable for both the User Profile Path and the Home Directory.

As an administrator, consider creating template user accounts for the various types of users that you plan to create. The template enables you to quickly create new user accounts when required. You should disable these template accounts to prevent their use for network access.

To use the template account to your advantage, just choose the template account in User Manager for Domains and create a copy of the account by choosing Copy from the User menu (or press F8). Doing so copies all properties of the template account except the following:

- Username
- Full Name
- Password
- Confirm Password

Template accounts also work best when you make use of the %username% environment variable for both the User Profile Path and the Home Directory. The environment enables the option User Must Change Password at Next Logon while it disables the Account Disabled box.

ANSWERS & EXPLANATIONS

8. The password for each username must be no longer than how many characters?

A. 14

8. CORRECT ANSWER: A

Each user has several property pages. When creating a new user, the first screen contains individual settings. Each setting in the upper User Properties dialog box in User Manager for Domains is described as follows:

- **Username.** The name that each user uses to log on to the network. The name must be unique, no longer than 20 characters, and cannot contain the following characters:

  "/\[]:;|=,+*?<>

  The goal of enterprise networking is for each user in the enterprise to have only *one* user account.

- **Full Name.** Enables the display of the user's full name. This can be used as a sort setting by choosing Sort by Full Name from the View menu.

- **Description.** Used to further describe a user, and if you use Description as a template, you can copy the description from account to account.

- **Password/Confirm Password.** The password can be up to 14 characters in length. If the user is working at an NT class system, the password is also case sensitive. If the user is at a Windows 95 or lower system, the password is case insensitive.

9. Which setting does not normally appear in the User Properties dialog box unless there is a problem?

D. Account Locked Out

9. CORRECT ANSWER: D

The settings in the lower User Properties dialog box in User Manager for Domains relate to how passwords are handled. The settings are as follows:

- **User Must Change Password at Next Logon.** Forces users to change their password when they next log on to the network. This option should not be selected if the account policy Users Must Log On in Order to Change Password has been set.

- **User Cannot Change Password.** Used in higher security networks in which the users are assigned passwords for their accounts.

- **Password Never Expires.** Overrides the account policy of password expiration and should only be used for service accounts in Windows NT.
- **Account Disabled.** The Account Disabled setting prevents users from using the disabled account.
- **Account Locked Out.** Active only if a user's account has been locked out by the operating system by failing the Account Lockout settings. To reactivate an account, simply clear the check box for this setting. An account can be locked out due to excessive failed logins, depending on the settings entered in account policies.

Answers A, B, and C are incorrect—these settings always appear in the dialog box.

10. Which two statements are true of the Password Never Expires setting in the User Properties dialog box?

    A. This setting overrides the account policy of password expiration.

    D. This setting should be used only for service accounts in Windows NT.

10. CORRECT ANSWERS: A-D

The Password Never Expires setting overrides the account policy of password expiration and should be used for service accounts in Windows NT.

Answer B is incorrect—this is done with the User Must Change Password at Next Logon setting. Answer C is incorrect—every user has a password assigned to their account in a Windows NT network.

11. The %username% variable must be unique in the domain, and no longer than how many characters?

    B. 20

11. CORRECT ANSWER: B

The %username% variable must be no longer than 20 characters.

12. Which feature enables an administrator to configure common drive mappings, run central batch files, and configure the system?

    C. Login scripts

12. CORRECT ANSWER: C

The login scripts enable an administrator to configure common drive mappings, run central batch files, and configure the system.

Answer A is incorrect—the User Manager for Domains is used to create and manage user and group accounts. Answer B is incorrect—Server Manager is used to manage computer accounts. Answer D is incorrect—User Manager is used to manage user accounts on an NT workstation.

13. When configuring a login script, what are the recommended extensions? Select two.

    A. *.bat
    B. *.cmd

13. CORRECT ANSWERS: A-B

When configuring a login script, recommended extensions are *.bat or *.cmd.

14. The logon scripts are stored by default in which directory?

    D. \%systemroot%\system32\repl\import\scripts

14. CORRECT ANSWER: D

The logon scripts are stored by default in the following directory:

\%systemroot%\system32\repl\import\scripts

15. The `netlogon` directory is which directory?

    D. \%systemroot%\system32\repl\import\scripts

15. CORRECT ANSWER: D

The `\%systemroot%\system32 \repl\import\scripts` directory is shared as the netlogon share.

The login script enables an administrator to configure common drive mappings, run central batch files, and configure the system. When configuring a login script, include the name of the *.bat or *.cmd file that you want to execute. The logon scripts are stored by default in the following directory:

\%systemroot%\system32\repl\import\scripts

This directory is shared as the netlogon share, and the logon script presents a common network layout to all clients on the network.

Chapter 3 MANAGING RESOURCES

16. Which Properties page enables the administrator to determine whether call-back security is to be implemented?

    B. Dial-In Properties

16. CORRECT ANSWER: B

The Dial-In Properties page in User Manager for Domains enables the administrator to determine which users are granted dial-in access to the network and whether call-back security should be implemented.

17. Which of the following is a call-back option commonly used in low-security networks and for users working out of hotel rooms?

    A. No Call Back

17. CORRECT ANSWER: A

If No Call Back is selected, the user can immediately use network resources.

The Dial-In Properties page enables administrators to determine which users are granted dial-in access to the network and whether the administrators should implement call-back security.

If you choose No Call Back, a user can immediately use network resources. No Call Back is commonly used in low-security networks and for users working out of hotel rooms.

If you choose Set by User, a user is prompted to enter her phone number, and the Remote Access Server calls her back at that number. If you choose Preset To, a user dials in to the office network. After connecting, the line is dropped, and the user is called back at a predefined phone number.

18. Which key should you press in User Manager for Domains to create a copy of the template account?

    C. F8

18. CORRECT ANSWER: C

F8 in User Manager for Domains creates a copy of the template account.

19. Global groups can contain what? Select the best answer.

    C. Users from the same domain

19. CORRECT ANSWER: C

Global groups can contain users from the local domain.

Answer A is incorrect—global groups cannot contain local groups. Answer B is incorrect—global groups cannot contain other global groups. Answer D is incorrect—global groups cannot contain users outside of the local domain.

ANSWERS & EXPLANATIONS

You create global groups by using the User Manager for Domains utility. When you create a global group, it is initially written to the SAM database on the Primary Domain Controller. Then the global group is synchronized with the Backup Domain Controllers during the synchronization process. The global groups are accessible from any domain controller.

To create a new global group, choose User, New Global Group from the menus of User Manager for Domains.

The New Global Group dialog box enables you to add and remove users as members of the global group in the current domain. After you have added all users, click the OK button to complete the creation of the global group.

20. Local groups can contain what? Select all that apply.

- B. Global groups from the same domain
- C. Global groups from a trusted domain
- D. Users from the same domain
- E. Users from a trusted domain

20. CORRECT ANSWERS: B-C-D-E

One of the most difficult enterprise concepts to get a handle on is the difference between global and local groups. In an Enterprise network, the acronym AGLP helps to define the use of global and local groups.

AGLP stands for Accounts/Global Groups/Local Groups/Permissions. This means that when you want to assign permissions to any resource, the following steps must be performed:

1. Make sure that user accounts exist for each user that needs access to the resource.

2. Assign all user accounts to a common global group. If the users are spread across multiple domains, you must create a global group in each domain because global groups can contain only users from the domain in which they are located.

3. Assign the global groups from each domain to a local group in the domain where the resource exists. If the resource is on a Windows NT domain controller, create the local group on a domain controller. If the resource is on a Windows NT Workstation or Windows NT Member Server, create the local group on that system's local account database.

4. Assign necessary permissions to the local group.

Local groups are the only groups that you should assign permissions. When assigning local group permissions, the administrator should always determine whether there is an existing local group with the appropriate permissions. For example, if you want to grant a user the capability to create new users or change group memberships, the Account Operators local group already has these permissions. You have no reason to create a new local group to perform this task. Instead, make the user a member of the Account Operators local group.

The following key words are important terms that were covered in this section. You should make sure you understand what each one is and what it does.

FURTHER REVIEW

MANAGING USER AND GROUP ACCOUNTS

Key Words

Global group

Local group

Replication

Replication service

User Manager

User Manager for Domains

Managing Windows NT User Rights

User rights define security rights when the user's activity cannot be associated with one particular object. Several predefined user rights can grant these nondiscretionary levels of access to the system.

The User Rights policy is implemented via the User Manager for Domain's User Rights option from the Policy menu.

The Default User Rights

User rights are automatically implemented in Windows NT 4. The user rights are stored in the SAM Account Database. This is in the Security hive of the HKEY_LOCAL_MACHINE subtree in the Registry. Table 3.1 describes each of the basic and advanced user rights as defined in Windows NT Workstation and Windows NT Server.

TABLE 3.1 USER RIGHTS ASSIGNMENTS IN WINDOWS NT 4

User Right	This Right:	Initially Assigned to:
Access This Computer from the Network	Enables users to connect to the computer via the network.	Administrators, Everyone, Power Users
Act as Part of the Operating System	Enables a process to perform as a secure, trusted part of the operating system. For example, the Microsoft Exchange 5.0 Server Service account requires this right to handle POP3 mail requests from clients.	None
Add Workstations to the Domain	Enables users to add workstations to the domain so that the workstation can recognize the domain's user and global accounts.	None, but this is a pre-defined right for all members of the Administrators and Server Operators local groups, and the right cannot be revoked.
Backup Files and Directories	Enables users to back up files and directories on the computer, no matter what file and directory permissions they have.	Administrators, Backup Operators, Server Operators
Bypass Traverse Checking	Enables users to change directories and traverse the directory structure, even if the user has no permissions for the traversed directory structures.	Everyone

continues

TABLE 3.1 CONTINUED

User Right	This Right:	Initially Assigned to:
Change System Time	Enables a user to set the time of the computer's internal clock.	Administrators, Server Operators, Power Users
Create a Pagefile	Determines which users can create a pagefile for the Virtual Memory Manager to use.	Administrators
Create a Token Object	Gives the right to create access tokens.	None; this is a predefined right of the Local Security Authority.
Create Permanent Shared Objects	Enables a user to create shared objects, such as \\Device, used within Windows NT. The right has nothing to do with creating file or printer shares.	None
Debug Programs	Enables a user to debug various low-level objects such as threads.	Administrators
Force Shutdown from a Remote System	Is not currently implemented in Windows NT 4, but it has been reserved for future use.	Administrators, Server Operators, Power Users
Generate Security Audits	Enables a process to generate security audit logs.	None
Increase Quotas	Is not currently implemented in Windows NT 4, but it has been reserved for future use. Products such as Disk Quota Manager might use this right.	Administrators
Increase Scheduling Priority	Enables a user to boost the execution priority of a process by using the Task Manager.	Administrators, Power Users
Load and Unload Device Drivers	Enables a user to install and remove device drivers.	Administrators
Lock Pages in Memory	Enables a user to lock pages into memory so that the pages cannot be paged out to the paging file.	None
Log On as a Batch Job	Is not currently implemented in Windows NT 4, but it has been reserved for future use.	None
Log On as a Service	Enables users to register with the systems as a Service. This right is automatically granted to any account set up as a service account.	None
Log On Locally	Enables users to log on to the system by typing their usernames and passwords into the User Authentication dialog box.	Account Operators, Administrators, Backup Operators, Everyone, Print Operators, Server Operators, Power Users, Guests, Users
Manage Auditing and Security Log	Enables users to specify which files to audit, and which printers to audit. The right does not enable the user to change the audit policy, but to work only within the framework defined by a member of the Administrators group. This right also enables the user to view and clear the security log in the event viewer.	Administrators
Modify Firmware Environment Variables	Enables a user to modify system environment variables stored in non-volatile RAM on RISC-based systems.	Administrators

User Right	This Right:	Initially Assigned to:
Profile Single Process	Enables a user to perform performance sampling on a process.	Administrators, Power Users
Profile System Performance	Enables a user to perform performance sampling on a computer.	Administrators
Replace a Process Level Token	Modifies a process's security access token. The right is used by the process of impersonation.	None
Restore Files and Directories	Enables users to restore backed-up files and directories regardless of their personal permissions on these files and directories.	Administrators, Backup Operators, Server Operators
Shut Down the System	Enables a user to shut down the Windows NT computer system.	Account Operators, Administrators, Backup Operators, Print Operators, Server Operators, Everyone Users, Power Users
Take Ownership of Files or Other Objects	Enables users to take ownership of any object on the computer, even if they do not have sufficient permissions to access the object.	Administrators

Modifying User Rights

Generally, you do not want to adjust the default user rights. If you do change the user rights, a possibility exists that the server could be rendered unusable. The following are some suggested guidelines to further secure your system's user rights. Two of the rights that have been granted default *access* rights are as follows:

- **Log on Locally.** The default membership includes the Everyone and Guest groups on Windows NT Workstation. Remove these two groups and replace them with the Users local group from the local account database. Be sure that the Domain's Domain Users global group is a member of the Users local group.

- **Shut Down the System.** The default membership in Windows NT Workstation includes the Everyone group. This group should not be assigned the shut-down privilege. You may also want to consider revoking this right from the Everyone group if you want all systems to run during the night.

Management of Global and Local Groups in a Multidomain Environment

The real art of using global and local groups emerges in a multidomain environment. When working with groups across trust relationships, the following guidelines are useful:

- Always gather users into global groups. Remember that global groups can contain only those user accounts from the same domain. You may have to create global groups with the same name in multiple domains.

- If you have multiple account domains, use the same name for a global group that has the same types of members as another global group in a separate domain. Remember that when multiple domains are involved, the group name is referred to as DOMAIN\GROUP.

- Before you create the local groups, determine whether an existing local group meets your needs. There is no sense in creating duplicate local groups.

- Remember that you must create the local group where the resource is located. If the resource is on a domain controller, create the local group in the Domain Account database. If the resource is on a Windows NT Workstation or Member Server, create the group in that system's local account database.

- Be sure to set the permissions for a resource before you make the global groups members of the local group assigned to the resource to ensure that security has been set for the resource.

Auditing Changes to the User Account Database

When an organization implements decentralized administration of the Windows NT Account database, you may want to audit all changes to the Accounts database. Remember, only members of the local groups Administrators and Account Operators can add, modify, and delete users in User Manager for Domains.

To enable auditing of changes to the Account database, a member of the Administrators group must enable Auditing User and Group Management. If you want to know exactly what files are being updated, enable File and Object Access.

The addition of File and Object Access helps you determine when Account Operators attempt to add a member to the Operators or Administrators local groups. When this attempt is made, a dialog box appears that states that the attempt was unsuccessful. Auditing User and Group Management will not "catch" this error. You must enable File and Object access so that you see the unsuccessful attempt to write to the SAM database.

PRACTICE QUESTIONS

CREATING AND MANAGING SYSTEM POLICIES AND USER PROFILES

1. What two items are used to assist in the centralization of management in a Windows NT Enterprise network?

    A. System policies

    B. Local groups

    C. User profiles

    D. Global groups

2. Which of the following helps an administrator implement common Registry settings across the enterprise? Select the best answer.

    A. System policies

    B. User profiles

    C. Regedt32

    D. Login scripts

3. Which of the following stores the user portion of the Registry? Select the best answer.

    A. System policies

    B. User profiles

    C. Regedt32

    D. Login scripts

4. User profiles can be implemented in which two ways?

    A. Local

    B. Global

    C. Roaming

    D. Group

5. Which user profile type enables users to have the user portion of their configurations follow them wherever they log on to the Windows NT network?

    A. Local

    B. Global

    C. Roaming

    D. Group

6. The user portion of the Windows NT Registry is stored in which file?

    A. USER.DAT

    B. USER.MAN

    C. NTUSER.DAT

    D. NTUSER.MAN

7. If you want to configure a user account to use a roaming profile, what is the first thing to do?

    A. Set the profile path in the User Manager for Domains for that account.

    B. Rename USER.DAT to USER.MAN.

    C. Move USER.DAT to the NETLOGON directory.

    D. Enable TTS.

8. An administrator can determine whether the user profiles stored on the local system are roaming or local profiles by viewing the User Profiles tab in which Control Panel applet?

    A. Network Neighborhood

    B. Passwords

    C. System

    D. Users

9. If a roaming profile is stored on only one specific server, where can the user be authenticated?

    A. Only on that server

    B. On any domain controller within the domain

    C. Only on the local workstation

    D. At any workstation within the domain

10. Implementing roaming profiles in Windows 95 differs from implementing roaming profiles in Windows NT in which of the following ways? Select all that apply.

    A. Separate user profiles are not implemented automatically in Windows 95; they are in Windows NT.

    B. The user portion of the Registry is saved in the file USER.DAT in Windows 95, whereas it is stored in NTUSER.DAT in Windows NT.

    C. The user profile path setting in the user's properties has no effect on Windows 95 clients.

    D. Windows NT roaming profile information is stored in the Windows NT Home Directory.

11. Amy is the network administrator at Cargo Masters, Inc. Recently, a number of users have experienced problems stemming from the users making incorrect changes to their profiles. What can Amy implement to reduce the problem of users performing incorrect configuration changes?

    A. Roaming profiles

    B. System policies

    C. Group assignments

    D. Login scripts

12. What is the System Policy file on NT named by default?

    A. CONFIG.POL

    B. NTCONFIG.POL

    C. SYSTEM.DAT

    D. SYSTEM.POL

13. Which of the following is used to implement system policies?

    A. System Policy Editor

    B. User Manager for Domains

    C. Server Manager

    D. Regedit

14. Which of the following best describes how the System Policy Editor is installed?

    A. From the Resource Kit

    B. On any Windows 95 workstation

    C. On any NT Workstation

    D. On any Windows NT domain controller

15. You can configure system policies to do all except which one of the following tasks?

    A. Implement defaults for hardware configuration for all computers.

    B. Restrict the capability to change specific parameters that affect the hardware configuration of the participating system.

    C. Eliminate the need for backups of user-specific information.

    D. Set defaults for all users on the areas of their personal settings that they can configure.

16. Using the System Policy Editor, you can create policies for which of the following? Select all that apply.

    A. Domain

    B. Computer

    C. User

    D. Group

17. The System Policy Editor can be found in what group of the Start menu?

    A. System

    B. User Manager

    C. Administrative Tools

    D. Programs

18. When you create a new policy file, what two default icons appear within the policy?

    A. Default Computer

    B. Default User

    C. Default Domain

    D. Default Group

19. Which item is used to configure all machine-specific settings?

    A. Default Computer

    B. Default User

    C. Default Domain

    D. Default Group

20. All property changes within the Default Computer section affect which subtree of the Registry?

    A. HKEY_USER

    B. HKEY_SYSTEM

    C. HKEY_CURRENT_USER

    D. HKEY_LOCAL_MACHINE

ANSWER KEY

1. A-C
2. A
3. B
4. A-C
5. C
6. C
7. A
8. C
9. B
10. A-B-C
11. B
12. B
13. A
14. D
15. C
16. B-C-D
17. C
18. A-B
19. A
20. D

ANSWERS & EXPLANATIONS

CREATING AND MANAGING SYSTEM POLICIES AND USER PROFILES

1. What two items are used to assist in the centralization of management in a Windows NT Enterprise network?

    A. System policies
    C. User profiles

1. CORRECT ANSWERS: A-C

The use of system policies and user profiles assists in the centralization of management in a Windows NT Enterprise network.

Answer B is incorrect—local groups do not assist this. Answer D is incorrect—global groups do not assist centralized management.

Using policies and profiles allows an administrator to control what a user can change on his computer and what is available on the desktop. For example, a system policy can be implemented that would prevent a user from changing the network settings of a computer. This greatly assists in network management by reducing problems caused by incorrectly configured machines.

2. Which of the following helps an administrator implement common Registry settings across the enterprise?

    A. System policies

2. CORRECT ANSWER: A

System policies help an administrator implement common Registry settings across the enterprise.

Answer B is incorrect—profiles do not implement Registry settings enterprise-wide. Answer C is incorrect—REGEDT32.EXE is the program used to edit the Registry. Answer D is incorrect—login scripts are used to assist with drive mapping and other user functions.

System policies help the network administrator restrict the configuration changes users can perform to their profiles. By combining roaming profiles and system policies, the administrators cannot provide the users a consistent desktop, but they can control what the users can do to that desktop. Likewise, the administrator can ensure that the users cannot modify certain settings.

System policies work like a merge operation. Think of system policies as a copy of your Registry. When you log in to the network and the NTCONFIG.POL file exists on the domain controller, it merges its settings into your Registry, changing your Registry settings as indicated in the system policy.

3. Which of the following stores the user portion of the Registry?

B. User profiles

3. CORRECT ANSWER: B

User profiles store the user portion of the Registry.

Answer A is incorrect—system policies are not stored in the user part of the Registry. Answer C is incorrect—REGEDT32.EXE is used to edit the Registry. Answer D is incorrect—login scripts do not access the Registry.

The explanation for question 4 discusses user profiles.

4. User profiles can be implemented in which two ways?

A. Local
C. Roaming

4. CORRECT ANSWERS: A-C

You can implement user profiles as either local profiles or roaming profiles.

Answer B is incorrect—there aren't any global profiles. Answer D is incorrect—there aren't any group profiles.

When a user logs in at a system, he creates a local profile on that system. The local profile is implemented as a set of directory structures. This directory structure includes the desktop folder and the Start menu folder.

When a user logs in to the network, her desktop and Start menu are also based on the local system that she is logging in to. The desktop is based on the user's profile directory and the ALL USERS directory. The same is true for the Start menu directory.

The problem with local profiles is that every workstation that you log in to can have its own version of the local profile. The user's configuration settings must be set at each workstation that he logs in to.

To overcome this problem, you must implement roaming profiles. Roaming profiles include the user portion of the Registry, which is downloaded from a designated system to the system that the users are currently logged on to. Any changes to the user's settings are stored in the central location so that the next workstation can retrieve the settings.

Chapter 3 MANAGING RESOURCES

5. Which user profile type enables users to have the user portion of their configurations follow them wherever they log on to the Windows NT network?

C. Roaming

> **5. CORRECT ANSWER: C**
>
> A roaming profile enables users to have the user portion of their configurations follow them wherever they log on to the Windows NT network.
>
> Answer A is incorrect—a local profile is specific to one computer. Answers B and D are incorrect—these do not indicate valid profile types.

6. The user portion of the Windows NT Registry is stored in which file?

C. NTUSER.DAT

> **6. CORRECT ANSWER: C**
>
> The user portion of the Registry is stored in the file NTUSER.DAT.
>
> Answers A, B, and D indicate incorrect filenames.

7. If you want to configure a user account to use a roaming profile, what is the first thing to do?

A. Set the profile path in the User Manager for Domains for that account.

> **7. CORRECT ANSWER: A**
>
> If you want to configure a user account to use a roaming profile, the first thing to do is set the profile path in the User Manager for Domains for that account.
>
> Answer B is incorrect—you do not need to do this to configure a roaming profile. Answer C is incorrect—you would not move the USER.DAT file. Answer D is incorrect—there isn't a TTS parameter.
>
> To configure a roaming profile for a user account, first set the profile path in the User Manager for Domains for that account. If you are configuring a block of users, the best method is to make a group property change by choosing all users you want to have roaming profiles, and then choosing Properties from the User menu.
>
> The most common setting is to have a directory shared with a share name such as profiles. It should enable the local group USERS the permission FULL CONTROL. With this share, you can now set the user's profile path to \\server\share\%username%. The next time the users log on, their profile information is saved to this central profile directory.

ANSWERS & EXPLANATIONS   131

8. An administrator can determine whether the user profiles stored on the local system are roaming or local profiles by viewing the User Profiles tab in which Control Panel applet?

    C. System

8. CORRECT ANSWER: C

An administrator can determine whether the user profiles stored on the local system are roaming or local profiles by viewing the User Profiles tab in the System applet in Control Panel.

Answer A is incorrect—the Network applet does not contain the user profiles tab. Answer B is incorrect—there isn't a Passwords applet on Windows NT. Answer D is incorrect—there isn't a Users applet in Windows NT.

9. If a roaming profile is only stored on one specific server, where can the user be authenticated?

    B. On any domain controller within the domain

9. CORRECT ANSWER: B

Although the roaming profile is stored on a specific server, the user can be authenticated on any domain controller within the domain.

Answer A is incorrect—any domain controller can authenticate the user. Answer C is incorrect—the local workstation would not be authenticating the login. Answer D is incorrect—the workstations in the domain do not authenticate logins.

10. Implementing roaming profiles in Windows 95 differs from implementing roaming profiles in Windows NT in which of the following ways? Select all that apply.

    A. Separate user profiles are not implemented automatically in Windows 95; they are in Windows NT.
    B. The user portion of the Registry is saved in the file USER.DAT in Windows 95, whereas it is stored in NTUSER.DAT in Windows NT.
    C. The user profile path setting in the user's properties has no effect on Windows 95 clients.

10. CORRECT ANSWERS: A, B, C

Implementing roaming profiles in Windows 95 differs from implementing roaming profiles in Windows NT in the following ways: Separate User profiles are not implemented automatically in Windows 95 as they are in Windows NT. The user portion of the Registry is saved in the file USER.DAT in Windows 95, whereas it is stored in NTUSER.DAT in Windows NT. The user profile path setting in the user's properties has no effect on Windows 95 clients.

Answer D is incorrect—there isn't a Windows NT home directory.

Windows 95 users can also have roaming profiles configured so that their user-based configurations can follow them from workstation to workstation. Implementing roaming profiles in Windows 95 differs from Windows NT in the following ways:

- Separate user profiles are not implemented automatically in Windows 95; they are in Windows NT.

- The user portion of the Registry is saved in the file USER.DAT in Windows 95, whereas it is stored in NTUSER.DAT in Windows NT.

- The user profile path setting in the user's properties has no effect on Windows 95 clients. The roaming profile information is stored in their Windows NT Home Directory.

11. Amy is the network administrator at Cargo Masters, Inc. Recently, a number of users have experienced problems stemming from the users making incorrect changes to their profiles. What can Amy implement to reduce the problem of users performing incorrect configuration changes?

    B. System policies

11. CORRECT ANSWER: B

System policies help the network administrator restrict the configuration changes the users can perform to their profiles.

Answer A is incorrect—roaming profiles do not restrict configuration changes. Answer C is incorrect—group assignments do not deal with system configuration. Answer D is incorrect—login scripts are not used to restrict configuration changes.

Using system policies to reduce the capabilities of users to change their profiles and configurations is one of the best ways to reduce network administrative overhead.

See the explanation for question 13 for a discussion about the restrictions that can be implemented using system policies.

12. What is the System Policy file on NT named by default?

    B. NTCONFIG.POL

12 CORRECT ANSWER: B

NTCONFIG.POL is the default system policy filename on NT networks.

Answer A, C, and D indicate incorrect file names.

13. Which of the following is used to implement system policies?

    A. System Policy Editor

13. CORRECT ANSWER: A

System policies are implemented by using the System Policy Editor.

Answer B is incorrect—User Manager for Domains is used to manage user accounts. Answer C is incorrect—Server Manager is used to manage computer accounts. Answer D is incorrect—REGEDIT.EXE is the 16-bit version of the Registry Editor.

You can implement system policies by using the System Policy Editor. The System Policy Editor is automatically installed with any Windows NT domain controller.

You can configure system policies to do the following:

- Implement defaults for hardware configuration for all computers or for a specific machine by using the profile.

- Restrict the capability to change specific parameters that affect the hardware configuration of the participating system.

- Set defaults for all users on the areas of their personal settings that they can configure.

- Restrict the users from changing specific areas of their configurations to prevent them from tampering with the system. An example is disabling all Registry editing tools for a specific user.

- Apply all defaults and restrictions on a group level rather than on just a user level.

You can also use the System Policy Editor to change settings in the Registry of the system on which the System Policy Editor is executed. Many times it is easier to use the System Policy Editor because it has a better interface for finding common restrictions.

14. Which of the following best describes how the System Policy Editor is installed?

    D. On any Windows NT domain controller

14. CORRECT ANSWER: D

The System Policy Editor is automatically installed with any Windows NT domain controller.

Answer A is incorrect—the System Policy Editor is not installed from the Resource Kit CD. Answer B is incorrect—the Editor is not used on a Windows 95 computer. Answer C is incorrect, the Editor is not installed on a Windows NT Workstation.

To create Computer, User, and Group policies, you must use the System Policy Editor. The System Policy Editor is automatically installed on all domain controllers, and you can find the Editor in the Administrative Tools Group of the Start menu.

When you create a new policy file, you see two default icons within the policy:

- **Default Computer.** Used to configure all machine-specific settings. All property changes within this section affect the HKEY_LOCAL_MACHINE subtree of the Registry.

- **Default User.** Used for any client that uses the policy and does not have a specific machine entry created for itself in the policy file. Default User is used to specify default policy settings for all users that use the policy. It affects the HKEY_CURRENT_USER subtree of the Registry. If the users are configured to use a roaming profile, this information is stored in their centralized version of NTUSER.DAT in their profile directories.

15. You can configure system policies to do all except which one of the following tasks?

    C. Eliminate the need for backups of user-specific information.

15. CORRECT ANSWER: C

System policies do not eliminate the need for backups of user-specific information.

Answer A is incorrect—system policies are used to implement hardware configuration defaults. Answer B is incorrect—system policies can be used to restrict changing specific parameters. Answer D is incorrect—system policies can implement defaults for user's personal settings.

16. Using the System Policy Editor, you can create policies for which of the following? Select all that apply.

    B. Computer
    C. User
    D. Group

16. CORRECT ANSWERS: B, C, D

To create Computer, User, and Group policies, you must use the System Policy Editor.

Answer A is incorrect—there are no domain policies.

ANSWERS & EXPLANATIONS

17. The System Policy Editor can be found in what group of the Start menu?

C. Administrative Tools

17. CORRECT ANSWER: C

The System Policy Editor is automatically installed on all Domain Controllers, and you can find the Editor in the Administrative Tools Group of the Start menu.

Answer A is incorrect—this is not a valid group. Answer B is incorrect—this is not a valid group. Answer D is incorrect—the System Policy Editor is not found under the Programs root, but rather in the Administrative Tools group under Programs.

18. When you create a new policy file, what two default icons appear within the policy?

A. Default Computer
B. Default User

18. CORRECT ANSWERS: A-B

When you create a new policy file, it presents you with two default icons within the policy: Default Computer and Default User.

Answers C and D are incorrect—these do not indicate valid icons in the System Policy Editor.

When a new policy is created in the System Policy Editor, there are two icons designating the two different sections of the policy: Default Computer for machine settings, and Default User for user settings.

19. Which item is used to configure all machine-specific settings?

A. Default Computer

19. CORRECT ANSWER: A

Use the Default Computer item to configure all machine-specific settings.

Answer B is incorrect—the Default User icon is used to configure user policies, which are user-specific settings. Answers C and D do not indicate valid icon names.

The Default Computer icon in the System Policy Editor is used to set computer policies, which are machine-specific defaults and restrictions.

You can configure computer policies to lock down common machine settings that affect all users of a Windows NT system. Common settings that are configured include the following:

- Programs to automatically run at startup of the computer system. These can include virus scans. Opening the System/Run option in the Default Computer Properties sets this option.

- Ensuring that all Windows NT clients will have the administrative shares automatically created upon startup of these systems. This setting enhances the capability of the administrator to centrally manage the network. Opening the Windows NT Network/Sharing option in the Default Computer Properties sets this option.

- Implementing customized shared folders. These include the Desktop, Start menu, Startup, and Programs folders. These can be set to point to an actual network share location so that multiple machines have common desktops or Start menus. Opening the Windows NT Shell/Custom Shared Folders option in the Default Computer Properties sets this option.

- Presenting a customized dialog box called the Logon Banner, which you can use to inform users of upcoming maintenance to the network or for other network information. Opening the Windows NT System/Logon option in the Default Computer Properties sets this option.

- Removing the last logged on user from the Authentication dialog box. Many users choose predictable passwords, and knowing the user's login name can help lead to guessing their passwords. This is also set in the Windows NT System/Logon option in the Default Computer Properties.

You also can implement computer policies on a computer-by-computer basis by choosing Add Computer from the Edit menu. This adds a new icon to the policy with that computer's name.

You implement user policies through the System Policy Editor. These policies affect the HKEY_CURRENT_USER Registry subtree. Each user is affected individually by these settings.

ANSWERS & EXPLANATIONS 137

You can also implement user policies on a user-by-user basis. To create an individual user policy, choose Add User from the Edit menu. When a user logs in, NTCONFIG.POL is searched for a policy for the specific user. If there is not a policy for that user, the default user policy is used for the login process.

Some of the common implementations of user profiles are the following:

- Locking down display properties to prevent users from changing the resolution of their monitors. You can lock down display properties as a whole or on each individual property page of display properties. Adjust this setting in the Control Panel/Display/Restrict Display option of the Default User Properties sheet.

- Setting a default color scheme or wallpaper. You can set the default in the Desktop option of the Default User Properties sheet.

- Restricting access to portions of the Start menu or Desktop. You can do this via the Shell/Restrictions option of the Default User Properties sheet.

- Limiting the applications run at a workstation. Set this option in the System/Restrictions option of the Default User Properties sheet. You can use System/Restrictions to prevent users from modifying the Registry.

- Preventing users from mapping or disconnecting network drives. You can set the options in the Windows NT Shell/Restrictions option of the Default User Properties sheet.

---

20. All property changes within the Default Computer section affect which subtree of the Registry?

    D. HKEY_LOCAL_MACHINE

20. CORRECT ANSWER: D

All property changes within the Default Computer section affect the HKEY_LOCAL_MACHINE subtree of the Registry.

Answer A is incorrect—the HKEY_USER subtree contains user-specific settings. Answer B is incorrect—this is not a valid Registry subtree. Answer C is incorrect—this is where the user's current sessions settings are stored.

FURTHER REVIEW

CREATING AND MANAGING SYSTEM POLICIES AND USER PROFILES

The following key words are important terms that were covered in this section. You should make sure you understand what each one is and what it does.

Key Words

Backup Domain Controller
Domain controller
Local profiles
Primary Domain Controller
Roaming profiles
System policies
System Policy Editor
User policies
User profiles

Additional System Policies Information

The following sections expand further on specific system policy information, including group policies, processing order of system policies, and Windows 95 versus Windows NT profiles.

Implementing Group Policies

If you need to have user settings affect multiple users, you can implement group policies. Group policies add another level of complexity to the processing of the policies. Some of the additional considerations include the following:

- The System Policy Editor uses global groups for group membership. Appropriate trust relationships must be implemented to see the necessary global groups.

- Because a user can belong to multiple global groups, the order in which the groups are processed is very important. One group's settings could be the opposite of another group's. Set group priority in the Group Priority option of the Options menu.

Processing Order for System Policies

When a user logs on to a network in which system policies have been implemented, the following steps occur:

1. The user successfully logs in to the network.

2. The user profile is read from the NETLOGON share of the authenticating domain controller.

3. If a predefined policy exists for a user, that policy is merged into the HKEY_CURRENT_USER Registry subtree. Then, the processing moves to step 5.

   If no predefined user policy exists, the default user policy is processed.

4. The group priority list is examined. If the user is a member of any of the global groups for which policy exists, the account is processed according to the group priority

order. The priority is ordered from bottom to top of the group priority list. Each of the group policies is applied to the `HKEY_CURRENT_USER` Registry subtree.

5. After the user and group policies have been processed, the machine policies are determined. If there is a predefined machine policy, that policy is merged with the `HKEY_LOCAL_MACHINE` Registry subtree. If there is no predefined machine policy for the system from which the user is logging in, the default machine policy is merged with the `HKEY_LOCAL_MACHINE` subtree.

Differences Between Windows NT and Windows 95 Profiles

Although Windows NT automatically implements system policies in its clients, there is more configuration required for Windows 95 if you want Windows 95 to recognize group policies. First, you must individually configure the Windows 95 clients to recognize group policies, as follows:

1. Open the Windows 95 Control Panel.
2. In the Control Panel, open the Add/Remove Programs applet.
3. Change to the Windows Setup tab and click the Have Disk button.
4. The System Policy installation files are located on the Windows 95 CD in the directory `\ADMIN\APPTOOLS\POLEDIT`. Choose this directory by using the Browse button.
5. When the options to install appear, choose Group Policies.

Following these steps installs the necessary files. After you configure the client to use system policies, one more change is recommended in a Windows NT network environment. By default, the Windows 95 client only looks for the file `CONFIG.POL` on the Primary Domain Controller's NETLOGON share. If you want the Windows 95 client to be able to process the system policy from any domain controller as in Windows NT, you must enable the Load Balancing option under the Network, System Policies Update, Remote Update option.

PRACTICE QUESTIONS

ADMINISTERING REMOTE SERVERS FROM VARIOUS CLIENT COMPUTERS

1. Versions of the Remote Administration Tools for Windows NT that shipped on the Windows NT 4.0 Server CD enable you to administer Windows NT domains from which two of the following operating systems?

    A. Windows 95

    B. Windows for Workgroups

    C. Windows NT Workstation

    D. LAN Manager

2. When using the Windows 95 Remote Administration Tools, which of the following can you manage on a Windows NT Server Domain? Select all correct answers.

    A. Auditing

    B. Print permissions

    C. николайNTFS permissions

    D. Dial-up connections

3. Which tool do you use from Windows 95 Remote Administration to manage servers in a domain?

    A. Event Viewer

    B. User Manager for Domains

    C. Server Manager

    D. Network Neighborhood

4. Which tool do you use from Windows 95 Remote Administration to manage users in a domain?

    A. Event Viewer

    B. User Manager for Domains

    C. Server Manager

    D. Network Neighborhood

5. Which tool do you use from Windows 95 Remote Administration to troubleshoot servers in a domain?

    A. Event Viewer

    B. User Manager for Domains

    C. Server Manager

    D. Network Neighborhood

6. You can manage servers running File and Print Services for NetWare from the Windows 95 system through which of the following? Select the best answer.

    A. Network Neighborhood

    B. User Manager for Domains

    C. Event Viewer

    D. The FPNW property sheet of any drive on that server

7. **The Windows NT Server Tools for Windows NT Workstation include which of the following utilities? Select the best answer.**

    A. DHCP Manager

    B. System Policy Editor

    C. Remote Access Admin

    D. User Manager

8. **The Web Administration tools are available from what two sources?**

    A. The Microsoft web site

    B. The NT Server Resource Kit

    C. Through mail-order houses

    D. A subdirectory on the original distribution CDs

9. **What are the Web Administration tools implemented as?**

    A. A CMD script

    B. An ActiveX plug-in

    C. A DirectX extension

    D. An Internet Information Server extension

10. **When using the Web Administration tools, the person connecting to the NT Administration page must be a member of what group?**

    A. The domain's Administrators local group

    B. Any domain's Administrators local group

    C. The domain's Administrators global group

    D. Any domain's Administrators global group

ANSWER KEY

1. A-C
2. A-B-C
3. C
4. B
5. A
6. D
7. A
8. A-B
9. D
10. A

ANSWERS & EXPLANATIONS

ADMINISTERING REMOTE SERVERS FROM VARIOUS CLIENT COMPUTERS

1. Versions of the Remote Administration Tools for Windows NT that shipped on the Windows NT 4.0 Server CD enable you to administer Windows NT domains from which two of the following operating systems?

   A. Windows 95
   C. Windows NT Workstation

1. CORRECT ANSWERS: A-C

The Remote Administration Tools for Windows NT enable you to administer Windows NT domains from Windows 95 and from Windows NT Workstation.

Answers B and D are incorrect—the Remote Administration tools are not available for WFW or LAN Manager.

A common initial misconception is that you must be located at a Windows NT domain controller to manage a Windows NT Domain. On the contrary—you can choose from several versions of the Remote Administration Tools for Windows NT that enable you to administer Windows NT Domains from Windows 95 and from Windows NT Workstation.

2. When using the Windows 95 Remote Administration Tools, which of the following can you manage on a Windows NT Server Domain? Select all correct answers.

   A. Auditing
   B. Print permissions
   C. NTFS permissions

2. CORRECT ANSWERS: A-B-C

The Windows 95 Remote Administration Tools enable a client running Windows 95 to manage NTFS permissions, auditing, and print permissions through the Network Neighborhood.

Answer D is incorrect—the Windows 95 Remote Administration Tools do not contain the Remote Access Admin application.

3. Which tool do you use from Windows 95 Remote Administration to manage servers in a domain?

   C. Server Manager

3. CORRECT ANSWER: C

Manage Windows NT servers and workstations in the domain by using Server Manager.

Answer A is incorrect—Event Viewer is used to monitor and troubleshoot events on the server. Answer B is incorrect—User Manager for Domains is used to manage user accounts. Answer D is incorrect—Network Neighborhood is not part of the Remote Administration Tools.

ANSWERS & EXPLANATIONS

4. Which tool do you use from Windows 95 Remote Administration to manage users in a domain?

B. User Manager for Domains

4. CORRECT ANSWER: B

You can manage users in the domain by using User Manager for Domains.

Answer A is incorrect—Event Viewer is used to monitor and troubleshoot events on the server. Answer C is incorrect—Server Manager is used to manage machine accounts. Answer D is incorrect—Network Neighborhood is not part of the Remote Administration Tools.

5. Which tool do you use from Windows 95 Remote Administration to troubleshoot servers in a domain?

A. Event Viewer

5. CORRECT ANSWER: A

You can troubleshoot servers by using the Event Viewer to view System, Application, and Audit Logs.

Answer B is incorrect—User Manager for Domains is used to manage user accounts. Answer C is incorrect—Server Manager is used to manage machine accounts. Answer D is incorrect—Network Neighborhood is not part of the Remote Administration Tools.

6. You can manage servers running File and Print Services for NetWare from the Windows 95 system through which of the following?

D. The FPNW property sheet of any drive on that server

6. CORRECT ANSWER: D

You can manage servers running File and Print Services for NetWare from the Windows 95 system through the FPNW property sheet of any drive on that server.

Answer A is incorrect—Event Viewer is used to monitor and troubleshoot events on the server. Answer B is incorrect—User Manager for Domains is used to manage user accounts. Answer C is incorrect—Server Manager is used to manage machine accounts.

The Windows 95 Remote Administration Tools allow a client running Windows 95 to manage the following aspects of a Windows NT Server domain:

- You can manage users in a domain with User Manager for Domains.
- Manage servers in the domain using Server Manager.

Chapter 3 MANAGING RESOURCES

- Troubleshoot servers using the Event Viewer to view System, Application, and Audit Logs.

- Extensions to the Windows 95 Explorer enable you to manage NTFS permissions, auditing, and print permissions through the Network Neighborhood.

- Manage servers running File and Print Services for NetWare from the Windows 95 system through the FPNW property sheet of any drive on that server.

7. The Windows NT Server Tools for Windows NT Workstation include which of the following utilities? Select the best answer.

   A. DHCP Manager

7. CORRECT ANSWER: A

The Windows NT Server Tools for Windows NT Workstation include User Manager for Domains and not User Manager (a Workstation utility).

Answer B is incorrect—they do not include the System Policy Editor. Answer C is incorrect—Remote Access Admin is not included. Answer D is incorrect—User Manager is in the NT Workstation Administrative Tools and is used for local user account management.

The Windows NT Server Tools for Windows NT Workstation enable you to manage a Windows NT domain from either a Windows NT Workstation or a Windows NT Member Server. The Windows NT Server Tools for Windows NT Workstation include the following utilities:

- **DHCP Manager.** Covered in Chapter 4, "Connectivity."

- **System Policy Editor.** As discussed in the previous section, you implement system policies by using the System Policy Editor.

- **Remote Access Admin.** Covered in Chapter 4.

- **Remote Boot Manager.** Covered in Chapter 2, "Installation and Configuration."

- **Server Manager.** Covered in Chapter 2.

- **User Manager for Domains.** As discussed in Section 3.1, you create Windows NT user accounts in the User Manager for Domains.
- **WINS Manager.** Covered in Chapter 4.
- **Extensions for Managing Services for Macintosh.** Covered in Chapter 2.

8. The Web Administration tools are available from what two sources?
   A. The Microsoft web site
   B. The NT Server Resource Kit

8. CORRECT ANSWERS: A-B

The Web Administration tools are available from the Microsoft web site or on the Server Resource Kit.

Answer C is incorrect—the utility is not from a mail-order house. Answer D is incorrect—it is not included on the Windows NT CD-ROM.

The Windows NT Server Resource Kit includes a new utility that enables you to remotely administer Windows NT Servers from Windows, Macintosh, and UNIX hosts running web browser software. This utility is also available for download from the Microsoft web site. Implement Web Administration tools as an Internet Information Server extension. The only caveat is that the person connecting to the NT Administration page must be a member of the Domain's Administrators local group.

To install the Web Administration tools on a Domain Controller, use the following steps:

1. Insert the Windows NT Server Resource Kit CD into the CD drive of the domain controller to be managed.
2. From the autorun screen presented, choose the Web Administration link.
3. On the next screen, choose the Install Now link.
4. To continue the installation, you must agree to the End User License Agreement by clicking the Yes button.
5. To start the installation, click the Continue button.

Chapter 3 MANAGING RESOURCES

6. To complete the installation, click the Exit to Windows button. The Readme file for the Web Administration tools is displayed to finalize the installation.

7. To access the web-based administration tools, start your web browser and go to the address http://<your_server_name>/ntadmin/ntadmin.htm.

9. What are the Web Administration tools implemented as?

   D. An Internet Information Server extension

9. CORRECT ANSWER: D

The Web Administration tools are implemented as an Internet Information Server extension.

10. When using the Web Administration tools, the person connecting to the NT Administration page must be a member of what group?

    A. The domain's Administrators local group

10. CORRECT ANSWER: A

The person connecting to the NT Administration page must be a member of the domain's Administrators local group.

Answer B is incorrect—there is not an Administrator local group in the domain. Answer C is incorrect—there is not an Administrator global group. Answer D is incorrect—there is not an Administrator global group for any domains.

The Web Administration tools are intended for an experienced NT administrator. These tools allow limited administration of a Windows NT domain controller using HTML forms. Management tasks that can be performed from Web Administration tools include the following:

- Managing user accounts.
- Managing global and local accounts.
- Adding and removing Windows NT computer accounts to/from a domain.
- Stopping and starting devices on the system.
- Viewing the System, Audit, and/or Application.
- Managing shared directories and their permissions.
- Managing NTFS file and directory permissions.

- Sending a broadcast message to all users with open sessions to the server.
- Setting up the server to run the Windows NT Resource Kit Remote Console Utility.
- Rebooting the server using the web page.
- Setting the preferences for the Web Administration Tools.
- Managing printers hosted by the server.
- Stopping, starting, and configuring services running on the server.
- Managing all active sessions. This includes disconnecting all or specific sessions.
- Viewing the server configuration. This makes use of the WINMSDP utility from the resource kit. This utility provides the same information as the graphical WINMSD utility, but in text-only format.
- Viewing a report format on selected performance counters.
- Viewing server statistics.

FURTHER REVIEW

ADMINISTERING REMOTE SERVERS FROM VARIOUS CLIENT COMPUTERS

The following key words are important terms that were covered in this section. You should make sure you understand what each one is and what it does.

Key Words

Remote server

Web Administration tools

PRACTICE QUESTIONS

MANAGING DISK RESOURCES

1. Which two of the following are the levels of security for protecting your disk resources in Windows NT?

   A. Share permissions
   B. NTFS permissions
   C. User permissions
   D. Attributes

2. Which of the following enables Windows NT administrators to protect their resources from unauthorized access?

   A. Share-level security
   B. Volume-level security
   C. Resource security
   D. Attributes

3. Which of the following is used to assign access permissions to shared directory resources on a Windows NT system for users?

   A. Share-level security
   B. Volume-level security
   C. Resource security
   D. Attributes

4. Which of the following explicit share permissions can you implement? Select all that apply.

   A. Modify
   B. Read
   C. Full Control
   D. No Access

5. Which is the minimum permission that enables users to connect to a resource and run programs?

   A. Full Control
   B. Read
   C. No Access
   D. Change

6. Which permission enables users to view documents that are stored in the share, but does not enable them to make changes to the documents?

   A. Full Control
   B. Read
   C. No Access
   D. Change

7. Which minimum share permission enables users to connect and to create new documents and subfolders?

   A. Full Control
   B. Read
   C. No Access
   D. Change

8. Which minimum permission enables users to modify existing documents and delete documents?

   A. Full Control
   B. Read
   C. No Access
   D. Change

9. Which permission enables users to do anything they want in the share?

   A. Full Control
   B. Read
   C. No Access
   D. Change

10. Which permission is sufficient for most day-to-day business needs?

    A. Full Control
    B. Read
    C. No Access
    D. Change

11. As a general rule, which permission is considered the most powerful?

    A. Full Control
    B. Read
    C. No Access
    D. Change

12. Users to whom you assign varying levels of permissions through group memberships have effective shared permissions of what?

    A. The accumulation of their individual shared permissions.
    B. The lowest possible permissions.
    C. Those permissions assigned the highest priority.
    D. The permissions assigned to the highest priority group to which they belong.

13. At what level do share permissions affect users? Select the best answer.

    A. Locally.
    B. When logged across the network.
    C. When running other operating systems locally.
    D. Share permissions do not affect users.

14. At what levels do NTFS permissions affect users? Select all that apply.

    A. Locally.
    B. When logged across the network.
    C. When running other operating systems locally.
    D. NTFS permissions do not affect users.

15. Which of the following NTFS directory permissions enable users to view the contents of a directory and to navigate to its subdirectories? Select all that apply.

    A. No Access
    B. List
    C. Read
    D. Add

16. Which of the following NTFS directory permissions overrides all other permissions?

    A. No Access
    B. List
    C. Read
    D. Add

17. Which of the following NTFS directory permissions enables users to add new subdirectories and files to the directory, but does not enable them to access files within the directory?

    A. No Access
    B. List
    C. Read
    D. Add

18. Which sets of NTFS directory permissions enable users to add new files to the directory structure, and restrict the users to read-only access to these files? Select all that apply.

    A. No Access
    B. List
    C. Read
    D. Add

19. If an NTFS file is moved to a new directory on the same volume, what will become of the permissions?

    A. The file will maintain its existing permissions.
    B. The file will assume permissions from the source.
    C. The file will assume permissions from the target.
    D. The file will abandon permissions.

20. If an NTFS file is copied to a new directory on the same volume, what will become of the permissions?

    A. The file will maintain its existing permissions.
    B. The file will assume permissions from the source.
    C. The file will assume permissions from the target.
    D. The file will abandon permissions.

ANSWER KEY

1. A-B
2. A
3. A
4. B-C-D
5. B
6. B
7. D
8. D
9. A
10. D
11. C
12. A
13. B
14. A-B
15. B-C
16. A
17. D
18. C-D
19. A
20. C

ANSWERS & EXPLANATIONS

MANAGING DISK RESOURCES

1. Which two of the following are the levels of security for protecting your disk resources in Windows NT?

   A. Share permissions
   B. NTFS permissions

1. CORRECT ANSWERS: A, B

Windows NT has two levels of security for protecting disk resources: Share permissions and NTFS permissions.

Answers C and D are incorrect—user permissions and attributes are not Windows NT security levels.

After you create your groups in Windows NT, the next step in securing your system is to protect your disk resources. Windows NT has two levels of security for protecting disk resources:

- Share permissions
- NTFS permissions

The management of both sets of permissions protects your Windows NT system from inappropriate access.

2. Which of the following enables Windows NT administrators to protect their resources from unauthorized access?

   A. Share-level security

2. CORRECT ANSWER: A

Share-level security allows administrators to assign explicit permissions to users and groups in regard to access shared directory resources on a Windows NT Server. The explanation for question 5 lists the explicit permissions that can be assigned to a directory share.

Answer B is incorrect—volume-level security is not part of the Windows NT security model. Answer C is incorrect—resource security is not an NT security level. Answer D is incorrect—attributes do not protect resources.

3. Which of the following is used to assign access permissions to shared directory resources on a Windows NT system for users?

   A. Share-level security

3. CORRECT ANSWER: A

Share-level security enables a Windows NT administrator to protect resources from Network users.

Answer B is incorrect—volume-level security is not part of the Windows NT security level. Answer C is incorrect—resource security is not an NT security level. Answer D is incorrect—attributes are not used as an entry point.

4. Which of the following explicit share permissions can you implement? Select all that apply.
   - B. Read
   - C. Full Control
   - D. No Access

4. CORRECT ANSWERS: B, C, D

There are four explicit share permissions that can be implemented. They are Read, Change, Full Control, and No Access.

Answer A is incorrect—Modify is not an explicit share permission.

See the explanation for question 5 for an explanation of the explicit share permissions.

5. Which is the minimum permission that enables users to connect to a resource and run programs?
   - B. Read

5. CORRECT ANSWER: B

The Read permission enables a user to connect to the resource and run programs.

Answer A is incorrect—Full Control is not the minimum permission required to connect to a resource. Answer C is incorrect—No Access will not allow a user to connect to a resource. Answer D is incorrect—Change is not the minimum permission required to connect.

Windows NT allows an administrator to assign permissions to any shared directory resource.

The four share permissions are described in the following list:

- **Read.** Enables users to connect to the resource and run programs. Users also can view any documents that are stored in the share, but they cannot make any changes to the documents.

- **Change.** Enables users to connect to a resource and run programs. this permission also enables users to create new documents and subfolders, modify existing documents, and delete documents.

- **Full Control.** Enables users to do anything they want in the share. Full Control also enables users to change the share permissions to affect all users. The Full Control permission generally is not required for most users. Change is sufficient for most day-to-day business needs.

Chapter 3 MANAGING RESOURCES

- **No Access.** The most powerful permission. When it is implemented, the user assigned this permission has no access to the specified resource. It does not matter what other permissions are assigned. The No Access permission overrides any other assigned permissions.

6. Which permission enables users to view documents that are stored in the share, but does not enable them to make changes to the documents?

   B. Read

6. CORRECT ANSWER: B

With the Read permission, users can view any documents that are stored in the share, but they cannot make any changes to the documents.

Answer A is incorrect—Full Control would allow the user to make changes. Answer C is incorrect—with No Access the user could not connect to the share. Answer D is incorrect—Change would allow the user to make changes.

7. Which minimum share permission enables users to connect and to create new documents and subfolders?

   D. Change

7. CORRECT ANSWER: D

The Change permissions setting enables users to connect to a resource and run programs. This permission also enables users to create new documents and subfolders, modify existing documents, and delete documents.

Answer A is incorrect—Full Control is not the minimum permission required. Answer B is incorrect—Read would not allow the user to create documents and folders. Answer C is incorrect—No Access would not allow the user to connect to the share.

8. Which minimum permission enables users to modify existing documents and delete documents?

   D. Change

8. CORRECT ANSWER: D

The Change permissions setting enables users to connect to a resource and run programs. This setting also enables users to create new documents and subfolders, modify existing documents, and delete documents.

Answer A is incorrect—Full Control is not the minimum permission required. Answer B is incorrect—Read would not allow the user to modify and delete existing documents.

ANSWERS & EXPLANATIONS

Answer C is incorrect—No Access would not allow the user to connect to the share.

9. Which permission enables users to do anything they want in the share?

   A. Full Control

9. CORRECT ANSWER: A

The Full Control permission enables users to do anything they want in the share.

Answer B is incorrect—Read only allows the user to view the contents of the share and execute programs. Answer C is incorrect—No Access would not allow the user to do anything. Answer D is incorrect—The Change permission would not allow the user to modify permissions in the share.

10. Which permission is sufficient for most day-to-day business needs?

    D. Change

10. CORRECT ANSWER: D

The Change permission is sufficient for most day-to-day business needs. This allows the user to create documents and folders, but not modify the permissions for the share.

Answer A is incorrect—Full Control would allow users to modify the share permissions. Answer B is incorrect—Read access would not allow users to create folders or documents. Answer C is incorrect—No Access would not allow the users to connect to the share.

11. As a general rule, which permission is considered the most powerful?

    C. No Access

11. CORRECT ANSWER: C

The No Access permission is the most powerful permission. When it is implemented, the user that you assign this permission has no access to that resource.

12. Users to whom you assign varying levels of permissions through group memberships have effective shared permissions of what?

    A. The accumulation of their individual shared permissions

12. CORRECT ANSWER: A

When users, through group membership, have been assigned varying levels of share permissions, the users' effective shared permissions are the accumulation of their individual shared permissions.

Answer B is incorrect—the user would have the accumulated permissions, not the lowest. Answer C is incorrect—permissions cannot be assigned priorities. Answer D is incorrect—permissions cannot be assigned to priority groups.

The only time that this is not the case is when you assign the user or a group to which the user belongs the explicit permission of No Access. The No Access permission always takes precedence over any other permissions you assign.

Remember, you must create the local groups in the accounts database where the resource is located. If the resource is located on a domain controller, you can create the local group in the domain's accounts database. If the resource is located on a Windows NT Workstation or a Windows NT Member Server, you must create the local group in that system's accounts database.

13. At what level do share permissions affect users? Select the best answer.

B. When logged across the network.

13. CORRECT ANSWER: B

Share permissions are in effect only when the user connects to the resource via the network.

Answer A is incorrect—share permissions are not in effect locally. Answer C is incorrect—the operating system does not affect that share permissions are not in effect locally. Answer D is incorrect—share permissions do affect users.

14. At what levels do NTFS permissions affect users? Select all correct answers.

A. Locally.
B. When logged across the network.

14. CORRECT ANSWERS: A-B

NTFS permissions can affect users logged on locally or across the network to the system where the NTFS permissions apply.

Answer C is incorrect—NTFS permissions are only in effect locally on the Windows NT operating system. Answer D is incorrect—NTFS permissions do affect users.

NTFS permissions enable you to assign more comprehensive security to your computer system. NTFS permissions can protect you at the file level. Share permissions, on the other hand, can apply only to the directory level. NTFS permissions can affect users logged on locally or across the network to the

ANSWERS & EXPLANATIONS

system where you apply the NTFS permissions. Share permissions are in effect only when the user connects to the resource via the network.

15. Which of the following NTFS directory permissions enable users to view the contents of a directory and to navigate to its subdirectories? Select all that apply.

    B. List
    C. Read

15. CORRECT ANSWERS: B-C

List and Read enables the user to view the contents of a directory and to navigate to its subdirectories. See the explanation for question 18 for an explanation of NTFS permissions.

Answer A is incorrect—No Access will not allow a user to view or navigate directories. Answer D is incorrect—Add will not allow the user to navigate the directories.

16. Which of the following NTFS directory permissions overrides all other permissions?

    A. No Access

16. CORRECT ANSWER: A

No Access overrides all other permissions. See the explanation for question 18 for an explanation of NTFS permissions.

Answers B, C, and D are incorrect—List, Read, and Add do not override all other permissions.

17. Which of the following NTFS directory permissions enables users to add new subdirectories and files to the directory, but does not enable them to access files within the directory?

    D. Add

17. CORRECT ANSWER: D

Add enables the user to add new subdirectories and files to the directory, but does not enable the user to access files within the directory.

Answer A is incorrect—No Access prevents the user from doing anything. Answer B is incorrect—List would allow the user to access files. Answer C is incorrect—Read would allow the user to access files.

18. Which sets of NTFS directory permissions enable users to add new files to the directory structure, and restrict the users to read-only access to these files? Select all that apply.

    C. Read
    D. Add

18. CORRECT ANSWERS: C-D

Add enables a user to add new files to the directory structure. After the files have been added, the users have read-only access to the files.

Answer A is incorrect—No access would not allow the user to add or read files. Answer B is incorrect—List would not allow the user to add files.

You can apply NTFS permissions, when applied at the directory level, as one of the following default assignments shown in Table 3.2:

TABLE 3.2   NTFS DIRECTORY PERMISSIONS

NTFS Permission	Meaning
No Access (None) (None)	The No Access NTFS permission means that the user will have absolutely No Access to the directory or its files. This will override any other NTFS permissions that may have been assigned to him through other group memberships.
List (RX) (Not Specified)	The List NTFS permission enables the user to view the contents of a directory and to navigate to its subdirectories. List does not grant users access to the files in these directories unless specified in file permissions.
Read (RX) (RX)	The Read NTFS permission enables the user to navigate the entire directory structure, view the contents of the directory, view the contents of any files in the directory, and execute programs.
Add (WX) (Not Specified)	The Add NTFS permission enables the user to add new subdirectories and files to the directory. Add does not give the user access to the files within the directory unless specified in other NTFS permissions.
Add & Read (RWX) (RX)	The Add & Read NTFS permission enables a user to add new files to the directory structure. After the file has been added, the user has read-only access to the files. This permission also enables the user to run programs.
Change (RWXD) (RWXD)	The Change NTFS permission enables the user to do the most data manipulation. Users can view the contents of directories and files, run programs, modify the contents of data files, and delete files.
Full Control (All) (All)	The Full Control permission gives the user all the capabilities of the Change permission. In addition, the user can change the permissions on that directory or any of its contents. He also can take ownership of the directory or any of its contents.
Special Directory	You can set the NTFS permissions as desired to any combination of (R)ead, (W)rite, E(x)ecute, (D)elete, Change (P)ermissions, and Take (O)wnership.

ANSWERS & EXPLANATIONS

You can apply NTFS permissions to individual files in directories. The NTFS file permissions are shown in Table 3.3:

TABLE 3.3 NTFS FILE PERMISSIONS

NTFS Permission	Meaning
No Access (None)	The No Access NTFS file permission means that the users have absolutely No Access to that file. This overrides any other NTFS directory and file permissions assigned to the users through other group memberships.
Read (RX)	The Read NTFS file permission enables the users to view the contents of files but to make no changes to the contents. The users can also execute the file if it is a program.
Change (RWXD)	The Change NTFS file permission enables the users to make any editing changes they want to a data file, including deleting the file.
Full Control (All)	The Full Control file permission gives the users all the capabilities of the Change permission. The users can also change the permissions on that file and take ownership of that file, if they are not the present owner.
Special File	You can set the NTFS file permissions as desired to any combination of (R)ead, (W)rite, E(x)ecute, (D)elete, Change (P)ermissions, and Take (O)wnership.

19. If an NTFS file is moved to a new directory on the same volume, what will become of the permissions?

    A. The file will maintain its existing permissions.

19. CORRECT ANSWER: A

If a file is moved from one directory to another directory on the same NTFS volume, it retains the same NTFS permissions it had.

Answer B is incorrect—the file will not assume permissions from the source. Answer C is incorrect—the file will not assume permissions from the target. Answer D is incorrect—the file will not lose all permissions.

20. If an NTFS file is copied to a new directory on the same volume, what will become of the permissions?

    C. The file will assume permissions from the target.

20. CORRECT ANSWER: C

If a file is copied from one directory to another on a single NTFS volume, the file inherits the directory permissions for new files of the target directory.

Answer A is incorrect—the file will not maintain its existing permissions. Answer B is incorrect—the file will not assume permissions from the source. Answer D is incorrect—the file will not lose all permissions.

As with NTFS permissions, the task of copying and moving files directly affects the auditing on files. If you copy a file from one NTFS directory to another NTFS directory, the new copy of the file inherits the auditing set on the target directory.

If you move a file from one NTFS directory to another NTFS directory on the same logical volume, the file maintains the same auditing settings that it had in the first directory.

If you move a file from one NTFS directory to another NTFS directory but they reside on different NTFS logical volumes, the file inherits the audit settings of the new folder. Any time a file is moved between volumes on Windows NT, the actual chain of events is a copy, verify, and delete. That is, a copy of the original file is placed in the new directory. This copy is verified against the original copy of the file. Finally, if they match, the original file is deleted.

> **FURTHER REVIEW**

MANAGING DISK RESOURCES

The following key words are important terms that were covered in this section. You should make sure you understand what each one is and what it does.

Key Words

Access Control Entries
Access Control List
Security log

The Windows NT Security Model

In the Windows NT security model, users are associated with resources. Each resource has an Access Control List (ACL) that contains Access Control Entries (ACEs). When you determine whether you should grant users access to resources, the users' access tokens are compared to the ACL for the resources they are trying to access.

When users log in to the system, they receive access tokens that are attached to any processes that they run during the logon session. The access tokens contain their security IDs (SID) and all their group memberships. The access tokens serve as the credentials for the logon session. Whenever users try to access an object, they present the access tokens as their credentials. Because the access token is built during the logon process, group membership is not modified until the next user logon.

When the user attempts to open a resource, the user's access token is compared to the Access Control List for the resource. The Access Control Entries within the Access Control List are, by default, sorted with all No Access permissions at the top of the list. The evaluation of whether the user should be granted access to the resource is as follows:

1. If the users or any group that they belong to is explicitly denied access (assigned the No Access permission), the access to the resource is denied.

2. The ACEs are next checked to see whether any of the entries explicitly assigns the users or a group to which the users belong the type of access that they are attempting. If there is such an entry, access is granted to the resource.

3. Each entry in the ACL is investigated to determine whether the accumulated permissions enable the users to have the access that they attempt.

4. If the necessary rights cannot be accumulated from the ACL, the users are denied the access that they have attempted.

When a user opens the object successfully, the user's process is given a handle to the object. The handle is used to identify the user accessing the object. The system also creates a list of granted access rights to the object. This way, if the user attempts different transactions with the object, only the list of granted rights needs to be evaluated. The entire process of checking the object's ACL does not have to be performed on every transaction attempt.

Not checking the object's ACL is both good and bad. It is good because subsequent actions on a resource do not require a check against the ACL every time that the user attempts to manipulate the data. This reduces network traffic, because the Windows NT Challenge/Response transaction does not have to perform over and over again. It is bad because the users have the same access to the object as they did when they opened the object, even if the ACL is modified for the object after access occurs. The list of granted rights to the object stored in the users' process tables for that handle is not modified. They have the same level of access until they close the object and ultimately close the handle to the object.

Implementing File-level Auditing

File-level auditing enables an administrator to review the security log to determine who may have created, deleted, or modified a specified file or directory. This can help identify problems in the security model implemented in a domain. To set up file-level auditing, two separate steps are required:

1. Enable File and Object Access Auditing in the domain's Audit policy.
2. Enable the detail of file level auditing you want to employ on specific file and directory objects on an NTFS volume.

A member of the Administrators local group must enable the File and Object Access auditing. After this has been enabled, administrators and any users or groups to whom you assign the User Right Manage Auditing and Security Log can set auditing on specific directories and review the security log for audit successes and failures.

To set up auditing on a specific directory or file on an NTFS volume, the person to whom you assign the task of setting up auditing must bring up the properties for that directory or file object. After choosing the Security tab of the object, that person can click the Auditing button to set the auditing levels for that object.

The administrator must answer the following questions:

- Whom are you going to audit?
- What actions are you going to audit?
- Do you want to apply this auditing to files and subfolders?

When determining the users to audit, remember that you are more likely to determine who performed a task by auditing the Everyone group rather than a smaller local group. The Everyone group is preferred when auditing because it includes all users that connect to the network (whether they are a known user is not important). However, if you know that only members of the local group Accounting_Users have access to a folder and its subfolders, for example, it is fine to audit just that group.

After you select the users to audit, you now must select the actions to audit. Auditing is always based on either successes or failures. Be careful what you choose here. The actions that you can audit for a file or folder directly match the six different NTFS permissions. You must choose the correct combination of permissions that are being used to determine who is performing the task that causes the need for an audit. For example, if you are trying to determine who has been deleting the General Ledger, you must audit delete successes (as they have been very successful in deleting the file). The actions that you can audit include the following:

- By enabling the Read event, you can determine whether an attempt was made to open a file.
- By enabling the Write event, you can determine when a user attempted to modify the contents of a file.
- By enabling the Execute event, you can determine when a user attempted to run a program.
- By enabling the Delete event, you can determine when a user attempted to delete a file object.
- By enabling the Change Permissions event, you can determine when a user tried to change the permissions on a file or directory.
- By enabling the Take Ownership event, you can determine when a user attempted to take ownership of a file or directory object.
- After you set the auditing, you can check the Event Viewer's Security Log to determine the access done to the file or directory on which auditing was enabled.

Auditing Logons and Logoffs

If you feel that your network has been compromised and unwanted users are accessing the network, the auditing of logons and logoffs can help determine what account they are using to access the network and what computer they are accessing the network from.

By auditing the successes and failures of the Logon and Logoff audit category, you can determine the location of the access point to your network. It is recommended that you monitor both successes and failures, because you want to know where the attempts to access the network are taking place and whether the attempts are successful.

SUMMARY

You should know have a good understanding of the many different parts of Windows NT administration in an enterprise environment. Although the test does not heavily focus on this subject, it is one of the most important in a real-world network implementation.

Most specifically, the points you should take away from this chapter are as follows:

- How to manage Windows NT User and Group Accounts
- How to implement and manage Windows NT share-level and user-level security
- Managing NTFS permissions

CHAPTER 4

Connectivity

Microsoft Windows NT 4.0 was designed to interoperate with many other systems in an enterprise environment. This chapter will introduce you to the tools Windows NT has to offer to communicate with these systems. The exam will contain various questions relating to solutions to different connectivity scenarios.

OBJECTIVES

This chapter helps you prepare for the exam by covering the following objectives:

Configure Windows NT Server for interoperability with NetWare servers using Gateway Services for NetWare and Migration Tool for NetWare.

▶ Although organizations continue to rapidly deploy Windows NT in the enterprise, many still have legacy NetWare systems that must be able to interoperate with Windows NT. Microsoft ensured compatibility with NetWare servers by including the NWLink IPX/SPX-compatible protocol, but they did not end there. Microsoft bundles in the Gateway Services for NetWare (GSNW) and also includes a utility to help smooth the conversion from NetWare into Windows NT Server. In the following sections you learn about:

continues

OBJECTIVES (continued)

- Gateway Services for NetWare (GSNW)
- Installing and configuring GSNW
- NWCONV.EXE: Migration Tool for NetWare

Install and configure multiprotocol routing to serve various functions including Internet Router, BOOTP/DHCP Relay Agent, and IPX Router.

▶ This section discusses installing and configuring multiprotocol routing, including Internet router and IPX router. Multiprotocol routing enables you to send more than one protocol across the router.

Install and configure Internet Information Server (IIS).

▶ Internet Information Server is bundled into Windows NT 4, and you can automatically install it during the initial installation of your Windows NT Server system.

▶ Internet Information Server, or IIS, serves primarily as a World Wide Web (WWW) server, but it also offers FTP and Gopher support. Because this software is included with the Windows NT Server software, it makes perfect sense to learn about what IIS can do for you. The enterprise exam has a few questions relating to installation and configuration of IIS. Before you can look into the installation and configuration of IIS, though, you must understand the different components and functions of IIS.

Install and configure Internet services including World Wide Web, DNS, and Intranet.

▶ Installing and configuring Internet services can be broken into a number of components: installing the World Wide Web, FTP, or Gopher service (WWW is used for all the examples here, as it is the most popular) and configuring DNS services. Intranet services are identical to Internet with the exception of the clients accessing them, and thus only Internet is examined here.

Install and configure Remote Access Service (RAS) including communications, protocols, and security.

▶ The Windows NT Remote Access Service (RAS) extends the power of Windows NT networking to anywhere you can find a phone line. Using RAS, a Windows NT computer can connect to a remote network via a dial-up connection and fully participate in the network as a network client. RAS also enables your Windows NT computer to receive dial-up connections from remote computers.

▶ RAS supports SLIP and PPP line protocols, and NetBEUI, TCP/IP, and IPX network protocols. Windows NT supports SLIP only as a client. PPP, on the other hand, is supported as both a server and client protocol. Because so many Internet users access their service providers using a phone line, RAS often serves as an Internet interface.

▶ The enterprise exam contains questions on the use of RAS. To be successful with these questions, you must have a solid understanding of RAS, including installation and configuration.

PRACTICE QUESTIONS

INTEROPERABILITY WITH NETWARE

1. Microsoft ensured compatibility with NetWare servers by including what protocol with Windows NT Server?

    A. NWLINK

    B. IPX/SPX

    C. TCP/IP

    D. NetBEUI

2. What utility has Microsoft bundled with Windows NT to help Windows NT Server interact with NetWare servers?

    A. Migration Tool for NetWare

    B. NetBEUI

    C. Gateway Services for NetWare

    D. IIS

3. How many connections to the NetWare server does GSNW require?

    A. 1

    B. 2

    C. 4

    D. 8

4. What utility transfers file and directory information, as well as user and group account information, from a NetWare server to a Windows NT domain controller?

    A. Gateway Services for NetWare

    B. Migration Tool for NetWare

    C. NTFS

    D. NetBEUI

5. For the Migration Tool for NetWare to maintain directory and file permissions, what type of partition must the target be?

    A. FAT

    B. VFAT

    C. NTFS

    D. CDFS

6. For the Migration Tool for NetWare to maintain directory and file permissions, what type of partition must the source be?

    A. FAT

    B. VFAT

    C. NTFS

    D. CDFS

7. To what NetWare permission does the Windows NT Full Control permission map?

    A. Read

    B. Write

    C. Modify

    D. Supervisor

8. To what NetWare permission does the Windows NT Read permission map?

    A. Read

    B. Write

    C. Modify

    D. Supervisor

9. To what NetWare permission does the Windows NT Change permission map? Choose all that apply.

    A. Read

    B. Write

    C. Modify

    D. Erase

10. To what Windows NT permission does NetWare's Create permission map?

    A. Read

    B. List

    C. Add

    D. Change

11. To what Windows NT permission does NetWare's File Scan permission map?

    A. Read

    B. List

    C. Add

    D. Change

12. To what Windows NT permission does NetWare's Access Control permission map?

    A. Change Permissions

    B. List

    C. Add

    D. Change

13. What rights and permissions are maintained when migrating from NetWare to a Windows NT FAT partition?

    A. All rights and permissions

    B. All rights but no permissions

    C. No rights but all permissions

    D. No rights and no permissions

14. What utility is used to start the Migration Tool for NetWare?

    A. NWCONV.EXE

    B. MIGRATE.COM

    C. MIGRATE.EXE

    D. MGTOOL.EXE

15. What becomes of passwords from the NetWare server during migration?

    A. Duplicate ones are discarded.

    B. Duplicate ones are written to an error file.

    C. All passwords are maintained.

    D. All passwords are discarded.

16. **What is the result of selecting Password is Username in the Migration Tool?**

    A. Migrated users have no passwords assigned to them.

    B. Migrated users' passwords are the same as their usernames.

    C. A single password is assigned to all migrated users.

    D. Migrated users are forced to change their passwords the first time they log on to the Windows NT Server.

ANSWER KEY

1. A
2. C
3. A
4. B
5. C
6. A
7. D
8. A
9. B-C-D
10. C
11. B
12. A
13. D
14. A
15. D
16. B

ANSWERS & EXPLANATIONS

INTEROPERABILITY WITH NETWARE

1. Microsoft ensured compatibility with NetWare servers by including what protocol with Windows NT Server?

    A. NWLINK

1. CORRECT ANSWER: A

NWLink was created by Microsoft to be fully compatible with the IPX/SPX protocol and NetWare.

Answer B is incorrect; IPX/SPX is Novell's NetWare protocol. Answers C and D are incorrect; TCP/IP and NetBEUI are not used by Windows NT to communicate with NetWare.

2. What utility has Microsoft bundled with Windows NT to help Windows NT Server interact with NetWare servers?

    C. Gateway Services for NetWare

2. CORRECT ANSWER: C

Microsoft bundles Gateway Services for NetWare (GSNW) to provide interoperability and help smooth the conversion from NetWare to Windows NT Server.

Gateway Services for NetWare performs the following functions:

- Enables Windows NT Server to access NetWare file and print resources.

- Enables Windows NT Server to act as a gateway to the NetWare file and print resources. The Windows NT Server can share the connection to the NetWare server.

Answer A is incorrect; the Migration utility is used to migrate from NetWare to Windows NT. Answer B is incorrect; NetBEUI is a protocol, not a utility. Answer D is incorrect; IIS is a Web server for Windows NT.

3. How many connections to the NetWare server does GSNW require?

    A. 1

3. CORRECT ANSWER: A

GSNW enables multiple Windows NT clients to share a single connection.

ANSWERS & EXPLANATIONS

GSNW can provide Windows NT networks with convenient access to NetWare resources. GSNW enables one single connection to be shared by multiple Windows NT clients. This sharing of a connection is very convenient. However, it also causes a significant performance loss for the NetWare resource. GSNW is ideal for occasional NetWare resource access, but it is not recommended for large-scale routing.

4. What utility transfers file and directory information, as well as user and group account information, from a NetWare server to a Windows NT domain controller?

B. Migration Tool for NetWare

4. CORRECT ANSWER: B

The Migration Tool for NetWare transfers file and directory information, as well as user and group account information, from a NetWare server to a Windows NT domain controller.

Answer A is incorrect; GSNW allows Windows NT to interact with a NetWare server. Answer C is incorrect; NTFS is the Windows NT file system. Answer D is incorrect; NetBEUI is a network protocol.

5. For the Migration Tool for NetWare to maintain directory and file permissions, what type of partition must the target be?

C. NTFS

5. CORRECT ANSWER: C

The Migration Tool for NetWare can preserve the directory and file permissions if it is being transferred to a Windows NTFS partition.

Answer A is incorrect; a FAT partition will not maintain file and directory partitions. Answer B is incorrect; VFAT is not supported by Windows NT. Answer D is incorrect; CDFS is the Windows NT CD-ROM file system.

6. For the Migration Tool for NetWare to maintain directory and file permissions, what type of partition must the source be?

A. FAT

6. CORRECT ANSWER: A

NetWare partitions are always FAT.

7. To what NetWare permission does the Windows NT Full Control permission map?

D. Supervisor

7. CORRECT ANSWER: D

Full Control equates to NetWare's Supervisor permission.

Answer A is incorrect; the NetWare Read permission is identical to the Read permission in Windows NT. Answer B is incorrect; the NetWare Write permission equates to part of the Windows NT Change permission. Answer C is incorrect; the NetWare Modify permission also equates to part of the Windows NT Change permission.

8. To what NetWare permission does the Windows NT Read permission map?

   A. Read

8. CORRECT ANSWER: A

The Read permission is identical on both NetWare and Windows NT.

Answer B is incorrect; the NetWare Write permission equates to part of the Windows NT Change permission. Answer C is incorrect; the NetWare Modify permission also equates to part of the Windows NT Change permission. Answer D is incorrect; the NetWare Supervisor permission equates to the Windows NT Full Control permission.

9. To what NetWare permission does the Windows NT Change permission map? Choose all that apply.

   B. Write
   C. Modify
   D. Erase

9. CORRECT ANSWERS: B-C-D

Windows NT's Change permission equates to NetWare's Write, Erase, and Modify permissions.

Answer A is incorrect; the NetWare Read permission is identical to the Read permission in Windows NT.

10. To what Windows NT permission does NetWare's Create permission map?

    C. Add

10. CORRECT ANSWER: C

Windows NT's Add permission equates to NetWare's Create permission.

Answer A is incorrect; the Windows NT Read permission equates to the NetWare Read permission. Answer B is incorrect; the Windows NT List permission equates to the NetWare File Scan permission. Answer D is incorrect; the Windows NT Change permission equates to the NetWare Write, Erase, and Modify permissions.

ANSWERS & EXPLANATIONS

11. To what Windows NT permission does NetWare's File Scan permission map?

  B. List

11. CORRECT ANSWER: B

Windows NT's List permission equates to NetWare's File Scan permission.

Answer A is incorrect; the Windows NT Read permission equates to the NetWare Read permission. Answer C is incorrect; the Windows NT Add permission equates to the NetWare Create permission. Answer D is incorrect; the Windows NT Change permission equates to the NetWare Write, Erase, and Modify permissions.

12. To what Windows NT permission does NetWare's Access Control permission map?

  A. Change Permissions

12. CORRECT ANSWER: A

NetWare's Access Control permission equates to Windows NT's Change Permissions permission. See Table 4.1 for a complete list of Novell NetWare permissions and the corresponding Windows NT NTFS permissions.

Answer B is incorrect; the Windows NT List permission equates to the NetWare File Scan permission. Answer C is incorrect; the Windows NT Add permission equates to the NetWare Create permission. Answer D is incorrect; the Windows NT Change permission equates to the NetWare Write, Erase, and Modify permissions.

13. What rights and permissions are maintained when migrating from NetWare to a Windows NT FAT partition?

  D. No rights and no permissions

13. CORRECT ANSWER: D

If the partition to which you are migrating is a FAT partition, no rights or permissions are maintained.

To retain permissions when migrating from a NetWare volume, the target partition must be formatted with NTFS.

14. What utility is used to start the Migration Tool for NetWare?

  A. NWCONV.EXE

14. CORRECT ANSWER: A

To start the Migration Tool for NetWare, you must run the NWCONV.EXE file from the command prompt.

Answers B, C, and D are incorrect executables (or *aren't* executables) for running the Migration Tool for NetWare.

The Migration Tool for NetWare transfers file and directory information, as well as user and group account information, from a NetWare server to a Windows NT domain controller. The Migration Tool can preserve the directory and file permissions if it is being transferred to a Windows NTFS partition. Table 4.1 displays the NetWare permissions and the corresponding Windows NT NTFS permissions.

TABLE 4.1 NETWARE PERMISSIONS AND CORRESPONDING NTFS PERMISSIONS

Novell NetWare Permission	Windows NT Permission
Supervisor	Full Control (All)
Read	Read (RX)
Write	Change (RWXD)
Erase	Change (RWXD)
Modify	Change (RWXD)
Create	Add (WX) Custom right
File Scan	List (RX) Custom right
Access Control	Change Permissions

If the partition to which you are migrating is a FAT partition, no rights or permissions are maintained.

To start the Migration Tool for NetWare, run the NWCONV.EXE file. For test purposes, it must be executed from a command prompt or from the Start, Run command.

15. What becomes of passwords from the NetWare server during migration?

    D. All passwords are discarded.

15. CORRECT ANSWER: D

For security reasons you cannot migrate the passwords from the NetWare server.

ANSWERS & EXPLANATIONS   175

16. What is the result of selecting Password is Username in the Migration Tool?

    B. Migrated users' passwords are the same as their usernames.

16. CORRECT ANSWER: B

Password is Username means that the migrated users' passwords are the same as their usernames.

Answer A is incorrect; the users will have their usernames assigned as passwords. Answer C is incorrect; no one single password would be assigned. Answer D is incorrect; the Password is Username selection will not make the users change their passwords. However, there is a specific selection in the Migration Tool to force users to change their passwords the first time they log on.

All the user accounts from your NetWare server are migrated by default to the Windows NT domain controller. To disable the transfer of users and groups, click the Transfer Users and Groups check box located at the top of the User and Group Options dialog box.

The User and Group Options dialog box holds all the options available on four pages: Passwords, User Names, Group Names, and Defaults.

The passwords from the NetWare server cannot be migrated across for security reasons; however, the Migration Tool can be used to specify how the passwords for the migrated users should be handled:

- No Password: The migrated users have no passwords assigned to them.

- Password Is Username: The migrated users have passwords the same as their usernames.

- Password Is: Assigns a single password to all migrated users.

- User Must Change Password: Forces the migrated users to change their passwords the first time they log on to the Windows NT Server.

You need to configure the Migration Tool in case it runs into a duplicate username or group name during the migration. The User Names page enables you to select how the Migration Tool should react to the duplicates:

- Log Error: Adds an error to the ERROR.LOG file.
- Ignore: Causes the account to be skipped with no error messages or warnings. This is the default option.
- Overwrite with New Information: The existing account would be overwritten with the new NetWare user information.
- Add Prefix: Includes a prefix with the user account to enable you to distinguish between the existing account and the migrated account.

The Defaults page tab contains two options:

- Use Supervisor Defaults: You can use the supervisor account restrictions for the migrated users instead of using the account policies in the Windows NT Server.
- Add Supervisors to the Administrators Group: The migrated users who have supervisor-equivalent access are added into the Windows NT domain's Administrators group. By default, the supervisors from the NetWare system are not added into this group.

FURTHER REVIEW

INTEROPERABILITY WITH NETWARE

The following key words are important terms that were covered in this section. You should make sure you understand what each one is and what it does.

Key Words

File and Print Sharing
IPX/SPX
NetWare
NWLink

Steps for Migrating from NetWare

When the Migration Tool for NetWare is first started, a dialog box displays that enables you to select the NetWare and Windows NT Server domain controller with which you will be working.

▼ **NOTE**

To be able to accomplish the migration from the NetWare server to your Windows NT Server computer, you must have supervisor access to the NetWare system, and you must be an administrator in the Windows NT domain to which you will be migrating.

To complete the migration from a NetWare server to a Windows NT Server, follow these steps:

1. From the Start menu choose the Run command, type NWCONV, and press Enter.

2. Click the Add button and select your NetWare server and Windows NT domain controller, and then click OK.

3. You then have the option to configure the User Options or the File Options. After you configure each of these sections, you can either click the Start Migration button, or you can do a trial migration first to verify your settings (which is highly recommended).

PRACTICE QUESTIONS

INSTALLING AND CONFIGURING MULTIPROTOCOL ROUTING

1. To set up Windows NT as an Internet router, what two steps should you follow? Choose two.

    A. Install two network adapters in the system.

    B. Enable IP routing.

    C. Start GSNW.

    D. Enable the NetBEUI protocol.

2. A Windows NT router cannot exchange Routing Information Protocol (RIP) routing packets with other IP RIP routers unless which of the following is true?

    A. GSNW is running.

    B. The RIP routing software is installed.

    C. NetBEUI is enabled.

    D. DHCP is running.

3. After you enable RIP, how often are RIP packets sent?

    A. Every 5 seconds

    B. Every 30 seconds

    C. Every minute

    D. Every 5 minutes

4. What is the purpose of the RIP packets?

    A. To exchange queued messages

    B. To exchange email

    C. To exchange routing information

    D. To verify host existence

5. To whom are the RIP packets sent?

    A. Hosts

    B. Clients

    C. Other routers

    D. Domain controllers

6. Without the RIP protocol, router tables are maintained _____.

    A. By OSPF

    B. Manually

    C. Automatically

    D. At startup

7. If administrators decide to manually add an entry to the routing table, what command must they use?

    A. ROUTE ADD

    B. TRACERT

C. NBSTAT

D. NETSTAT

8. After the DHCP Server Service has been installed, you can configure the service using which tool?

   A. Server Manager

   B. DHCP Manager

   C. DHCP Administrator

   D. DHCP Client Configuration

9. The DHCP database is created in which format?

   A. Access

   B. JET

   C. DNS

   D. IP

10. Where is the DHCP database stored?

    A. \%systemroot%\system32\dhcp

    B. \%systemroot%\system32\jet

    C. \%systemroot%\dhcp

    D. \%systemroot%\jet

11. Spencer, the new administrator, is complaining about the size of the DHCP database. Which command should Spencer use to clear deleted records from the DHCP database?

    A. COMPRESS

    B. DELETE

    C. JETPACK

    D. CLEAR

12. What is the primary purpose for the DHCP Relay tab?

    A. To allow a Windows NT system to relay DHCP broadcasts for clients across an IP router

    B. To block broadcast messages from foreign networks

    C. To relay alerts regarding the DHCP database to the administrator

    D. To relay inventory messages to a central JET database

13. Under normal conditions, IP routers are configured to do what with broadcasts?

    A. Forward them.

    B. Ignore them.

    C. Answer them.

    D. Send them continuously.

14. Given the situation in question 13, if a client asks for an IP address on a local segment when the DHCP server is located on another network segment, what becomes of the request?

    A. It goes unanswered.

    B. It is answered immediately.

    C. It is routed for answer.

    D. It is continuously sent until an answer is received.

15. When the IPX RIP router is installed, Windows NT can route IPX packets over the installed network adapters. What does it use to exchange routing table information?

A. IP
B. RIP
C. TCP/IP
D. UDP

ANSWER KEY

1. A-B
2. B
3. B
4. C
5. C
6. B
7. A
8. B
9. B
10. A
11. C
12. A
13. B
14. A
15. B

ANSWERS & EXPLANATIONS

INSTALLING AND CONFIGURING MULTIPROTOCOL ROUTING

1. To set up Windows NT as an Internet router, what two steps should you follow? Choose two.

    A. Install two network adapters in the system.
    B. Enable IP routing.

1. CORRECT ANSWERS: A-B

To set up Windows NT as an Internet router, install two network adapters in the system, and then enable IP routing.

Answer C is incorrect; GSNW is used to interact with NetWare. Answer D is incorrect; NetBEUI is not used in Internet communications.

2. A Windows NT router cannot exchange Routing Information Protocol (RIP) routing packets with other IP RIP routers unless which of the following is true?

    B. The RIP routing software is installed.

2. CORRECT ANSWER: B

A Windows NT router cannot exchange Routing Information Protocol (RIP) routing packets with other IP RIP routers unless the RIP routing software is installed.

Answer A is incorrect; GSNW is used to interact with NetWare. Answer C is incorrect; NetBEUI is not used in Internet communications. Answer D is incorrect; DHCP is not required to use RIP.

Windows NT can act as a router between the Internet and the internal network. With a router, all incoming packets from the Internet are forwarded into the network.

Setting Windows NT up as an Internet router is as simple as installing two network adapters in the system, and then enabling IP routing via Control Panel, Networks, the TCP/IP protocol configuration. This option enables Windows NT to act as a static router. Windows NT cannot exchange Routing Information Protocol (RIP) routing packets with other IP RIP routers unless the RIP routing software is installed. RIP is installed as a service through the Network applet. Once RIP is installed, there is no further configuration necessary to activate it.

Chapter 4 CONNECTIVITY

3. After you enable RIP, how often are RIP packets sent?

B. Every 30 seconds.

3. CORRECT ANSWER: B

RIP packets are sent out once every 30 seconds to exchange information with other RIP-enabled routers.

4. What is the purpose of the RIP packets?

C. To exchange routing information

4. CORRECT ANSWER: C

RIP packets are used to exchange routing information between routers. This dynamically builds routing tables, which precludes entering all necessary routes manually into a static routing table.

Answer A is incorrect; RIP packets do not exchange messages. Answer B is incorrect; RIP is not used by email. Answer D is incorrect; RIP packets are not used to verify host existence.

5. To whom are the RIP packets sent?

C. Other routers

5. CORRECT ANSWER: C

RIP packets are sent to other dynamic RIP-routing routers to exchange and update routing information.

Answer A is incorrect; RIP packets are not sent to other hosts. Answer B is incorrect; RIP packets are not sent to clients. Answer D is incorrect; RIP packets are not sent to domain controllers.

6. Without the RIP protocol, router tables are maintained _____.

B. Manually

6. CORRECT ANSWER: B

Without the RIP protocol, router tables must be set up manually when using Windows NT to route information.

Answer A is incorrect; OSPF is not used by Windows NT. Answer C is incorrect; RIP is required to automatically build routing tables. Answer D is incorrect; router tables are not maintained at startup.

7. If administrators decide to manually add an entry to the routing table, what command must they use?

A. ROUTE ADD

7. CORRECT ANSWER: A

The ROUTE ADD command is used from a MS-DOS prompt to manually maintain routing tables on a Windows NT system.

ANSWERS & EXPLANATIONS 183

Answer B is incorrect; TRACERT is used to trace the route of a packet, not to maintain routing tables. Answer C is incorrect; NBSTAT is not used for routing table maintenance. Answer D is incorrect; NETSTAT is not a valid command in Windows NT.

▼ **NOTE**

Windows NT supports RIP I routing. Steelhead (RRAS) supports RIP II routing.

8. After the DHCP Server Service has been installed, you can configure the service using which tool?

B. DHCP Manager

8. CORRECT ANSWER: B

After you install the DHCP Server Service, you can configure the service using the DHCP Manager option.

Answer A is incorrect; Server Manager is used to manage computer accounts. Answers C and D are incorrect; these are not valid application names.

9. The DHCP database is created in which format?

B. JET

9. CORRECT ANSWER: B

The DHCP database is created in JET format. The JET database was originally created for Access, and is used by Windows NT for the DHCP and WINS databases.

Answer A is incorrect; Access is a database program, not a format. Answer C is incorrect; DNS is used for host name resolution. Answer D is incorrect; IP is part of the TCP/IP protocol suite.

10. Where is the DHCP database stored?

A. \%systemroot%\system32\dhcp

10. CORRECT ANSWER: A

The DHCP database is stored in the \%systemroot%\system32\dhcp subdirectory.

Chapter 4 CONNECTIVITY

11. Spencer, the new administrator, is complaining about the size of the DHCP database. Which command should Spencer use to clear deleted records from the DHCP database?

    C. JETPACK

11. CORRECT ANSWER: C

Spencer should back up the database occasionally using the JETPACK command, which also clears out deleted records.

Answers A, B, and D are not valid database commands.

DHCP is a service available on Windows NT that dynamically assigns IP addresses to clients. Instead of manually assigning an IP address to each new computer you purchase, DHCP can assign an IP address to the computer each time it boots. This simplifies administration tremendously.

Setting up the DHCP Server Service requires Windows NT Server, with DHCP installed as a service. To install the DHCP Server Service, add the service using the Network applet in Control Panel.

After you install the DHCP Server Service, you can configure the service using the Administrative Tools, DHCP Manager option.

The local machine always appears on the list, but you can remotely administer other servers by adding a server using the Servers menu option. After clicking on the local machine (or any other server that might appear in the list), you set up the DHCP scope—the range of available IP addresses.

The DHCP database is created in JET format and stored in the `\%systemroot%\system32\dhcp` subdirectory. You should back up the database occasionally using the JETPACK command, which also clears out deleted records.

12. What is the primary purpose for the DHCP Relay tab?

    A. To allow a Windows NT system to relay DHCP broadcasts for clients across an IP router

12. CORRECT ANSWER: A

The DHCP Relay tab enables a Windows NT system to relay DHCP broadcasts for clients across an IP router.

Answer B is incorrect; the DHCP Relay will not block broadcast messages. Answer C is incorrect; the DHP Relay tab does not relay alerts. Answer D is incorrect; the DHP Relay tab does not relay inventory messages.

ANSWERS & EXPLANATIONS 185

13. Under normal conditions, IP routers are configured to do what with broadcasts?

    B. Ignore them

13. CORRECT ANSWER: B

Normally, you configure IP routers to ignore broadcasts.

Answer A is incorrect; you would usually not want to forward broadcasts, as this can produce a broadcast storm. Answer C is incorrect; routers would not respond to broadcasts. Answer D is incorrect; routers will not produce broadcast messages.

14. Given the situation in question 13, if a client asks for an IP address on a local segment when the DHCP server is located on another network segment, what becomes of the request?

    A. It goes unanswered.

14. CORRECT ANSWER: A

A client broadcasting for an IP address on a local segment when the DHCP server is located on a different network segment does not receive an answer.

Answer B is incorrect; the client will not be answered. Answer C is incorrect; the broadcast would not be routed. Answer D is incorrect; the client would continuously send the broadcast message.

The DHCP Relay tab enables a Windows NT system to relay DHCP messages for clients across an IP router. Normally, you configure IP routers not to forward broadcasts, so a client asking (broadcasting) for an IP address on a local segment when the DHCP server is located on a remote segment does not receive an answer. You can also specify optional timeout parameters in the DHCP Relay tab.

Add the addresses of any DHCP servers on the DHCP Relay tab so that DHCP requests (IP packets) can be directed appropriately.

▼ **NOTE**

The DHCP protocol originated as an expansion of the BOOTP protocol, which enables diskless workstations to get their boot information from a server.

15. When the IPX RIP router is installed, Windows NT can route IPX packets over the installed network adapters. What does it use to exchange routing table information?

    B. RIP

15. CORRECT ANSWER: B

Windows NT uses RIP to exchange its routing table information with other RIP routers.

Answer A is incorrect; IP is part of the TCP/IP protocol suite. Answer C is incorrect; TCP/IP is the protocol suite used for network and Internet communication, not for communication with IPX/SPX systems, such as NetWare. Answer D is incorrect; UDP is part of the TCP/IP protocol suite.

IPX is another protocol common to networks interacting with NetWare's IPX/SPX protocol. You enable the IPX router by installing the RIP for IPX service using the Network applet in Control Panel.

After installing the IPX RIP router, Windows NT can route IPX packets over the installed network adapters. It uses the RIP to exchange its routing table information with other RIP routers. The default sending interval is once every 30 seconds, so you must be careful in deploying hundreds of RIP routers in an enterprise environment; these packets can consume a big chunk of network bandwidth (especially on WANs, where the bandwidth commonly is limited to 64 Kbps).

The configuration screen for the IPX RIP router is straightforward, and only prompts for whether the administrator wants to propagate NetBIOS broadcasts (type 20 packets) over the router.

You have to propagate NetBIOS broadcasts over the router only if both sides of the Windows NT router contain Microsoft Clients (such as Windows 95 or Windows for Workgroups) that need to communicate browsing information over the router.

Although RIP does offer a number of benefits—including a reduction in administrative overhead associated with updating router tables—it does have a drawback in that RIP can increase network traffic in large networks as it routes table updates.

FURTHER REVIEW

INSTALLING AND CONFIGURING MULTIPROTOCOL ROUTING

The following key words are important terms that were covered in this section. You should make sure you understand what each one is and what it does.

Key Words

Gateway Services for NetWare

Migration Tool for NetWare

DHCP Scope

RIP for IP

RIP Packets

Multiprotocol Routing

DHCP Server Service

INSTALLING AND CONFIGURING INTERNET INFORMATION SERVER

PRACTICE QUESTIONS

1. Internet Information Server, or IIS, serves primarily as a server of what?

   A. World Wide Web (WWW)

   B. DNS

   C. DHCP

   D. Archie

2. What version of IIS ships with Windows NT Server 4.0?

   A. 2.0

   B. 3.0

   C. 4.0

   D. 5.0

3. What are the services that Internet Information Server provides on the Windows NT platform? Choose all that apply.

   A. HTTP

   B. HTML

   C. FTP

   D. Gopher

4. Which of the following is a client/server protocol used on the World Wide Web?

   A. HTTP

   B. HTML

   C. FTP

   D. Gopher

5. John is a network administrator at Sprockets, Inc. He has been asked to set up a server to allow people on the Internet to download files. What server service does IIS provide that can be used to fill this need?

   A. HTTP

   B. HTML

   C. FTP

   D. Gopher

6. Which of the following is a means to create a set of hierarchical links to other computers?

   A. HTTP

   B. HTML

   C. FTP

   D. Gopher

7. What is the graphical administration tool provided with IIS called?

   A. Internet Tool

   B. Server Manager

   C. User Manager

   D. Internet Service Manager

8. Using the Internet Service Manager, you can centrally perform what three functions? Choose three.

   A. Manage

   B. Add and delete

   C. Control

   D. Monitor

9. The Internet Service Manager has three views that you can select to enable you to easily monitor the information you need. What are the three main views? Choose three.

   A. Report view

   B. Log view

   C. Servers view

   D. Services view

10. In the Internet Service Manager, which is the default view?

    A. Report view

    B. Log view

    C. Servers view

    D. Services view

ANSWER KEY

1. A
2. A
3. A-C-D
4. A
5. C
6. D
7. D
8. A-C-D
9. A-C-D
10. A

ANSWERS & EXPLANATIONS

INSTALLING AND CONFIGURING INTERNET INFORMATION SERVER

1. Internet Information Server, or IIS, serves primarily as a server of what?

    A. World Wide Web (WWW)

1. CORRECT ANSWER: A

Internet Information Server, or IIS, serves primarily as a World Wide Web (WWW) server.

Answer B is incorrect; IIS does not provide DNS services. Answer C is incorrect; IIS does not provide DHCP services. Answer D is incorrect; IIS does not provide Archie server capability.

Internet Information Server uses Hypertext Transfer Protocol (HTTP), File Transfer Protocol (FTP), and the Gopher services to provide Internet publishing services to your Windows NT Server computer.

2. What version of IIS ships with Windows NT Server 4.0?

    A. 2.0

2. CORRECT ANSWER: A

IIS 2.0 ships with Windows NT Server 4.0.

Installing IIS is very simple. During the initial install of your Windows NT Server software, you were prompted about whether you wanted to install IIS at that time. However, if you responded no, you still have the opportunity to install it at any time from a working installation of Windows NT Server.

To install IIS after Windows NT has been installed, simply go to the Network applet in the Control Panel and install IIS under the Services property page.

When the installation steps are complete, your Windows NT Server is ready to host your Internet publications. If you want to test your IIS installation, from a Web browser enter `http://your_computername` and verify that you can see the default Web page installed with IIS. If you can see this Web page, your installation and all the Internet services are functional. If you do not see the default Web page, begin the process anew and look for errors along the way.

ANSWERS & EXPLANATIONS 191

▼ **NOTE**

Service Pack 3 for Windows NT 4.0 will upgrade IIS to version 3.0. The Windows NT Option Pack contains IIS 4.0 and no longer supports the Gopher service.

3. What are the services that Internet Information Server provides on the Windows NT platform? Choose all that apply.

   A. HTTP
   C. FTP
   D. Gopher

3. CORRECT ANSWERS: A-C-D

Internet Information Server uses Hypertext Transfer Protocol (HTTP), File Transfer Protocol (FTP), and the Gopher services to provide Internet publishing services to your Windows NT Server computer. See answers 4–6 for more detailed information about HTTP, FTP, and Gopher.

Answer B is incorrect; HTML (Hypertext Markup Language) is used to create Web pages.

4. Which of the following is a client/server protocol used on the World Wide Web?

   A. HTTP

4. CORRECT ANSWER: A

HTTP is a client/server protocol used on the World Wide Web.

Answer B is incorrect; HTML (Hypertext Markup Language) is used to create Web pages. Answer C is incorrect; FTP is used to transfer files using TCP/IP. Answer D is incorrect; Gopher is used to build a set of hierarchical links to other computers.

HTTP is a client/server protocol used on the World Wide Web. HTTP Web pages allow the client and server machines to interact and be updated very quickly using Windows Sockets. HTTP is, of course, pervasive on the Internet, and more information on this standard can be found at http://www.ics.uci.edu/pub/ietf/http/.

5. John is a network administrator at Sprockets, Inc. He has been asked to set up a server to allow people on the Internet to download files. What server service does IIS provide that can be used to fill this need??

   C. FTP

5. CORRECT ANSWER: C

FTP is the protocol used to transfer files from one computer to another using the TCP/IP protocol.

Answer A is incorrect; HTTP is a client/server protocol used on the World Wide Web. Answer B is incorrect; HTML (Hypertext Markup Language) is used to create Web pages.

Chapter 4 CONNECTIVITY

Answer D is incorrect; Gopher is used to build a set of hierarchical links to other computers.

FTP is widely used to provide a way to transfer files over the Internet. In any FTP file transfer, the two computers must each play a role in the connection. One system must be designated the FTP server and the other the FTP client. The FTP client does all the work in the transfer; the FTP server is a depository only. This protocol is very handy for quick transfer of files across the Internet.

6. Which of the following is a means to create a set of hierarchical links to other computers?

   D. Gopher

6. CORRECT ANSWER: D

The Gopher service provides a means to create a set of hierarchical links to other computers or to annotate files or directories.

Answer A is incorrect; HTTP is a client/server protocol used on the World Wide Web. Answer B is incorrect; HTML (Hypertext Markup Language) is used to create Web pages. Answer C is incorrect; FTP is used to transfer files using TCP/IP.

The Gopher service provides a means to create a set of hierarchical links to other computers or to annotate files or directories. This service is not as common as FTP or HTTP, but is included with IIS for backward compatibility with the older Gopher Internet technology.

7. What is the graphical administration tool provided with IIS called?

   D. Internet Service Manager

7. CORRECT ANSWER: D

Internet Information Server provides a graphical administration tool called the Internet Service Manager.

Answer A is incorrect; this is not a valid application name. Answer B is incorrect; Server Manager is used to manage computer accounts. Answer C is incorrect; User Manager is used on Windows NT Workstation to manage local user accounts.

8. Using the Internet Service Manager, you can centrally perform what three functions? Choose three.

   A. Manage
   C. Control
   D. Monitor

8. CORRECT ANSWERS: A-C-D

Using Internet Service Manager, you can centrally manage and monitor the Internet services in your Windows NT network.

Answer B is incorrect; you cannot add or delete services with the Internet Service Manager.

Internet Information Server provides a graphical administration tool called the Internet Service Manager. With this tool, you can centrally manage and monitor the Internet services in your Windows NT network. The Internet Service Manager uses the built-in Windows NT security model, so it offers a secure method of remotely administering your Web sites and other Internet services. To start the Internet Service Manager from the Start menu, click Programs, Microsoft Internet Information Server, and then select the Internet Service Manager icon. When the Internet Service Manager has started, you can view the status of your Internet services.

The Internet Service Manager allows you to start and stop Web and FTP services, set directory and access permissions, configure log settings, and other advanced functions.

9. The Internet Service Manager has three views that you can select to enable you to easily monitor the information you need. What are the three main views? Choose three.

   A. Report view
   C. Servers view
   D. Services view

9. CORRECT ANSWERS: A-C-D

The three main views are Report view, Servers view, and Services view.

10. In the Internet Service Manager, which is the default view?

    A. Report view

10. CORRECT ANSWER: A

Report view is the default view.

Answer B is incorrect; Log view is not an Internet Service Manager view. Answers C and D are valid Internet Service Manager views, but are not the default view.

The Internet Service Manager has three views that you can select to more easily monitor the information you need. The three main views are as follows:

- Report view: This is the default view. The report view lists each computer alphabetically with each Internet service shown on a separate line in the screen.

- Servers view: This view groups all the services on each server and lists only computers with an Internet service loaded on them. The servers can then be expanded to display the loaded services.

- Services view: Each Internet service is listed with the corresponding servers grouped by service.

In each of the views, you can double-click on an entry to view the Properties dialog box for the selected item. You can configure the servers and services in these dialog boxes.

FURTHER REVIEW

INSTALLING AND CONFIGURING INTERNET INFORMATION SERVER

The following key words are important terms that were covered in this section. You should make sure you understand what each one is and what it does.

Key Words

FTP
Gopher
HTML
HTTP
Internet Information Server (IIS)
Internet Service Manager

PRACTICE QUESTIONS

INSTALLING AND CONFIGURING INTERNET SERVICES

1. Internet services can be broken into what three components? Choose three.

    A. Reverse lookup

    B. WWW

    C. Gopher

    D. FTP

2. In the Internet Service Manager application, which page enables you to set user logon and authentication requirements?

    A. The Services Property page

    B. The Directories Property page

    C. The Logging Property page

    D. The Advanced Property page

3. In the Internet Service Manager application, which page enables you to select logging of the activity of the services?

    A. The Services Property page

    B. The Directories Property page

    C. The Logging Property page

    D. The Advanced Property page

4. In the Internet Service Manager application, which page shows you the location of your home directories and the location in which to place all your Internet publications?

    A. The Services Property page

    B. The Directories Property page

    C. The Logging Property page

    D. The Advanced Property page

5. In the Internet Service Manager application, on which page do you set the name of the default document to be used and whether to enable directory browsing?

    A. The Services Property page

    B. The Directories Property page

    C. The Logging Property page

    D. The Advanced Property page

6. In the Internet Service Manager application, which page enables you to prevent access to the service based on IP addresses?

    A. The Services Property page

    B. The Directories Property page

    C. The Logging Property page

    D. The Advanced Property page

7. In the Internet Service Manager application, which page can you use to limit the network bandwidth available for outbound traffic from the server?

    A. The Services Property page

    B. The Directories Property page

    C. The Logging Property page

    D. The Advanced Property page

8. What is the primary use of the DNS Service on the Internet and Unix-based systems?

   A. Page delivery

   B. FQDN name resolution to IP addresses

   C. Management statistics

   D. Monitoring and optimization of existing resources

9. DNS is the abbreviation for which of the following?

   A. Domain Name System

   B. Domain Name Service

   C. Dynamic Name System

   D. Dynamic Name Service

10. The DNS Service Search Order section lists the DNS servers. These servers contain a database that Windows NT searches to find the name assigned to your computer or other hosts on the internetwork. Servers are searched in what order?

    A. Alphabetically

    B. By region

    C. Order listed

    D. Frequency

ANSWER KEY

1. B-C-D
2. A
3. C
4. B
5. B
6. D
7. D
8. B
9. A
10. C

ANSWERS & EXPLANATIONS

INSTALLING AND CONFIGURING INTERNET SERVICES

1. Internet services can be broken into what three components? Choose three.

   B. WWW
   C. Gopher
   D. FTP

1. CORRECT ANSWERS: B-C-D

Internet services can be broken into three components: World Wide Web services (HTTP), FTP services, and Gopher services. These services were discussed in the previous sections.

Answer A is incorrect; reverse lookup is not a valid Internet service.

2. In the Internet Service Manager application, which page enables you to set user logon and authentication requirements?

   A. The Services Property page

2. CORRECT ANSWER: A

The Services Property page tab enables you to set user logon and authentication requirements, as well as port and connection information for the service.

3. In the Internet Service Manager application, which page enables you to select logging of the activity of the services?

   C. The Logging Property page

3. CORRECT ANSWER: C

The Logging Property page enables you to select logging of the activity of the services. You can select a log filename and the log format, and you can also specify how often you should start a new log file. A nice feature of this page is the option to log to a SQL/ODBC database. This option is available only if the ODBC drivers are installed on your system.

4. In the Internet Service Manager application, which page shows you the location of your home directories and the location in which to place all your Internet publications?

   B. The Directories Property page

4. CORRECT ANSWER: B

The Directories Property page shows you the location of your home directories and the location in which to place all your Internet publications.

5. In the Internet Service Manager application, on which page do you set the name of the default document to be used and whether to enable directory browsing?

   B. The Directories Property page

5. CORRECT ANSWER: B

The Directories Property page enables you to set the name of the default document to use and whether to enable directory browsing.

6. In the Internet Service Manager application, which page enables you to prevent access to the service based on IP addresses?

   D. The Advanced Property page

6. CORRECT ANSWER: D

The Advanced Property page enables you to prevent access to the service based on IP addresses.

7. In the Internet Service Manager application, which page can you use to limit the network bandwidth available for outbound traffic from the server?

   D. The Advanced Property page

7. CORRECT ANSWER: D

You can use the Advanced Property page to limit the network bandwidth available for outbound traffic from the server.

The Advanced Property page enables you to prevent access to the service based on IP addresses. This enables you to secure an intranet very easily by selecting an IP address range and then limiting the access allowed to the site. You can also use this page to limit the network bandwidth available for outbound traffic from the server.

8. What is the primary use of the DNS service on the Internet and UNIX-based systems?

   B. FQDN name resolution to IP addresses

8. CORRECT ANSWER: B

You use the Domain Name Server Service on the Internet and UNIX-based systems primarily to resolve Fully Qualified Domain Names (FQDN) to IP addresses.

Answer A is incorrect; page delivery is not the primary use of DNS. Answer C is incorrect; management statistics are not provided by DNS. Answer D is incorrect; resource monitoring and optimization is not provided by DNS.

9. DNS is the abbreviation for:

A. Domain Name System

10. The DNS Service Search Order section lists the DNS servers. These servers contain a database that Windows NT searches to find the name assigned to your computer or other hosts on the internetwork. Servers are searched in what order?

C. Order listed

9. CORRECT ANSWER: A

DNS is the abbreviation for Domain Name System.

10. CORRECT ANSWER: C

Servers are searched in the order listed in the file. For example, suppose you have the following servers listed in your DNS properties:

10.10.10.1

10.10.36.1

10.10.86.200

The 10.10.10.1 entry would be accessed first. If the 10.10.10.1 server did not respond with the IP address of the name being requested, Windows NT would try the 10.10.36.1 server next, and would continue trying until it reached the last server in the list. The DNS property page has up and down buttons that allow you to change the order of the servers listed.

Answer A is incorrect; servers are not searched alphabetically.
Answer B is incorrect; servers are not searched by region.
Answer D is incorrect; there is not a server frequency setting.

You use the Domain Name Server Service on the Internet and UNIX-based systems primarily to resolve Fully Qualified Domain Names (FQDN) to IP addresses. You install the service via Control Panel, Networks. This installs the service into the service database, and after rebooting, starts the service automatically. The service is configured using the DNS Manager application in the Administrative Tools menu. After you install it, you must set up the records in the DNS database.

You set up information concerning DNS (Domain Name System) servers on the DNS tab. The first two optional entries are the Host Name and Domain fields. You can use the Domain field to identify your computer on a smaller, local network, such as the one in your company. By default, this is your Windows NT computer name, but the network administrator can assign a different name. The host name is combined with a domain name or suffix to create your Fully Qualified Domain Name.

▼ **NOTE**

Take note that a DHCP server can supply the DNS Service information as well. If a DHCP server supplies the DNS server information, you can leave these fields empty.

The next entries are more important, especially if your machine is connected to the Internet. The DNS Service Search Order section lists the Domain Name System (DNS) servers. These servers contain a database that Windows NT searches to find the name assigned to your computer or other hosts on the internetwork. Servers are searched in the order listed.

▼ **NOTE**

The servers are searched in the order listed until the first server is contacted. If you always contact the first DNS server in the list, the second server will never be used for Internet name resolution. It only checks the second DNS server listed when a connection cannot be made to the first server in the list.

FURTHER REVIEW

INSTALLING AND CONFIGURING INTERNET SERVICES

The following key words are important terms that were covered in this section. You should make sure you understand what each one is and what it does.

Key Words

Domain Name System (DNS)
Fully Qualified Domain Name (FQDN)

PRACTICE QUESTIONS

REMOTE ACCESS SERVICE (RAS)

1. Karen, a network administrator, needs to install and configure RAS. Where is this done?

    A. System applet in Control Panel

    B. Network applet in Control Panel

    C. Server Manager

    D. Administrative Tools

2. To justify additional expenses, you need to gather statistics on RAS. Which of the following tools displays statistics on current conditions of RAS?

    A. Performance Monitor

    B. The Status tab of the Dial-Up Networking Monitor in Control Panel

    C. Event Viewer

    D. User Manager for Domains

3. A sure way to find problems with RAS is to check the PPP.LOG. Which of the following statements are true of PPP logging? Choose two.

    A. It is enabled by default.

    B. Information is written to the PPP.LOG.

    C. You must edit the Registry to turn it on.

    D. It also contains logging information on modems.

4. Susan, a remote user, can connect using clear text, but cannot connect using encryption. What is the most likely problem?

    A. Connection speeds are too slow to support verification.

    B. Encryption is not enabled at both client and server.

    C. The client and server encryption methods are incompatible.

    D. The server requires additional resources.

5. If you, as the RAS administrator, suspect that the client and server encryption methods are incompatible and cause problems, what should you do?

    A. Try to connect using the Allow Any Authentication Including Clear Text option.

    B. Try to avoid using any form of encryption.

    C. Try to discourage users from seeking dial-in functionality.

    D. Try to connect using the Incompatible Encryption Methods option.

6. Which of the following statements is true with regard to Callback with Multilink?

    A. RAS can use multiple phone numbers for callback.

B. RAS can use only one phone number for callback by default, but can use multiple phone numbers with the Multilink function enabled.

C. RAS can utilize callback only over ISDN lines.

D. RAS can use only one phone number for callback.

7. If a non-ISDN client makes a connection using Multilink over multiple phone lines with Callback enabled, the server will call back using using which of the following?

   A. Only a single phone line
   B. Multiple phone lines
   C. An ISDN line
   D. One phone line, unless the default has been changed to Utilize Multiple

8. Jerry complains that AutoDial spontaneously attempts to dial a remote connection during his logon. How should an administrator address this problem?

   A. Move Jerry to another machine
   B. Disable AutoDial
   C. Restrict Jerry's profiles and groups
   D. Reinstall Windows NT

9. RAS can use which protocols for dial-in connections? Choose all that apply.

   A. TCP/IP
   B. NWLink
   C. NetBEUI
   D. AppleTalk

10. Which of the following best describes a node in a SLIP connection?

    A. Has its own phone number
    B. Has a static IP address
    C. Is PPP-enabled
    D. Is DHCP-configured

11. Which of the following protocols cannot be used on DHCP and WINS?

    A. PPP
    B. TCP/IP
    C. SLIP
    D. PPTP

12. Which of the following protocols does PPP support? Choose all that apply.

    A. TCP/IP
    B. NetBEUI
    C. IPX
    D. AppleTalk

13. Which protocol enables you to securely transmit PPP packets over a TCP/IP network?

    A. SLIP
    B. PPP
    C. PPTP
    D. UDP

14. Which protocol is part of an emerging technology called Virtual Private Networks?

    A. SLIP
    B. PPP

C. PPTP

D. UDP

15. **What is the purpose of Virtual Private Networks (VPNs)?**

    A. To provide corporate networks with the same security over the Internet that they would have over a direct connection

    B. To provide corporate networks with the same support over the Internet that they would have over a direct connection

    C. To provide corporate networks with the same speed over the Internet that they would have over a direct connection

    D. To provide corporate networks with the same access over the Internet that they would have over a direct connection

ANSWER KEY

1. B
2. B
3. B-C
4. C
5. A
6. D
7. A
8. B
9. A-B-C
10. B
11. C
12. A-B-C
13. C
14. C
15. A

ANSWERS & EXPLANATIONS

REMOTE ACCESS SERVICE (RAS)

1. Karen, a network administrator, needs to install and configure RAS. Where is this done?

    B. Network applet in Control Panel

1. CORRECT ANSWER: B

RAS is installed and configured from the Network applet in Control Panel.

Answer A is incorrect; you cannot install RAS from the System applet. Answer C is incorrect; Server Manager is used to manage computer accounts. Answer D is incorrect; Administrative Tools is the program group where the Windows NT administration tools are located.

Remote Access Service is installed using the Services tab of the Network Properties dialog box. Prior to the installation, you should gather some basic information that you use during the installation of RAS:

- The type of modem to be used by RAS
- Whether the device will be used for outgoing RAS communication, incoming RAS communication, or both
- The protocols to be used by RAS
- Whether the callback security feature needs to be configured

After you have all the required information, you are ready to begin the installation of RAS. To complete the RAS installation, follow these steps:

1. In Control Panel, double-click on the Network Application icon.

2. In the Network dialog box, choose the Services tab. Click on the Add button, invoking the Select Network Service dialog box.

3. In the Select Network Service dialog box, choose Remote Access Service from the service list and click OK. Windows NT prompts you for the path to the

Windows NT Installation CD-ROM. Enter the path to the Windows NT installation files and click OK.

4. Windows NT prompts you for the name of an RAS-capable device and an associated communication port. A modem installed on your system typically appears as a default value. Click OK to accept the modem, or click on the down arrow to choose another RAS-capable device on your system. You also can install a new modem or an X.25 Pad using the Install Modem and Install X25 Pad buttons.

5. The Remote Access Setup dialog box appears. Click on the Configure button to specify whether to use the port for dial-out connections, dial-in connections, or both. The Port Usage options apply only to the port. In other words, you could configure COM1 for dial-out only and COM2 for receive only. In the Remote Access Setup dialog box, you also can add or remove a port entry from the list. The Clone button enables you to copy a port configuration.

6. Click on the Network button to specify the network protocols for your Remote Access Service to support. The Server Settings options in the lower portion of the Network Configuration dialog box only appear if you configure the port to receive calls. Select one or more dial-out protocols. If you want RAS to take care of receiving calls, select one or more server protocols, and choose an encryption setting for incoming connections. You also can select Multilink, which enables one logical connection to use several physical pathways.

   A Configure button follows each of the Server Settings protocol options. Each Configure button opens a dialog box that enables you to specify configuration options for the protocol, as follows:

   - The RAS Server NetBEUI dialog box enables you to specify whether the incoming caller will have access to the entire network or to only the RAS server.

- By confining a caller's access to the RAS server, you improve security (because the caller can access only one PC), but you reduce functionality because the caller can't access information on other machines.

- The RAS Server TCP/IP Configuration dialog box enables you to define how the RAS server assigns IP addresses to dial-up clients. You can use DHCP to assign client addresses, or you can configure RAS to assign IP addresses from a static address pool. If you choose to use a static address pool, input the beginning and ending addresses in the range. To exclude a range of addresses within the address pool, enter the beginning and ending addresses in the range you're excluding in the From and To boxes. Then click on the Add button. The excluded range appears in the Excluded Ranges list box.

- The RAS Server TCP/IP Configuration dialog box enables you to specify whether a client can access the entire network or only the RAS server. By confining a caller's access to the RAS server, you improve security (because the caller can only access one PC), but you reduce functionality because the caller cannot access information on other machines.

- The RAS Server IPX Configuration dialog box enables you to specify how the RAS server assigns IPX network numbers.

- You can also specify whether a client can access the entire network or only the RAS server. By confining a caller's access to the RAS server, you improve security (because the caller can only access one PC), but you reduce functionality because the caller can't access information on other machines.

7. After you define the RAS settings to your satisfaction, click OK.

8. The Network Services tab appears in the foreground. You should see Remote Access Service in the list of services. Click the Close button.

9. Windows NT asks whether you want to restart your computer. Choose Yes.

When configuring Remote Access Service, you need to configure the communication ports, network protocols, and encryption settings required for remote users when they dial into your Windows NT Server using the RAS as a server.

The RAS server is configured using the Control Panel Network icon located on the Services page tab. Locate the Remote Access Service and click the Properties button. The Remote Access Setup dialog box opens. A number of configuration options are available from this dialog box:

- Add: Add a port to be used by RAS. May be accessed by a modem or X.25 pad.

- Remove: Remove a port being used by RAS.

- Configure: Change the settings for a port being used by RAS.

- Clone: Copy the settings being used from one port to another.

- Network: Configure the network protocols and encryption to be used by RAS.

To make configuration changes to an existing port being used by RAS, click the Configure button. The following list describes each of the options:

- Dial Out Only: Port only used for outgoing RAS connections

- Receive Calls Only: Port only used for receiving calls from RAS clients

- Dial Out and Receive: Port used for both outgoing and incoming RAS connections

You can configure each port that is listed in the RAS Setup dialog box for different roles. Com1 can be configured for dial-out only, whereas Com2 is used to receive calls only. By allowing each port to be configured separately, you have a great deal of flexibility in the Remote Access Service.

After you configure the ports, you must configure the network settings. Start from the Remote Access Setup dialog box. Click the Network Button to view the Network Configuration dialog box.

The Network Configuration settings apply to all the ports that are enabled in RAS. Notice in the top section of the screen that you can select which protocols to use for dial-out calls. By clicking the check box next to the required protocols, you can enable or disable each of the protocols.

For the RAS server settings, you must configure the middle section of the screen. As an RAS server, you can control how far each of the selected protocols can go or whether RAS clients accept the protocols at all. Again, the check box directly next to each of the protocols enables or disables the protocols.

Clicking the Configure button located to the right of the listed protocols can also restrict each of the protocols. You can configure each protocol slightly differently.

2. To justify additional expenses, you need to gather statistics on RAS. Which of the following tools displays statistics on current conditions of RAS?

  B. The Status tab of the Dial-Up Networking Monitor in Control Panel

2. CORRECT ANSWER: B

In Control Panel, the Status tab of the Dial-Up Networking Monitor displays statistics on current conditions, including connection statistics and device errors.

Answer A is incorrect; Performance Monitor does not display current RAS statistics. Answer C is incorrect; the Event Viewer does not display statistics. Answer D is incorrect; User Manager for Domains is used to manage domain user accounts.

The Dial-Up Networking application (in the Accessories program group) enables you to create phonebook entries. A phonebook entry is a preconfigured dial-up connection to a specific site. The Control Panel Telephony application enables the remote user to preconfigure dialing properties for different dialing locations.

RAS can connect to a remote computer using any of the following media:

- Public Switched Telephone Network (PSTN): (Also known as the phone company.) RAS can connect using a modem through an ordinary phone line.

- X.25: A packet-switched network. Computers access the network via a Packet Assembler Disassembler device (PAD). X.25 supports dial-up or direct connections.

- Null modem cable: A cable that connects two computers directly. The computers then communicate using their modems (rather than network adapter cards).

- ISDN: A digital line that provides faster communication and more bandwidth than a normal phone line. (It also costs more, which is why not everybody has it.) A computer must have a special ISDN card to access an ISDN line.

3. A sure way to find problems with RAS is to check the PPP.LOG. Which of the following statements are true of PPP logging? Choose two.

   B. Information is written to the PPP.LOG.
   C. You must edit the Registry to turn it on.

3. CORRECT ANSWERS: B-C

If you have problems with PPP, you can log PPP debugging information to a file called PPP.LOG in the \<winnt_root>\System32\Ras directory. To log PPP debugging information to PPP.LOG, change the Registry value for \HKEY_LOCAL_MACHINE\System\CurrentControlSet\Services\Rasman\PPP\Logging to 1.

Answer A is incorrect; PPP logging is not enabled by default. Answer D is incorrect; the PPP log does not contain modem logging information.

4. Susan, a remote user, can connect using clear text, but cannot connect using encryption. What is the most likely problem?

   C. The client and server encryption methods are incompatible.

4. CORRECT ANSWER: C

RAS authentication problems often stem from incompatible encryption methods.

Answer A is incorrect; connection speeds would not cause an authentication problem. Answer B is incorrect; both client and server would always have an encryption setting, even if it is clear text. Answer D is incorrect; server resources would not cause an authentication problem.

RAS authentication problems often stem from incompatible encryption methods. If you can connect using clear text and you can't connect using encryption, you know the client and server encryption methods are incompatible. You should try to connect using the Allow Any Authentication Including Clear Text option.

5. If you, as the RAS administrator, suspect that the client and server encryption methods are incompatible and cause problems, what should you do?

   A. Try to connect using the Allow Any Authentication Including Clear Text option.

5. CORRECT ANSWER: A

If you can connect using clear text, and you can't connect using encryption, you know the client and server encryption methods are incompatible. You should try to connect using the Allow Any Authentication Including Clear Text option.

Answer B is incorrect; there is always a form of encryption, even if it is clear text. Answer C is incorrect; asking users to avoiding dialing in would not fix the encryption issue and could be fatal to your job. Answer D is incorrect; there isn't an Incompatible Encryption Methods option.

Like everything else in Windows NT, RAS is designed for security. As standard practice, all events are written to the system log, and you can view them with Event Viewer (which is used to view event logs). The following are some of RAS's other security features:

- Auditing: RAS can leave an audit trail, enabling you to see when users logged in and what authentication they provided.

- Callback security: You can enable the RAS server to use callback (hang up all incoming calls and call the caller back), and you can limit callback numbers to pre-arranged sites that you know are safe.

- Encryption: RAS can encrypt logon information, or it can encrypt all data crossing the connection.

- Security hosts: In case Windows NT isn't safe enough, you can add an extra dose of security by using a third-party intermediary security host—a computer that stands between the RAS client and the RAS server and requires an extra round of authentication.

- PPTP filtering: You can tell Windows NT to filter out all packets except ultra-safe PPTP packets (described later in this chapter).

6. Which of the following statements is true in regards to Callback with Multilink?

   D. RAS can use only one phone number for callback.

6. CORRECT ANSWER: D

RAS can use only one phone number for callback.

Answer A is incorrect; RAS cannot use multiple lines for callback. Answer B is incorrect; RAS cannot use one callback number and multiple lines with Multilink. Answer C is incorrect; RAS does not require ISDN to utilize the callback feature.

7. If a non-ISDN client makes a connection using Multilink over multiple phone lines with Callback enabled, the server will call back using which of the following?

   A. Only a single phone line

7. CORRECT ANSWER: A

If a client makes a connection using Multilink over multiple phone lines with Callback enabled, the server calls back using only a single phone line—in other words, Multilink functionality is lost.

Answer B is incorrect; the server will not use multiple phone lines. Answer C is incorrect; the server will not use an ISDN line to call back a non-ISDN client. Answer D is incorrect; you cannot change any settings to affect the number of lines (one) that RAS will use to call back.

Windows NT also includes a new feature called Multilink. Using Multilink, a Windows NT computer can form an RAS connection using more than one physical pathway. One Multilink connection, for example, can use two modems at once (or one modem line and one ISDN line) to form a single logical link. By using multiple pathways for one connection, Multilink can greatly increase bandwidth. Of course, the computer has to have access to more than one pathway (that is, it must have two modems installed). Multilink, however, is not supported for callback features; you can configure only one number for callback.

8. Jerry complains that AutoDial spontaneously attempts to dial a remote connection during his logon. How should an administrator address this problem?

   B. Disable AutoDial

8. CORRECT ANSWER: B

At logon, when Explorer initializes, it might reference a shortcut or some other target that requires an AutoDial connection, causing AutoDial to spontaneously dial a remote connection. The only ways to prevent the AutoDial are to disable AutoDial or to eliminate the shortcut or other targets causing the AutoDial to occur.

Answer A is incorrect; moving the user to another machine would not fix the problem on the original machine. Answer C is incorrect; restricting the user profile and groups would not change AutoDial. Answer D is incorrect; reinstalling the operating system might fix the problem, but is very inefficient, to say the least.

9. RAS can use which protocols for dial-in connections? Choose all that apply.

   A. TCP/IP
   B. NWLink
   C. NetBEUI

9. CORRECT ANSWERS: A-B-C

RAS supports TCP/IP, NWLink, and NetBEUI protocols for both dial-in and dial-out connections.

Answer D is incorrect; RAS does not support the AppleTalk protocol.

10. Which of the following best describes a node in a SLIP connection?

    B. Has a static IP address

10. CORRECT ANSWER: B

Each node in a SLIP connection must have a static IP address.

Answer A is incorrect; a SLIP node does not require an assigned phone number. Answer C is incorrect; a SLIP connection cannot be PPP-enabled, as PPP has replaced the SLIP line protocol. Answer D is incorrect; SLIP cannot use DHCP.

11. Which of the following protocols cannot be used on DHCP and WINS?

    C. SLIP

11. CORRECT ANSWER: C

SLIP cannot be used with DHCP and WINS.

Answer A is incorrect; PPP can use DHCP and WINS. Answer B is incorrect; TCP/IP is not a line protocol. Answer D is incorrect; PPTP is a tunneling protocol over PPP.

ANSWERS & EXPLANATIONS   215

Serial Line Interface Protocol (SLIP) is a standard protocol for serial line connections over TCP/IP networks. SLIP is relatively old for the computer age—it was developed in 1984—and, although it is not yet completely obsolete, it does lack some of the features that are available in PPP. Each node in a SLIP connection must have a static IP address; that is, you can't use Windows NT features such as DHCP and WINS. Unlike PPP, SLIP does not support NetBEUI or IPX. You must use TCP/IP with SLIP. Also, SLIP cannot encrypt logon information.

12. Which of the following protocols does PPP support? Choose all that apply.

    A. TCP/IP
    B. NetBEUI
    C. IPX

12. CORRECT ANSWERS: A-B-C

PPP supports TCP/IP, NetBEUI, and IPX. Point-to-Point Protocol (PPP) was originally conceived as a deluxe version of SLIP. Like SLIP, PPP is an industry standard for point-to-point communications, but PPP offers several advantages over SLIP. Most notably, PPP isn't limited to TCP/IP. PPP also supports IPX and NetBEUI. Because PPP supports so many protocols, it enables you to have much more flexibility in configuring network communications, and also provides secure authentication.

13. Which protocol enables you to securely transmit PPP packets over a TCP/IP network?

    C. PPTP

13. CORRECT ANSWER: C

PPTP is a protocol that enables you to securely transmit PPP packets over a TCP/IP network.

Answer A is incorrect; SLIP will not allow you to securely transfer PPP packets. Answer B is incorrect; PPP by itself does not transmit PPP packets over a network, but simply provides the network connection. Answer D is incorrect; UDP is part of the TCP/IP protocol suite.

14. Which protocol is part of an emerging technology called Virtual Private Networks?

    C. PPTP

14. CORRECT ANSWER: C

PPTP is part of an emerging technology called Virtual Private Networks (VPNs).

Answer A is incorrect; SLIP is not used with VPN. Answer B is incorrect; PPP by itself does not support VPN. Answer D is incorrect; UDP is part of the TCP/IP protocol suite.

15. What is the purpose of Virtual Private Networks (VPNs)?

   A. To provide corporate networks with the same security over the Internet that they would have over a direct connection

15. CORRECT ANSWER: A

The point of VPNs is to provide corporate networks with the same (or close to the same) security over the Internet that they would have over a direct connection.

Answer B is incorrect; a VPN does not provide any specific support. Answer C is incorrect; a VPN does not increase speeds. Answer D is incorrect; a VPN does not provide any additional access.

PPTP is a protocol that enables you to securely transmit PPP packets over a TCP/IP network. Because the Internet is a TCP/IP network, PPTP enables highly private network links over the otherwise highly public Internet. PPTP connections are encrypted, making them nearly impenetrable to virtual voyeurs.

In fact, PPTP is part of an emerging technology called Virtual Private Networks (VPNs). The point of VPN is to provide corporate networks with the same (or close to the same) security over the Internet that they would have over a direct connection.

Another exciting advantage of PPTP (and another reason that it fits nicely into the scheme of the VPN) is that PPTP doesn't discriminate among protocols. Because PPP supports NetBEUI and IPX, and because PPTP operates on PPP packets, PPTP actually lets you transmit non-TCP/IP protocols over the Internet.

Because PPTP provides intranet privacy over the open Internet, it can significantly reduce costs in some situations. Networks that once would have depended on extravagant direct connections now can hook up via a local Internet service provider.

FURTHER REVIEW

REMOTE ACCESS SERVICE (RAS)

The following key words are important terms that were covered in this section. You should make sure you understand what each one is and what it does.

Key Words

Dial-Up Networking
Event Viewer
ISDN
Phonebook Entry
RAS
Virtual Private Networks

SUMMARY

You should now have a good working knowledge of the utilities included with Windows NT that provide connectivity with heterogeneous systems. You also should have experience in implementing these tools in a working environment. Make sure before you take the exam that you fully understand the concepts behind the following tasks:

- Installing Internet Information Server and understanding the services it provides
- Installing and configuring Remote Access Service, including PPTP support
- Installing and configuring DNS
- Installing and configuring DHCP
- Integrating and converting Novell NetWare networks

CHAPTER 5

Monitoring and Optimization

Although not a large part of the NT Enterprise exam, monitoring and optimization is an important piece in getting your systems to operate at the highest level of performance possible. To do this, you use monitoring tools to gather information about your systems and network.

Windows NT 4 provides a number of network services that enable users to carry out specific requirements on their networks. Table 5.1 lists some of the more commonly installed network components. Some are installed by default; others are not.

TABLE 5.1   NETWORK COMPONENTS

Component	Description
Computer browser	Enables users to find or browse resources on the network without having to remember specific paths or the correct syntax
DHCP	The automatic distribution and administration of TCP/IP addresses and related parameters to DHCP clients
Directory Replicator	The automatic duplication of directories among Windows NT computers
Domain Name System (DNS)	The resolution of TCP/IP host names to IP addresses
Internet Explorer	An Internet browser that provides access to the World Wide Web (WWW) to view and download files
Netlogon	Service that performs user account logon validation and synchronization of user accounts in a domain
Server	Enables network clients to access shared resources
WINS	A centralized database that resolves NetBIOS names to TCP/IP addresses
Workstation	Provides network access to shared resources

This chapter discusses the tools to use to gather information and how to use that information to optimize your systems and network components.

OBJECTIVES

This chapter covers the following Microsoft exam objectives:

Establish a baseline for measuring system performance. Tasks include creating a database of measurement data.

▶ Whenever you analyze a system's performance, you must first create a baseline from which to measure. After you have an established baseline, you can compare system performance to that baseline whenever changes are made to the system, whether they are good or bad.

▶ The method in which data is collected can provide a wide variety of information. Taking a measurement, for example, adding all the components, and then measuring again displays the effect of having all the components working together. Another way of measuring is to take a separate measurement as each component is added. This provides data about how each individual component affects the performance of the

continues

OBJECTIVES (continued)

system. Yet another way is to add components one at a time, but in different combinations, thus providing a better understanding of how each component affects the performance of the others.

▶ Some of the tools Microsoft provides for monitoring system performance are as follows:

- Server Manager: Monitors the number of users connected, open files, idle time, shared resources, and so on.
- Windows NT Diagnostics: Displays the current configuration for the processor, memory, disk, and network.
- Response Probe: A utility used to apply a controlled stress on a system and monitor the response.
- Performance Monitor: An administrative tool for monitoring NT workstations and servers. Performance Monitor helps you better plan for future use and, at the same time, optimize its current performance.
- Task Manager: Enables the viewing, stopping, and starting of applications and processes. It also contains the Performance Monitor capabilities that enable the viewing of memory and CPU utilization.
- Network Monitor: Captures and views the network traffic going in and out of the system on which Network Monitor is running.
- All these tools come with Windows NT 4 (Network Monitor must be installed) except Response Probe, which comes with the Resource Kit.

Monitor performance of various functions by using Performance Monitor. Functions include Processor, Memory, Disk, and Network.

▶ To conduct analysis and optimization, do the following:

- Create a baseline of current use.
- Monitor the use over a period of time.
- Analyze data to determine non-optimal system use.
- Determine how the system should be used.
- Determine whether additional resources should be added to the system or whether the system needs to be upgraded.
- Performance Monitor helps you plan better for future use and, at the same time, optimize your system's current performance.

Monitor network traffic by using Network Monitor. Tasks include collecting, presenting, and filtering data.

▶ Network Monitor is a tool that enables monitoring of the network traffic going in and out of the system running the monitor. A second format that comes with Systems Management Server permits traffic to be monitored anywhere on the network.

Identify performance bottlenecks.

▶ Bottlenecks are the problem areas that need to be addressed to improve the performance of the system. Trends are useful for capacity planning and preparing for future needs.

▶ Any spreadsheet or database application can be used to analyze the data collected.

OBJECTIVES

Optimize performance for various results. Results include controlling network traffic and controlling server load.

- The most common and now the least expensive method of optimizing performance is to add more physical memory (RAM). Adding more memory to a server, whatever function that server serves, helps performance. Also, adding additional NICs and controlling bandwidth available to services and applications can greatly affect the performance of a Windows NT system.

PRACTICE QUESTIONS

ESTABLISHING A BASELINE FOR MEASURING SYSTEM PERFORMANCE

1. Which is the primary tool used for creating a baseline in Windows NT Server? Choose the best answer.

   A. Server Manager

   B. User Manager

   C. Network Monitor

   D. Performance Monitor

2. Which monitoring tool that Microsoft provides does not come on the Microsoft Windows NT Server CD?

   A. Task Manager

   B. Response Probe

   C. Network Monitor

   D. Performance Monitor

3. What is a baseline?

   A. The performance specifications for all hardware components.

   B. The performance specifications for all software components.

   C. A collection of performance information to which all future measurements can be compared.

   D. A baseline in Microsoft Windows NT is like "Safe Mode" in Windows 95. It is the minimum standard configuration for the system.

4. How many baselines should be created? Choose the best answer.

   A. One for each server, even if they have "identical" configurations

   B. One for each Primary Domain Controller

   C. One for each domain controller (Primary and Backup)

   D. One for each computer on the network

5. Which components should be included in the creation of the baseline? Choose all that apply.

   A. Memory

   B. Processor

   C. Disk

   D. Network

6. Which component is the most important when creating a baseline? Choose all that apply.

   A. Memory

   B. Processor

   C. Disk

   D. Network

7. **When should a baseline be created?**

    A. When the server is first configured

    B. After two months, so that the system has stabilized

    C. At the first sign of problems on the network

    D. At the first sign of problems on the server

8. **At what time of day should data for the baseline be recorded? Choose the best answer.**

    A. 7:00 a.m. to 10:00 a.m.

    B. 2:30 p.m. to 6:30 p.m.

    C. All day

    D. 10:00 a.m. to 2:00 p.m.

9. **How often should the baseline be upgraded? Choose the best answer.**

    A. Every two weeks.

    B. Whenever changes have been made to the server or the network.

    C. Once a year.

    D. The baseline does not need to be upgraded.

10. **When Sean creates a baseline for his application server by using Performance Monitor, which view should he use?**

    A. Chart

    B. Report

    C. Log

    D. Alert

11. This is a scenario question. First, you must review the scenario, then review the required and optional results. Following that is a solution. You must pick the best evaluation of that solution. Note that question 12 also deals with the same scenario.

    Scenario:
    Alice has taken over as administrator of a small network. The network consists of 150 users with two domains that fully trust each other. Three file servers are in DomainA, of which the Primary Domain Controller is one. In DomainB, the Primary Domain Controller is a print server, and an application server also exists. No baseline has been created for the domain controllers of either domain.

    Required Result:
    A baseline must be created for each of the domain controllers.

    Optional Results:
    A baseline must be created for the application server.

    A baseline must be created for the print server.

    Proposed Solution:
    Alice uses Performance Monitor on each domain controller and file server each day, throughout the day, for two weeks. She uses the Log view so that a log file can be created and referenced at a later date.

    Evaluation of Proposed Solution:
    (Choose the most correct answer.)

    A. The required result is met, and both optional results are also met.

    B. The required result and one optional result are met.

C. The required result is met, and neither optional result is met.

D. None of the results is met.

12. **This applies to the same scenario as number 11.**

    Scenario:
    Alice has taken over as administrator of a small network. The network consists of 150 users with two domains that fully trust each other. Three file servers are in DomainA, of which the Primary Domain Controller is one. In DomainB, the Primary Domain Controller is a print server, and an application server also exists. No baseline has been created for the domain controllers of either domain.

    Required Result:
    A baseline must be created for each of the domain controllers.

    Optional Results:
    A baseline must be created for the application server.

    A baseline must be created for the print server.

    Proposed Solution:
    Alice uses Performance Monitor on each file server, print server, and application server each day, throughout the day, for two weeks. She uses the Log view so that a log file can be created and referenced at a later date.

    Evaluation of Proposed Solution:
    (Choose the most correct answer.)

    A. The required result is met, and both optional results are also met.

    B. The required result and one optional result are met.

    C. The required result is met, and neither optional result is met.

    D. None of the results is met.

ANSWER KEY

1. D
2. B
3. C
4. A
5. A-B-C-D
6. A-B-C-D
7. A
8. C
9. B
10. C
11. B
12. A

ANSWERS & EXPLANATIONS

ESTABLISHING A BASELINE FOR MEASURING SYSTEM PERFORMANCE

1. Which is the primary tool used for creating a baseline in Windows NT Server? Choose the best answer.

    D. Performance Monitor

1. CORRECT ANSWER: D

Performance Monitor can capture data for all aspects of the computer performance.

Answer A is incorrect; Server Manager is used to manage computer accounts. Answer B is incorrect; User Manager is used to manage local user accounts. Answer C is incorrect; Network Monitor is used to analyze network traffic.

Performance Monitor is used to gather information from many objects to create a baseline to be used to compare computer performance with information gathered later. This baseline is used to monitor server load and can be used to decide when you need to upgrade or replace the server. A baseline is also useful for deciding initial tuning settings on the server.

You should always include memory, processor, disk, and network objects in the baseline. After the initial set of data is captured, use the same settings and capture data on a regular basis. Place this information in a database and analyze the performance of the system.

2. Which monitoring tool that Microsoft provides does not come on the Microsoft Windows NT Server CD?

    B. Response Probe

2. CORRECT ANSWER: B

Response Probe is available on the Resource Kit for Windows NT 4.

Answer A is incorrect; Task Manager is not a monitoring tool. Answers C and D are incorrect; these tools are included with Windows NT.

Response Probe is a utility available on the Resource Kit that enables Performance Monitor to be started as a service to automate the collection of data.

3. What is a baseline?

C. A collection of performance information to which all future measurements can be compared.

3. CORRECT ANSWER: C

A baseline is a collection of performance information to which all future measurements can be compared.

Answer A is incorrect; a baseline is not just hardware components. Answer B is incorrect; a baseline is not just software components. Answer D is incorrect; there isn't a "Safe Mode" in Windows NT.

A baseline includes both hardware components, such as processor and memory, and software components, such as network counters and services. This provides an overall view of the server's performance that can be used to compare with future measurements of the server.

4. How many baselines should be created? Choose the best answer.

A. One for each server, even if they have "identical" configurations

4. CORRECT ANSWER: A

One baseline should be created for each server even if hardware and software seem to be "identical," because nothing is ever really "identical."

Answer B and C are incorrect; you should create baselines for all servers, not just PDCs. Answer D is incorrect; it is not necessary to create baselines for each computer.

You should create a baseline for every server on your network. Separate baselines are needed because no two servers will be alike. Each server will have different roles and different services running that affect performance.

5. Which components should be included in the creation of the baseline? Choose all that apply.

A. Memory
B. Processor
C. Disk
D. Network

5. CORRECT ANSWERS: A-B-C-D

Memory, processor, disk, and network should all be included when creating a baseline.

All answers are correct.

All aspects of a server should be included when creating a baseline. This allows you to track changes in performance in all areas.

6. Which component is the most important when creating a baseline? Choose all that apply.

   A. Memory
   B. Processor
   C. Disk
   D. Network

6. CORRECT ANSWERS: A-B-C-D

All components are important because any one of them could cause a computer to perform poorly.

All answers are correct.

Any component could have an adverse effect on performance. If any of the four main components is at higher than optimum levels, it will affect the performance of the server as a whole.

7. When should a baseline be created?

   A. When the server is first configured.

7. CORRECT ANSWER: A

A baseline should be created when a server is first configured so configuration changes can be evaluated for performance.

Answer B is incorrect; a baseline should be created immediately, not after a period of time. Answers C and D are incorrect; you should not wait for problems to occur.

The baseline should be created when the server is first installed and configured. This provides an initial benchmark from which future changes in performance can be gauged.

8. At what time of day should data for the baseline be recorded? Choose the best answer.

   C. All day

8. CORRECT ANSWER: C

The performance should be monitored at all times during the day to compare "load" to "no load" times.

Answers A, B, and D are incorrect; the baseline should be created over an entire day to measure both load and no-load times on the server.

Measurements can also be taken for a full week at different times of the day so information can be recorded at both peak and slack times. Ideally, you should have enough data to know whether the different counters experience significant changes during different times of the day.

9. How often should the baseline be upgraded? Choose the best answer.

   B. Whenever changes have been made to the server or the network.

9. CORRECT ANSWER: B

The baseline should be upgraded each time the configuration has been changed.

Chapter 5 MONITORING AND OPTIMIZATION

Answer A is incorrect; a baseline is not required every two weeks. Answer C is incorrect; a baseline is not required once a year. Answer D is incorrect; the baseline needs to be upgraded every time a change is made to the server's configuration.

When a server's configuration has been changed, such as additional hardware resources or changes in services being used, a new baseline should be created that takes into account these changes. This will also help gauge the effect the changes have had on the server.

10. When Sean creates a baseline for his application server by using Performance Monitor, which view should he use?

C. Log

10. CORRECT ANSWER: C

The Log view creates a file that can be referenced at a later date.

You must use the Log view to create a baseline measurement; this is the only way to create a log of activity. While measuring, you log, relog, and append logs to get a complete set of information. Objects that should be included are as follows:

- Cache
- Logical disk
- Memory
- Network adapter
- Network segment activity on at least one server in the subnet
- Physical disk (if using a RAID system)
- Processor
- Server
- System

Please refer to complete scenario for questions 11 and 12.

11. **Proposed Solution:**
    Alice uses Performance Monitor on each domain controller and file server each day, throughout the day, for two weeks. She uses the Log view so that a log file can be created and referenced at a later date.

    B. The required result and one optional result are met.

11. CORRECT ANSWER: B

Baselines were created for both domain controllers and the print server. The application server did not get a baseline created.

All servers in a network should have a separate baseline created. This is needed because each server will have either a different role or different needs to fulfill, such as the number of users connecting to the server.

12. **Proposed Solution:**
    Alice uses Performance Monitor on each file server, print server, and application server each day, throughout the day, for two weeks. She uses the Log view so that a log file can be created and referenced at a later date.

    A. The required result is met, and both optional results are also met.

12. CORRECT ANSWER: A

Baselines were created for both domain controllers as well as for both the print server and the application server.

This solution provides a separate baseline for all servers in the network.

FURTHER REVIEW

ESTABLISHING A BASELINE FOR MEASURING SYSTEM PERFORMANCE

The following key words are important terms covered in this section. You should make sure you understand what each one is and what it does.

Key Words

Baseline
Log
Performance Monitor

PRACTICE QUESTIONS

PERFORMANCE MONITORING

1. How is Performance Monitor installed on a Primary Domain Controller?

    A. Performance Monitor is installed from the Windows NT 4.0 Resource Kit.

    B. Performance Monitor is automatically installed as part of Windows NT 4.

    C. Performance Monitor is purchased as an add-on package.

    D. Performance Monitor is a separate service that must be installed after Windows NT has been installed.

2. Performance Monitor can be used to monitor the activity of the disk. To activate the disk counters, `diskperf -y` must first be run. What must be run if you want to monitor a RAID disk system?

    A. `diskperf -yr`

    B. `diskperf -y stripe`

    C. `diskperf -ye`

    D. `diskperf -raid`

3. Which is the default window in Performance Monitor?

    A. Report

    B. Chart

    C. Objects, Counters, Instances

    D. Sessions, Real Time, Transfer Statistics

4. What does a Counter represent in Performance Monitor?

    A. A process that executes a set of program instructions

    B. A mechanism for identifying system resources

    C. The type of data available from an object

    D. The type of data available from a thread

5. What does an object represent in Performance Monitor?

    A. A process that executes a set of program instructions

    B. A mechanism for identifying system resources

    C. The type of data available from a type of object

    D. The type of data available from a thread

6. What does an instance represent in Performance Monitor?

    A. The type of data available from a thread

    B. The type of data available from an object

    C. One of multiple installed objects

    D. One of multiple installed counters

7. **What is used to enable the TCP/IP network counters in Performance Monitor?**

    A. `perfnet -y`

    B. `perfnet /yes`

    C. `netperf -y`

    D. SNMP service

8. **How often do you have to enable the disk counters for Performance Monitor?**

    A. Each time Performance Monitor is restarted.

    B. Each time the computer is restarted.

    C. The disk counters never have to be re-enabled.

    D. Each time an administrator logs on to the server.

9. **Susan wants to get the most accurate reading on the network counters on her file and print server. What should she do? Choose the best answer.**

    A. Run Performance Monitor on the file and print server while running multiple applications on the server.

    B. Run Performance Monitor on a different server while running multiple applications on the server.

    C. Run Performance Monitor on the file and print server while transferring files to another computer.

    D. Run Performance Monitor on a different server while transferring files to another computer.

10. **Mike wants to get the most accurate reading on the network counters on his application server. What should he do? Choose the best answer.**

    A. Run Performance Monitor on the application server while running multiple applications on the server.

    B. Run Performance Monitor on a different server while running multiple applications on the server.

    C. Run Performance Monitor on the application server while transferring files to another computer.

    D. Run Performance Monitor on a different server while transferring files to another computer.

ANSWER KEY

1. B
2. C
3. B
4. C

5. B
6. C
7. D
8. C

9. C
10. A

ANSWERS & EXPLANATIONS
PERFORMANCE MONITORING

1. How is Performance Monitor installed on a Primary Domain Controller?

   B. Performance Monitor is automatically installed as part of Windows NT 4.

1. CORRECT ANSWER: B

Performance Monitor is a built-in utility of Windows NT 4.

Answer A is incorrect; Performance Monitor is included with NT, so it is not necessary to install it from the Resource Kit. Answer C is incorrect; you do not need to purchase Performance Monitor. Answer D is incorrect; Performance Monitor is a built-in application, not a separate service.

The Performance Monitor utility is included in all Windows NT systems. This utility can be used to monitor many areas of the system, including processor, RAM, network traffic, and disk usage.

2. Performance Monitor can be used to monitor the activity of the disk. To activate the disk counters, `diskperf -y` must first be run. What must be run if you want to monitor a RAID disk system?

   C. `diskperf -ye`

2. CORRECT ANSWER: C

The `-y` enables the disk counters and the `e` indicates that every drive should be monitored.

Answers A, B, and D are incorrect; these are not valid switches for the `diskperf` command.

The `diskperf` command enables the disk counters in Performance Monitor. These counters can affect system performance and should be active only when you're creating a baseline or monitoring performance. The switches include `-y`, which activates the counters on the first drive, `-ye`, which activates the counters on all drives, and `-n`, which shuts off the counters.

3. Which is the default window in Performance Monitor?

   B. Chart

3. CORRECT ANSWER: B

The chart view is the default view in Performance Monitor.

You can view data in Performance Monitor in various ways. The Chart, Report, Log, and Alert views are described in Table 5.2.

Chapter 5 MONITORING AND OPTIMIZATION

TABLE 5.2 VARIOUS WAYS TO VIEW DATA IN PERFORMANCE MONITOR

View	Description
Chart	A chart is a graphic display of the value of a counter over a period of time.
Report	A report shows the value of the counter. A report of all the counters can be created.
Log	The selected data is stored in a file on a disk for future analysis.
Alert	An alert can be set on an individual counter. This causes an event to display if the counter attains the specified value.

The four views are always available, but only one can be viewed at a time. The default view is the Chart view. To highlight an individual chart line, select the desired line in the legend and press Ctrl+H. This turns the corresponding line white and makes it much wider than the other lines. After the highlight is enabled, you can move it from one chart line to another by using either the up/down arrow keys or the mouse. To disable the highlight, press Ctrl+H again.

If you want to view the contents of the log while it is still collecting data, open a second instance of Performance Monitor. Switch to the desired view (Chart or Report) and change the Data values displayed from option to the name of the running log file.

4. What does a Counter represent in Performance Monitor?

   C. The type of data available from an object

4. CORRECT ANSWER: C

A counter represents the type of data that is available from an object.

Answer A is incorrect; a counter is not a process. Answer B is incorrect; a counter is not a mechanism. Answer D is incorrect; a counter is not a type of data available from a thread.

A counter defines the type of data available from a type of object. Performance Monitor can display, collect, and average data from counters by using the Windows NT Registry and the Performance Library DLLs. Counters can be divided into three types:

- Instantaneous: Instantaneous counters always display the most recent measurement. In the case of the Process:Thread Count, the number of threads found in the last measurement is displayed.

- Averaging: Averaging counters measure a value over a period of time and display the average of the last two measurements.

- Difference: Difference counters subtract the last measurement from the preceding measurement and display the difference if it is a positive value. A negative value is shown as zero.

Other performance-monitoring applications can read the data gathered from Performance Monitor and can display and use the negative values.

Data is broken down into either absolute or relative information, with the difference being that an absolute value is exactly the duration taken or the amount reached, whereas a relative value is one measurement compared to another. See Table 5.3 for an example of absolute values.

TABLE 5.3 ABSOLUTE TRANSFER RATES

Counter	5-Second Interval	5-Minute Interval
Disk time	4.652 seconds	263.89 seconds
Bytes transferred	82,524 bytes	4,978,335 bytes

Determining which measurement is showing a faster rate of transfer is difficult. If you look at the same information using relative counters, as in Table 5.4, it is easier to compare the results.

TABLE 5.4 RELATIVE TRANSFER RATES

Counter	5-Second Interval	5-Minute Interval
Disk time	93.04%	87.96%
Bytes transferred	16,504.8 bytes/sec	16,594.45 bytes/sec

Chapter 5 MONITORING AND OPTIMIZATION

A brief description displays at the bottom of the dialog box if the Explain button is selected. This is useful if you are unsure to what a counter refers.

5. What does an object represent in Performance Monitor?

  B. A mechanism for identifying system resources

5. CORRECT ANSWER: B

An object represents a mechanism for identifying system resources.

Answer A is incorrect; an object is not a process. Answer C is incorrect; an object is not data from another object. Answer D is incorrect; an object is not data from a thread.

When you monitor a computer system, what is really being monitored is the behavior of its objects. An object is a standard mechanism for identifying and using a system resource. Objects are created to represent individual threads, processes, physical devices, and sections of shared memory. Performance Monitor groups counters by their object type, and each object has a unique set of counters assigned to it. Certain objects and their respective counters are available on all systems; others are available only when the computer is running the associated software or service.

Each object type can have more than one component installed on the computer. These components are referred to as instances and are displayed in the Instance box of any Add To dialog box. The Instance box can also contain the Total Instance, which represents the total of all instances. Some objects are dependent on or part of another object; this type of object can also be referred to as a child object. An object that has one or more dependent objects can be referred to as a parent object.

A thread is an object with a process that executes program instructions. By having multiple threads, a process can carry out different parts of its program on different processes concurrently. Threads that are dependent on a process or parent object are indicated with an arrow from parent object to child object.

Microsoft designed Performance Monitor to cause as little impact on Windows NT as possible; however, it does have an effect on the system. Therefore, when you are monitoring anything other than network performance, monitoring the server system from a different computer is recommended. When you are monitoring for network performance, it is best to do so in Log mode.

The core objects that can be monitored on any Windows NT 4 system are described in Table 5.5.

TABLE 5.5 CORE OBJECTS CAPABLE OF BEING MONITORED

Core Object Name	Description of Object
Cache	An area of physical memory that holds recently used data
LogicalDisk	Partitions and other logical views of disk space
Memory	Physical random access memory used to store code and data
Objects	Certain system software objects
Paging file	File used to back up virtual memory locations to increase memory
PhysicalDisk	A single spindle-disk unit or RAID device
Process	Software object that represents a running program
Processor	Hardware unit (CPU) that executes program instructions
Redirector	File system that diverts file requests to the network servers; also referred to as the Workstation service
System	Contains counters that apply to all system hardware and software
Thread	The part of a process that uses the processor for executing program instructions

6. What does an instance represent in Performance Monitor?

  C. One of multiple installed objects

6. CORRECT ANSWER: C

An instance represents one of multiple installed objects. For example, if two disk drives exist, two instances exist for the object Physical Disk.

Answer A is incorrect; an instance is not data from a thread. Answer B is incorrect; an instance is not data from an object. Answer D is incorrect; an instance is not one of multiple counters.

In Performance Monitor, multiple identical objects can be monitored, such as multiple disk counters, one for each physical disk. An instance is one of multiple installed objects and is used to differentiate between them. For example, if you were monitoring Disk Reads/sec for three hard drives, each drive's counter would be an instance.

7. What is used to enable the TCP/IP network counters in Performance Monitor?

   D. SNMP service

7. CORRECT ANSWER: D

The SNMP service enables the TCP/IP network counters in Performance Monitor.

Answers A and B are incorrect; `perfnet` is not a valid command. Answer C is incorrect; `netperf` is not a valid command.

The TCP/IP counters in Performance Monitor are available when the SNMP service is installed from the Network control panel.

8. How often do you have to enable the disk counters for Performance Monitor?

   C. The disk counters never have to be re-enabled.

8. CORRECT ANSWER: C

The disk counters remain enabled until an administrator disables them by running `diskperf -n`.

Answer A is incorrect; you do not have to enable counters each time Performance Monitor is started. Answer B is incorrect; you do not have to enable the counters every time the computer is restarted. Answer D is incorrect; you do not have to enable the counters when an administrator logs on.

You enable the disk performance counters by using the `diskperf` command with the `-y` switch (for one disk) or `-ye` switch (for multiple disks). The disk counters do have an adverse effect on disk performance and should not be enabled unless needed for testing or benchmarking. To turn the counters off, you would run the `diskperf` command with the `-n` switch.

ANSWERS & EXPLANATIONS   239

9. Susan wants to get the most accurate reading on the network counters on her file and print server. What should she do? Choose the best answer.

   C. Run Performance Monitor on the file and print server while transferring files to another computer.

9. CORRECT ANSWER: C

Susan should run Performance Monitor on the file and print server while transferring files so that additional network traffic is not generated by monitoring.

Answer A is incorrect; running multiple applications would be used to test an applications server. Answers B and D are incorrect; you need to run Performance Monitor on the server that is being tested.

File and print servers generally are accessed for data storage and retrieval and sometimes for loading applications across the network; therefore, the largest load applied is from users who access the server at the same time and demand resource requirements. Events that need to be monitored for this type of server are listed in Table 5.6.

TABLE 5.6   FILE AND PRINT SERVER MONITORING

Workload Unit	Performance Monitor Counter
Concurrent user sessions	Server: Server Sessions
The number of open files	Server: Files Open
Average transaction size	PhysicalDisk: Avg. Disk Bytes/Transfer
Amount of disk activity	PhysicalDisk: %Disk Time
Type of disk activity	PhysicalDisk: %Disk Read Time PhysicalDisk: %Write Time
Network use	Network Segment: %Network Utilization

In addition to the preceding, you might find that additional resources (such as memory) are being consumed and should also be monitored. All four of the main system components are important in any server; however, some resources are more important than others, depending on the type of server being analyzed. For a file and print server, the order of importance is explained in Table 5.7.

Chapter 5 MONITORING AND OPTIMIZATION

TABLE 5.7 ORDER OF IMPORTANCE IN A FILE AND PRINT SERVER

Priority	Resource	Implications
1	Memory	Memory is used for caching opened files; if RAM is insufficient for caching, performance takes a big hit.
2	Processor	The processor is used for each network connection. This means all network traffic must pass through the processor.
3	Disk	The disk drive is the primary resource that users are going to access. The speed of the disk drives affects the general perception of how the server operates.
4	Network	A number of factors affect the network system (adapter type, number of adapters, protocols used, and so on). It does not matter, however, how fast the disk drive is, how much RAM exists, or how many processors exist if the network adapter is slow.

When forecasting resource requirements, keep the following in mind:

- Monitor the number of user sessions and the effect each session has on the four main system resources.
- If the server is used to retrieve and update data files, monitor the disk and network resources.
- If the server is used for data files and to load applications, monitor memory, disk, and network resources.
- Make sure Maximize Throughput for File Sharing is selected in the Server dialog box. This is found in the Network Applet of the Control Panel on the Services tab.

10. Mike wants to get the most accurate reading on the network counters on his application server. What should he do? Choose the best answer.

   A. Run Performance Monitor on the application server while running multiple applications on the server.

10. CORRECT ANSWER: A

Mike should run Performance Monitor on the application server while running multiple applications to generate workload units.

Answer B is incorrect; you must run Performance Monitor on the server being tested. Answer C is incorrect; file transfers are not used to test application servers. Answer D is incorrect; you must run Performance Monitor on the server being tested.

Workload units are key when analyzing an application server. Workload units that need to be monitored are shown in Table 5.8.

TABLE 5.8 MONITORING WORKLOAD

Workload Unit	Performance Monitor Counter
Concurrent user sessions	Server: Server Sessions
Processor usage	Processor: %Processor Time
Average disk transaction size	PhysicalDisk: Avg. Disk Bytes/Transfer
Amount of disk activity	PhysicalDisk: %Disk Time
Network use	Network Segment: %Network Utilization
Average network transaction	NetBEUI: Frame Bytes/sec (similar size counter for each protocol)
Available memory	Memory: Available Bytes
Amount of paging	Memory: Pages/sec
Usage of cache	Cache: Copy Read Hits %
Processes waiting for processor availability	System: ProcessorQueueLength

In addition to the counters that Performance Monitor provides, certain applications (such as Microsoft Exchange Server) provide additional counters and predefined charts. If application-specific counters are available, be sure to utilize them when analyzing the server.

Table 5.9 lists the four main resources in order of importance and briefly describes their roles in an application server.

TABLE 5.9 RESOURCES AND THEIR ROLES IN AN APPLICATION SERVER

Priority	Resource	Roles
1	Processor	Applications run on the server instead of the client side of the network.
2	Memory	Memory is needed at the server to support both the server needs and the application needs.
3	Disk	Client/server applications typically access large amounts of data; therefore, they demand more of the disk drives.
4	Network	Client/server applications transfer many requests across the network. These requests often are queries or commands that are small in size.

> **FURTHER REVIEW**
PERFORMANCE MONITORING

The following key words are important terms covered in this section. You should make sure you understand what each one is and what it does.

Key Words

Cache
Counter
Logical disk
Object
Pagefile
RAID
Striping
Thread

An Overview of Performance Monitor

This section identifies some of the options available in Performance Monitor for monitoring, analyzing server performance, and gathering specific data. Some of the options include

- Viewing data from multiple computers simultaneously
- Seeing how changes affect the computer
- Changing charts of current activity while viewing them
- Starting a program or procedure automatically or sending a notice when a threshold is exceeded
- Exporting Performance Monitor data to spreadsheets or database programs or using it as raw input for programs
- Saving different combinations of counter and option settings for quick starts and changes
- Logging data about various objects from multiple computers over time
- Creating reports about current activity or trends over time

A number of other factors can adversely affect the data gathered by using Performance Monitor:

- If the sample interval is too short, the log file becomes very large.
- If sampled too often, the processor has additional burden.
- If the interval is too long, significant changes in data might be missed.
- Monitoring too soon after startup records all processes and services being initiated.
- Leaving the computer on the network during monitoring burdens other network resources and skews their performance.

What Resources Should You Monitor?

The throughput of each resource should be monitored both individually during installation and after installation is complete with all resources in use.

The following four resources have the greatest impact on the performance of the server:

- Memory
- Processor
- Disk
- Network

Monitoring the four resources—memory, processor, disk, and network—simultaneously shows the effects the resource combinations have on each other and on the server system.

Memory

Two main types of memory need to be considered when analyzing server performance:

- Physical random access memory (RAM)
- Virtual memory (pagefile)

The more physical memory available, the better, because the disk drive does not have to be accessed as often for the pagefile. The pagefile can be moved to another partition to reduce access to the boot partition, but moving the pagefile prevents debugging of system problems if the system tends to crash often. The best option is to leave the pagefile in its default location, with its size set to be the same as physical memory, and to create a large secondary pagefile on another physical drive.

Processor

The type and number of processors greatly affects the performance of the system. Windows NT Server 4 can scale up to 32 processors.

Disk

A number of factors affect disk performance, and you should take all of them into account when analyzing and optimizing the system. The factors include

- Type and number of controllers: Whether they are IDE, EIDE, SCSI, fast SCSI, and so on, can make a big difference.
- Types of drives implemented: Disk drives come with varying specs relative to access speed and rotation speed.
- Controllers that support RAID: RAID can provide fault tolerance.
- Disk striping with parity: If you are using Microsoft's disk striping with parity, read performance can improve greatly.
- Busmaster controllers: Have a processor on board to handle requests and reduce the load on the system processor.
- Caching: Read and write performance can improve when requests are held in onboard memory until free time is available.
- Type of work being performed: Application server, file and print server, network protocol(s) being used, number of users, type of network adapter(s), services being run (DHCP, WINS, IIS, and so on).
- Matching disk controllers to disk types: Ensure that disk controllers are matched to the disk types. A fast-wide SCSI disk should be used with a fast-wide SCSI controller.

Network

A number of topologies and network architecture standards is available. The two main architectures in use today are Ethernet and Token Ring:

- Ethernet is the most commonly implemented type of network and operates anywhere from 10 MHz to 100 MHz and more.

- Token Ring is a standard that was developed by IBM and operates anywhere from 4 MHz to 16 MHz and more.

Whether Ethernet or Token Ring is used, using the fastest network card with the largest bus is always advisable. Both Ethernet and Token Ring are available in 32-bit formats, and 64-bit cards should be available soon if they are not already.

Performance Analysis

Analysis of a system takes four steps:

- Determine what is normal for the system and how to deal with the abnormal.
- Set expectations of how the system or resource should respond under specific conditions.
- Help plan for upgrades and additions.
- Provide better input into system budgeting requirements.

When a system is to be analyzed, you should first determine what functions the server performs. Three types of Windows NT Servers exist, as described in Table 5.10.

TABLE 5.10 Windows NT Servers

Server Type	Description
File and print server	Used for data storage and retrieval. It also can be used for loading application software over the network.
Application server	The server runs the application engine that users access by using a local version of the application front end.
Domain server	A domain server validates user account logons. Domain controllers synchronize the account database among themselves.

To set expectations, you must know what is to be expected of a system. This is referred to as workload characterization. A workload unit is a list of requests made on the system or a resource. An example of a workload unit might be the number of bytes transferred per second.

To determine workload characterization, you must understand what is taking place in each environment.

▼ **NOTE**

Many Windows NT installations have the servers acting in one, two, or all three server roles. In these situations, the administrator might have to sacrifice or reduce the performance of one server role to bring the performance of another role up to a satisfactory level to get the best overall performance.

A resource that restricts the workflow is referred to as a bottleneck. Sometimes, the performance of one resource makes another resource appear to be the bottleneck. For example, if a server does not have sufficient physical memory, this could also affect the physical drive because the system accesses the paging file.

Because Windows NT is self-tuning to a certain degree, a good percentage of optimization involves upgrading hardware, not changing Registry settings. It is important, however, to know what needs to be upgraded and what doesn't.

PRACTICE QUESTIONS

ANALYSIS USING NETWORK MONITOR

1. Nancy is trying to verify that logon requests are reaching the server with the correct user name, because a number of users are not getting validated. How can she verify that particular user names are being forwarded to the logon server?

   A. Have each user go to the server and log on locally.

   B. Have Nancy watch users enter their names and passwords to ensure they are not making typos.

   C. Run Network Monitor on the logon server and check the Hexadecimal pane to see whether the names are getting to the server.

   D. Verification that the information is reaching the server is not possible.

2. What are the areas of the Network Monitor window when it is capturing data?

   A. Network Statistics, Session Statistics, Counters

   B. Graph, Session Statistics, Total Statistics, Station Statistics

   C. Objects, Counters, Instances

   D. Sessions, Real Time, Transfer Statistics

3. What areas can be displayed while you are viewing the captured data in Network Monitor?

   A. Resource pane, Data pane

   B. Summary pane, Detail pane, Hexadecimal pane

   C. Report pane, Alert pane, Detail pane

   D. None of the above

4. What are the two versions of the Network Monitor?

   A. Real mode and Protected mode

   B. Local traffic only and full network traffic

   C. Promiscuous mode and Server mode

   D. LAN mode and WAN mode

5. Dave wants to monitor the traffic his clients and servers are generating on the network interacting with the network servers. How can he do this?

   A. Use Performance Monitor to monitor the network bindings.

   B. Use Network Monitor to monitor the network traffic on the servers.

   C. Turn off file- and print-sharing on the desktop systems.

   D. Install SNMP.

6. What are the three frame types in Network Monitor?

   A. Broadcast

   B. Directed

C. Multicast

D. Sequential

7. **What Microsoft product contains an enhanced version of Network Monitor?**

    A. Exchange.

    B. SQL.

    C. Systems Management Server.

    D. There is no enhanced version.

8. **The Hexadecimal pane in Network Monitor shows what?**

    A. Network broadcasts

    B. Frames coming into the server

    C. Client computer NetBIOS names

    D. User names

9. **A computer used to capture traffic and send it to a computer running Network Monitor must be running what service?**

    A. SNMP

    B. Network Analyzer

    C. Network Monitor Agent

    D. SMS Client

10. **How is the Network Monitor installed on a Windows NT system?**

    A. Automatically

    B. As a protocol

    C. From the Windows NT Resource Kit

    D. As a service

ANSWER KEY

1. C
2. B
3. B
4. B
5. B
6. A-B-C
7. C
8. B
9. C
10. D

ANSWERS & EXPLANATIONS

ANALYSIS USING NETWORK MONITOR

1. Nancy is trying to verify that logon requests are reaching the server with the correct user name, because a number of users are not getting validated. How can she verify that particular user names are being forwarded to the logon server?

    C. Run Network Monitor on the logon server and check the Hexadecimal pane to see whether the names are getting to the server.

1. CORRECT ANSWER: C

Nancy should run Network Monitor at the logon server and view the Hexadecimal pane to see whether the names are getting to the server correctly.

Answer A is incorrect; users should not log on to the server. Answer B is incorrect; you do not need to watch a user log on. Answer D is incorrect; you can verify that the information is reaching the server.

One of the first provisions to a user is the capability to log on to the network and be validated by a server. Other considerations for the network administrator follow:

- When do people log on? Are they all logging on at 8 a.m. or randomly over an hour during the morning from 7:30 a.m. to 8:30 a.m.?

- Are all users logging on from a local network computer, or are some users logging on from remote sites?

The first action that must take place is finding the logon server. In a Windows NT network, the logon server can be found in two ways, depending on what has been implemented:

- Send a broadcast message across the network to the NETLOGON mail slot (only located on domain controllers).

- Send a query to the WINS server for all registered domain controllers in the selected domain (appears as a domain [1C] entry in WINS). If found, send a request through directed frames.

After the requests have all been sent out, the client computer then accepts the first server response to that request. Whether the request was generated from a broadcast or from a directed message does not matter. Four factors are involved in validating the logon:

- The amount of traffic generated by establishing the session
- The amount of traffic generated if the client is at a Windows 95 computer
- The amount of traffic generated if the client is at a Windows NT computer
- The termination of the session

The Hexadecimal pane in Network Monitor shows the frames coming into the server, thus allowing the administrator to monitor what logon requests are being sent to the server for authentication.

2. **What are the areas of the Network Monitor window when it is capturing data?**

    B. Graph, Session Statistics, Total Statistics, Station Statistics

2. CORRECT ANSWER: B

The Network Monitor window shows the Graph, Session Statistics, Total Statistics, and Station Statistics areas when capturing data.

Capturing data by using Network Monitor is quite simple and can be initiated in one of three ways:

- Select Capture, Start from the menu bar.
- Click the Start Capture button in the toolbar.
- Press F10, the function key.

Stopping the capture of data is just as simple as starting it and can been done in one of four ways:

- Select Capture, Stop from the menu bar.
- Click the Stop Capture button in the toolbar.
- Press F11, the function key.
- Click the Stop and View button in the toolbar.

The Capture Window is the default view of Network Monitor. Table 5.11 describes each area of the Network Monitor window.

ANSWERS & EXPLANATIONS 249

TABLE 5.11 NETWORK MONITOR WINDOW AREAS

Window Area	Description
Graph	A horizontal bar chart that displays the current activity as a percentage of network utilization
Session Statistics	A summary of the transactions between two hosts and a display of which host initiated the broadcasts or multicasts
Total Statistics	Statistics for the traffic on the network as a whole, the frames captured, the per-second statistics, and the network adapter statistics
Station Statistics	A summary of the number of frames and bytes sent and received, the number of frames initiated by a host, and the number of broadcasts and multicasts

To control the amount of data captured, the user can set a capture filter. A filter describes what type of data should be captured and displayed. The most common items to filter are either the protocol (NetBEUI, IPX, TCP/IP, and so on) or the destination or source address (MAC address, IP address, and so on).

Captured data can be displayed for analysis, or it can be saved to a capture file (*.CAP) for analysis later. After the data is captured, it needs to be analyzed. To analyze the data, it must be displayed. Displaying the data can be done in one of three ways:

- Select Capture, Display Captured Data from the menu bar.
- Click the Display Captured Data button in the toolbar.
- Press F12, the function key.

3. What areas can be displayed while you are viewing the captured data in Network Monitor?

    B. Summary pane, Detail pane, Hexadecimal pane

3. CORRECT ANSWER: B

The Summary pane, Detail pane, and Hexadecimal pane can be displayed while you are viewing the captured data in Network Monitor.

As with capturing data, filters can be applied while you are viewing the data. Filters enable the capture of numerous types of information, but also permit the user to filter for frames of particular interest during analysis. The following three areas make up the display window for Network Monitor:

- The Summary pane: Shows a list of all frames captured and information about each of them.

- The Detail pane: Shows protocol information for the frame selected in the Summary pane.

- The Hexadecimal pane: Displays the contents of the frame in hexadecimal format. The actual contents of data sent can be viewed in this area.

4. What are the two versions of the Network Monitor?

   B. Local traffic only and full network traffic

4. CORRECT ANSWER: B

The two versions of the Network Monitor are local traffic only and full network traffic.

Answer A is incorrect; Network Monitor is a network packet analyzer that comes with Windows NT Server and with Microsoft Systems Management Server. The advantage of the version that comes with Systems Management Server is that any system on the network can be monitored from a single location.

Network Monitor does not require special hardware other than a network adapter supported by the system on which it is installed. Windows NT 4 supports NDIS 4 and allows the viewing of local traffic only or full network traffic with the version of Network Monitor available in Microsoft Systems Management Server.

Network Monitor is made up of two components:

- Network Monitor application: Enables a system to capture and display network data, to display network statistics, and to save the captured data for future analysis

- Network Monitor Agent: Enables a computer to capture all network traffic and to send it over the network to the computer running the Network Monitor application

5. Dave wants to monitor the traffic his clients and servers are generating on the network interacting with the network servers. How can he do this?

   B. Use Network Monitor to monitor the network traffic on the servers.

5. CORRECT ANSWER: B

Network Monitor can be used to monitor the network traffic on the servers.

Answer A is incorrect; Performance Monitor would not be used to monitor network traffic. Answer C is incorrect; turning off sharing would not indicate the network traffic. Answer D is incorrect; the SNMP service would not help monitor the network traffic.

Network Monitor allows the administrator to monitor the actual network traffic on a system, but Performance Monitor can only monitor traffic statistics.

File Session Traffic

Almost all communication between computers requires the establishment of a session before the communication actually takes place. For example, accessing a file on a server, running an application that accesses a SQL server, or accessing a mailbox on an Exchange server requires establishing a session. DHCP, WINS, and DNS are a few of the communications in a Windows NT network that do not require an established session before communication starts. Establishing a session occurs in five steps:

1. Resolve the NetBIOS name (computer name) to an IP address.
2. Resolve the IP address to the MAC address (hardware address) of the computer.
3. Establish a TCP session.
4. Establish a NetBIOS session.
5. Negotiate the computer's SMB protocols.

Please refer to the Further Review section of this objective for more information regarding server traffic.

Chapter 5 MONITORING AND OPTIMIZATION

6. **What are the three frame types in Network Monitor?**

   A. Broadcast

   B. Directed

   C. Multicast

6. CORRECT ANSWERS: A-B-C

Three frame types are monitored by Network Monitor.

Answer D is incorrect; Sequential is not a valid frame type.

Network Monitor can be used to provide traffic analysis and perform optimization on a network by monitoring the frames being sent across the network. Different services and actions generate different frame types, depending on the requirements of what is being done.

To optimize or capacity-plan your network, as with optimizing a server, the administrator must know what traffic is currently being generated. Analysis involves determining the effect each Windows NT Server service has on the network and is done with a network analyzer. You can optimize network traffic in two ways:

- Provide users with better response time by implementing network services that can increase network traffic.
- Provide users with more bandwidth on the network by reducing network traffic generated by services.

Each method is valid and deserves consideration, but a properly optimized network is going to strike a compromise between the two. Capacity-planning is the method of analyzing the network as various factors are increased. As the network grows, new services are added.

Classifying services enables an administrator to better predict the effects on a network as changes are made. Each of the Windows NT Server services can be classified by answering three simple questions:

- What kind of traffic does this service generate?
- How often is this traffic generated?
- What impact does this traffic have on the network?

Frames are divided into three types: broadcast, multicast, and directed. Table 5.12 provides a description of each frame type.

ANSWERS & EXPLANATIONS 253

TABLE 5.12   FRAME TYPES

Frame Type	Description
Broadcast	Broadcasts are sent with the destination FFFFFFFFFFFF. No host can be configured with this address, but all hosts on the network (subnet) accept this frame and process it. The frame is passed up the stack until it is determined whether the frame is meant for that computer.
Multicast	Multicasts are sent to a portion of the computers on the network. Like broadcast frames, multicast frames are not sent to a specific Media Access Control (MAC) address but to a select few addresses on the network. Each host on the network must register its multicast address to become a member of a multicast set. NetBEUI and some TCP/IP applications utilize multicasting.
Directed	Directed frames are the most common type of frame. Each directed frame has a specific address for a host on the network. All other hosts disregard a directed frame because it does not contain the host's MAC address.

All frames are broken down into different pieces, or fields, that can be analyzed. Some contain addressing information, others contain data, and so on. By analyzing the addressing portion of the frame, you can determine whether the frame is a broadcast type. This helps administrators determine which service created the frame and whether it can be optimized.

The type of network traffic generated often depends on the protocol used to send the frames. As more companies want connectivity over WANs and more people want access to the Internet, TCP/IP has become the protocol of choice.

7. What Microsoft product contains an enhanced version of Network Monitor?

   C. Systems Management Server.

7. CORRECT ANSWER: C

Answer A is incorrect; Exchange does not include Network Monitor. Answer B is incorrect; SQL does not include Network Monitor. Answer D is incorrect; Network Monitor does have an enhanced version.

Microsoft's System Management Server product includes an enhanced version of Network Monitor that can operate in "promiscuous" mode, which means it can monitor network traffic between two remote machines. The Windows NT version can only monitor traffic to and from the machine running Network Monitor.

Chapter 5 MONITORING AND OPTIMIZATION

8. The Hexadecimal pane in Network Monitor shows what?

    B. Frames coming into the server

8. CORRECT ANSWER: B

The Hexadecimal pane in Network Monitor shows the actual content of the frames coming into the server.

Answer A is incorrect; the hexadecimal pane does not display network broadcasts. Answer C is incorrect; the hexadecimal pane does not display NetBIOS names. Answer D is incorrect; user names are not displayed by Network Monitor.

9. A computer used to capture traffic and send it to a computer running Network Monitor must be running what service?

    C. Network Monitor Agent

9. CORRECT ANSWER: C

The Network Monitor Agent enables a computer to capture all network traffic and send it over the network to the computer running Network Monitor. This capability is automatically installed on any system running Network Monitor. The Network Monitor Agent is available for computers running both Windows 95 and Windows NT.

10. How is the Network Monitor installed on a Windows NT system?

    D. As a service

10. CORRECT ANSWER: D

Answer A is incorrect; Network Monitor is not installed automatically. Answer B is incorrect; Network Monitor is not a protocol. Answer C is incorrect; Network Monitor is included with Windows NT.

Network Monitor is installed from the Services property page in the Network control applet. You have the choice of installing only the Network Monitor Agent or installing the Network Monitor and Agent.

FURTHER REVIEW

ANALYSIS USING NETWORK MONITOR

The following key words are important terms covered in this section. You should make sure you understand what each one is and what it does.

Key Words

Broadcast
Frames
Network Monitor
Promiscuous

Client-to-Server Browser Traffic

Client-to-server traffic is the communication a client has with a server. Browser traffic is all traffic generated during the browser process, both in announcing available resources and in retrieving lists of available resources. The entire process is as follows:

1. Servers (any computer with sharing enabled) are added to the browse list by announcing themselves to the master browser.
2. The master browser shares the list of servers with the backup browsers and the master browsers of other domains.
3. The client computer retrieves a list of backup browsers from the master browser.
4. The client retrieves a list of servers from a backup browser.
5. The client retrieves a list of shared resources from the server.

Server-to-Server Traffic

A large amount of traffic is generated between servers. The basics of server browsing are as follows:

1. At startup, the PDC assumes the role of domain master browser for its domain.
2. At startup, each BDC becomes either a backup browser or the master browser of its subnet, if no PDC is on the subnet.
3. Every 12 minutes, each master browser announces itself to the master browsers of other domains on the local subnet.
4. Every 12 minutes, each domain master browser contacts the WINS server for a listing of all domains.
5. Every 12 minutes, each master browser contacts the domain master browser for an update of the browse list.
6. Every 15 minutes, each backup browser contacts its local master browser to retrieve an updated list.

Along with the announcement traffic a server generates, the server can create additional traffic by taking part in other browser traffic.

- Browser elections take place if a client cannot find a master browser, if the master browser announces it is being shut down, or if a domain controller is being initialized.
- Master browsers in different domains share their browse lists to permit servers and resources to be accessed throughout the network.

- Backup browsers retrieve updated browse lists from their local master browser.

The three areas in which Trust Relationships generate traffic are as follows:

- Creating the trust creates traffic (about 16,000 bytes), but only at the time the trust is created.

- Using trusted accounts creates traffic. When the administrator of the trusting domain assigns permissions to an account from the trusted domain, more traffic is generated.

- Pass-through authentication creates additional traffic. When a user accesses a resource in a trusting domain, the trusting domain controller must use pass-through authentication to validate the user.

PRACTICE QUESTIONS

IDENTIFYING AND RESOLVING PERFORMANCE BOTTLENECKS

1. **What is a bottleneck? Choose the best answer.**

   A. A slow network card

   B. A faulty memory SIMM

   C. A crashed disk drive

   D. A resource that restricts workflow

2. **Jackie wants to check to see whether the disk drive in the server is a bottleneck. What should she do?**

   A. Use Performance Monitor to compare byte transfer rates to the baseline.

   B. Use Task Manager to view the amount of memory being used.

   C. Use Windows NT Diagnostics to verify the size, speed, and type of disk drive installed.

   D. Open Disk Administrator to adjust the cluster size being used on the disk drive.

3. **Chuck has been running some tests on one of his file and print servers and has come to the conclusion that the disk drives are the bottleneck. What is the best solution for Chuck's network?**

   A. Add another disk to his server.

   B. Add a faster disk to his server.

   C. Redistribute the load across more file and print servers.

   D. Reinstall Windows NT Server 4, making sure to choose the disk optimization option during installation.

4. **John discovered that the processor was the bottleneck on his application server, but when he added another processor to the system, the server's performance did not improve. What could be the problem?**

   A. John forgot to activate the new processor in the System dialog box.

   B. The application is not written to be multithreaded.

   C. More memory has to be added to enable the new processor.

   D. Windows NT cannot work with multiple processors unless it is an OEM version.

5. **Sharon found that the processor in her server was a bottleneck and upgraded to a faster one. Although the processor was rated much faster, the performance did not improve as expected. What other option did Sharon have?**

   A. Install the latest Service Pack.

   B. Upgrade to Windows NT 4 b-release.

   C. Add a second processor instead of upgrading the existing processor.

   D. Have the application rewritten.

6. What two counters make up the %Processor Time?

    A. %Privileged Time

    B. Bytes Processed/sec

    C. %Free Time

    D. %User Time

7. When you are monitoring memory, to what does Available Bytes refer?

    A. The amount of space available in the pagefile that has not been committed to an application

    B. The amount of space available on the disk drive that has not been committed to the pagefile

    C. The amount of cache that has not been written back to the disk

    D. The amount of physical memory that has not been used

8. When monitoring memory, to what does Committed Bytes refer?

    A. The amount of physical memory being used

    B. The difference between the amount of physical memory and the amount of virtual memory

    C. The amount of virtual memory that has been allocated either to physical RAM for storage or to the pagefile

    D. The total amount of both physical and virtual memory being used

9. This is a scenario question. First, you must review the scenario, then review the required and optional results. Following that is a solution. You must pick the best evaluation of that solution. Note that question 10 also deals with the same scenario.

    Scenario:
    A file server is being used by 65 users for storing files, as well as for installation source files. The server has 64 MB of RAM, a 9.2 GB fast SCSI drive, a 16-bit network card, and enabled shadow RAM. The users complain that access to the server is slow at some times of the day.

    Required Result:
    Determine whether the processor is the bottleneck.

    Optional Results:
    Determine whether memory is the bottleneck.

    Improve the performance of the server.

    Proposed Solution:
    Run Performance Monitor at different times throughout the day for a number of days, watching the counters of %Processor Time, Page Faults/sec, and Processor Queue Length.

    Evaluation of Proposed Solution:
    (Choose the most correct answer.)

    A. The required result is met, and both optional results are also met.

    B. The required result and one optional result are met.

    C. The required result is met, and neither optional result is met.

    D. The required result is not met, and one optional result is met.

10. **This applies to the same scenario as number 9.**

    Scenario:
    A file server is being used by 65 users for storing files, as well as for installation source files. The server has 64 MB of RAM, a 9.2 GB fast SCSI drive, a 16-bit network card, and enabled shadow RAM. The users complain that access to the server is slow at some times of the day.

    Required Result:
    Determine whether memory is the bottleneck.

    Optional Results:
    Determine whether the processor is the bottleneck.

    Improve the performance of the server.

    Proposed Solution:
    Run Performance Monitor at different times throughout the day for a number of days, watching the counters of %Processor Time, Page Faults/sec, and Processor Queue Length.

    Evaluation of Proposed Solution:
    (Choose the most correct answer.)

    A. The required result is met, and both optional results are also met.

    B. The required result and one optional result are met.

    C. The required result is met, and neither optional result is met.

    D. The required result is not met, and one optional result is met.

ANSWER KEY

1. D
2. A
3. C
4. B

5. C
6. A-D
7. D
8. C

9. C
10. B

ANSWERS & EXPLANATIONS

IDENTIFYING AND RESOLVING PERFORMANCE BOTTLENECKS

1. What is a bottleneck? Choose the best answer.

    D. A resource that restricts workflow

1. CORRECT ANSWER: D

A bottleneck is a resource that restricts workflow.

Answer A is incorrect; a bottleneck is not a slow network card. Answer B is incorrect; a bottleneck is not a faulty SIMM. Answer C is incorrect; a bottleneck is not a crashed hard drive.

Bottlenecks are the problem areas that need to be addressed to improve the performance of the system. Trends are useful for capacity planning and preparing for future needs.

Any spreadsheet or database application can be used to analyze the data collected.

2. Jackie wants to check to see whether the disk drive in the server is a bottleneck. What should she do?

    A. Use Performance Monitor to compare byte transfer rates to the baseline.

2. CORRECT ANSWER: A

Use Performance Monitor to compare byte transfer rates to the baseline.

Answer B is incorrect; memory being used is not indicative of a disk bottleneck. Answer C is incorrect; NT Diagnostics is not used to gauge disk bottlenecks. Answer D is incorrect; cluster size does not directly pertain to performance, but rather to efficiency.

Performance Monitor has counters for both the PhysicalDisk and LogicalDisk objects. The LogicalDisk monitors the logical partitions of physical drives that indicate when a service or application is making excessive requests. The PhysicalDisk is used to monitor the physical disk drive as a whole.

▼ NOTE

Remember to activate Performance Monitor disk counters before trying to monitor the disk drives. By default, the counters are not enabled and do not show activity when added in Performance Monitor.

Type **diskperf -y** at a command prompt to enable the counters on the local computer.

Type **diskperf -y \\servername** at a command prompt to enable the counters on a remote computer.

Type **diskperf -ye** at a command prompt to enable the counters on the local computer with a RAID implementation.

Type **diskperf -n** at a command prompt to disable the counters on the local computer.

Table 5.13 shows some of the counters to use and the values to watch for when monitoring the physical disk. Logical disks also have similar counters.

TABLE 5.13 DISK MONITORING

Counter	Description
%Disk Time	This is the amount of time the disk is busy with reads and writes. An acceptable value is around 50%.
Disk Queue Length	This is the number of waiting disk I/O requests. If this value is consistently 2 or more, upgrade the disk.
Avg. Disk Bytes/ Transfer	This is the average number of bytes transferred to or from the system during read and write operations.
Disk Bytes/sec	This is the rate at which bytes are transferred to or from the disk during read and write operations.

3. Chuck has been running some tests on one of his file and print servers and has come to the conclusion that the disk drives are the bottleneck. What is the best solution for Chuck's network?

   C. Redistribute the load across all the file and print servers.

3. CORRECT ANSWER: C

Redistribute the load across multiple file and print servers so that they have more equal usage.

Answer A is incorrect; adding another disk will not reduce the drive load on the server. Answer B is incorrect; although adding a faster disk might have a small effect, it will not fix the underlying problem that the server is overloaded. Answer D is incorrect; there is not a disk optimization option during the Windows NT installation.

When a file server becomes overloaded, the problem usually manifests itself in overloaded disk drives when more people try to access the server than the server can handle. The quickest way to rectify this is to distribute the load across more file and print servers.

Chapter 5 MONITORING AND OPTIMIZATION

4. John discovered that the processor was the bottleneck on his application server but when he added another processor to the system, the server's performance did not improve. What could be the problem?

   B. The application is not written to be multithreaded.

4. CORRECT ANSWER: B

If the application is not written to be multithreaded, all requests must go through one processor.

Answer A is incorrect; you do not have to activate a new processor. Answer C is incorrect; additional memory is not needed. Answer D is incorrect; all versions of Windows NT 4.0 are multiprocessor capable.

An application must be multithreaded to take advantage of multiple processors. Otherwise, to increase performance, you would usually have to add additional application servers.

5. Sharon found that the processor in her server was a bottleneck and upgraded to a faster one. Although the processor was rated much faster, the performance did not improve as expected. What other option did Sharon have?

   C. Add a second processor instead of upgrading the existing processor.

5. CORRECT ANSWER: C

If the application is written to be multithreaded, it is more beneficial to have multiple processors than to have one processor that is fast.

Answer A is incorrect; installing a service pack will not change a processor's performance. Answer B is incorrect; there is not a NT 4 b-release. Answer D is incorrect; rewriting the application will not affect processor performance.

It is better to add additional processors than to just upgrade a single processor. With multithreaded applications, Windows NT can take advantage of multiprocessors to greatly increase the performance over a single processor.

6. What two counters make up the %Processor Time?

   A. %Privileged Time
   D. %User Time

6. CORRECT ANSWER: A-D

%Privileged Time and %User Time together make up %Processor Time.

Answer B is incorrect; Bytes Processed/sec is not part of %Processor Time. Answer C is incorrect; %Free Time is not part of processor time.

The two most common problems when the processor is a bottleneck are CPU-bound applications and drivers and excessive interrupts generated by inadequate disk or network components.

Table 5.14 shows the counters to watch and the types of values for which to look.

TABLE 5.14 BOTTLENECK INDICATORS

Counter	Description
Processor: %Processor Time	This is the amount of time the processor is busy. It is the %Privileged Time plus the %User Time. When the processor is consistently above 75%–80%, it has become a bottleneck.
Processor: %Privileged Time	This is the amount of time the processor spends performing operating system services. Like %Processor Time, this value should average below 75%.
Processor: %User Time	This is the amount of time the processor spends running user services such as desktop applications. Again, this value should average below 75%.
Processor: Interrupts/sec	This is the number of interrupts the processor is handling from applications and hardware devices.
System: Processor Queue Length	This is the number of requests the processor has in its queue. Each of these requests is a thread waiting to be processed. Normally, this value is at zero, but if the queue length is consistently 2 or greater, the queue has a problem.
Server Work Queues: Queue Length	This is the number of requests in the queue for a particular processor. Again, if the queue length is 2 or greater, the queue has a problem.

7. When you are monitoring memory, to what does Available Bytes refer?

   D. The amount of physical memory that has not been used

7. CORRECT ANSWER: D

Available Bytes refers to the amount of physical memory that is not being used.

Answer A is incorrect; you do not commit pagefile space to an application. Answer B is incorrect; available bytes does not mean the space on the drive committed to the pagefile. Answer C is incorrect; it does not mean the amount of cache written back to disk.

Chapter 5 MONITORING AND OPTIMIZATION

8. When monitoring memory, to what does Committed Bytes refer?

    C. The amount of virtual memory that has been allocated to either physical RAM for storage or to the pagefile

8. CORRECT ANSWER: C

Commited Bytes refers to the amount of virtual memory that has been allocated to either physical RAM for storage or to the pagefile.

Answer A is incorrect; committed bytes does not mean the amount of physical memory being used. Answer B is incorrect; committed bytes does not mean the difference between physical and virtual memory. Answer D is incorrect; committed bytes does not mean the total amount of physical and virtual memory.

Memory has the greatest impact on the system because a shortage of memory causes the system to read and write from the disk more often. The RAM in Windows NT is broken down into two categories:

- Nonpaged: Data placed directly into a specific memory location that cannot be written to or retrieved from disk
- Paged: Virtual memory, in which all applications believe they have a full range of memory addresses available

The best indicator that memory is the bottleneck is a sustained high rate of hard page faults. Table 5.15 shows some of the memory counters to watch and the range that is acceptable.

TABLE 5.15 PAGE FAULT COUNTERS

Counter	Description
Pages/sec	This is the number of requests that had to access the disk because the requested pages were not available in RAM.
Available Bytes	This is the amount of available physical memory.
Committed Bytes	This is the amount of virtual memory allocated either to physical RAM for storage or to the pagefile.
Pool Nonpaged Bytes	This is the amount of RAM in the pool nonpaged memory area, where space is used by operating system components as they carry out their tasks.

ANSWERS & EXPLANATIONS   265

9. **Proposed Solution:**
   Run Performance Monitor at different times throughout the day for a number of days, watching the counters of %Processor Time, Page Faults/sec, and Processor Queue Length.

   C. The required result is met, and neither optional result is met.

9. CORRECT ANSWER: C

Monitoring Page Faults/sec can help determine whether memory is a bottleneck.

Answers A, B, and D are incorrect; the required result was met but neither of the optional results.

Monitoring Page Faults/sec can help determine if memory is a bottleneck, and the %Processor Time and Processor Queue length counters will indicate if the processor is a bottleneck. Improving the performance of the server would depend on what is causing the performance degradation (for example, memory or processor).

10. **Proposed Solution:**
    Run Performance Monitor at different times throughout the day for a number of days watching the counters of %Processor Time, Page Faults/sec, and Processor Queue Length.

    B. The required result and one optional result are met.

10. CORRECT ANSWER: B

Monitoring Page Faults/sec is for memory and monitoring %Processor Time and Processor Queue Length is for the processor.

Answers A, C, and D are incorrect, because the required result and one optional result were met.

Improving the performance of the server would depend on what is causing the performance degradation (for example, memory or processor). Monitoring Page Faults/sec can help determine whether memory is a bottleneck, and monitoring %Processor Time and Processor Queue Length can help determine whether the processor is a bottleneck.

FURTHER REVIEW

IDENTIFYING AND RESOLVING PERFORMANCE BOTTLENECKS

The following key words are important terms that were covered in this section. You should make sure you understand what each one is and what it does.

Key Words

Bottleneck

Nonpaged Memory

Paged Memory

Bottleneck Indicators

Table 5.16 shows some counters to monitor and some values to watch for when a lot of activity from the network is at the server.

TABLE 5.16 FINDING NETWORK BOTTLENECKS

Counter	Description
Server: Bytes Total/sec	This is the number of bytes the server has sent and received over the network. If this value is low, try adding an adapter.
Server: Logon /sec	This is the number of logon attempts for local, across-the-network, and service-account authentication in the last second. Add domain controllers if the value is low.
Server: Logon Total	This is the number of logon attempts for local, across-the-network, and service-account authentication since the server was started.
Network Segment: % Network	This is the percentage of bandwidth in use for the local network segment. This is used to monitor the effects of different network operations, such as account synchronization and utilization and logon validation. Limit the number of protocols used if this number is high.
Network Interface: Bytes Sent/sec	This is the number of bytes sent by using the selected adapter. Upgrade the network adapter if a problem exists.
Network Interface: Bytes Total/sec	This is the number of bytes sent and received by using the selected adapter. Upgrade the network adapter if a problem exists.

▼ **NOTE**

To have the network segment available in Performance Monitor, the Network Monitor Agent service must first be installed.

PRACTICE QUESTIONS

PERFORMANCE OPTIMIZATION

1. Jane wants to optimize the network components on her server. What should she do?

    A. Remove unused adapter cards and protocols.

    B. Disable the Server service.

    C. Make sure that TCP/IP, IPX/SPX, and NetBEUI are all installed to create the maximum number of network paths possible.

    D. Nothing needs to be done because Windows NT is self-optimizing.

2. Which of the following items can make the system use virtual memory more efficiently? Choose all that apply.

    A. Move the pagefile to the partition where the Windows NT system files are located.

    B. Move the pagefile from the partition where the Windows NT system files are located.

    C. Spread the pagefile over multiple drives.

    D. Set the minimum pagefile size to that which it reaches during peak system load.

3. Optimum performance in Windows NT 4 depends on which two components?

    A. Pagefile location

    B. Software

    C. Hardware

    D. Processor type (PowerPC, Intel, MIPS)

4. What is the definition of optimal performance?

    A. To make threads process at a greater speed

    B. To make processors work at a higher-percentage capacity

    C. To have the maximum possible number of services running

    D. To get the best performance result with the available hardware and software

5. Which of the following components is automatically optimized by Windows NT? Choose the best answer.

    A. Pagefile

    B. Mouse

    C. File system

    D. Bindings

6. To optimize your network cards, what should you consider? Choose all that apply.

    A. Never use NetBEUI.

    B. Always use NetBEUI.

    C. Use a card with the fastest available bus.

    D. Split your network into multiple subnets, with each subnet attaching to a separate network card in the server.

7. **Hardware fault tolerance increases the performance of what system components? Choose all that apply.**

    A. Disk

    B. Network

    C. Processor

    D. Memory

8. **What is the main drawback of hardware fault tolerance?**

    A. Increases system overhead

    B. Requires special drivers

    C. Only available on Intel platforms

    D. Increases expense

9. **Why is hardware fault tolerance considered to be better than software fault tolerance?**

    A. Hardware fault tolerance does not work with the HAL of Windows NT.

    B. Windows NT's version of fault tolerance only works with NTFS.

    C. Software fault tolerance works only with FAT.

    D. Hardware fault tolerance removes the parity calculation from the processor.

10. **When you are choosing disk drives for a server, what should you consider? Choose all that apply.**

    A. Use the FAT file system.

    B. Use the fastest drives.

    C. Use stripe sets with parity when possible.

    D. Choose SCSI over IDE.

ANSWER KEY		
1. A	5. A	9. D
2. B-C-D	6. C-D	10. B-C-D
3. B-C	7. A-C	
4. D	8. D	

ANSWERS & EXPLANATIONS

PERFORMANCE OPTIMIZATION

1. Jane wants to optimize the network components on her server. What should she do?

   A. Remove unused adapter cards and protocols.

1. CORRECT ANSWER: A

Always remove unused hardware and software when trying to optimize a server.

Answer B is incorrect; disabling the Server service stops the server from sharing anything. Answer C is incorrect; you want the least number of protocols necessary. Answer D is incorrect; Windows NT is not self-optimizing.

To optimize the network components on a server, the first thing to do is remove all unused adapters and protocols. You should then adjust the order of the protocol bindings to reflect the ones used the most.

2. Which of the following items can make the system use virtual memory more efficiently? Choose all that apply.

   B. Move the pagefile from the partition where the Windows NT system files are located.

   C. Spread the pagefile over multiple drives.

   D. Set the minimum pagefile size to that which it reaches during peak system load.

2. CORRECT ANSWERS: B-C-D

Spread the pagefile across multiple drives. Move the pagefile from the boot partition. Set the minimum pagefile size to the size it needs to be during peak load.

Answer A is incorrect; you would not want to keep the pagefile on the same partition as the system files.

Setting the pagefile parameters can have a big effect on system virtual memory. Spreading the pagefile across multiple drives is recommended to speed up access. Setting the minimum pagefile size to what the system is requiring during peak load removes overhead because the system doesn't need to increase the pagefile size. The pagefile should never be kept on the system partition; this would slow down access to the pagefile because the system is also accessing the system files on that partition. The usual recommendation is to keep a pagefile on the boot partition to provide the capability to create a memory dump during a crash, and to install the system files on a separate partition.

270   Chapter 5   MONITORING AND OPTIMIZATION

> ▼ **NOTE**
> If the pagefile is not on the boot partition, the system cannot create a memory dump during a crash.

3. Optimum performance in Windows NT 4 depends on which two components?

   B. Software
   C. Hardware

3. CORRECT ANSWERS: B-C

Performance depends on both hardware and software because the hardware can restrict performance and, if the software is written to use the full potential of the hardware, it becomes a bottleneck (16-bit as opposed to 32-bit applications).

Answer A is incorrect; performance is not directly dependent on pagefile location. Answer D is incorrect; performance is not dependent on processor type.

Getting the maximum performance out of a system is a combination of optimizing both hardware and software components. The hardware components can include physical memory, processor, drive type, and network card speed. The software components can include network protocol bindings, virtual memory settings, and pagefile configuration.

4. What is the definition of optimal performance?

   D. To get the best performance result with the available hardware and software

4. CORRECT ANSWER: D

Optimal performance is a result of getting the best performance possible from the available hardware and software.

Answer A is incorrect; optimal performance is not just processing threads. Answer B is incorrect; processor capacity alone does not give optimal performance. Answer C is incorrect; more servers instead of well-running servers does not mean optimal performance, just a lot of wasted money.

Optimal performance is getting the best possible use out of your existing hardware and software. Although it sometimes seems easier just to "throw money" at the problem—buying more RAM, for example—this is usually not better in the long run. The way to get the best performance out of your systems is to tune each component to its optimal settings for the server's role.

5. Which of the following components is automatically optimized by Windows NT? Choose the best answer.

   A. Pagefile

5. CORRECT ANSWER: A

The pagefile is automatically optimized by Windows NT.

Answer B is incorrect; the mouse does not need to be optimized. Answer D is incorrect; the bindings must be modified manually through the Network applet in Control Panel.

Windows NT can automatically grow and shrink the pagefile, depending on the virtual memory requirements. It is usually recommended to set the initial pagefile size to the maximum required at peak load, however, because growing and shrinking the pagefile can affect system performance.

6. To optimize your network cards, what should you consider? Choose all that apply.

   C. Use a card with the fastest available bus.

   D. Split your network into multiple subnets, with each subnet attaching to a separate network card in the server.

6. CORRECT ANSWERS: C-D

Using a card with the fastest possible bus and subnetting the network to reduce the amount of traffic on each subnet will optimize your network cards.

Answer A is incorrect; NetBEUI is actually the fastest protocol—its main drawback is that it is nonroutable. Answer B is incorrect; you would not use NetBEUI in a WAN because it is nonroutable.

Using a network adapter with the fastest possible bus speed (such as PCI) will increase the speed of communication between the system and the NIC. Also, "smart" adapters are now available that will actually help with some of the communications processing, taking even more load from the system processor. If your system communicates with multiple networks, subnetting the networks and adding an additional network card for each one can greatly increase the speed of communication, because each card is handling information only for that particular subnet.

7. Hardware fault tolerance increases the performance of what system components? Choose all that apply.

   A. Disk

   C. Processor

7. CORRECT ANSWERS: A-C

Answer B is incorrect; hardware fault tolerance does not increase network adapter performance. Answer D is incorrect; hardware fault tolerance does not increase memory performance.

See question 9 for a complete explanation.

272 Chapter 5 MONITORING AND OPTIMIZATION

8. What is the main drawback of hardware fault tolerance?

   D. Increases expense

8. CORRECT ANSWER: D

Hardware fault tolerance solutions are considerably more expensive because a dedicated RAID processor card must be purchased. Windows NT includes a software-based solution.

Answer A is incorrect; system overhead is actually decreased. Answer B is incorrect; no special drivers are required. Answer C is incorrect; hardware fault tolerance can be used on any platform.

9. Why is hardware fault tolerance considered to be better than software fault tolerance?

   D. Hardware fault tolerance removes the parity calculation from the processor.

9. CORRECT ANSWER: D

Hardware fault tolerance is better because it removes the parity calculation from the processor.

Answer A is incorrect; hardware fault tolerance will work with Windows NT. Answer B is incorrect; fault tolerance will work with both FAT and NTFS. Answer C is incorrect; Windows NT's software fault tolerance will work with both FAT and NTFS.

Using a hardware-based fault tolerance, or RAID disk system, will increase the performance of both the disk subsystem and the processor because the processor no longer has to calculate the parity bits for stripe sets or track writing of multiple bits in a disk-mirroring solution. The main drawback to a hardware-based solution is the expense of the hardware components, whereas the Windows NT software solution is included with the operating system.

10. When you are choosing disk drives for a server, what should you consider? Choose all that apply.

    B. Use the fastest drives.
    C. Use stripe sets with parity when possible.
    D. Choose SCSI over IDE.

10. CORRECT ANSWERS: B-C-D

The use of faster drives and SCSI improves disk access time, and the use of stripe sets with parity adds fault tolerance.

Answer A is incorrect; the file system does not impact the decision of what drive type to use. Also, except for specific circumstances, such as sequential logs, the FAT file system is slower than the NTFS file system.

Using the fastest available drives and using stripe sets with parity for speed will provide an increase in drive performance and also provide fault tolerance. If the system is still experiencing a bottleneck with the disk drives, you have a number of possible solutions:

- Offload some of the processes to another system.

- Add a faster controller or an on-board caching controller.

- Add more memory to permit more caching by Windows NT.

- Add more disk drives in a RAID environment Spreading the data across multiple physical disks improves performance.

> **FURTHER REVIEW**

PERFORMANCE OPTIMIZATION

The following key words are important terms covered in this section. You should make sure you understand what each one is and what it does.

Key Words

Bottleneck

Optimize

SUMMARY

This chapter has discussed the tools used to gather information about your systems and network performance. This includes using the Performance Monitor and Network Monitor tools included with Windows NT and creating a baseline against which you can judge future performance readings. As stated in the introduction to the chapter, monitoring and optimization is not a large part of the exam, but is one of the most important things to learn and implement in real-world network administration. For the exam, make sure you know the following key points:

- Using the Performance Monitor to create baselines and identify bottlenecks

- Using Network Monitor to monitor network traffic and identify problem areas

- Optimizing a Windows NT system for peak performance

CHAPTER 6

Troubleshooting

This chapter covers a difficult subject. Troubleshooting sometimes can seem like a "black art." The best way to troubleshoot a problem is to systematically work through it, eliminating possibilities as you go. This chapter contains nine separate sections, each of which deals with a different subsystem of Windows NT and the areas available for troubleshooting.

OBJECTIVES

This chapter covers the following Microsoft exam objectives:

Choose the appropriate course of action to take to resolve installation failures.

▶ This section discusses choosing the appropriate course of action to solve installation failures. These failures occur for two basic reasons: hardware-related problems and configuration-related problems. This section also discusses some of the methods available for automating the installation process.

Choose the appropriate course of action to take to resolve boot failures.

▶ When configuration changes take place on a Windows NT system, they sometimes result in the inability to restart Windows NT. This section reviews common problems that occur during the boot process as well as their resolutions. This section discusses the boot process, the emergency repair process, and using the Last Known Good (LKG) configuration.

continues

OBJECTIVES (continued)

Choose the appropriate course of action to take to resolve configuration failures. Tasks include backing up and restoring the Registry and editing the Registry.

▶ The Registry stores most of the configuration information for Windows NT. It is organized as a series of keys, subkeys, and values. A file system is similar in organization: a file is stored with a filename consisting of a drive letter, a directory, and a filename (C:\USERS\MYFILE.TXT), and the file can contain data. In much the same way, the Registry stores information as a key, subkey, and value (HKEY_LOCAL_MACHINE\MySubkey\My Value).

Choose the appropriate course of action to take to resolve printer problems.

▶ Before examining the print model, it is necessary to discuss the vocabulary used by Microsoft to explain the model. Microsoft does not use the same terminology as other network operating systems. This can lead to confusion when first working with the Windows NT print model.

▶ *Print devices* are the actual hardware devices that produce hard-copy output. *Printers* are the software interfaces between the operating system and the print device. A printer can be configured to send output to multiple physical print devices. Multiple printers also can be configured to send output to the same print device at different priority levels or at different hours of the day. A *print spooler* is the software responsible for receiving, distributing, and processing print jobs. A spooler consists of many components that perform these functions.

▶ A *print job* is data destined for a print device. It can be sent in various formats in the Windows NT print model. A *queue* is a series of print jobs waiting to be printed. *Print processors* work with the print drivers to de-spool the spooled print jobs during print spool file playback. The print processor also makes the final alterations to print jobs, based on the data type of each job. Data types include Text, Enhanced Metafile (EMF), RAW FF (Appended), and RAW FF (Auto).

Choose the appropriate course of action to take to resolve RAS problems.

▶ One of the many challenges faced by network administrators today is the user's need to dial in to the network. The popularity and convenience of laptops and telecommuting makes this process necessary. Windows NT comes with a dial-in service known as Remote Access Service (RAS). RAS also provides the capability for the server to dial out, which enables dial-up networking. This section presents an overview of RAS and investigates troubleshooting the RAS client and server.

Choose the appropriate course of action to take to resolve connectivity problems.

▶ Network connectivity problems center around the inability of a client to find the destination server on the network. This can be due to the following:

- The protocol does not allow routing in a wide area network.

- The client and the server do not share a common protocol.

OBJECTIVES

- The protocol is configured improperly.
- Name resolution is not being performed correctly.
- The network has a physical problem.

Choose the appropriate course of action to take to resolve resource access and permission problems.

▶ When resources cannot be accessed and there is not a network connectivity problem, it generally can be attributed to incorrect share or NTFS permissions. This section discusses how to troubleshoot resource-access problems that result from incorrect permissions and how share and NTFS permissions interact with each other.

▶ Another issue covered in this section is group usage in a multidomain environment. Planning your domain environment for growth and using groups in your security assignments can assist you in creating a security environment that will expand into a multidomain environment.

Choose the appropriate course of action to take to resolve fault-tolerance failures. Fault-tolerance methods include tape backup, mirroring, and stripe set with parity.

▶ Two levels of fault tolerance are built into Windows NT Server: disk mirroring/duplexing (RAID 1) and disk striping with parity (RAID 5). Each fault-tolerant method has advantages and issues when being implemented. No matter which fault-tolerant method you implement, a good backup strategy is essential to prevent data loss in an organization. This section details issues with disk mirroring, stripe sets with parity, and backup strategies.

Perform advanced problem resolution. Tasks include diagnosing and interpreting a blue screen, configuring a memory dump, and using the Event Log service.

▶ Advanced problem resolution requires the use of the Event log, the System log, and the Application log to determine what is causing the problem. What the user sees often is the result of a more significant failure. The following three event logs are maintained by Windows NT:

- **The System Event log:** Records events generated by Windows NT system components, such as drivers and services.
- **The Security Event log:** Records events related to system security. In the case of the security log, the system audit policy determines which events are logged. System audit policies are created and maintained with User Manager for Domains.
- **The Application Event log:** Records messages generated by applications.

▶ The first place you should look for information is the Event Viewer. You will see three basic events in the logs. The first is informational items that let you know when things are happening on the system. These are represented by blue circles with the letter "i" in them. Warning messages indicate more severe problems but do not stop the system. These are yellow circles with an exclamation point (!) in them. Warnings often lead to a STOP error. Most STOP errors indicate that some part of Windows NT is not functioning, and they are shown as red stop signs. Event fields are described in the following list:

continues

OBJECTIVES (continued)

Date: The date the event message was logged

Time: The time the event message was logged

User: The user who caused the event

Computer: The name of the computer on which the event occurred

Event ID: A numeric value for a specific message as defined by the source of the message

Source: The application or system component that logged the event

Type: A Windows NT classification of the event, such as an Error, Warning, or Information message

Category: A classification of the event, as defined by the source of the message

Description: A textual explanation of the event

Data: Binary data specific to an event, shown as a series of either byte or word values

PRACTICE QUESTIONS

SOLVING INSTALLATION FAILURES

1. What can be configured for a newly created BDC to communicate with a PDC on a remote TCP/IP subnetwork? Select all that apply.

   A. WINS server IP address

   B. DNS server IP address

   C. LMHOSTS file

   D. HOSTS file

2. During Windows NT Server installation, you accidentally chose to install the computer as a member server. How do you change the role of the computer to a backup domain controller? Select the best response.

   A. Reinstall Windows NT Server.

   B. In Server Manager, promote the member server to a backup domain controller.

   C. Edit the Registry.

   D. In the Networks applet, change the role of the computer on the Identification tab.

3. Which situation causes the installation of a backup domain controller named MARKETING in the HEAD_OFFICE domain to fail? Select all that apply.

   A. The PDC for the HEAD_OFFICE domain is not available.

   B. The MARKETING BDC does not share a common protocol with the PDC.

   C. There are no other BDCs in the domain.

   D. Another computer named MARKETING already exists on the network.

   E. All the above.

4. If the incorrect video driver is selected during Windows NT Workstation installation, what should be the next course of action?

   A. Reinstall Windows NT Server.

   B. Select the LastKnownGood boot option.

   C. Select the VGA Mode option from the Boot menu.

   D. Hold Shift during the boot process to enable the VGA driver.

5. If your CD-ROM drive is not on the Windows NT Hardware Compatibility List, what alternative method can be used to install Windows NT? Select all that apply.

   A. Run the installation over the network using WINNT /B.

   B. Generate the three startup disks using WINNT32 /OX.

   C. Copy the installation files to a local directory and run WINNT /B from the directory.

   D. Order the 3 1/2-inch floppy installation disk set from Microsoft.

6. Which of the following systems meet the minimum hardware specifications to run Windows NT Server? Select all that apply.

   A. Pentium 100 MHz, 16 MB RAM, 100 MB free disk space

   B. 486-33 MHz, 16 MB RAM, 200 MB free disk space

   C. DEC Alpha 166MHz, 12 MB RAM, 300 MB free disk space

   D. Pentium II 233 MHz, 32 MB RAM, 500 MB free disk space

7. Which program is used to speed up the installation of client software during the deployment of computers?

   A. APPDIFF.EXE

   B. USERDIFF.EXE

   C. SYSDIFF.EXE

   D. SOFTDIFF.EXE

8. This is a scenario question. First you must review the scenario, then review the required and optional results. Following that is a solution. You must pick the best evaluation of that solution. Note that question 9 deals with the same scenario.

   Scenario:
   The Orion Organization has hired a consultant to assist with the deployment of 1,000 new computer systems, all of which will be running Windows NT 4 Workstation.

   Required Result:
   The IS Manager wants the installations to be completely automated and to be consistent between computers.

   Optional Results:
   The workstations should be installed to different resource domains based on their geographic locations, and they should have the correct time zone settings.

   All applications used in the Orion Organization should be included in the deployment process.

   Proposed Solution:
   Create an unattended script file for the installation process. Install all necessary software onto the first system using the unattended script file. Run the SYSDIFF utility to take a snapshot of all the software installed. Perform all remaining installations using the unattended script file and the SYSDIFF snapshot.

   Evaluation of Proposed Solution:
   (Choose the most correct answer.)

   A. Meets the required result and both optional results

   B. Meets the required result and only one optional result

   C. Meets only the required result

   D. Does not satisfy any required or optional results

9. This question deals with the same scenario as number 8.

   Scenario:
   The Orion Organization has hired a consultant to assist with the deployment of 1,000 new computer systems, all of which will be running Windows NT 4 Workstation.

   Required Result:
   The IS Manager wants the installations to be completely automated and to be consistent between computers.

Optional Results:
The workstations should be installed to different resource domains based on their geographic locations, and they should have the correct time zone settings.

All applications used in the Orion Organization should be included in the deployment process.

Proposed Solution:
Create an unattended script file for the installation process. Create a uniqueness database file to store the computer names, domains, and time zone settings for each computer. Install the first system using the unattended script file. Run the SYSDIFF utility using the /SNAP option to capture the current configuration of the system. Install all necessary software onto the system. Run the SYSDIFF utility using the /DIFF option to take a snapshot of all the software installed. Run the SYSDIFF utility a third time using the /INF option to create an OEM directory structure. Modify the unattended script file to include this software in the installation. Perform all remaining installations using the unattended script file and the uniqueness database file.

Evaluation of Proposed Solution:
(Choose the most correct answer.)

A. Meets the required result and both optional results

B. Meets the required result and only one optional result

C. Meets only the required result

D. Does not satisfy any required or optional results

10. When installing Windows NT onto a SCSI drive, what issue can arise that does not come into play when installing to IDE/EIDE drives?

A. Unique SCSI IDs.

B. Master/slave settings.

C. Whether the SCSI controller is BIOS-enabled.

D. There are no issues when using SCSI drives.

ANSWER KEY

1. A-C
2. A
3. A-B-D
4. C
5. A-C
6. B-D
7. C
8. D
9. A
10. A

ANSWERS & EXPLANATIONS

SOLVING INSTALLATION FAILURES

1. What can be configured for a newly created BDC to communicate with a PDC on a remote TCP/IP subnetwork? Select all that apply.

   A. WINS server IP address
   C. LMHOSTS file

1. CORRECT ANSWERS: A-C

Both WINS and LMHOSTS provide NetBIOS name resolution.

Answer B is incorrect because a DNS server would not provide NetBIOS name resolution. Answer D is incorrect because a HOSTS file does not provide NetBIOS name resolution.

For a BDC to be installed successfully, it must be able to communicate with the PDC, even if it is on a remote subnet. The NetBIOS name of the PDC must be resolved to an IP address for this to occur.

2. During Windows NT Server installation, you accidentally chose to install the computer as a member server. How do you change the role of the computer to a backup domain controller?

   A. Reinstall Windows NT Server.

2. CORRECT ANSWER: A

To change the role of an NT Server computer from member server to backup domain controller, you must reinstall the software.

Answer B is incorrect because you cannot promote a member server to a domain controller. Answer C is incorrect because there is not a Registry change available to change the server role. Answer D is incorrect because you cannot change the role of the server in the network applet.

During Windows NT Server installation, the installer is asked what role the computer will play in the network. The choices are primary domain controller, backup domain controller, and standalone server. This selection is critical because an incorrect selection generally requires reinstallation of the NT Server product into a new directory. Installing a primary domain controller requires that a unique domain name be entered. This name must be a unique NetBIOS name on the network (including computer names and other domain names). When installing a backup domain controller, make sure the domain name is entered correctly.

3. Which situation causes the installation of a backup domain controller named MARKETING in the HEAD_OFFICE domain to fail? Select all that apply.

   A. The PDC for the HEAD_OFFICE domain is not available.
   B. The MARKETING BDC does not share a common protocol with the PDC.
   D. Another computer named MARKETING already exists on the network.

3. CORRECT ANSWERS: A-B-D

The installation of a BDC will fail if the BDC cannot communicate with the PDC. Lack of a common protocol or the unavailability of the PDC can cause this. Likewise, if another computer named MARKETING exists on the network, the networking services on the BDC will fail. This also prevents communication with the PDC.

Answer C is incorrect because multiple BDCs are not required to install another BDC. Answer E is incorrect because answer C is not correct.

If you install a backup domain controller (BDC) or a stand-alone server that participates in the domain, the Windows NT Server computer requires communication with the primary domain controller (PDC). The BDC needs to communicate with the PDC at two stages of the installation:

- During the creation of the computer account for the BDC
- During the initial synchronization of the Accounts database

A member server that participates in the domain requires communication with the PDC during the creation of the computer account in the PDC's Accounts database. If the PDC is not available during installation, a member server can initially be installed as a member of a workgroup. The member server then can join a domain when the PDC is available on the network.

4. If the incorrect video driver is selected during a Windows NT Workstation installation, what should be the next course of action?

   C. Select the VGA Mode option from the Boot menu.

4. CORRECT ANSWER: C

You can choose to boot Windows NT using the /BASEVIDEO option.

Answer A is incorrect because you do not need to reinstall Windows NT to fix a video driver problem. Answer B is incorrect because the LastKnownGood option does not switch video drivers. Answer D is incorrect because holding the Shift key does not modify video drivers.

Choosing the VGA Mode option on the boot menu starts Windows NT with the `BOOT.INI /BASEVIDEO` option, which loads Windows NT using a VGA 16-color, 600 × 480 display driver. This enables you to change to the correct video driver and then to reboot the machine using the new video driver.

5. If your CD-ROM drive is not on the Windows NT Hardware Compatibility List, what alternative method can be used to install Windows NT? Select all that apply.
   A. Run the installation over the network using `WINNT_/B`.
   C. Copy the installation files to a local directory and run `WINNT_/B` from the directory.

5. CORRECT ANSWERS: A-C

Without the generation of boot disks, the installation of Windows NT can be performed from a local folder or from a network share if the CD-ROM is not on the HCL.

Answer B is incorrect because you still need the capability to access the source files. The startup disks just boot into installation mode. Answer D is incorrect because Windows NT no longer is available on disk.

Even if Windows NT does not support your CD-ROM drive, it still is possible to perform the installation. Assuming you have DOS or Windows 95 drivers for your CD-ROM, you can copy the `\i386` directory from the CD-ROM to the local hard disk. You then can run the command `winnt_ /b` from the newly created directory. The `/b` parameter installs the Windows NT boot files to the local hard disk in the directory `c:\$WIN_NT$.~bt` instead of generating the three boot disks. Windows NT also can be installed from a network share of the target computer participating in a network.

6. Which of the following systems meet the minimum hardware specifications to run Windows NT Server? Select all that apply.
   B. 486-33 MHz, 16 MB RAM, 200 MB free disk space
   D. Pentium II 233 MHz, 32 MB RAM, 500 MB free disk space

6. CORRECT ANSWERS: B-D

The only systems that meet the minimum requirements for installing Windows NT Server are the 486-33 and Pentium II systems.

Answer A is incorrect because the Pentium 100 does not meet the minimum disk space requirement. Answer C is incorrect because all RISC-based installations require 16 MB of RAM.

Windows NT supports a wide variety of hardware. As such, a variety of problems can occur with these hardware devices. Windows NT has very specific minimum hardware requirements, as you can see in the following list:

- CPU: For Intel-based systems, any 486 or higher processor is sufficient. For RISC-based systems, any supported RISC processor (MIPS 4 × 00, Alpha, PreP-compliant PPC) is sufficient.

- Video adapter: A VGA or better is required.

- Hard disk drive: A minimum of 110 MB of free space is required.

- Floppy disk drive: A 3 1/2- or 5 1/4-inch floppy drive for Intel systems is required. (It is used for setup boot disks.)

- CD-ROM drive: A supported CD-ROM drive is necessary. It can be located either on the system on which NT Server is being installed or on another computer connected by a network.

- Memory: At least 16 MB is recommended for Intel- and RISC-based systems (although 12 MB is sufficient for installation of NT Workstation on an Intel platform). The price of memory has decreased dramatically, and it significantly improves system performance. Therefore, a larger quantity is advisable (32 MB being a more reasonable minimum).

- Network adapter: Although a network adapter is not absolutely necessary, networking is not available unless a network adapter is installed.

- Pointing device: A mouse or other pointing device is not absolutely necessary, but it is highly recommended.

In addition to the minimum hardware requirements, it is essential to consider the Windows NT Hardware Compatibility List (HCL). If your system and all its installed components are on the HCL, many potential difficulties can be avoided. Before installing Windows NT, make a list of all the components on your system and the resources they use. Having this information available can greatly simplify the installation process.

Chapter 6 TROUBLESHOOTING

▼ **NOTE**

If you are unsure whether your computer's hardware is on the Windows NT HCL, you can use the Hardware Quantifier tool. This tool itemizes and identifies all hardware on your system necessary for Windows NT. The program runs from a floppy disk created by running the `MAKEDISK.BAT` batch file in the `\SUPPORT\HQTOOL` directory on the Windows NT Server CD-ROM.

7. Which program is used to speed up the installation of application software during the deployment of computers?

   C. SYSDIFF.EXE

7. CORRECT ANSWER: C

The SYSDIFF utility captures the files, the *.ini settings, and the Registry entries associated with a software installation.

The Windows NT Server CD includes a deployment application that assists with the installation of application software during unattended installations. The application is called SYSDIFF.EXE and is located in the `\support\deptools\%platform%` directory of the Windows NT Server CD-ROM.

The SYSDIFF utility is run in three phases. The first phase takes a snapshot of a computer before any applications are installed. The second phase takes a snapshot of all changed files, *.ini configuration files, and Registry entries after the applications have been installed. The final phase applies these changes to other systems that do not yet have the applications installed. The parameters of the SYSDIFF utility are as follows:

- `SYSDIFF /SNAP snapfile`: Creates the original snapfile that contains the current files, the *.ini configuration files, and the Registry settings before applications are installed.

- `SYSDIFF /DIFF snapfile diff-file`: After all applications are installed, this command creates the difference file based on the original snapfile. The file outlines what files, *.ini settings, and Registry entries have been added during the installation of the application software.

- `SYSDIFF /APPLY diff-file`: This command is used to apply the difference file to a workstation on which applications have not yet been installed.

- `SYSDIFF /INF diff-file oemroot`: This command applies the contents of a difference file to an installation directory. It generates an .inf file to perform .ini file and Registry changes contained in a SYSDIFF package. It also generates an OEM\ directory tree for file changes contained in a SYSDIFF package. This information can be incorporated into an automated installation.

8. **Proposed Solution:**
   Create an unattended script file for the installation process. Install all necessary software onto the first system using the unattended script file. Run the SYSDIFF utility to take a snapshot of all the software installed. Perform all remaining installations using the unattended script file and the SYSDIFF snapshot.

   D. Does not satisfy any required or optional results

8. CORRECT ANSWER: D

Although this solution appears to satisfy the required result, a uniqueness database file is required to do 1,000 installs. The UDF provides the unique settings required by each computer. Without the UDF, the computers would have to be renamed manually after the install is completed. In addition, the SYSDIFF procedure is performed incorrectly. The initial snapshot must be performed before the software is installed to the master template system.

9. **Proposed Solution:**
   Create an unattended script file for the installation process. Create a uniqueness database file to store the computer names, domains, and time zone settings for each computer. Install the first system using the unattended script file. Run the SYSDIFF utility using the /SNAP option to capture the current configuration of the system. Install all necessary software onto the system. Run the SYSDIFF utility using the /DIFF option to take a snapshot of all the software installed. Run the SYSDIFF utility a third time using the /INF option to create an OEM directory structure. Modify the unattended script file to include this software in the installation. Perform all remaining installations using the unattended script file and the uniqueness database file.

   A. Meets the required result and both optional results

9. CORRECT ANSWER: A

This solution meets all the business requirements. The unattended script file and the UDF file methodology meet the required results. The first optional result also is met with the UDF file. The second optional result is met with the proper use of the SYSDIFF utility.

When performing large numbers of Windows NT installations, the main areas of concern are speed and consistency. Windows NT enables you to script, or automate, installation. This provides a consistent method of performing the installations and reduces the amount of user interaction required during the installation process. Automated installation makes use of two files: an unattended script file and a uniqueness database file.

Chapter 6 TROUBLESHOOTING

The unattended script file can be configured using the SETUPMGR.EXE utility. This application is located on the Windows NT Server CD in the \support\deptools\ %platform% directory. SETUPMGR.EXE generates a text file containing all the basic information required for installation of Windows NT. The script can be configured for either Windows NT Workstation or Windows NT Server.

The uniqueness database file defines unique parameter settings for individual computers when multiple installations are performed using the same unattended script. The uniqueness database file defines which definitions are included in the file and which included sections are referenced by the definitions.

10. When installing Windows NT onto a SCSI drive, what issue can arise that does not come into play when installing to IDE/EIDE drives?

   A. Unique SCSI IDs.

10. CORRECT ANSWER: A

When installing SCSI drives, each drive must have a unique SCSI ID to be accessible. EIDE drives are configured using a master/slave relationship.

Answer B is incorrect because master/slave settings do not pertain to SCSI drives. Answer C is incorrect because the controller can be either BIOS enabled or not; Windows NT supports both. Answer D is incorrect because there are issues with SCSI drives.

Installation failure most commonly occurs because of media errors or hardware problems such as hard disk errors. Problems also can arise from unsupported CD-ROMs and network adapters. Boot sector viruses affect the master boot record and can cause problems with Windows NT. Therefore, you might want to scan each of your hard drives for viruses.

The actual boot error you receive when a boot sector virus is encountered during installation is reported as 0x4000. This error message occurs after the first reboot during an installation. To fix this error, you can boot using a write-protected disk with antivirus software loaded. Another method is to run the command fdisk /mbr after booting into DOS. This command rewrites the master boot record for the hard disk.

If you are using small computer system interface (SCSI) drives, make sure your SCSI chain is properly terminated. The BIOS on the boot SCSI adapter should be enabled, and the BIOS on all other SCSI adapters should be disabled. All SCSI devices should have unique SCSI IDs.

For enhanced integrated drive electronics (EIDE) drives, make sure the system drive is on the first controller on the motherboard. In addition, the file I/O and disk access should be set to standard.

For IDE/EIDE or EDSI drives, the controller should be functional before installing Windows NT. If the disk lights come on briefly upon starting the computer, you know the controller is working. You also will hear the disk start up. If the drives are larger than 1,024 cylinders, make sure Windows NT supports the disk configuration utility you are using. Finally, the jumpers should be set correctly for master or slave drives.

FURTHER REVIEW

SOLVING INSTALLATION FAILURES

The following key words are important terms that were covered in this section. You should make sure you understand each one and what it does.

Key Words

Enhanced integrated drive electronics (EIDE)
Hardware Compatibility List (HCL)
Hardware Quantifier tool
NetBIOS name
Small computer system interface (SCSI)
SYSDIFF

PRACTICE QUESTIONS

SOLVING BOOT FAILURES

1. Which files are located in the root directory of C: on a Windows NT Intel system? Select all that apply.

   A. SYSTEM.INI

   B. NTLDR

   C. BOOT.INI

   D. NTOS2.EXE

2. Which Registry subkey is used to determine the order in which device drivers and services are started?

   A. HKEY_CURRENT_USER\Software\Microsoft\Windows NT

   B. HKEY_LOCAL_MACHINE\Software\Microsoft\Windows NT

   C. HKEY_LOCAL_MACHINE\System\CurrentControlSet\Control\ServiceGroupOrder

   D. HKEY_LOCAL_MACHINE\System\CurrentControlSet\Services\ServiceGroupOrder

3. When is the Last Known Good configuration saved?

   A. When control is passed to the NTOSKRNL

   B. When the kernel has completed initialization

   C. When the user successfully logs on to the computer

   D. When the Control + Alt + Delete to Logon dialog box appears

4. If Windows NT was installed on the second partition of the slave disk in a directory named WINNT, the ARC name in the BOOT.INI for this installation would be which of the following?

   A. SCSI(0)disk(1)rdisk(0)partition(1)\WINNT

   B. MULTI(0)disk(1)rdisk(0)partition(1)\WINNT

   C. SCSI(0)disk(0)rdisk(2)partition(2)\WINNT

   D. MULTI(0)disk(0)rdisk(1)partition(2)\WINNT

5. Your system encounters frequent STOP errors resulting in a blue screen on the computer. What settings can be added to BOOT.INI to assist in debugging the problem? Select all that apply.

   A. /SOS

   B. /DEBUG

   C. /ENABLEDEBUG

   D. /BAUDRATE

292 Chapter 6 TROUBLESHOOTING

6. **When creating a boot disk for a RISC-based system, what files must be included on the boot disk? Select all that apply.**

   A. `NTLDR`

   B. `OSLOADER.EXE`

   C. `HAL.DLL`

   D. `BOOT.INI`

7. **After adding a new network adapter to your Windows NT Workstation computer, the computer suffers a blue screen STOP error when restarting. To repair this problem, you have to do which of the following? Select the best answer.**

   A. Use a Windows NT boot disk and remove the adapter using the Network applet in the Control Panel.

   B. Perform an emergency repair process.

   C. Use the Last Known Good configuration.

   D. Reinstall Windows NT Workstation.

8. **To create the three startup disks for Windows NT, which command do you use?**

   A. `WINNT /B`

   B. `WINNT /O`

   C. `WINNT /OX`

   D. `RDISK /S`

9. **To back up the entire Registry to the Emergency Repair Disk, which command do you use?**

   A. `REGBACK.EXE`

   B. `RDISK`

   C. `RDISK /E`

   D. `RDISK /S`

10. **After performing an emergency repair process, all the user accounts in the domain have been lost. This most likely is due to which of the following? Select the best answer.**

    A. Somebody has deleted all the accounts.

    B. The SAM database was restored.

    C. The Registry is still corrupt.

    D. The emergency repair process always removes all user accounts from the domain.

ANSWER KEY

1. B-C
2. C
3. C
4. D
5. B-D
6. B-C
7. C
8. C
9. D
10. B

ANSWERS & EXPLANATIONS

SOLVING BOOT FAILURES

1. **Which files are located in the root directory of C: on a Windows NT Intel system? Select all that apply.**

   B. NTLDR

   C. BOOT.INI

1. CORRECT ANSWERS: B-C

Remember that the Windows NT boot partition is where the operating system is located.

Answer A is incorrect because the SYSTEM.INI is not located in the root directory. Answer D is incorrect because NTOS2.EXE is not a valid file.

The Windows NT boot process involves several files working together to start the Windows NT operating system. On Intel and RISC platforms, the initialization files initially are platform specific but then are common during the later stages of the boot process. The platform-specific files required for the startup of an Intel-platform Windows NT system are as follows:

- **NTLDR**: The NTLDR file loads the Windows NT operating system. It is located in the root directory of the C: drive.

- **BOOT.INI**: This text file contains the entries for the Operating System Selection menu that appears during the startup of the computer. It is located in the root directory of the C: drive.

- **BOOTSEC.DOS**: This file contains the boot sector of the hard disk that existed before Windows NT was installed. It is machine specific and should not be copied between systems. It is loaded by NTLDER if an operating system other than Windows NT is selected during the boot process. It is located in the root directory of the C: drive.

- **NTDETECT.COM**: This file examines the available hardware on the system and builds the hardware list that will be contained in the HKEY_LOCAL_MACHINE\ Hardware key of the Registry. It is located in the root directory of the C: drive.

294 Chapter 6 TROUBLESHOOTING

- NTBOOTDD.SYS: This driver is used by Windows NT systems that have a non-BIOS–enabled SCSI adapter. This driver is used to access devices attached to the adapter. It is located in the root directory of the C: drive. It is not required for BIOS-enabled SCSI adapters.

2. Which Registry subkey is used to determine the order in which device drivers and services are started?

   C. HKEY_LOCAL_MACHINE\System\
   CurrentControlSet\Control\
   ServiceGroupOrder

2. CORRECT ANSWER: C

The List value is found in HKEY_LOCAL_MACHINE\System\CurrentControlSet\Control\ServiceGroupOrder. It sets the order for starting services.

The kernel load phase is the actual loading of NTOSKRNL.EXE. The HAL is loaded after the kernel to mask differences in the underlying hardware. Finally, the SYSTEM hive is loaded and scanned again. This time, it is scanned for device drivers and services configured to a system startup type. The drivers and services are loaded into memory but are not initialized. They are loaded in the order set by the ServiceGroupOrder subkey found in the Registry:

```
HKEY_LOCAL_MACHINE\System\CurrentControlSet\Control\
ServicesGroupOrder
```

3. When is the Last Known Good configuration saved?

   C. When the user successfully logs on to the computer

3. CORRECT ANSWER: C

The Last Known Good configuration is saved after a user successfully logs on to the system.

Answer A is incorrect because the configuration is not saved when control is passed to the NTOSKRNL. Answer B is incorrect because the configuration is not saved when the kernel is initialized. Answer D is incorrect because the configuration is not saved when the logon box appears.

When the Win32 subsystem starts, the WINLOGON.EXE process is started. The WINLOGON.EXE process calls the local security authority that displays the Press Control + Alt + Delete logon dialog box.

The service controller makes a final pass through the SYSTEM hive, looking for services configured to start automatically. The services are loaded based on their configured dependencies. The Last Known Good configuration is not saved until the user successfully logs on to the system.

4. If Windows NT was installed on the second partition of the slave disk in a directory named WINNT, the ARC name in the BOOT.INI for this installation would be which of the following?

D. MULTI(0)disk(0)rdisk(1)
   partition(2)\WINNT

4. CORRECT ANSWER: D

Because Windows NT was installed to a slave disk, the disk is not a SCSI disk. Therefore, the first parameter in the ARC name must be MULTI. Remember that partitions start numbering at 2; therefore, answer D is correct in referring to the second partition as partition(2).

The BOOT.INI file makes use of Advanced RISC Computing (ARC) names to represent the locations of installed operating systems on a computer. A typical ARC name is as follows:

```
multi(0)disk(0)rdisk(1)partition(1)
```

The ARC name components can be described as follows:

- MULTI/SCSI: This component identifies the hardware adapter/disk controller that is controlling the disk on which the operating system is installed. SCSI is used as the first parameter only if the adapter is a SCSI adapter with BIOS disabled. All other controllers (including SCSI controllers with BIOS enabled) use the designation MULTI.

▼ NOTE

The MULTI() syntax indicates to Windows NT that it should rely on the system BIOS to load system files. This means that NTLDR, the boot loader for x86-based computers, will be using interrupt (INT) 13 BIOS calls to find and load NTOSKRNL.EXE and any other files it needs to get the system running. The SCSI() syntax indicates that Windows NT needs to load a SCSI device driver and to use that driver to access the boot partition.

- DISK: The SCSI bus number (or ID) of the disk. If the first parameter is MULTI, the value is set to 0.

- RDISK: The ordinal number of the disk. If the disk is a SCSI disk (controlled by a BIOS-enabled SCSI controller), it is the SCSI ID of the disk.

- PARTITION: The ordinal number of the partition on which the operating system is installed.

5. Your system encounters frequent STOP errors resulting in a blue screen on the computer. What settings can be added to BOOT.INI to assist in debugging the problem? Select all that apply.

   B. /DEBUG
   D. /BAUDRATE

5. CORRECT ANSWERS: B-D

To enable debugging on a Windows NT system, you need to add /DEBUG, /BAUDRATE, and /DEBUGPORT to an ARC name in the BOOT.INI.

Answer A is incorrect because /SOS is not a debugging setting. Answer C is incorrect because this is not a valid setting.

Within BOOT.INI, a series of options can be added to entries for troubleshooting and debugging purposes. The following switch options can be appended to the multiline in the BOOT.INI file:

- /SOS: Displays kernel and driver names during system startup. If you suspect a driver is missing or corrupted, append the /SOS switch to the BOOT.INI line that loads Windows NT.

- /MAXMEM:##: Enables you to specify the quantity of memory Windows NT will use. If you suspect a problem with a faulty memory chip, for example, this option enables you to boot your system using less than the total quantity of available RAM. A value of less than 12 MB should never be specified because Windows NT Workstation requires at lest 12 MB for normal operation. (NT Server requires 16 MB.) If you want to limit the amount of memory to 16 MB, enter the parameter as /MAXMEM:16.

- /BASEVIDEO: Forces Windows NT to use the standard VGA display driver. If your display no longer appears correctly or if a driver upgrade has made your display unreadable, this option can be added to BOOT.INI.

- /DEBUG: Tells NT to load the kernel debugger during boot and to keep it in memory.

- /CRASHDEBUG: This is similar to the /DEBUG option, except the debugging code is available only if the system crashes. In most cases, this is a better option because the debugger code will not be in memory and, therefore, won't interfere with the problem.

- /DEBUGPORT: Indicates the communications port you use.
- /BAUDRATE: Selects the baud rate for the connection you use for debugging.
- /NOSERIALMICE: This parameter disables NTDETECT from looking for serial mice on the designated serial port. This often is used when a UPS is connected to a COM port. The technique that NTDETECT.COM uses can cause many UPSs to think a power failure has occurred. The setting /NOSERIALMICE:COM1 indicates not to detect serial mice on COM1. If no COM port is indicated, no COM ports are searched for serial mice.

6. **When creating a boot disk for a RISC-based system, what files must be included on the boot disk? Select all that apply.**

   B. OSLOADER.EXE
   C. HAL.DLL

6. CORRECT ANSWERS: B-C

The boot disk for a RISC system requires the OSLOADER.EXE, HAL.DLL, and *.pal files. The *.pal files are required only on an Alpha system.

Answer A is incorrect because NTLDR does not need to be included on a RISC boot disk. Answer D is incorrect because a boot disk does not require a BOOT.INI.

A boot disk can be created for a Windows NT system. This disk enables you to reboot your system if the startup files located in the system partition are damaged or missing. The procedure to create a boot disk is quite straightforward, as follows:

- Format the disk from within Windows NT. This is required because the boot sector must look for the NTLDR file, not the IO.SYS file as under DOS or Windows 95.
- For Intel systems: Using My Computer, Windows NT Explorer, or a command prompt, copy the following files to the disk: NTLDR, BOOT.INI, NTDETECT.COM, and possibly NTBOOTDD.SYS (if you are using a non-BIOS–enabled SCSI controller).

- For RISC systems: Copy the following files to the newly formatted disk: OSLOADER.EXE, HAL.DLL, and *.pal (for Alpha systems only). Note that, for RISC systems, a few more steps are required. To boot from a disk, you have to add an alternate boot selection in your system firmware. Refer to your system's documentation for information about how to add a boot selection.

7. After adding a new network adapter to your Windows NT Workstation computer, the computer suffers a blue screen STOP error when restarting. To repair this problem, you have to do which of the following? Select the best answer.

   C. Use the Last Known Good configuration.

7. CORRECT ANSWER: C

When the computer prompts you to press the spacebar for the Last Known Good configuration, do so. Also remember to press L to select the Last Known Good configuration.

Answer A is incorrect because you cannot access the Network applet using a boot disk. Answer B is incorrect because you do not need to perform an emergency repair. Answer D is incorrect because you do not need to reinstall Windows NT.

The LastKnownGood option can be used during the boot process to select the prior successful boot configuration. Basically, the LastKnownGood option enables you to boot your system using the Registry settings in effect the last time you successfully booted your system and logged on. If your system configuration has changed and you no longer are able to boot your computer, this option reverts your configuration to the settings in effect the last time you successfully booted your computer.

It should be noted that the Last Known Good configuration is available to users only when they have successfully logged on to the system. To use the LastKnownGood option, press the spacebar when prompted during the Windows NT boot sequence. You will be presented with a screen informing you that the LastKnownGood option can be used. Press the L key to use the Last Known Good configuration.

8. To create the three startup disks for Windows NT, which command do you use?

C. WINNT /OX

8. CORRECT ANSWER: C

The command WINNT /OX generates the three startup disks for Windows NT. They are used to install Windows NT from CD and to perform emergency repairs. You would use WINNT32 on a Windows NT system.

Answer A is incorrect because you would not use the /B switch. Answer B is incorrect because you would not use the /O switch. Answer D is incorrect because the RDISK /S command is used to create a repair disk with Registry information.

For Intel-based systems, place the Windows NT CD-ROM into a system running Windows NT or any other operating system and then locate either WINNT.EXE or WINNT32.EXE. (WINNT is for 16-bit operating systems and Windows 95; WINNT32 is for 32-bit operating systems.) Execute the appropriate file using the /OX command-line parameter. You are prompted to insert startup disks 3, 2, and then 1. These disks can be used to install the operating system or to perform an emergency repair process. RISC-based systems, unlike Intel systems, do not require startup disks. Instead, the firmware is used to provide a series of boot options.

9. To back up the entire Registry to the Emergency Repair Disk, which command do you use?

D. RDISK /S

9. CORRECT ANSWER: D

The parameter /S, when included with the RDISK command, also backs up the SECURITY and SAM hives that normally are not backed up.

Answer A is incorrect because REGBACK.EXE is not a valid command. Answer B is incorrect because the RDISK command, by itself, will not back up the entire Registry. Answer C is incorrect because RDISK /E is the wrong switch.

The Emergency Repair Disk is created during the actual installation of the Windows NT operating system. It should be updated whenever changes are made to the computer. The application file for creating and updating the emergency repair disk is RDISK.EXE. This executable file starts the repair disk utility.

Update Repair Info updates the data files stored in the `%SystemRoot%\System32\Config` directory. If no Emergency Repair Disk is provided during an emergency repair process, the information in this directory is used.

By default, the `SECURITY` and `SAM` hives are not updated when updating the repair information. If you want this information to be updated, you must run `RDISK /S`.

Create Repair Disk is used for the initial creation of a recovery disk, and it requires a blank floppy disk. Note that the disk need not be formatted (or even blank) because RDISK formats the disk.

A recovery disk contains copies of a Windows NT system's configuration files. Thus, a recovery disk created for one specific computer cannot be used on a different computer. In addition, recovery disks should be updated whenever your system configuration changes. The recovery disk contains the following files:

- `SETUP.LOG`: A log of files installed and the cyclic redundancy check (CRC) checksums for each file. This file is Read Only, Hidden, and System.

- `SYSTEM._`: The contents of the `HKEY_LOCAL_MACHINE\SYSTEM` Registry key in compressed format.

- `SOFTWARE._`: The contents of the `HKEY_LOCAL_MACHINE\SOFTWARE` Registry key in compressed format.

- `SECURITY._`: The contents of the `HKEY_LOCAL_MACHINE\SECURITY` Registry key in compressed format.

- `SAM._`: The contents of the `HKEY_LOCAL_MACHINE\SAM` Registry key in compressed format.

- `DEFAULT._`: The contents of the `HKEY_LOCAL_MACHINE\DEFAULT` Registry key in compressed format.

- `NTUSER.DA_`: The contents of `%systemroot%\Profiles\Default User\Ntuser.day` in compressed format.

- `AUTOEXEC.NT`: A copy of `%systemroot%\System32\Autoexec.nt` (a configuration file for the MS-DOS environment under Windows NT).

- `CONFIG.NT`: A copy of `%systemroot%\System32\Config.nt` (a configuration file for the MS-DOS environment under Windows NT).

10. After performing an emergency repair process, all the user accounts in the domain have been lost. This most likely is due to which of the following? Select the best answer.

    B. The SAM database was restored.

10. CORRECT ANSWER: B

If all Registry files are recovered, the SAM will be restored to its initial state from installation. The SAM now must be either re-created or restored from backup. If RDISK /S has been run, the accounts created until that point in time are restored.

Answer A is incorrect because nobody has deleted the accounts. Answer C is incorrect because the Registry is not corrupt. Answer D is incorrect because the emergency repair process does not usually remove all user accounts.

The following options apply to standard emergency repair on an Intel-based machine. These options, however, are similar to the options for other systems. Insert the Windows NT Server Disk 1 and boot the computer. When prompted, insert Disk 2 and proceed. At the next prompt, select R to begin the recovery process. The following four options are presented:

- Inspect Registry Files
- Inspect Startup Environment
- Verify Windows NT System Files
- Inspect Boot Sector

All four tasks are selected by default, but tasks can be deselected as required. Note that to select or deselect items, you must use the cursor keys because no mouse driver is loaded at this point. These four tasks perform the following operations:

- Inspect Registry Files: This option can be used to repair Registry keys. When this option is selected, you are provided with a list of Registry files it can restore. A warning also is shown, indicating that information can be lost. Proceed until you are prompted with a list of information that can be restored. Select the Registry keys you want to restore and then click Continue.

- Inspect Startup Environment: This option verifies that the Windows NT files in the system partition are not missing or corrupted. If required, Repair will replace them with files from the Windows NT Server CD. On Intel-based systems, Repair ensures that Windows NT is listed in BOOT.INI. If this is not the case (or if BOOT.INI is missing), Repair changes or creates it as required. On RISC-based systems, startup information in NVRAM is inspected and repaired if required.

- Verify Windows NT System Files: This option verifies that the Windows NT system files are not corrupt or missing. The file SETUP.LOG on the recovery disk contains a list of every file installed. It also has a cyclic redundancy check (CRC) checksum for every file. The checksums are computed for each file present on the system and are compared with SETUP.LOG. If the checksums do not match, the repair process asks whether it should place the files from the Windows NT Server CD. If you have applied service packs to your system, these might need to be reinstalled after the repair process is completed.

- Inspect Boot Sector: On Intel systems, this option verifies that the boot sector on the system partition is configured to load NTLDR on startup. If this is not the case, the boot sector will be repaired. This part of the recovery process is not required for RISC systems. After the entire process has been completed, your system is configured as a bootable system, and all errors encountered are repaired.

FURTHER REVIEW

SOLVING BOOT FAILURES

The following key words are important terms that were covered in this section. You should make sure you understand each one and what it does.

Key Words

BOOT.INI
LastKnownGood option
RDISK
SETUP.LOG

PRACTICE QUESTIONS

SOLVING CONFIGURATION AND REGISTRY FAILURES

1. What information is stored in the Registry? Select all that apply.

   A. Programs

   B. Configuration information

   C. Hardware detected during the startup process

   D. Only application information

2. What is the organization of the Registry?

   A. Keys, values

   B. Keys, text, values

   C. Values

   D. Keys, subkeys, values

3. Which Windows NT Resource Kit file can be used to research an unknown Registry entry?

   A. SERVERGUIDE.HLP

   B. GUIDE.TXT

   C. RESGUIDE.HLP

   D. REGENTRY.HLP

4. Using REGEDT32.EXE, where do you look to determine which subkey contains the Last Known Good configuration?

   A. The LastKnownGood subkey in the HKEY_LOCAL_MACHINE subtree.

   B. The LastKnownGood value located in HKEY_LOCAL_MACHINE\ Select.

   C. The LastKnownGood value located in HKEY_LOCAL_MACHINE\System\CurrentControlSet.

   D. The LastKnownGood value located in HKEY_LOCAL_MACHINE\System\Select.

5. Which editing tool can be used to edit the Registry?

   A. Notepad

   B. CONFIGREG

   C. REGEDT32

   D. SysEdit

6. Which of the following data types can be used in the Registry? Select all that apply.

   A. REG_HEX

   B. REG_BYTE

   C. REG_BINARY

   D. REG_SZ

7. The text string values in the Registry are stored as which type?

   A. REG_SZ

   B. REG_TEXT

   C. REG_WORD

   D. REG_EXPAND

8. On the Intel platform, the information collected by NTDETECT.COM during the startup process is stored in which key of the HKEY_LOCAL_MACHINE **subtree?**

   A. SAM

   B. SOFTWARE

   C. HARDWARE

   D. SECURITY

9. **What does RDISK /S do?**

   A. Copies only selected Registry keys

   B. Copies boot files but not Registry files

   C. It is not a valid program

   D. Makes a complete copy of the Registry, including SAM and SECURITY

10. **From within REGEDT32, which of the following is true?**

    A. You can save the entire Registry.

    B. You cannot save or restore the entire Registry.

    C. You can save only selected keys.

    D. You cannot save the information.

ANSWER KEY

1. B-C
2. D
3. D
4. D
5. C
6. C-D
7. A
8. C
9. D
10. B

ANSWERS & EXPLANATIONS
SOLVING CONFIGURATION AND REGISTRY FAILURES

1. What information is stored in the Registry? Select all that apply.
   - B. Configuration information
   - C. Hardware detected during the startup process

1. CORRECT ANSWERS: B-C

The Registry contains information about hardware detected during startup as well as configuration information for installed devices, services, and applications.

Answer A is incorrect because programs are not stored in the Registry. Answer D is incorrect because the Registry contains more than just application information.

The Registry stores most of the configuration information for Windows NT. It is organized as a series of keys, subkeys, and values. A file system is similar in organization: a file is stored with a filename consisting of a drive letter, a directory, and a filename (`C:\USERS\ MYFILE.TXT`), and the file can contain data. In much the same way, the Registry stores information as a key, subkey, and value (`HKEY_LOCAL_MACHINE\MySubkey\MyValue`).

2. What is the organization of the Registry?
   - D. Keys, subkeys, values

2. CORRECT ANSWER: D

The Registry is organized into keys, subkeys, and values contained in the subkeys.

Answer A is incorrect because subkeys also are part of the Registry's organization. Answer B is incorrect because text is not part of the Registry's organization. Answer C is incorrect because the Registry contains keys and subkeys in addition to values.

The Registry is organized in a hierarchical fashion with keys being the top level. Subkeys are specific areas within the keys, and values are information contained within each subkey.

3. Which Windows NT Resource Kit file can be used to research an unknown Registry entry?
   - D. REGENTRY.HLP

3. CORRECT ANSWER: D

The Windows NT Resource Kit contains a help file named `REGENTRY.HLP` that holds all Registry entries, data types, and default values.

Answers A, B, and C are not valid filenames.

The REGENTRY.HLP file lists all available Registry information. This file can be extremely useful for finding specific values to enter that are not part of the default Registry, such as the DontDisplayLastLogon entry. This entry stops Windows NT from displaying the last logon name used to log on to a system.

4. Using REGEDT32.EXE, where do you look to determine which subkey contains the Last Known Good configuration?

　D. The LastKnownGood value located in HKEY_LOCAL_MACHINE\System\Select.

4. CORRECT ANSWER: D

Answers A, B, and C are incorrect Registry values for the Last Known Good configuration information.

The LastKnownGood value stored in the HKEY_LOCAL_MACHINE\System\Select subkey has a REG_DWORD data type that contains a number. If the number is 2, HKEY_LOCAL_MACHINE\System\Current ControlSet002 contains the Last Known Good configuration information.

5. Which editing tool can be used to edit the Registry?

　C. REGEDT32

5. CORRECT ANSWER: C

You can use the REGEDT32 program to edit the Registry.

Answer A is incorrect because you cannot edit the Registry with Notepad. Answer B is incorrect because CONFIGREG is not a valid program name. Answer D is incorrect because SysEdit is not a valid program name.

The Registry can be viewed using REGEDT32, a tool provided with Windows NT. This tool provides a graphical interface to examine and modify Registry information on either local or remote computers. All information in the Registry can be edited using this tool. Much of the key information, however, also can be changed using standard administrative tools such as the Control Panel. It is preferable to use standard tools to modify the Registry; this reduces the likelihood of accidental changes or deletions. The mostly used common standard tools are the applets in the Control Panel.

Whenever possible, use administrative tools such as the Control Panel and the System Policy Editor to make configuration changes rather than editing the Registry. It is safer to use administrative tools because they are designed to store values properly in the Registry. You are not warned if you make errors while changing values with a Registry editor. Registry-editing applications do not recognize and cannot correct errors in syntax or other semantics.

▼ **NOTE**

Note that REGEDIT also can be used to edit Registry files. REGEDIT has better search capabilities than REGEDT32 but cannot edit all value types. In addition, you cannot set security permissions on the Registry using the `REGEDIT` command.

6. Which of the following data types can be used in the Registry? Select all that apply.
   C. REG_BINARY
   D. REG_SZ

6. CORRECT ANSWERS: C-D

`REG_BINARY` and `REG_SZ` are recognized data types in the Windows NT Registry.

Answer A is incorrect because `REG_HEX` is not a valid data type. Answer B is incorrect because `REG_BYTE` is not a valid data type.

Each value in the Registry stores data as a specific value type. Some value types, however, can be used only for certain types of data. The value types used in Windows NT are as follows:

- `REG_BINARY`: Binary information, entered either as a sequence of binary digits or as hexadecimal digits.
- `REG_SZ`: A string value (human-readable text).
- `REG_EXPAND_SZ`: A string value that also contains a variable, such as `%SystemRoot%`.
- `REG_DWORD`: A four-byte hexadecimal value.
- `REG_MULTI_SZ`: A large string value (multiple lines of text, such as a list of configured IP addresses).

Values can be added anywhere in the Registry by selecting the desired key and then selecting Edit, Add Value from the REGEDT32 menu. You then are asked for the name of the new value, its data type, and the data itself.

ANSWERS & EXPLANATIONS

Existing Registry values can be modified by double-clicking the desired value in its Registry key. Depending on the value type of the selected value, you are presented with an appropriate editor. After the desired modifications have been completed, click OK to save the new value.

7. The text string values in the Registry are stored as which type?

  A. REG_SZ

7. CORRECT ANSWER: A

String values in the Registry are stored in the REG_SZ data type.

Answers B, C, and D are invalid string values.

See the explanation of Registry string values after question 6.

8. On the Intel platform, the information collected by NTDETECT.COM during the startup process is stored in which key of the HKEY_LOCAL_MACHINE subtree?

  C. HARDWARE

8. CORRECT ANSWER: C

The information collected by NTDETECT is stored in the HARDWARE subkey. This information is volatile and is rebuilt every time Windows NT is restarted.

Answers A, B, and D are the wrong Registry subkeys.

NTDETECT stores information in the HARDWARE Registry subkey of the HKEY_LOCAL_MACHINE key every time Windows NT is started.

9. What does RDISK /S do?

  D. Makes a complete copy of the Registry, including SAM and SECURITY.

9. CORRECT ANSWER: D

Running RDISK with the /S parameter backs up the entire Registry to the %SystemRoot%\Repair directory. It also includes updated copies of the SAM and SECURITY hives.

Answer A is incorrect because RDISK /S does not copy only selected Registry keys. Answer B is incorrect because RDISK /S does not copy only boot files. Answer C is incorrect because RDISK /S is a valid program.

One way to back up the Registry is to use the RDISK utility. The RDISK utility saves the current configuration to the %SystemRoot\Repair directory, and it can be used by the emergency repair process. The RDISK utility saves all information except the SAM and SECURITY hives. If you want to save the complete Registry using RDISK, you must run RDISK /S.

This also creates a backup, compressed version of the Registry that includes updated versions of the SAM and SECURITY hives.

The Windows NT Resource Kit includes the REGBACK and REGREST utilities, which also can be used to back up and restore the Registry. These utilities enable you to back up the entire Registry to a specified directory. A separate file is created for each hive of the Registry.

A final method to back up the Registry is to use the Windows NT Backup program. If you select the Backup Local Registry option and at least one file on the Windows NT boot partition, Windows NT Backup also can back up the local Registry. If you are running NTBACKUP from a batch file, you must include the /B option to back up the local Registry. Remember, you must include at least a single file from the boot partition of Windows NT to back up the Registry.

▼ **NOTE**

The Backup Local Registry option cannot be used to back up remote Registries. NT Backup only can back up the local Registry.

10. From within REGEDT32, which of the following is true?

   B. You cannot save or restore the entire Registry.

10. CORRECT ANSWER: B

You cannot restore or save the entire Registry using the REGEDT32 utility because a portion of the Registry always is open when operating Windows NT.

Answer A is incorrect because you cannot save the entire Registry. Answer C is incorrect because you cannot save selected keys. Answer D is incorrect because you can save some of the Registry information.

The REGEDT32 tool can be used to back up the Registries of other computers in the domain as well. In REGEDT32, select Save from the Registry menu. You are prompted to enter a filename. This procedure creates a binary file containing the selected Registry information.

Select Restore from the Registry menu to restore this information at a later time. You are prompted to select a file to be restored. Note that, because the Registry is open when Windows NT is running, you cannot restore the entire Registry from within REGEDT32. This is because some of the keys currently are opened by the operating system. After a file has been selected, a warning message displays before the Registry values are restored.

FURTHER REVIEW

SOLVING CONFIGURATION AND REGISTRY FAILURES

The following key words are important terms that were covered in this section. You should make sure you understand each one and what it does.

Key Words

Hive
NT Backup
RDISK
REGEDIT
REGEDT32

PRACTICE QUESTIONS

SOLVING PRINTER PROBLEMS

1. Which service must be installed to enable a UNIX system to print to a Windows NT printer?

   A. TCP/IP

   B. Simple TCP/IP services

   C. SNMP Service

   D. TCP/IP Print service

2. If a job in the printer will not print and cannot be deleted, how can you remove this job from the printer?

   A. Delete all files in the %System Root%\System32\spool\PRINTERS directory.

   B. Log on as Administrator and delete the job. The Administrator account has the right to delete stuck jobs.

   C. Ignore the job. After the configured timeout period has passed, the job removes itself from the queue.

   D. Stop and start the Spooler service.

3. Windows NT Server supports the automatic downloading of which client print drivers on the same print server? Select all that apply.

   A. MIPS

   B. PowerPC

   C. Intel

   D. None of the above

4. What is the main difference in the printing process between when a Windows 3.x client prints to a Windows NT print share and when a Windows NT client prints to a Windows NT print share?

   A. There is no difference.

   B. Windows 3.x clients cannot print to a Windows NT print share.

   C. Windows 3.x clients only can submit text jobs.

   D. Windows 3.x clients fully process their jobs before submitting them to a Windows NT print share.

5. You have installed the TCP/IP Print service on your print server and have restarted the print server, yet UNIX clients cannot print to any of the print shares. Which of the following could be the reason for this?

   A. Windows NT does not support printing for UNIX clients.

   B. The SNMP Service also must be installed.

   C. The TCP/IP Print service is set to be started manually. It should be switched to start automatically.

   D. The UNIX clients must first capture the print port.

6. **What must be installed to enable Macintosh clients to print to a Windows NT printer?**

    A. TCP/IP Print Server service

    B. Services for Macintosh

    C. Mac Print Services

    D. AppleTalk protocol

7. This is a scenario question. First you must review the scenario, then review the required and optional results. Following that is a solution. You must pick the best evaluation of that solution. Note that question 8 also deals with the same scenario.

    Scenario:
    The Xavier group has offices in Boston, Montreal, and Seattle. Each office has its own domain, with the Boston domain functioning as the master domain in a Master Domain Model. Global groups have been created to represent the Boston users, the Montreal users, and the Seattle users. The resource domains each have their own printer resources that are shared throughout the entire enterprise.

    Required Result:
    The Systems group comprised of Bob, Mary, and Jane should be the only group with Full Control on all printers in the enterprise.

    Optional Results:
    The Xavier group wants all print servers to be capable of hosting jobs sent by UNIX computers.

    The Xavier group wants to provide printing support to all Macintosh clients in the enterprise.

    Proposed Solution:
    When a printer is installed, change the permissions on each print share to assign Bob, Mary, and Jane to manage all documents for the printer. Be sure to install the TCP/IP and AppleTalk Protocols on each print server. This enables print support for UNIX and Macintosh clients.

    Evaluation of Proposed Solution:
    (Choose the most correct answer.)

    A. Meets the required result and both optional results

    B. Meets the required result and only one optional result

    C. Meets only the required result

    D. Does not satisfy any required or optional results

8. **This question deals with the same scenario as number 7.**

    Scenario:
    The Xavier group has offices in Boston, Montreal, and Seattle. Each office has its own domain, with the Boston domain functioning as the master domain in a Master Domain Model. Global groups have been created to represent the Boston users, the Montreal users, and the Seattle users. The resource domains each have their own printer resources that are shared throughout the entire enterprise.

    Required Result:
    The Systems group comprised of Bob, Mary, and Jane should be the only users with Full Control on all printers in the enterprise.

    Optional Results:
    The Xavier group wants all print servers to be capable of hosting jobs sent by UNIX computers.

    The Xavier group wants to provide printing support to all Macintosh clients in the enterprise.

Proposed Solution:
In each domain, add the user accounts for Bob, Mary, and Jane to the Print Operators local group. At each print server, install the TCP/IP protocol and the SNMP Service. Also add the services for Macintosh service.

Evaluation of Proposed Solution:
(Choose the most correct answer.)

   A. Meets the required result and both optional result

   B. Meets the required result and only one optional result

   C. Meets only the required result

   D. Does not satisfy any required or optional results

9. You have updated the HP LaserJet 4 print driver on your print server for Windows 95 to enable duplex printing. Your Windows 95 clients are not able to take advantage of this new option. What is the problem?

   A. Windows 95 clients do not support duplex printing.

   B. You must load Windows 95 print drivers at the client systems.

   C. You must restart the Windows 95 system for the changes to take effect.

   D. You must delete and then reconnect to the existing printer to download the newer version of the driver.

10. If a physical printing device has broken down, and the printer that was sending jobs to the printing device still has jobs in its queue, how do you redirect the jobs to a similar printing device?

    A. You cannot redirect jobs.

    B. Have the users recall their jobs and readdress them to a different printer.

    C. Add a new local port to the printer using the UNC name of a printer that prints to a similar printing device.

    D. Use the Redirect option in the printer's property pages.

ANSWER KEY

1. D
2. D
3. A-B-C
4. D
5. C
6. B
7. D
8. B
9. D
10. C

ANSWERS & EXPLANATIONS

SOLVING PRINTER PROBLEMS

1. Which service must be installed to enable a UNIX system to print to a Windows NT printer?

    D. TCP/IP Printing service

1. CORRECT ANSWER: D

The TCP/IP Printing service enables a UNIX system to print to a Windows NT printer. After installation, it is referred to as the TCP/IP Print Server service in the list of installed services.

Answer A is incorrect because TCP/IP is a protocol, not a service. Answer B is incorrect because Simple TCP/IP services are not installed to enable TCP/IP printing. Answer C is incorrect because the SNMP Service is for network management not TCP/IP printing.

Windows NT includes an LPD service (the Microsoft TCP/IP Print Server service) that can accept print jobs from UNIX clients using Line Printer Remote (LPR) clients. Windows NT clients also can use the LPR command when they have installed the TCP/IP Print Server service. The syntax of the LPR command is as follows:

```
lpr -S{server} -P{printer} -J{job} -C{class} -o {option} -x -d {filename}
```

▼ NOTE

The options -S and -P are case sensitive. They must be uppercased.

Another command included with the TCP/IP Print Server service is the LPQ command, which can display the queue information for an LPD Print Server. The syntax of the LPQ command is

```
<C1>lpq -S{server} -P{printer}
```

2. If a job in the printer will not print and cannot be deleted, how can you remove this job from the printer?

    D. Stop and start the Spooler service.

2. CORRECT ANSWER: D

Stopping and starting the Spooler service flushes all jobs from the printer.

Answer A is incorrect because you do not delete files to reset a print queue. Answer B is incorrect because, if a job is hung, it doesn't matter who you are logged on as. Answer C is incorrect because the job will not clear on its own.

If a print job is hung and cannot be deleted, stopping and starting the Spooler service from the Services applet in the Control Panel flushes all jobs from the print queue.

3. Windows NT Server supports the automatic downloading of which client print drivers on the same print server? Select all that apply.

    A. MIPS
    B. PowerPC
    C. Intel

3. CORRECT ANSWERS: A-B-C

You must install print drivers for each platform that will connect to the print server for printing.

Answer D is incorrect because Windows NT does support the downloading of these client print drivers.

Automatic downloading of print drivers can be configured for the following platforms:

- Windows NT Alpha platforms (Windows NT versions 3.1, 3.5x, and 4.0)
- Windows NT MIPS platforms (Windows NT versions 3.1, 3.5x, and 4.0)
- Windows NT PPC platforms (Windows NT 3.51 and 4.0)
- Windows NT Intel platforms (Windows NT versions 3.1, 3.5x, and 4.0)
- Windows 95 (true 32-bit print drivers only)

When a Windows NT client connects to a printer on a remote print server, its version of the print driver is compared to the version on the print server. If the version on the print server is newer, the newer version is downloaded and used on the client. This also occurs if the driver does not exist on the client.

Chapter 6 TROUBLESHOOTING

4. What is the main difference in the printing process between when a Windows 3.x client prints to a Windows NT print share and when a Windows NT client prints to a Windows NT print share?

   D. Windows 3.x clients fully process their jobs before submitting them to a Windows NT print share.

4. CORRECT ANSWER: D

Windows for Workgroups uses its own 16-bit drivers to fully process a job before sending the job to a Windows NT print share. Windows NT clients partially process their print jobs and then send them to the print share. The print share's spooler completes the processing of the job.

Answer A is incorrect because there is a difference. Answer B is incorrect because Windows 3.x clients can print to a Windows NT print share. Answer C is incorrect because Windows 3.x clients can submit any print job not just text.

5. You have installed the TCP/IP Print service on your print server and have restarted the print server, yet UNIX clients cannot print to any of the print shares. Which of the following could be the reason for this?

   C. The TCP/IP Print service is set to be started manually. It should be switched to start automatically.

5. CORRECT ANSWER: C

The TCP/IP Print service is not configured to start automatically after installation. You must change its startup setting to start the service automatically.

Answer A is incorrect because Windows NT does support printing for UNIX clients. Answer B is incorrect because you do not need to install the SNMP service. Answer D is incorrect because UNIX clients do not capture printer ports.

6. What must be installed to enable Macintosh clients to print to a Windows NT printer?

   B. Services for Macintosh

6. CORRECT ANSWER: B

Services for Macintosh includes the Services for Macintosh print processor (SFMPSPRT), which enables Macintosh clients to print to Windows NT print shares.

Answer A is incorrect because the TCP/IP Print Server service is not required for Macintosh printing. Answer C is incorrect because this service does not exist. Answer D is incorrect because the AppleTalk protocol is installed with Services for Macintosh not separately.

The Services for Macintosh print processor (SFMPSPRT.DLL) enables Macintosh clients to send print jobs to Windows NT printers. This print processor has a specific data type named PSCRIPT1. This data type enables Macintosh clients to send Level 1 PostScript jobs to nonPostScript printers.

The spooler sends the PostScript code through a Microsoft TrueImage raster image processor (RIP) supplied with Services for Macintosh. The raster image processor creates a series of one-page, monochrome bitmaps at a maximum of 300 DPI. The Windows NT print spooler sends the rasterized images, or bitmaps, to the print driver for the target printer. The print driver returns a job that prints the bitmaps on the page. If the printer is a PostScript printer, the Services for Macintosh print processor sends the job using the RAW data type.

7. **Proposed Solution:**
When a printer is installed, change the permissions on each print share to assign Bob, Mary, and Jane to manage all documents for the printer. Be sure to install the TCP/IP and AppleTalk protocols on each print server. This enables print support for UNIX and Macintosh clients.

  D. Does not satisfy any required or optional results

7. CORRECT ANSWER: D

According to the requirements, Bob, Mary, and Jane require Full Control permissions, not Manage Documents permissions. This can achieved without granting excess permissions by making them members of the Print Operators local group in each of the three domains.

As with any other resource on a Windows NT network, printers can be configured with permissions to restrict access. The following permissions can be used to control access to print devices under Windows NT:

- Full Control: Enables full access and administrative control.

- Manage Documents: Enables a user/group to change the status of any print job.

- Print: Permits a user to send print jobs to a print device and to pause, resume, or delete any of his or her own jobs.

- No Access: Denies all access to a print device.

When a printer is created under Windows NT, the following permissions are assigned:

- The Administrator, Server Operator, and Print Operator groups are granted Full Control permissions.

- The Creator Owner group is granted Manage Documents permissions.
- All users are granted Print permissions.

8. **Proposed Solution:**
In each domain, add the user accounts for Bob, Mary, and Jane to the Print Operators local group. At each print server, install the TCP/IP protocol and the SNMP Service. Also add the Services for Macintosh service.

B. Meets the required result and only one optional result

8. CORRECT ANSWER: B

This solution grants the three users sufficient permissions to meet the primary requirement. Only Macintosh clients, however, can access the print shares. You need the TCP/IP Print Server service to grant print access to UNIX hosts.

See question 1's explanation regarding TCP/IP printing.

See question 6's explanation regarding Macintosh printing.

See question 7's explanation regarding printer permissions.

9. You have updated the HP LaserJet 4 print driver on your print server for Windows 95 to enable duplex printing. Your Windows 95 clients are not able to take advantage of this new option. What is the problem?

D. You must delete and then reconnect to the existing printer to download the newer version of the driver.

9. CORRECT ANSWER: D

Windows 95 clients only download the server's version of the print driver when they initially connect to the printer. You must delete the printer and then reinstall it to download the new version of the driver. Windows NT clients do compare their driver to the version stored on the print server. If the version on the print server is newer, the clients download the newer version.

Answer A is incorrect because Windows 95 clients do support duplex printing. Answer B is incorrect beacuse you do not need to load drivers at each client system. Answer C is incorrect because you do not need to restart the Windows 95 systems.

10. If a physical printing device has broken down, and the printer that was sending jobs to the printing device still has jobs in its queue, how do you redirect the jobs to a similar printing device?

C. Add a new local port to the printer using the UNC name of a printer that prints to a similar printing device.

10. CORRECT ANSWER: C

A local port can be added that points to the UNC name of a printer. The printer must use the same print driver as the original printer because the job will be fully processed when downloaded to the new printer.

Answer A is incorrect because you can redirect print jobs. Answer B is incorrect because the users do not need to recall their jobs. Answer D is incorrect because there is not a Redirect option in the printer property page.

FURTHER REVIEW

SOLVING PRINTER PROBLEMS

The following key words are important terms that were covered in this section. You should make sure you understand each one and what it does.

Key Words

LPD Service

LPQ

LPR

Print device

Print drivers

Print job

Print spooler

Printer

Queue

Files Involved in the Windows NT Print Process

Most files involved in printing are in the `%systemroot%\SYSTEM32` directory. One notable exception is the spooler's workspace, which can be placed on any given drive or directory. By default, it is located in `%systemroot%\SYSTEM32\SPOOL\Printers`.

You can change this location in the Advanced Property page of the Server Properties dialog box. You can access this dialog box from the Printers applet by selecting Server Properties from the File menu. The following list shows the major print-related files used in Windows NT:

- The print spooler uses `WINSPOOL.DRV`, `SPOOLSS.EXE`, and `SPOOLSS.DLL`.

- Local print providers (used for printers connected to a local port, such as LPT1 or COM1) use `LOCALSPL.DLL`.

- Remote print providers (used for printers not connected to a local port, such as a printer equipped with a network interface card) use `WIN32SP.DLL` for NT print servers. For NetWare print servers, `NWPROVAU.DLL` is used instead. For AppleTalk print servers, `SFMPSPRT.DLL` is used.

- Print monitors (used to send jobs from the spooler to the print device) can use one of a series of files, depending on how the printer is connected. For local printers, `LOCALMON.DLL` is used. For network-connected printers, a DLL specific to the network connection is used (`HPMON.DLL` or `LPRMON.DLL`).

PRACTICE QUESTIONS

TROUBLESHOOTING REMOTE ACCESS SERVICE

1. You have purchased a new modem for use with Dial-Up Networking in Windows NT Workstation. There is only a Windows 95 driver on the modem driver disk, and the Windows NT Workstation CD-ROM does not contain a driver for your new modem. How do you configure your modem for use?

   A. Edit the SWITCH.INF file.

   B. Edit the MODEM.INF file.

   C. Use a driver for an older version of the modem.

   D. Use the Windows 95 driver.

2. How can RAS Server be configured to auto assign IP addresses to dial-in clients? Select all that apply.

   A. Use a DHCP server.

   B. Use the current IP address of the client.

   C. Have its own pool of IP addresses to assign to clients.

   D. This cannot be done. Clients must request their own IP addresses.

3. You want to install Internet tunnels to provide access to the corporate network over the Internet. What must be installed before you configure RAS to provide this capability?

   A. VPN Service.

   B. PPTP protocol.

   C. L2TP protocol.

   D. This functionality is built into RAS and just needs to be configured.

4. Ruby is dialing in to the RAS server on your network. She complains that the line disconnects right after her user name has been authenticated. This happens every time she attempts to connect to the network, and no further communication exists. This is most likely due to which of the following? Select the best answer.

   A. The client is using the wrong network protocol.

   B. Ruby has entered the wrong password for her account.

   C. Ruby does not have dial-in permissions.

   D. Call-back security has been set to a specific phone number for the client and is configured incorrectly.

5. This is a scenario question. First you must review the scenario, then review the required and optional results. Following that is a solution. You must pick the best evaluation of that solution.

   Scenario:
   Your office wants to enable users to access the office network from home. The office is connected to the Internet through a fractional T1 line.

Required Result:
The office has decided to provide only managers with dial-in access to the network.

Optional Results:
Because the network is being accessed from the homes of personnel, the office wants to encrypt all information transferred to and from the network.

Because of the nature of the files the managers have access to on the network, it has been determined that call-back security will be implemented. The managers will be called back at a predetermined phone number.

Proposed Solution:
Install a RAS Server, which contains a digiboard, on the local network. Set up four modems to enable the users to access the network. In User Manager for Domains, create a global group containing all the managers' accounts. In Remote Access Admin, assign the newly created global group the Dial-in permission. Set call-back security on the global group so the users can set the number at which to be called back.

Evaluation of Proposed Solution:
(Choose the most correct answer.)

   A. Meets the required result and both optional results

   B. Meets the required result and only one optional result

   C. Meets only the required result

   D. Does not meet the required result or either optional result

6. **A user notes that, when logging on to the network using Dial-Up Networking, it seems to take an exceptionally long time for the logon process to complete. This is most likely due to which of the following? Select the best answer.**

   A. A roaming profile is being downloaded.

   B. A login script is being executed.

   C. A virus scan is being run.

   D. Authentication always is slow over a dial-in connection.

7. **A user dials in to your RAS Server using multilink. The server uses call-back security to a user-specified number. The server successfully calls the user back, but the connection is not using multilink anymore. This is due to which of the following?**

   A. The user must provide both phone numbers for multilink to work.

   B. The call-back security feature only works with multilink if it is configured to call back a preconfigured phone number.

   C. The user's modems are not on the multilink HCL.

   D. Multilink is not supported for call-back security.

8. **Which service needs to be running to enable AutoDial functionality?**

   A. Server Service

   B. AutoDial Service

   C. Remote Access AutoDial Manager

   D. Dial-Up Networking Service

9. Where can a network administrator view which users have connected to the network using the RAS service, how much data they transferred to and from the network, and how long the users were connected to the RAS server?

   A. PPP.LOG

   B. Remote Access Admin

   C. Event Viewer's System Log

   D. Dial-Up Network Monitor

10. A remote client has connected to the office's RAS Server using a NetBEUI PPP connection. The RAS Server is running the NWLink, TCP/IP, and NetBEUI protocols. The DATA server is running only the TCP/IP protocol, and the OFFICE server is running only the NWLink protocol. The MAIL server is running only the NetBEUI protocol. Which servers can the remote client connect to (and use file shares from) if the NetBEUI protocol has been configured to allow access to the entire network? Select all that apply.

    A. The RAS server

    B. The DATA server

    C. The OFFICE server

    D. The MAIL server

ANSWER KEY

1. D
2. A-C
3. B
4. D
5. D
6. A
7. D
8. C
9. C
10. A-B-C-D

ANSWERS & EXPLANATIONS

TROUBLESHOOTING REMOTE ACCESS SERVICE

1. You have purchased a new modem for use with Dial-Up Networking in Windows NT Workstation. There is only a Windows 95 driver on the modem driver disk, and the Windows NT Workstation CD-ROM does not contain a driver for your new modem. How do you configure your modem for use?

   D. Use the Windows 95 driver.

1. CORRECT ANSWER: D

Windows 95 and Windows NT Workstation can use the same modem configuration files.

Answer A is incorrect because there is no SWITCH.INF file. Answer B is incorrect because you do not edit the MODEM.INF file. Answer C is incorrect because you do not use a older modem driver.

Windows NT can use Windows 95 configuration files to install a modem. If you are unable to find a Windows NT 4 driver, you can use a Windows 95 driver in its place.

Installing a modem is simple in Windows NT. After the hardware is connected, go to the Control Panel and double-click the Modems icon. If no modem is installed, the modem installer starts automatically. This wizard steps you through the installation of the modem.

If you already have used the installer once and it was unable to detect the modem, you probably have one of two problems. Either the modem cannot be detected and you will have to install it manually, or the system can't see the modem and you should check the port. If you need to install the modem manually, check the option Don't Detect My Modem, I Will Select It from a List. This selection brings up a screen that enables you to select the modem.

2. How can RAS Server be configured to auto assign IP addresses to dial-in clients? Select all that apply.

   A. Use a DHCP server.
   C. Have its own pool of IP addresses to assign to clients.

2. CORRECT ANSWERS: A-C

When using TCP/IP as a dial-in protocol, a RAS server can assign IP addresses using the network's DHCP server or using its own private pool.

Answer B is incorrect because you do not use the client's current IP address. Answer D is incorrect because clients do not need to request a specific IP address.

If you are encountering problems with clients connecting to RAS using TCP/IP, first check whether any addresses are available to assign for the client. If the address pool allocated for RAS is full, the client cannot connect. It is a good rule of thumb to make sure enough addresses are allocated for the RAS ports available. When you add additional RAS ports, you also need to add additional addresses to be allocated.

3. You want to install Internet tunnels to provide access to the corporate network over the Internet. What must be installed before you configure RAS to provide this capability?

   B. PPTP protocol.

3. CORRECT ANSWER: B

By installing the PPTP protocol, you can add Virtual Private Networks (VPNs) to RAS Server.

Answer A is incorrect because there is not a VPN service. Answer C is incorrect because there is not an L2TP protocol. Answer D is incorrect because PPTP is not included in RAS.

The PPTP protocol allows the creation of Virtual Private Networks (VPNs). This enables clients to dial in to a standard Internet service provider and then connect to their corporate network using a "tunnel." The "tunnel" actually is a second protocol link, which is connected using encryption over the first protocol (TCP/IP). You must set up RAS, install the PPTP protocol, and configure inbound VPN ports using the RAS setup to enable this capability.

4. Ruby is dialing in to the RAS server on your network. She complains that the line disconnects right after her username has been authenticated. This happens every time she attempts to connect to the network, and no further communication exists. This is most likely due to which of the following? Select the best answer.

   D. Call-back security has been set to a specific phone number for the client and is configured incorrectly.

4. CORRECT ANSWER: D

This situation can occur when call-back security has been implemented for a specific user, and it is set to call the user back at a predetermined number. In this case, the predetermined number either is incorrect or is entered incorrectly.

Answer A is incorrect because the client does not authenticate when the wrong protocol is specified. Answer B is incorrect because a wrong password does not immediately cause a disconnect. Answer C is incorrect because Ruby does have dial-in permissions or the system would not authenticate the logon.

You also can set call-back options in the Dial-in property pages of User Manager for Domains or Remote Access Admin. Call-back adds another level of security to your network. It also assigns long-distance charges primarily to the RAS server rather than to the dial-in clients. The following call-back levels can be set:

- No Call Back: This is the default; it means the call-back feature is disabled.

- Set By Caller: With this option, the user can specify the number to use when the server calls back. This is useful if a large number of users travel and you want to centralize long distance.

- Preset To: This enhances the security of the network by forcing the user to be at a predetermined phone number. If this option is set, the user can call only from that location.

▼ NOTE

In some cases, call-back security cannot be implemented. If the user dials in from a hotel that does not have direct lines to the rooms, call-back security cannot be implemented.

5. **Proposed Solution:**
Install a RAS Server, which contains a digiboard, on the local network. Set up four modems to enable the users to access the network. In User Manager for Domains, create a global group containing all the managers' accounts. In Remote Access Admin, assign the newly created global group the Dial-in permission. Set call-back security on the global group so the users can set the number at which to be called back.

D. Does not meet the required result or either optional result

5. CORRECT ANSWER: D

Dial-in permissions are granted to individual users, not to groups.

As with all other aspects of Windows NT, security is built into the RAS server. At a minimum, a user requires an account in Windows NT, and that account needs to have Dial-in permissions set.

You can grant users dial-in permissions using the User Manager (or User Manager for Domains) or through the Remote Access Admin program. If you are having problems connecting to the RAS server, this is one of the first things you should check. The following are the steps to set or check dial-in permissions:

ANSWERS & EXPLANATIONS

1. Open the User Manager (Start, Programs, Administrative Tools, User Manager).

2. Select the account you are using and choose User, Properties.

3. Click the Dial-in button. This brings up the Dial-in Permissions dialog box.

4. Check the Grant Dial-in Permission to User box to enable the user to dial in.

You also can check permissions from the Remote Access Admin utility. Use the following steps to do this:

1. Start the Remote Access Admin (Start, Programs, Administrative Tools, RAS Admin).

2. Choose Users, Permissions from the menu.

3. In the Remote Access Permissions dialog box, select the user and make sure Dial-in permission is granted.

6. A user notes that, when logging on to the network using Dial-Up Networking, it seems to take an exceptionally long time for the logon process to complete. This is most likely due to which of the following? Select the best answer.

   A. A roaming profile is being downloaded.

6. CORRECT ANSWER: A

If a roaming profile has been configured for a user, configure the client to use a locally cached version of the profile if a slow connection is detected. This can be set on the User Profiles tab of the System applet in the Control Panel.

Answer B is incorrect because a login script does not execute until the logon process itself is complete. Answer C is incorrect because a virus scan does not run during the logon process. Answer D is incorrect because authentication is not necessarily slow over a dial-in connection.

If roaming profiles are enabled on your network, you should configure the remote clients to use cached profile information. Otherwise, every time the user dials in, the system will download a new copy of the profile. Roaming profiles can grow to be extremely large (in excess of 200 KB); over a regular modem connection, they can take a very long time to download.

Chapter 6 TROUBLESHOOTING

7. A user dials in to your RAS Server using multilink. The server uses call-back security to a user-specified number. The server successfully calls the user back, but the connection is not using multilink anymore. This is due to which of the following?

D. Multilink is not supported for call-back security.

7. CORRECT ANSWER: D

Multilink is not supported for call-back security when using modems over Public Switched Telephone Networks.

Answer A is incorrect because the user does not need to provide both phone numbers. Answer B is incorrect because multilink does not work with call-back security. Answer C is incorrect because there is not a multilink HCL.

If you configure call–back security for your RAS installation, you cannot support multilink connections. The client can dial in with multiple modems, but the call–back feature only calls back on one port.

8. Which service needs to be running to enable AutoDial functionality?

C. Remote Access AutoDial Manager

8. CORRECT ANSWER: C

The Remote Access AutoDial Manager must be running for AutoDial to be available. AutoDial is used mostly for single computers or for branch offices that only connect on an as-needed basis. If using AutoDial is necessary, you should set the Remote Access AutoDial Manager to start automatically in the Services applet in Control Panel.

Answer A is incorrect because the Server service is not related to AutoDial functionality. Answer B is incorrect because this is not a valid service. Answer D is incorrect because Dial-Up Networking is not part of AutoDial.

9. Where can a network administrator view which users have connected to the network using the RAS service, how much data they transferred to and from the network, and how long the users were connected to the RAS server?

C. Event Viewer's System Log

9. CORRECT ANSWER: C

The Windows NT Event Viewer shows an information event after a RAS session has ended. The event contains information about who was connected, how long they were connected, and how much data was transferred over the connection.

Answer A is incorrect because the PPP.LOG does not show this information. Answer B is incorrect because Remote Access Admin only shows currently connected users. Answer D is incorrect because the Dial-Up Network Monitor shows client-side dial-in information.

10. A remote client has connected to the office's RAS Server using a NetBEUI PPP connection. The RAS Server is running the NWLink, TCP/IP, and NetBEUI protocols. The DATA server is running only the TCP/IP protocol, and the OFFICE server is running only the NWLink protocol. The MAIL server is running only the NetBEUI protocol. Which servers can the remote client connect to (and use file shares from) if the NetBEUI protocol has been configured to allow access to the entire network? Select all that apply.

   A. The RAS server
   B. The DATA server
   C. The OFFICE server
   D. The MAIL server

10. CORRECT ANSWERS: A-B-C-D

All servers can be accessed because RAS functions as a NetBIOS gateway, enabling access to servers not running the NetBEUI protocol. This is especially helpful because NetBEUI is the fastest dial-up protocol that can be used. The drawback is that a user cannot connect through the dial-up to the Internet or to any other external systems. The gateway only communicates with other systems on the WAN.

> **FURTHER REVIEW**

TROUBLESHOOTING REMOTE ACCESS SERVICE

The following key words are important terms that were covered in this section. You should make sure you understand each one and what it does.

Key Words

Call-back security

Multilink Protocol (MP)

PPP

PPTP

RAS

Troubleshooting Other Issues with the Client

As previously mentioned, Windows NT acts as a PPP server. This means the client station and the server undergo a negotiation during the initial phase of the call.

During the negotiation, the client and the server decide on the protocol to be used and the parameters for the protocol. If there are problems when attempting to connect, you might want to set up PPP logging to actually watch the negotiation between the server and the client. This can be set up on the server by changing the Logging option, as follows:

```
HKEY_LOCAL_MACHINE\SYSTEM\
CurrentControlSet\Services\RASMAN\PPP\
Parameters
```

The log file is in the system32\RAS directory. Like the modem log, it can be viewed using any text editor. Other obstacles you might encounter when dialing in to the network include the following:

- You must make sure the protocol you are requesting is available on the RAS server. There must be at least one common protocol or the connection fails.

- If you are using NetBEUI, make sure the name used on the RAS client is not in use on the network to which you are attempting to connect.

- If you are attempting to connect using TCP/IP, the RAS server must be configured to provide an address or to allow you to request your own address.

Other Issues That Affect RAS Connections

Other issues can affect a RAS connection, such as authentication problems and the use of multilink when call-back security is enabled. Authentication can be a problem in two areas. First, a client might attempt to connect using an incorrect username and password. This can happen easily if the user is dialing from a home system. The RAS client can be set to attempt the connection using the current username and password, or it might have to unsave the previous password if it has changed on the network.

The other authentication problem occurs if the security settings on the server and the client do not match. You can get around this using the Allow Any Authentication setting or also by using the After Dial terminal window. If connection can be achieved using clear text, you must increase the encryption level on both the client and the server to use the highest level of encryption shared by both.

Using call-back security with the multilink protocol is not supported over a Public Switched Telephone Network. The initial connection to the server can use multilink. When the server hangs up, however, only one number is configured for the call-back configuration. The client only uses one line from this point on.

▼ **NOTE**

The only situation in which call-back security can be enabled for a multilink session is over an ISDN connection using two channels. The two channels must share the same phone number for this to work.

PRACTICE QUESTIONS

SOLVING CONNECTIVITY PROBLEMS

1. The two offices of MNO Office Supplies are linked by a dedicated T1 line. The network is configured to use NetBEUI as its network protocol. Users can connect to any servers on their network segment, but they cannot view resources on the remote network segment. This is due to which of the following? Select the best answer.

    A. They require a WINS server.

    B. They need to configure LMHOSTS files at each computer.

    C. A static route needs to be added on the router to direct traffic between the two segments.

    D. NetBEUI does not support routing.

2. You cannot connect to a client/server application on a NetWare server. What must be configured on your Windows NT Workstation to enable connectivity? Select the best answer.

    A. NWLink protocol

    B. RIP for IPX

    C. Client Services for NetWare

    D. SAP Agent

3. You cannot connect to a printer hosted by a NetWare server. What must be configured on your Windows NT Workstation to enable connectivity? Select all that apply.

    A. NWLink protocol

    B. RIP for IPX

    C. Client Services for NetWare

    D. SAP Agent

4. Your network has a mix of NetWare 3.x and NetWare 4.x servers. A Windows NT Workstation cannot connect to all the NetWare servers, even though Client Services for NetWare and NWLink appear to be configured properly. What potentially is the problem?

    A. There are frame type issues.

    B. Preferred Server is configured incorrectly.

    C. The default context is set incorrectly.

    D. You need to switch the default network provider to NetWare from Microsoft.

5. This is a scenario question. First you must review the scenario, then review the required and optional results. Following that is a solution. You must pick the best evaluation of that solution.

    Scenario:
    The Cosmos Corporation wants to use TCP/IP as the primary protocol on the wide area network between two sites. The corporation has had issues assigning IP addresses to all the hosts on its network and has brought in your consulting firm to assist with the IP address rollout.

Required Result:
The Cosmos Corporation wants to reduce the number of hosts that require manual IP address configuration.

Optional Results:
The Cosmos Corporation wants to provide fault tolerance in case the primary IP address-assignment server fails.

The Cosmos Corporation wants to reduce the broadcast traffic on the network.

Proposed Solution:
Set up two DHCP servers on separate segments with the Scope of IP addresses set as shown in Table 6.1.

Also configure a DHCP relay agent on each network segment to forward any DHCP packets to the DHCP server on the remote segment.

TABLE 6.1   IP ADDRESS SETS BY SERVER

	Server1	Server2
Scope1	192.168.2.10–192.168.2.200 with subnet mask 255.255.255.0	192.168.3.10–192.168.3.200 with subnet mask 255.255.255.0
Scope2	192.168.3.201–192.168.3.254 with subnet mask 255.255.255.0	192.168.2.201–192.168.2.254 with subnet mask 255.255.255.0
Scope1 Options	Default Gateway–192.168.2.1	Default Gateway–192.168.3.1
	WINS Server–192.168.2.8	WINS Server–192.168.2.8
	WINS Node Type–Hybrid	WINS Node Type–Hybrid
Scope2 Options	Def Gateway–192.168.3.1	Def Gateway–192.168.2.1
	WINS Server–192.168.2.8	WINS Server–192.168.2.8
	WINS Node Type–Hybrid	WINS Node Type–Hybrid

Evaluation of Proposed Solution:
(Choose the most correct answer.)

A. Meets the required result and both optional results

B. Meets the required result and only one optional result

C. Meets only the required result

D. Does not meet the required result

6. You use the Network Monitor to diagnose why clients on a remote subnet are taking a long time to authenticate on the network. It is discovered that the clients all are authenticating with a BDC on a remote subnet rather than with the local BDC. What setting should you use to configure the NetBIOS node type on this subnet to speed up authentication, yet enable authentication from remote BDCs if the local BDC is down?

   A. Pointed

   B. Broadcast

   C. Mixed

   D. Hybrid

7. Which command can be used to determine how many routers are crossed when communicating with a remote TCP/IP network?

   A. ROUTE.EXE

   B. TRACERT.EXE

   C. NETSTAT.EXE

   D. NET DISPLAY

8. Which command can be used to determine what ports are in use during a network session?

   A. ROUTE.EXE

   B. NBTSTAT.EXE

   C. NETSTAT.EXE

   D. NET CONFIG

9. Which commands can be used to view your network adapter's MAC address? Select all that apply.

   A. IPCONFIG /ALL

   B. ARP -A

   C. NBTSTAT -n

   D. NET CONFIG WORKSTATION

10. You can ping all computers on your local network segment but not any computers on remote network segments. Which of the following is the likely cause of this problem?

    A. Incorrect subnet mask

    B. Incorrect default gateway

    C. Incorrect DNS setting

    D. Incorrect WINS setting

ANSWER KEY

1. D
2. A
3. A-C
4. A
5. D
6. C
7. B
8. C
9. A-D
10. B

ANSWERS & EXPLANATIONS

SOLVING CONNECTIVITY PROBLEMS

1. The two offices of MNO Office Supplies are linked by a dedicated T1 line. The network is configured to use NetBEUI as its network protocol. Users can connect to any servers on their network segment, but they cannot view resources on the remote network segment. This is due to which of the following? Select the best answer.

    D. NetBEUI does not support routing.

1. CORRECT ANSWER: D

NetBEUI is fast performing and requires no configuration, but it does not support routing. This protocol cannot be used to link two remote offices.

Answer A is incorrect because a WINS server is not required. Answer B is incorrect because LMHOSTS files do not need to be configured. Answer C is incorrect because a static route does not need to be entered.

NetBEUI is the simplest protocol to use on the network because it automatically configures itself to perform at its best possible level. The major issue with NetBEUI is that it is non-routable. If your network is broken into separate segments, clients using NetBEUI cannot communicate with servers on remote segments of the network. The only physical device that enables this connectivity is a bridge. A bridge logically connects two physical network segments into one large segment.

2. You cannot connect to a client/server application on a NetWare server. What must be configured on your Windows NT Workstation to enable connectivity? Select the best answer.

    A. NWLink protocol

2. CORRECT ANSWER: A

Connecting to a client/server application on a NetWare server only requires the NWLink protocol.

Answer B is incorrect because RIP for IPX does not need to be installed. Answer C is incorrect because Client Services for NetWare is not required for applications. Answer D is incorrect because there is not a SAP Agent.

NWLink is Microsoft's 32-bit implementation of the IPX/SPX protocol standard. NWLink is a routable network protocol commonly associated with Novell NetWare networks.

By default, NWLink by itself enables you to interact with client/server class applications running on NetWare servers. It also enables a NetWare client to connect to a SQL server running on a Windows NT box. (The client must be running NetBIOS, which is optional in NetWare.)

3. **You cannot connect to a printer hosted by a NetWare server. What must be configured on your Windows NT Workstation to enable connectivity? Select all that apply.**
   A. NWLink protocol
   C. Client Services for NetWare

The only configuration that needs to be checked when NWLink is installed is the frame type. NetWare servers use different frame types depending on the network topology and the version of NetWare in use. If you are having problems communicating with a Novell server, make sure the frame types are the same.

When the frame type is set to Automatic, only a single frame type is loaded. If both Ethernet 802.2 (the default for NetWare 3.12 and later versions) and Ethernet 802.3 (the default for NetWare 3.11 and later versions) are loaded, Windows NT defaults to the Ethernet 802.2 frame type. This prevents communication with any NetWare servers using only the 802.3 frame type.

3. CORRECT ANSWERS: A-C

To use file and print services on a NetWare server, a Windows NT Workstation computer requires both the NWLink protocol and Client Services for NetWare.

Answer B is incorrect because RIP for IPX does not need to be installed. Answer D is incorrect because there is not a SAP Agent.

If you want to be able to work with the file and print services of a Novell NetWare system, you need to add either Client Services for NetWare (on Windows NT Workstation) or Gateway (and Client) Services for NetWare (on Windows NT Server). These services enable your Windows NT system to become a Novell client.

If you want NetWare clients to use file and print services on a Windows NT Server, you must load File and Print Services for NetWare. This enables a Windows NT server to emulate a NetWare 3.12 server, which a NetWare client can connect to using its native protocols.

ANSWERS & EXPLANATIONS

▼ **NOTE**

Client Services for NetWare enables a user to authenticate to a Novell NetWare 4.x server by indicating the Preferred Tree and the default context. Unfortunately, you cannot manage the Directory Services using NetAdmin or NWAdmin because you have not fully authenticated into the Directory Services. You can do this only if you use NetWare's Windows NT client.

4. Your network has a mix of NetWare 3.x and NetWare 4.x servers. A Windows NT Workstation cannot connect to all the NetWare servers, even though Client Services for NetWare and NWLink appear to be configured properly. What potentially is the problem?

   A. There are frame type issues.

4. CORRECT ANSWER: A

If Windows NT is set to autodetect frame types, it defaults to an Ethernet 802.2 frame when it detects both Ethernet 802.2 and Ethernet 802.3 frame types on the network. NetWare 3.11 (and earlier versions) use 802.3 as the default frame type. NetWare 3.12 and 4.x use Ethernet 802.2 as the default frame type.

Answer B is incorrect because the preferred server configuration does not stop the client from connecting. Answer C is incorrect because there is not a default context to set. Answer D is incorrect because there is no default network provider.

5. Proposed Solution:
   Set up two DHCP servers on separate segments with the Scope of IP addresses set as shown in Table 6.1.

   Also configure a DHCP relay agent on each network segment to forward any DHCP packets to the DHCP server on the remote segment.

   D. Does not meet the required result

5. CORRECT ANSWER: D

This solution does not work. You do not want to create overlapping scopes on the two servers. Even though the DHCP relay agent would pass requests to the other server, the clients would receive incorrect default-gateway information if they received an IP address from the other subnet's server.

Overlapping scopes on multiple DHCP servers can cause massive network problems, especially if the DHCP Relay Agent is used to relay requests between subnets. Microsoft recommends that, if you need multiple DHCP servers for redundancy, you should configure 75 percent of the scope on one server and 25 percent of the scope on the backup server.

6. You use the Network Monitor to diagnose why clients on a remote subnet are taking a long time to authenticate on the network. It is discovered that the clients all are authenticating with a BDC on a remote subnet rather than with the local BDC. What setting should you use to configure the NetBIOS node type on this subnet to speed up authentication, yet enable authentication, from remote BDCs if the local BDC is down?

    C. Mixed

6. CORRECT ANSWER: C

If you use Mixed for the NetBIOS node type, the client first broadcasts and then uses a WINS lookup.

Answer A is incorrect because Pointed is not a valid node type. Answer B is incorrect because Broadcast does not allow authentication by remote BDCs. Routers, by default, do not transmit broadcasts. Answer D is incorrect because Hybrid does not try the local servers first. It accepts the first available authentication.

The Mixed node type first tries a broadcast on the local subnet for a domain controller to provide network authentication. If a domain controller does not respond, the machine tries to reach a known remote domain controller.

7. Which command can be used to determine how many routers are crossed when communicating with a remote TCP/IP network?

    B. TRACERT.EXE

7. CORRECT ANSWER: B

The TRACERT command indicates how many routers are crossed when communicating with a remote host.

Answer A is incorrect because the ROUTE command is used to modify the routing table. Answer C is incorrect because NETSTAT displays the ports in use. Answer D is incorrect because NET DISPLAY is not a valid command.

The TRACERT command can be used to determine what route is taken when a computer attempts to communicate with a host on a remote network. It also reports how many routers have been crossed when the remote host is communicated with. This is invaluable in TCP/IP troubleshooting because it can show you exactly where a break might occur if a remote system cannot be accessed.

8. Which command can be used to determine what ports are in use during a network session?

    C. NETSTAT.EXE

8. CORRECT ANSWER: C

The NETSTAT command can be used to determine what ports are in use when a communication session is taking place. TCP/IP Winsock applications use preconfigured ports to connect. Many networks now have firewalls in place that prevent certain ports from being used. The NETSTAT command can be used to determine which ports might need to be opened on a firewall.

Answer A is incorrect because the ROUTE command does not show what ports are in use. Answer B is incorrect because NBTSTAT shows NetBIOS information not port information. Answer D is incorrect because NET CONFIG does not show what ports are in use.

9. Which commands can be used to view your network adapter's MAC address? Select all that apply.

   A. IPCONFIG /ALL
   D. NET CONFIG WORKSTATION

9. CORRECT ANSWERS: A-D

The IPCONFIG /ALL and NET CONFIG WORKSTATION commands can be used to view your network adapter's MAC address.

Answer B is incorrect because ARP -A is not a valid command. Answer C is incorrect because NBTSTAT -n does not display the MAC address.

To verify that the configuration has been entered, you can use IPCONFIG. If you type **IPCONFIG** at a prompt, it displays the IP address, the subnet mask, and the default gateway for you. You also can use the following three switches with IPCONFIG:

- /ALL: You normally use this to see all the configuration information for a computer.

- /RELEASE: If you are using DHCP, this drops the IP address you got from the DHCP server. You should do this before you move a client to a different network. When the computer next attempts to initialize the TCP/IP stack, it will request a new address from a DHCP server.

- /RENEW: DHCP works by leasing an address. The RENEW option forces the computer to attempt to renew the lease on the address. You can use this to verify that the client can see the DHCP server as well as to bring down any changes made to the configuration that were obtained from the DHCP server.

10. You can ping all the computers on your local network segment but not any computers on remote network segments. Which of the following is the likely cause of the problem?

   B. Incorrect default gateway

10. CORRECT ANSWER: B

If the default gateway is configured incorrectly, you can connect only to local hosts.

Answer A is incorrect because, if the subnet mask is incorrect, you cannot connect to all the computers on your local subnet. Answer C is incorrect because an invalid DNS does not stop connection to computers by IP address. Answer D is incorrect because an incorrect WINS setting does not stop connection by IP address.

As a basic rule of thumb, if you cannot connect outside your own subnet, it is related to the default gateway. The default gateway is the address to which your computer forwards packets for any destination outside your local subnet. If the default gateway address is incorrect, the packets cannot be forwarded correctly; hence, connection outside the subnet is not possible.

FURTHER REVIEW

SOLVING CONNECTIVITY PROBLEMS

The following key words are important terms that were covered in this section. You should make sure you understand each one and what it does.

Key Words

Client Services for NetWare (CSNW)
File and Print Services for NetWare
Frame types
Gateway Services for NetWare
IPCONFIG
NBTSTAT
NetBEUI
NetBIOS
NETSTAT
NWLink
PING
TCP/IP
TRACERT

Tools for Troubleshooting Connectivity Problems

Windows NT contains several tools that can be used to troubleshoot connectivity problems. These tools include the following:

- The Network Monitor
- The Server Manager
- The TRACERT command
- The NETSTAT command
- The PING command

The Network Monitor application can be used to examine network traffic and to monitor network performance. The Network Monitor is a network sniffer that can be used to check for the following:

- Bad packet cyclic redundancy checks (CRCs): A packet with a bad CRC value indicates that the packet is corrupted.

- Network saturation: This is caused by a network card constantly sending broadcast packets.

- Packet recognition: Understanding what common traffic flows should look like can help in diagnosing a communication error. Detecting where communication is breaking down can assist in determining where the problem lies and can lead to a quicker resolution. You might notice, for example, that the DHCP client is placing Discover packets onto the network, but the DHCP server is not sending offers. You can rule out that the problem is on the client.

The Server Manager program can be used to manage services running on a Windows NT computer.

The TRACERT command can be used to determine what route is taken when a computer attempts to communicate with a host on a remote network. It also reports how many routers have been crossed when the remote host is communicated with.

The NETSTAT command can be used to determine what ports are in use when a communication session is taking place. TCP/IP Winsock applications use preconfigured ports to connect. Many networks now have firewalls in place that prevent certain ports from being used. The NETSTAT command can be used to determine which ports might need to be opened on a firewall.

PING is a tool used to test the validity of an IP address and verify a client's TCP/IP configuration. It test the connectivity between two systems.

PRACTICE QUESTIONS

SOLVING RESOURCE ACCESS AND PERMISSIONS PROBLEMS

1. What are the default permissions assigned to a new file share?

    A. Users, Change

    B. Everyone, Change

    C. Users, Full Control

    D. Everyone, Full Control

2. When Jim attempts to log on to a Windows NT Workstation, he receives the message that he cannot log on locally. What configuration change must be made to grant Jim permission to log on locally?

    A. Make Jim a member of the Administrators local group.

    B. Configure Jim's account so he can log on only to the workstation to which he has problems logging on.

    C. Configure Jim's account to ignore warnings.

    D. Grant Jim's account the user right Log on Locally.

3. A confidential file in the Accounting local group that is assigned NTFS Change permissions was moved from the C:\ACCTG to the D:\DATA directory, with D: being a FAT partition. The directory is shared as DATA with Everyone having Full Control. What are the permissions after the file is moved?

    A. Everyone, Full Control

    B. Users, Change

    C. Administrators, Full Control

    D. Users, Change, Administrators, Full Control

4. When you log on to Windows NT Workstation as an Administrator, you notice that the sharing symbol no longer appears on any of your shared folders. Which of the following is the probable cause of this? Select the best answer.

    A. The View options in Windows NT Explorer have been configured to not show the shared folder symbol.

    B. The Server service has stopped.

    C. The Workstation service has stopped.

    D. On Windows NT Workstation, shares only are viewed in the Server Manager.

5. A file within the Users local group that is assigned NTFS Change permissions is located in the C:\USERS directory. The directory D:\DATA has been assigned the NTFS Administrators permissions with Full Control permissions. If the file is moved to the D:\DATA directory, what are the permissions after the file is moved?

    A. Everyone, Full Control

    B. Users, Change

C. Administrators, Full Control

D. Users, Change, Administrators, Full Control

6. A file in the Users local group that is assigned NTFS Change permissions is located in the C:\USERS directory. The directory C:\DATA has been assigned the NTFS Administrators permissions with Full Control permissions. If the file is moved to the C:\DATA directory, what are the permissions after the file is moved?

    A. Everyone, Full Control

    B. Users, Change

    C. Administrators, Full Control

    D. Users, Change Administrators, Full Control

7. All users' home directories have been generated using the setting \\SERVER\USERS\%USERNAME% in the home directory field of each user's properties. Harvey, who is part of the Administrators group, gets an error when he tries to delete a user's home directory. What permissions are assigned to the home directories by default?

    A. Users, Full Control

    B. Everyone, Full Control

    C. %USERNAME%, Change

    D. %USERNAME%, Full Control

8. The file DATA.TXT has been assigned the NTFS permissions Users, Read. The directory the file is in has the NTFS permissions Users, Change. The share permissions for the folder are set to Administrators, Full Control and Users, Full Control. What are the effective permissions on the file DATA.TXT?

    A. Users, Read

    B. Users, Change

    C. Users, Full Control

    D. Users, Full Control Administrators, Full Control

9. An organization has three domains named Alberta, Saskatchewan, and Manitoba. The trust relationships have been established so that Alberta trusts Saskatchewan and Saskatchewan trusts Manitoba. The Manitoba domain admins group is part of the Saskatchewan domain admins group, and the Saskatchewan domain admins group is part of the Alberta domain admins group.

   Max is a domain admin in the Manitoba domain. When he tries to access the Alberta domain, he receives an error. What is the problem?

    A. Max needs to log on as the Manitoba Administrator.

    B. Max cannot access the Alberta domain because trusts are nontransitive.

    C. The trust relationships must be rebuilt.

    D. Max needs to log on to the Manitoba domain controller.

10. Harry, a user who resigned three weeks ago, had his account deleted. He now has returned to his former job. When you re-create his account, he no longer can access the files he accessed before his resignation. Why is this?

A. The account should have been undeleted in the User Manager for Domains.

B. The account now has a new SID.

C. The password has changed.

D. The account must be regenerated.

ANSWER KEY

1. D
2. D
3. A
4. B
5. C
6. B
7. D
8. A
9. B
10. B

ANSWERS & EXPLANATIONS

SOLVING RESOURCE ACCESS AND PERMISSIONS PROBLEMS

1. What are the default permissions assigned to a new file share?

   D. Everyone, Full Control

1. CORRECT ANSWER: D

The default permissions assigned to a shared directory are Everyone, Full Control.

In Windows NT networking, shares provide an access point into a server's file stores. Setting share permissions determines which users have access to a file share and what level of access they have.

Share permissions do not change from the entry-point directory. In other words, if a user only has Read access to a shared directory, that user also only has Read access to all subdirectories. The shared permissions that can be assigned to a directory include the following:

- No Access: No Access permissions override all other permissions assigned to a shared directory. If a user (or a group the user is a member of) is assigned No Access permissions, he cannot gain access to the file share.

- Read: Read permissions enable the assigned user to view documents, to copy information from the shared directory, and to run programs.

- Change: Change permissions include all the privileges of Read permissions, plus the capability to modify and to delete any files contained in the shared directory.

- Full Control: Full Control permissions include all the privileges of Change permissions, plus the capability to change the share permissions on the shared directory.

By default, a newly created file share is assigned to the EVERYONE special group with Full Control permissions. This default generally should be changed because it grants access rights to the file share.

ANSWERS & EXPLANATIONS 349

▼ **NOTE**

It is recommended that you never use the EVERYONE special group when assigning permissions. The EVERYONE special group includes all users that connect to the file share, including users you do not know about. It is better to use the local group USERS.

The following are some issues that must be considered when you use share permissions:

- Share permissions can be applied only to directory objects. You cannot apply share permissions to the file's level of access.

- On FAT volumes, share permissions are the only level of security that can be applied.

- Share permissions can be applied only to users connecting through the network. Share permissions do not apply to local security.

2. When Jim attempts to log on to a Windows NT Workstation, he receives the message that he cannot log on locally. What configuration change must be made to grant Jim permission to log on locally?

D. Grant Jim's account the user right Log on Locally.

2. CORRECT ANSWER: D

If you grant the users' accounts (or groups that they have membership in) the user right Log on Locally, users can log on to the NT Workstation computer.

Answer A is incorrect because you do not need to add Jim to the Administrators group. Answer B is incorrect because you should not restrict the account to a specific workstation. Answer C is incorrect because you cannot configure an account to ignore warnings.

You can enable a specific account to log on to a machine locally that the account's group membership does not have access to by giving the user the Log on Locally right. This can be done in the Account Rights property page of User Manager for Domains.

Chapter 6 TROUBLESHOOTING

3. **A confidential file in the Accounting local group that is assigned NTFS Change permissions was moved from the `C:\ACCTG` to the `D:\DATA` directory, with D: being a FAT partition. The directory is shared as DATA with Everyone having Full Control. What are the permissions after the file is moved?**

   A. Everyone, Full Control

> **3. CORRECT ANSWER: A**
>
> Because the file is moved to a directory on a FAT partition, the NTFS permissions are not retained. FAT does not support file-level security, so the only security available is what has been configured for the share.

4. **When you log on to Windows NT Workstation as an Administrator, you notice that the sharing symbol no longer appears on any of your shared folders. Which of the following is the probable cause of this? Select the best answer.**

   B. The Server service has stopped.

> **4. CORRECT ANSWER: B**
>
> If the Server service stops operating, share symbols do not appear below shares because they are not being shared at that time. When you restart the Server service, the share symbols reappear.
>
> Answer A is incorrect because there is not a view option to eliminate the sharing symbol. Answer C is incorrect because stopping the Workstation service does not eliminate the sharing symbol. Answer D is incorrect because shares are not viewed only with Server Manager.

5. **A file within the Users local group that is assigned NTFS Change permissions is located in the `C:\USERS` directory. The directory `D:\DATA` has been assigned the NTFS Administrators permissions with Full Control permissions. If the file is moved to the `D:\DATA` directory, what are the permissions after the file is moved?**

   C. Administrators, Full Control

> **5. CORRECT ANSWER: C**
>
> Because the file is moved between NTFS partitions, the file assumes the NTFS permissions of the target directory.
>
> When a file is copied or moved on an NTFS partition, the permissions might change. This can lead to unexpected resource access problems when the NTFS permissions are not what was expected. Remember the following rules for moving and copying files:
>
> - When a file is copied into an NTFS directory, the file assumes the NTFS permissions of the target directory.
> - If a file is moved to an NTFS directory on the same NTFS partition, the file retains its original NTFS permissions.

ANSWERS & EXPLANATIONS 351

- If a file is moved to an NTFS directory on a different NTFS partition, the file assumes the NTFS permissions of the target directory.

- If a file is moved or copied to a nonNTFS partition, all NTFS permissions are lost.

6. A file in the Users local group that is assigned NTFS Change permissions is located in the C:\USERS directory. The directory C:\DATA has been assigned the NTFS Administrators permissions with Full Control permissions. If the file is moved to the C:\DATA directory, what are the permissions after the file is moved?

   B. Users, Change

6. CORRECT ANSWER: B

Because the file is moved to a directory on the same NTFS partition, it retains its original permissions.

See the explanation for question 5.

7. All users' home directories have been generated using the setting \\SERVER\USERS\%USERNAME% in the home directory field of each user's properties. Harvey, who is part of the Administrators group, gets an error when he tries to delete a user's home directory. What permissions are assigned to the home directories by default?

   D. %USERNAME%, Full Control

7. CORRECT ANSWER: D

When a home directory is generated on an NTFS partition, only the user's account is granted the Full Control permission.

By default, home directory permissions are %USERNAME%, Full Control. For an administrator to delete a home directory, either the user has to assign permission to the administrator or the administrator has to take ownership of the directory. This gives the administrator Full Control permission for that directory.

8. The file data.txt has been assigned the NTFS permissions Users, Read. The directory the file is in has the NTFS permissions Users, Change. The share permissions for the folder are set to Administrators, Full Control and Users, Full Control. What are the effective permissions on the file DATA.TXT?

   A. Users, Read

8. CORRECT ANSWER: A

File permissions always take precedence over directory permissions in NTFS permissions assignments. Because the share permissions are effectively Full Control, the Read permissions on the file DATA.TXT are the most restrictive and are the effective permissions.

See the NTFS permissions explanation in question 5.

9. An organization has three domains named Alberta, Saskatchewan, and Manitoba. The trust relationships have been established so that Alberta trusts Saskatchewan and Saskatchewan trusts Manitoba. The Manitoba domain admins group is part of the Saskatchewan domain admins group, and the Saskatchewan domain admins group is part of the Alberta domain admins group.

   Max is a domain admin in the Manitoba domain. When he tries to access the Alberta domain, he receives an error. What is the problem?

   B. Max cannot access the Alberta domain because trusts are non-transitive.

9. CORRECT ANSWER: B

An account can only use resources in its own domain or in a domain that explicitly trusts its domain. Trust relationships are not transitive.

Answer A is incorrect because logging on as administrator does not provide access. Answer C is incorrect because the trust relationships do not need to be rebuilt. Answer D is incorrect because logging on to the domain controller does not provide access.

Any time a user encounters an error when trying to access a remote domain, first check permissions and trust relationships. You should make sure that the domain the user is attempting to access explicitly trusts the user's domain. The most important thing to remember is that trusts are nontransitive.

Trusts are explained more thoroughly in Chapter 1, "Planning."

10. Harry, a user who resigned three weeks ago, had his account deleted. He now has returned to his former job. When you re-create his account, he no longer can access the files he accessed before his resignation. Why is this?

    B. The account now has a new SID.

10. CORRECT ANSWER: B

When you delete an account and re-create it with the same User ID, the account has a different SID and does not retain any of its previous group memberships. It usually is recommended that an account be disabled until the administrator is sure it no longer will be used. If you re-create a user account, you need to give that user permissions to all resources again.

Answer A is incorrect because you cannot undelete an account. Answer C is incorrect because a changed password is not the problem. Answer D is incorrect because you cannot regenerate accounts.

FURTHER REVIEW

SOLVING RESOURCE ACCESS AND PERMISSIONS PROBLEMS

The following key words are important terms that were covered in this section. You should make sure you understand each one and what it does.

Key Words

Accounts-Global Groups-Local Groups-Permissions (AGLP) global group

Local group

NTFS permissions

Share permissions

SID

Combining Permissions

To complicate matters, you can assign both NTFS permissions and share permissions to a folder. In addition, the files in a share also can have NTFS file permissions. The effective permissions are the most restrictive of the share and NTFS permissions. Evaluate each set of permissions separately and then compare them to determine which is most restrictive.

A good rule of thumb is to set the share permissions to the maximum level of NTFS permissions required within the directory structure. If you use this rule, you only have to troubleshoot the NTFS permissions. This is because the NTFS permissions always are the most restrictive.

Implementing Permissions in a Multidomain Environment

When assigning permissions, make sure you use the Account-Global Groups-Local Groups-Permissions (AGLP) methodology, as follows:

- An account is created for each user.

- The accounts are grouped together into global groups. Global groups can contain only accounts from the same domain. If multiple domains exist, you need to create a global group in each domain.

- The global groups are made members of local groups in the domain in which the resource exists. If the resource exists on a domain controller, the local group is created in the domain account database. If the resource exists on a Windows NT member server or an NT Workstation, create the local group in the account database of that system.

▼ **NOTE**

You do not have to go to the specific system to add a local group to a member server or NT Workstation account database. In User Manager for Domains, you can modify a computer's account database by typing \\`computername` in the dialog box presented when you choose Select Domain from the User menu.

- The local group(s) is assigned the appropriate permissions.

This methodology should be applied to both NTFS and share permissions. If you use this methodology, it expands well into a multidomain environment.

Remember that, in a multidomain environment, appropriate trust relationships must be established. A trust relationship should be established so the Resource domains trust the Account domains. In this case, local groups in the Resource domains can have global groups from the Account domains assigned as members.

PRACTICE QUESTIONS

SOLVING FAULT-TOLERANCE FAILURES

1. What software-fault-tolerant solutions can be used to protect the System and boot partitions of Windows NT? Select all that apply.

   A. Disk mirroring

   B. Stripe set

   C. Disk duplexing

   D. Stripe set with parity

2. How do you recover from a MIRROR failure?

   A. Use the `Disk Regenerate` command in Disk Administrator.

   B. Use the `Rebuild Mirror` command in Disk Administrator.

   C. Break the mirror, replace the defective disk, and re-establish the mirror.

   D. Replace the defective disk. The Disk Administrator automatically re-creates the mirror set.

3. What happens if a single disk fails in a mirrored solution on a Windows NT system?

   A. The system keeps running.

   B. The drive controller generates a stop error (a blue screen).

   C. All users are logged off and the system reboots.

   D. The second disk will fail.

4. Two disks fail in a stripe set with parity solution. What happens?

   A. The system stops.

   B. The drive controller generates a stop error (a blue screen).

   C. All users are logged off and the system reboots.

   D. The system keeps running.

5. What disk driver does Windows NT use when implementing a mirror set?

   A. NTFS.SYS

   B. FTDISK.SYS

   C. MIRROR.SYS

   D. DISK.SYS

6. Your stripe set with parity is running out of disk space. You add a new 4-GB drive to your system, and you want to expand the stripe set with parity to include the new disk. What must be done?

   A. In Disk Administrator, select the previous stripe set with parity, Ctrl + click the free space in the new disk, and select Disk Regenerate from the Fault Tolerant menu.

   B. In Disk Administrator, select the previous stripe set with parity, Ctrl + click the free space in the new disk, and select Disk Expand in the Fault Tolerant menu.

C. Back up all the data on the existing stripe set with parity, delete the partition, and create a new stripe set with parity using all the disks of the previous stripe set with parity, including the new disk. After the system has been restarted, restore all data and re-create any shares that were on the partition.

D. In Disk Administrator, select previous stripe set with parity, Ctrl + click the free space in the new disk, and select Expand Stripe Set with Parity from the Disk Menu.

7. What can be used to protect against both a disk and a disk controller failure?

    A. Stripe set

    B. Stripe set with parity

    C. Disk mirroring

    D. Disk duplexing

8. A disk has failed in a stripe set with parity. How do you recover?

    A. Replace the disk, restart the system, and allow automatic recovery to take place.

    B. Replace the disk, re-create the stripe set with parity, and restore from a tape backup.

    C. Replace the disk and select the `Disk Regenerate` command from the Fault Tolerant menu in Disk Administrator.

    D. Replace the disk. Start the Disk Administrator, right-click the remaining disks in the stripe set with parity, and select Rebuild.

9. What steps are required to recover from a failed disk in a mirror set? Select all that apply.

    A. Boot with a fault-tolerant boot disk.

    B. Replace the defective disk.

    C. Select Regenerate from the Fault Tolerant menu.

    D. Re-create the mirror.

10. This is a scenario question. First you must review the scenario, then review the required and optional results. Following that is a solution. You must pick the best evaluation of that solution.

    Scenario:
    The Omega Organization needs to establish a backup strategy. It has two Windows NT Server computers named PDC and BDC; these computers require that backups be performed. Both computers have the System and boot partitions on the C: drive, and all organizational data is stored to the D: drive. The tape backup device is on the Windows NT HCL and is located on the PDC. The following requirements have been defined:

    Required Result:
    The backup of the PDC must include the Registry.

    Optional Results:
    The backup process should be automated.

    The backup process should restrict data file access to the owner or to an administrator.

Proposed Solution:
Create the following batch file to perform the backup:

```
Ntbackup backup c:\boot.ini
d:\*.*  \\BDC\D$\*.*/t:normal
/r /b /23:00
```

Evaluation of Proposed Solution:
(Choose the most correct answer.)

A. Meets the required solution and both optional solutions

B. Meets the required solution and only one optional solution

C. Meets only the required solution

D. Does not meet the required solution

ANSWER KEY

1. A-C
2. C
3. A
4. A
5. B
6. C
7. D
8. C
9. A-B-D
10. B

ANSWERS & EXPLANATIONS

SOLVING FAULT-TOLERANCE FAILURES

1. What software-fault-tolerant solutions can be used to protect the System and boot partitions of Windows NT? Select all that apply.
   A. Disk mirroring
   C. Disk duplexing

1. CORRECT ANSWERS: A-C

Windows NT only can protect the System and boot partitions using disk mirroring or disk duplexing when using a software raid solution.

Answer B is incorrect because a stripe set is not fault tolerant. Answer D is incorrect because a stripe set with parity cannot contain the boot or System partition.

Disk mirroring writes the contents of a single disk onto two physical disks. Mirroring duplicates each write action to both disks in the mirror set. This protects against a disk failure because the system can continue to function using the other disk in the mirror set. If the disks are on separate controllers, this also protects against a controller failure. If they are on separate controllers, this commonly is known as disk duplexing. The cost associated with disk mirroring is 50 percent. This means that 50 percent of the total disk space in the mirror set is used to maintain fault-tolerant information.

Disk mirroring is the only fault-tolerant partitioning scheme provided with Windows NT that can contain the System and boot partitions. There are some issues to consider, however, when you mirror the System or boot partitions. It is possible that the disk the computer uses to start the system might not be functioning at that time. You then would need a fault-tolerant boot disk.

▼ **NOTE**

Remember that any time you update the disk configuration, you must update the Emergency Repair Disk. Doing so copies the disk configuration changes so you can recover the fault-tolerant set in case of Registry problems.

2. **How do you recover from a MIRROR failure?**

   C. Break the mirror, replace the defective disk, and re-establish the mirror.

2. CORRECT ANSWER: C

You must replace the defective disk and then re-establish the mirror using the remaining disk of the mirror set and the free space on the new disk.

Answer A is incorrect because you do not use `Disk Regenerate`. Answer B is incorrect because there is not a `Rebuild Mirror` command. Answer D is incorrect because the mirror set is not automatically re-created.

If a mirror set fails, you might need to use a fault-tolerant boot disk. You only need to do so if the Boot or system partitions of Windows NT are located on the failed drive in the mirror set. If the boot or System partitions were located on the failed disk, the following steps must be taken:

1. Diagnose which disk is the failed hard disk in the mirror set. This disk probably needs to be replaced.

2. Start the system using the fault-tolerant boot disk. Select the startup entry for the functioning disk in the system.

3. Start the Disk Administrator program.

4. Select the mirror set. (You might not be able to determine which disk has failed until you start the Disk Administrator program.)

5. From the Fault Tolerant menu, select Break Mirror.

6. Assign to the remaining member of the mirror set the original drive letter assigned to the mirror set.

7. After the defective drive has been replaced, you should re-establish the mirror. This can be done by selecting the remaining member of the mirror set and then Ctrl + clicking an area of free disk space on the newly installed disk. This area should be the same size or larger than the original member of the mirror set.

8. When prompted, restart the computer.

Chapter 6 TROUBLESHOOTING

3. What happens if a single disk fails in a mirrored solution on a Windows NT system?

   A. The system keeps running.

3. CORRECT ANSWER: A

See the explanation for question 1.

Answer B is incorrect because the controller does not generate a stop error. Answer C is incorrect because the users are not logged off and the system does not reboot. Answer D is incorrect because the second disk does not fail.

4. Two disks fail in a stripe set with parity solution. What happens?

   A. The system stops.

4. CORRECT ANSWER: A

Stripe sets with parity only protect against a single-disk failure.

Disk striping with parity protects against the failure of a single disk on a Windows NT system. A stripe set with parity writes data across all the disks in a 64-KB stripe. On a different disk in each stripe, parity information is written that assists in recovering from a disk failure. The movement of the parity information between the drives in the stripe set with parity helps to improve performance when a disk fails. If a disk fails, the information that was on the missing disk can be rebuilt using the information on the remaining disk and the parity information for that stripe. For some stripes, the parity information will have been stored on the disk that failed. No calculations are required to read information for stripes where this scenario occurs.

Windows NT–created stripe sets with parity cannot be used to store the Windows NT System and boot partitions. For data partitions, they offer better write and read performance because of the additional disk controllers involved in a stripe set with parity. A stripe set with parity requires a minimum of three disks and can be created using up to 32 disks. These disks can be any mix of disk formats, including SCSI, IDE, EIDE, and ESDI.

5. What disk driver does Windows NT use when implementing a mirror set?

   B. FTDISK.SYS

5. CORRECT ANSWER: B

Windows NT uses the fault-tolerant disk driver (FTDISK.SYS) when implementing a mirrored set.

Answers A, C, and D are not valid filenames.

It is important to know what the FTDISK.SYS file does because, if you need to create a boot disk to access a Windows NT system running a fault-tolerant solution, this file must be on the repair disk. The FTDISK file is located on the boot partition. The FTDISK file allows fault-tolerant drive arrays to be accessed with the repair disk.

6. Your stripe set with parity is running out of disk space. You add a new 4-GB drive to your system, and you want to expand the stripe set with parity to include the new disk. What must be done?

C. Back up all the data on the existing stripe set with parity, delete the partition, and create a new stripe set with parity using all the disks of the previous stripe set with parity, including the new disk. After the system has been restarted, restore all data and re-create any shares that were on the partition.

6. CORRECT ANSWER: C

Windows NT does not support increasing the number of disks in the stripe set with parity without re-creating the stripe set with parity and reloading the contents from backup.

Answer A is incorrect because you cannot regenerate the set. Answer B is incorrect because there is not a Disk Expand menu option. Answer D is incorrect because there is not an Expand Drive Set option.

7. What can be used to protect against both a disk and a disk controller failure?

D. Disk duplexing

7. CORRECT ANSWER: D

A disk-duplexing scheme protects against both disk and controller failure because each disk in the mirror set is controlled by an independent disk controller. If a controller or drive fails, the system continues to operate.

Answer A is incorrect because a stripe set is not fault tolerant. Answer B is incorrect because a stripe set with parity does not protect against controller failure. Answer C is incorrect because disk mirroring uses the same drive controller, which still leaves a single point of failure.

8. A disk has failed in a stripe set with parity. How do you recover?

C. Replace the disk and select the `Disk Regenerate` command from the Fault Tolerant menu in Disk Administrator.

8. CORRECT ANSWER: C

When a disk fails in a stripe set with parity, the Windows NT system can continue to use the disk array. When reading information from a stripe, the computer rebuilds any missing information from the failed disk using the parity information and the remaining disks for that stripe.

Answer A is incorrect because there is not automatic recovery to a disk failure. Answer B is incorrect because you do not need to restore the data. Answer D is incorrect because there is not a Rebuild option in Disk Administrator.

An example might be the best way to explain how parity information is calculated and used when a single disk fails in a stripe set with parity. Stripe sets with parity use the `Exclusive OR` function to create the parity information for each stripe. The `Exclusive OR` function is based on the following series of calculations:

- 0 Exclusive OR 0 = 0
- 0 Exclusive OR 1 = 1
- 1 Exclusive OR 0 = 1
- 1 Exclusive OR 1 = 0

Table 6.2 shows how the parity information is calculated for a single stripe as the data is written to the stripe.

TABLE 6.2   CALCULATING THE PARITY INFORMATION FOR A STRIPE SET WITH PARITY

Drive	Drive Status	Bit Pattern
Data drive 1	Running	11100011
Data drive 2	Running	11101101 XOR
Check Byte drive	Running	00001110

If Data drive 1 fails, the calculation shown in Table 6.3 is used to re-create the data missing from Data drive 1.

TABLE 6.3   CALCULATING THE PARITY INFORMATION FOR A STRIPE SET WITH PARITY

Drive	Drive Status	Bit Pattern
Data drive 1	Running	11100011
Check Byte drive	Running	00001110 XOR
Data drive 2	Failed	11101101

The system regenerates the information from Data drive 2 in memory on the fly. Because of the amount of calculations required, system performance suffers. Therefore, you need to quickly replace the failed disk and regenerate the stripe set with parity.

▼ **NOTE**

If two or more disks fail in a stripe set with parity, the only way to recover is to restore from a backup tape.

If a stripe set with parity fails, you should replace the defective disk as quickly as possible. The following process is used:

1. Start the Disk Administrator program to determine which disk has failed.

2. Replace the failed disk. Windows NT does not support hot-swapping functionality; the system must be shut down to replace the drive with a new drive. The new drive must be at least the same size as the original drive.

3. Start the Disk Administrator again.

4. Click the stripe set with parity you need to repair and then Ctrl + click the free space of the drive you want to add to the stripe set with parity.

5. From the Fault Tolerant menu, select Regenerate. Note that this process can take some time, although it takes less time than restoring from tape.

6. If any other partitions were on the failed drive, they might need to be restored from a tape backup.

▼ **NOTE**

You cannot increase the size of a stripe set with parity unless you back up its information. To back up a stripe set with parity, delete the previous stripe set with parity and create a new one using additional disks. After the new stripe set with parity is running, you have to restore the original data from the backup.

Chapter 6 TROUBLESHOOTING

9. What steps are required to recover from a failed disk in a mirror set? Select all that apply.

   A. Boot with a fault-tolerant boot disk.
   B. Replace the defective disk.
   D. Re-create the mirror.

9. CORRECT ANSWERS: A-B-D

To recover from a failed mirror set, you might have to boot with a fault-tolerant disk if the failed disk is the disk and partition referenced in the BOOT.INI. You also must replace the defective disk and re-create the mirror set in Disk Administrator.

Answer C is incorrect because you do not use the regenerate command with mirror sets.

See the explanation for question 2.

10. Proposed Solution:
    Create the following batch file to perform the backup:

    ```
    Ntbackup backup c:\boot.
    ini d:\*.*\\BDC\D$\*.*/
    t:normal /r /b /23:
    ```

    B. Meets the required solution and only one optional solution

10. CORRECT ANSWER: B

The required objective is met because /b for backing up the Registry is included in the NTBACKUP statement, and a file is being backed up from the C: drive of the PDC. The /r parameter restricts access to the data to owners or an administrator. There is no such parameter as /time.

Answers A, C, and D are incorrect because the required results and only one of the optional results were met.

The Windows NT Backup program does not support the scheduling of backups. If you want to schedule backups, you must use the text version of the NTBACKUP command and the Automatic Transaction (AT.EXE) command that comes with Windows NT. The NTBACKUP command uses the following syntax:

```
NTBACKUP BACKUP paths [/A] [/V] [/R] [/D "TEXT"]
[/B] [/HC:ON¦OFF] [/T type] [/L "LOGFILE"]
```

In this syntax:

- /A indicates that the new backup operation should be appended to the tape.

- /V indicates that the backup set should be verified after the backup process is completed.

- /R indicates that restoration should be restricted to administrators or owners of the file.

- /D "TEXT" enables an electronic description to be associated with the backup.

- /B indicates that the local Registry should be included in the backup operation.

- /HC:ON|OFF turns the hardware compression feature on or off.

- /T sets the backup type. Options include Normal, Incremental, Differential, Copy, or Daily.

- /L "LOGFILE" indicates that logging should occur and should be written to the indicated log file.

A batch file can be written that can be called by the Windows NT AT.EXE command. The AT command enables you to schedule a batch file to be run at regular intervals.

```
AT time [ /EVERY:date[,...] | /NEXT:date[,...]] "command"
```

If you create a batch file named fullback.bat, for example, and you want it to run every Friday at 11:30 p.m., you would use the following command:

```
AT 23:30 /EVERY:Friday "FULLBACK.BAT"
```

▼ NOTE

The AT command requires that the Schedule service be running on the computer on which you want to run the scheduled backup.

FURTHER REVIEW

SOLVING FAULT-TOLERANCE FAILURES

The following key words are important terms that were covered in this section. You should make sure you understand each one and what it does.

Key Words

Disk duplexing

Disk mirroring

Disk striping

Disk striping with parity

`Exclusive OR` function

NTBackup

Backup Strategies

Some very common backup strategies can be implemented to make sure data is not lost on a system. These strategies include the following:

- Daily full backups
- Weekly full backups with differentials
- Weekly full backups with incrementals

A backup methodology of full backups can be implemented when the total amount of data that needs to be backed up can be handled by your tape backup device and can be performed in a timely fashion. As the size of your backup set increases, this backup methodology generally evolves into a weekly full backup set with differentials or incrementals occurring on the other days of the week. With the increases in data storage over the past few years, this often requires that a tape changer be in place to enable the automatic changing of tapes. If data is lost and needs to be restored from tape, it takes a single restore function to restore the entire system to the state it was in after the last completed backup.

When using the backup with differentials method, full backups usually are run once a week. On the other days of the week, a differential backup is run. The differential backs up all the files that have changed since the previous week's full backup. If the system needs to be restored fully from backup, it requires two restore operations—one from the previous week's full backup and one from the previous day's differential backup. A common practice is to store the full backups off-site to prevent loss of data from a natural disaster or fire.

When using the backup with incrementals method, full backups usually are run once a week. On the other days of the week, an incremental backup is run. The incremental backups save all the files that have changed since the last backup. It does not matter whether it was a full backup or the incremental backup from the day before. If the system needs to be restored fully from backup, it requires many restore operations. First you restore the previous week's full backup. You then restore the incremental backups in order. A common practice is to store the full backups off-site to prevent loss of data from a natural disaster or fire.

PRACTICE QUESTIONS

ADVANCED PROBLEM RESOLUTION

1. In Windows NT debugging, the host computer is which of the following?

    A. The computer suffering the STOP errors

    B. The computer running the kernel debugger

    C. The computer running the Remote Debug service

    D. The file in which the Windows NT Symbol files are stored on the network

2. In Windows NT debugging, the target computer is which of the following?

    A. The computer suffering the STOP errors

    B. The computer running the kernel debugger

    C. The computer running the Remote Debug service

    D. The file where the Windows NT Symbol files are stored on the network

3. What program writes the contents of memory to a disk file when a STOP error occurs?

    A. CRASHDUMP
    B. DUMPCHK.EXE
    C. DUMPFLOP.EXE
    D. DUMPEXAM.EXE

4. In which file are the contents of a CRASHDUMP stored by default?

    A. Paging file
    B. `%SystemRoot%\crashdmp.log`
    C. `%SystemRoot%\memdump.log`
    D. `%SystemRoot%\memory.dmp`

5. What utility can be used to reduce the size of a memory dump file by extracting the crucial information that Microsoft Technical services requires to diagnose a problem?

    A. CRASHDUMP
    B. DUMPCHK.EXE
    C. DUMPFLOP.EXE
    D. DUMPEXAM.EXE

6. What utility can be used to copy the contents of a memory dump to floppy disks to be sent to Microsoft technical support?

    A. DUMPDISK.EXE
    B. DUMPCHK.EXE
    C. DUMPFLOP.EXE
    D. DUMPEXAM.EXE

7. When running a kernel debugger, what command is entered to display all device drivers in use and their link dates?

    A. devices

    B. !devices

    C. drivers

    D. !drivers

8. When performing kernel debugging on a multiprocessor computer, what additional steps must be performed before starting the debugging process?

    A. Add the /MULTI parameter to the BOOT.INI file of the target computer.

    B. Set the environment variable _DEBUG_PROCESSOR to MULTI on the host computer.

    C. Rename the file NTKRNLMP.DBG to NTOSKRNL.EXE on the host computer.

    D. Rename the file NTKRNLMP.DBG to NTOSKRNL.EXE on the target computer.

9. What must be configured on both the host and target computers for successful kernel debugging to take place? Select all that apply.

    A. Debug ports

    B. Remote Debug service

    C. Port speed settings

    D. The NT Symbol path

10. If you have not configured your computer to store the results of a STOP error into a memory dump file, where might you look to see what the actual STOP error was?

    A. Server Manager

    B. DRWATSON.LOG

    C. MEMORY.DMP

    D. Windows NT Event Viewer

ANSWER KEY

1. B
2. A
3. A
4. D
5. D
6. C
7. D
8. C
9. A-C
10. D

ANSWERS & EXPLANATIONS

ADVANCED PROBLEM RESOLUTION

1. In Windows NT debugging, the host computer is which of the following?

B. The computer running the kernel debugger

1. CORRECT ANSWER: B

The host computer is the computer running the kernel debugging software.

Answer A is incorrect because the computer with the STOP errors is the target computer. Answer C is incorrect because there is not a Remote Debug service. Answer D is incorrect because the machine containing the Symbol file is not necessarily the host computer.

You can remotely debug a system by running the kernel debugger on another system, called the host computer. The system suffering the STOP errors is considered the target computer.

The host computer requires that the necessary tools for debugging be located on a local disk drive. The symbol tree is used in debugging to provide information about what the code does at various locations. This information is different for every version of Windows NT. The symbol library for a standard single-processor version of Windows NT is in the \support\debug\%platform%\symbols directory on the CD-ROM.

If you have installed a service pack or you are working with a HAL other than the basic single-processor HAL, you need to create a symbol set for the system. The following list outlines how to do this:

1. Copy the correct directory structure from the Support directory on the CD to your hard drive.

2. For the updates you have applied, copy the symbols from the distribution media in the same order you applied them. Depending on your service pack version, these might need to be expanded first.

3. For multiprocessor systems, you have to rename some of the symbol files. The standard kernel debugger files are named NTOSKRNL.DBG for kernel and HAL.DBG for the HAL. On a multiprocessor computer, you need to rename NTKRNLMP.DBG to NTOSKRNL.DBG. These files are in the \Exe subdirectory.

4. Next you need to set up the host with a series of environment variables so the debugger has the basic information it needs. You can do this using the SET command (for help on how to use this command, type **SET /?** at a prompt) along with the following switches:

    - _NT_DEBUG_PORT: The COM port being used
    - _NT_DEBUG_BAUD_RATE: The baud rate for the port
    - _NT_SYMBOL_PATH: The directory in which the symbols directory is located
    - _NT_LOG_FILE_OPEN: The name of a log file (optional)

▼ **NOTE**

To automate the process of performing kernel debugging, you might want to create a batch file that sets the preceding environment variables and starts the kernel debugger.

5. After you restart the host system, you can perform kernel debugging on the remote system. To do this, run the kernel debugger for the platform of the target machine. You need to be aware of the following command-line switches:

    - -b: Sends a debug breakpoint to the remote system, causing execution on the target computer to stop as soon as possible.
    - -c: Requests a communications resync when the systems connect.

- -m: Watches the modem control lines. This places the debugger in terminal mode if there is no CD (carrier detect).

- -n: Loads the symbols immediately. They usually are loaded in a deferred mode.

- -v: Activates verbose mode.

- -x: Forces the debugger to break in immediately when an exception occurs. The application usually is left to deal with it.

If you want to invoke the debugger, you must use the Ctrl + C combination. After you have started the debugger, you need to use some of the commands in Table 6.4 to diagnose the problems.

TABLE 6.4   KERNEL DEBUGGING COMMANDS

Command	Usage
!reload	Reloads the symbol files if an updated symbol file has been copied to the host system.
!trap	Dumps the computer state when the trap frame occurs. It shows the state of the computer when an access fault has occurred.
!errlog	Displays the contents of an error log that the system builds as kernel errors occur. If there are contents in the log, this can assist in determining which component or process caused the STOP error.
!process	Lists information about the current process running on the active processor.
!process 0 0	Lists all running processes and their headers.
!thread	Lists all the currently running threads.
!drivers	Displays a list of all drivers currently loaded. The most useful information often is the link date, which can be used to determine whether nonservice-pack versions of drivers are used correctly.
!vm	Lists the system's virtual memory usage.
g	Releases the target computer if kernel debugging was invoked by the person performing kernel debugging.
.reboot	Restarts the target computer.

2. **In Windows NT debugging, the target computer is which of the following?**

    A. The computer suffering the STOP errors.

> **2. CORRECT ANSWER: A**
>
> The target computer is the computer on which the STOP errors are occurring. This computer is the target of the kernel debugging.
>
> Answer B is incorrect because the computer running the debugger is the host computer. Answer C is incorrect because there is not a Remote Debug service. Answer D is incorrect because the machine containing the Symbol file is not the target computer.
>
> For the system you debug to properly route the information (to the serial port rather than to the screen), you need to modify the BOOT.INI file. The following list provides the switches you should add to the version of Windows NT you will boot:
>
> - /Debug: Tells NT to load the kernel debugger during boot and to kept it in memory.
>
> - /Crashdebug: Similar to the /Debug option, except the debugging code is available only if the system crashes. In most cases, this is a better option because the debugger code is not in memory and, therefore, doesn't interfere with the problem.
>
> - /Debugport: Indicates the communications port you use.
>
> - /Baudrate: Selects the baud rate for the connection you use for debugging.
>
> You also must configure the target computer to not reboot in the case of a STOP error so kernel debugging can be performed at that time. This can be done by deselecting the Automatically Reboot option on the Startup/Shutdown tab of the System applet in the Control Panel.

3. **What program writes the contents of memory to a disk file when a STOP error occurs?**

    A. CRASHDUMP

> **3. CORRECT ANSWER: A**
>
> Although not a true executable, the CRASHDUMP routine writes the contents of memory to the page file with an indicator that a memory dump has been written to the page file.

When the system is restarted, the contents of the page file are written to the file %SystemRoot%\Memory.dmp by default.

Answers B, C, and D are incorrect; these are utilities used for other debugging purposes. See the explanation for question 5.

4. In which file are the contents of a CRASHDUMP stored by default?

D. %SystemRoot%\memory.dmp

4. CORRECT ANSWER: D

The contents of a memory dump are stored in the file %SystemRoot%\memory.dmp by default. The actual memory dump originally is written to the page file on the boot partition in Windows NT with an indicator that a memory dump has taken place. When the system is restarted, the page file contents then are copied to the MEMORY.DMP file. You might receive a warning that you are running out of virtual memory space when the system initially restarts.

Answer A is incorrect because a CRASHDUMP is not stored in the paging file. Answers B and C are not valid filenames.

5. What utility can be used to reduce the size of a memory dump file by extracting the crucial information that Microsoft Technical services requires to diagnose a problem?

D. DUMPEXAM.EXE

5. CORRECT ANSWER: D

The DUMPEXAM utility reduces the size of a memory dump file for transport to Microsoft Technical support. It includes only the relevant information and, by default, stores the information in a file named MEMORY.TXT.

Answer A is incorrect because CRASHDUMP is not a true utility. (See the explanation for question 3.) Answers C and D are utilities used for other purposes.

Three utilities that come with Windows NT enable you to work with the memory dump files. These utilities are listed here with a brief description:

- DUMPCHK: Makes sure the dump file is in order by verifying all the addresses and listing the errors and system information.

- DUMPEXAM: Creates a text file to provide the same information that was on the blue screen at the time the STOP error occurred. You need the symbol files, the kernel debugger extensions, and `IMAGEHLP.DLL` to run a dump exam. The DUMPEXAM utility can be used only for STOP 0x0000000A and 0x0000001E errors.

- DUMPFLOP: Backs up and compresses the dump file to a series of floppies so they can be sent to Microsoft.

6. What utility can be used to copy the contents of a memory dump to floppy disks to be sent to Microsoft technical support?

   C. DUMPFLOP.EXE

6. CORRECT ANSWER: C

Not only does DUMPFLOP copy the entire `MEMORY.DMP` file to floppy disk, it also compresses the information.

Answer A is incorrect because this is not a valid utility name. Answers B and C are utilities used for other purposes.

See the explanation in question 5.

7. When running a kernel debugger, what command is entered to display all device drivers in use and their link dates?

   D. `!drivers`

7. CORRECT ANSWER: D

The command `!drivers` is executed within the kernel debugger. It is a Windows NT resource kit tool that displays the same results for the computer on which the program is run. For more information about the kernel debugger, see the explanation for question 1.

Answers A, B, and C are not valid commands for the kernel debugger.

8. When performing kernel debugging on a multiprocessor computer, what additional steps must be performed before starting the debugging process?

   C. Rename the file `NTKRNLMP.DBG` to `NTOSKRNL.EXE` on the host computer.

8. CORRECT ANSWER: C

You must rename the `NTKNRLMP.DBG` file on the host computer to `NTOSKRNL.EXE`. A multiprocessor computer uses the multiprocessor version of the `NTOS2KRNL.EXE`, and the symbol file must match the executable on the host computer.

Answer A is incorrect because there is not a `/MULTI BOOT.INI` parameter. Answer B is incorrect because you do not set a variable for multiprocessors. Answer D is incorrect because you do not rename the file on the host computer.

ANSWERS & EXPLANATIONS   375

9. **What must be configured on both the host and target computers for successful kernel debugging to take place? Select all that apply.**

   A. Debug ports
   C. Port speed settings

For further explanation of remote debugging, see the explanations for questions 1 and 2.

9. CORRECT ANSWERS: A-C

Both the target and host computers must configure which port and what speed will be used for debugging to take place.

Answer B is incorrect because there is not a Remote Debug service. Answer D is incorrect because the NT Symbol path does not need to be configured.

You can interactively debug a problematic computer using another computer, either with a RAS null modem cable or remotely by using a modem. The port-speed setting must be identical for the target and host computers.

In the \support\debug directory on the distribution CD, there is a kernel debugger for each platform that can be used for installation. The kernel debuggers use basic serial communications, and each needs some configuration. The following steps are involved in preparing for a debugging session:

1. Set up the serial connection.
2. Configure the problematic computer (target).
3. Place the symbol tree on the diagnostic computer (host).
4. Start the computer in debugging mode.
5. Start the debugger on the diagnostic computer.

You might not be able to use an off-the-rack null modem cable to perform kernel debugging. Table 6.5 shows the cabling requirements for a 9-pin cable. Table 6.6 shows the cabling specifications for a 25-pin cable. Kernel debugging does not function correctly if the null modem cable you use does not meet these specifications.

TABLE 6.5 9-PIN NULL MODEM CABLING

Remote Host	Calling System	Signal
3	2	Transmit Data
2	3	Receive Data
7	8	Request to Send
8	7	Clear to Send
6,1	4	Data Set Ready and Carrier Detect
5	5	Signal Ground
4	6,1	Data Terminal Ready

TABLE 6.6 25-PIN NULL MODEM CABLING

Remote Host	Calling System	Signal
3	2	Transmit Data
2	3	Receive Data
4	5	Request to Send
4	4	Clear to Send
6,8	20	Data Set Ready and Carrier Detect
7	7	Signal Ground
20	6,8	Data Terminal Ready

After you have created the null modem cable, connect the host and target computers. Be sure to plug the Remote Host end of the null modem cable into the target computer and the Calling System end of the cable into the host computer.

10. If you have not configured your computer to store the results of a STOP error into a memory dump file, where might you look to see what the actual STOP error was?

   D. Windows NT Event Viewer

10. CORRECT ANSWER: D

The Windows NT Event Viewer's System log can contain an entry with the actual STOP error message if the Startup/Shutdown tab in the System applet has been configured to write an event to the system log.

Answer A is incorrect because Server Manager does not display STOP error information. Answer B is incorrect because this is not a valid file. Answer C is incorrect because you cannot tell what the actual STOP error was from the MEMORY.DMP file.

Thousands of events can be listed in the event logs. To make finding the problem easier, you can filter the log. Filters can be set on any of the event fields in the preceding list. To filter the log, choose View, Filter from the menu.

Searching for an event is similar to filtering. In many cases, however, it is more useful for troubleshooting because it enables you to see the events around the one for which you are looking. You can find an event by going to View, Find.

The Find dialog box appears and enables you to enter search criteria. The options are almost the same as in the Filter Events dialog box. You will notice, however, that dates are missing. You now can look for any piece of text in the details of the event and can choose to search up or down.

Two other errors usually are found in the security log. Violations of security are shown as locks, and access events are shown as keys. Blue screen errors are cases in which the operating system fails to start or abruptly stops working.

There are two ways to deal with a blue screen. You can reboot the system, but if the problem continues, you might have to diagnose which driver or component of Windows NT is causing the STOP error. Interpreting the information reported when a STOP error has occurred can help in diagnosing which driver might be at fault. You also can use some of the tools provided by Windows NT to diagnose the problem and fix it.

Debug Port Status Indicators, Bugcheck Information, Driver Information, Kernel Build Number and Stack Dump, and Debug Port Information are the items used to determine the root of a system crash.

You also can configure the computer to create a dump file and debug it or to use a kernel debugger to isolate the problem. Boot options associated with a debug are /DEBUG, /CRASHDEBUG, /DEBUGPORT, and /BAUDRATE. You can keep the system debug-ready by setting the /DEBUG switch in the BOOT.INI. This enables the host computer running a kernel debugger to interrupt processing on the target computer whenever desired. If you use the /CRASHDEBUG switch, kernel debugging is enabled only after a STOP error has occurred.

When a STOP error occurs and the system gives the character mode stop screen, the following five main sections are on-screen:

- Debug Port Status Indicators: Describes the status of the serial port. If it is in use, that information is used for debugging.

- BugCheck Information: Displays the actual error code and any parameters included by the developer in the error-trapping routines. If only the top line is displayed, the error also has affected the areas used to display such information. This is the most useful information for diagnosing the cause of the STOP screen.

- Driver Information: This area lists the drivers that were loaded when the STOP error occurred. Three items of information are given for each driver, as follows:

  - The memory location into which the driver was loaded.

  - The time the driver was created. (This is the offset in seconds from Jan 1, 1970; use CVTIME.EXE to convert these to readable dates.)

  - The name of the driver. BugCheck Information sometimes includes a pointer to the instruction that caused the ABEND (abnormal end). You can use this information to discover which driver was involved.

- Kernel Build Number and Stack Dump: Provides information about the current build number and a dump of the last instructions executed.

- Debug Port Information: Indicates the baud rate and other COM settings for the debug port in use.

> **FURTHER REVIEW**

ADVANCED PROBLEM RESOLUTION

The following key words are important terms that were covered in this section. You should make sure you understand each one and what it does.

Key Words

- Application event log
- DUMPCHK
- DUMPEXAM
- DUMPFLOP
- Host computer
- Kernel debugger
- Memory dump file
- Security event log
- Stop event
- System event log
- Target computer

Analyzing Memory Dump Files

Sometimes you are unable to resolve the problem using the kernel debugger. When this happens, you might want to have Windows NT create a dump file and either try to analyze it yourself or send it to Microsoft for analysis.

To create a dump file, you must have the page file existing on the boot partition of Windows NT. The page file on this partition must be larger in size than the total memory installed on the computer because the contents of memory are copied into the page file when a STOP error occurs.

The system restarts and the contents of the page file are copied to the configured memory dump file. The default is `%SystemRoot%\memory.dmp`. This can be configured in the System applet of Control Panel on the Startup/Shutdown tab. You must make sure there is enough free disk space on the partition where the `MEMORY.DMP` file is to be created. It will be the size of the installed RAM on the system.

Configuring Windows NT to create a dump file is easy. You must configure the DumpCrash settings. Use the following steps to set this up:

1. Right-click the My Computer icon.
2. Choose the Startup/Shutdown tab.
3. Under Recovery, click the Write Debugging Information To check box.

    You can select to overwrite an existing dump file by checking Overwrite any Existing File.

    You can enter another location for the dump file by entering the location (and name) into the text box.

4. Click OK.

Finding More Information

If you have worked with the event logs in Windows NT, you know that the information displayed in the event details sometimes can be cryptic. This means you need to be able to find more information using the event ID or other clues in the information. The following are three very good sources for information about Windows NT errors:

- Microsoft TechNet is a solid and very current source of information, and it is available as a monthly subscription. TechNet probably is the best source for troubleshooting information for Windows NT and all Microsoft products. Shipped to subscribers on a monthly basis, it comes on at least two CDs.

- The Microsoft support site, at `http://www.microsoft.com/support`, has a full suite of information about problems other users already have experienced. One of the more helpful items on the support site is a group of troubleshooting wizards. These wizards step you through the process of troubleshooting, and they provide you with solutions that come from the Microsoft technical staff.

- The Microsoft Knowledge Base contains articles about errors in the Windows NT operating system and their solutions. The Knowledge Base is accessible on the Internet at `http://www.microsoft.com/kb`.

SUMMARY

This chapter examined the different areas of Windows NT you need to be able to troubleshoot. If you approach this systematically, you are likely to quickly find the problem. This chapter also showed the number and variety of tools available for troubleshooting Windows NT.

The different Windows NT areas you need to know how to troubleshoot include the following:

- Installation and boot failures
- Resource access failures
- Tracing network connectivity failures
- Recovering from fault-tolerant drive failures
- Debugging STOP errors

Practice Exam 1

The Windows NT Server Enterprise exam is an adaptive test—meaning that the number of questions you must answer is indeterminate. The following describes how an adaptive test works:

- The test covers six categories: Planning, Installation and Configuration, Managing Resources, Connectivity, Monitoring and Optimization, and Troubleshooting. Test questions are associated with these categories.

- The testing system asks an extremely difficult question for one of the five test categories. If you answer correctly, the testing system asks you a few easier questions to pass the category.

  If you answer incorrectly, the testing system presents you with at least one less difficult question for the category. If you continue to incorrectly answer questions for the category, the questions become increasingly less difficult until the testing system determines that you do not have sufficient knowledge to pass the category.

  If you finally answer a question correctly, the testing system asks increasingly difficult questions for the category until you correctly answer a certain number of questions (the number is unknown to you or me).

You are not asked the questions in any particular order; they are distributed randomly. The testing system presents questions for all six categories in a seemingly random order. The passing score is 784 out of 1,000. The following are the two types of questions in the test:

- **Multiple-choice questions.** Select the correct answer.
- **Scenario-based questions.** Select the response or best scenario from the scenario description.

It is suggested that you set a timer to track your progress while taking the practice exam, because the time restrictions on the tests are often the biggest obstacles to overcome. Begin the following practice exam after you set your timer.

Questions 1 and 2 are based on the following scenario:

Your company has chosen to replace its current network platform with Windows NT. The current network has 1,600 users and 21 file servers located at four wide-area sites.

Day-to-day business requires a substantial amount of file sharing and remote printing among sites.

To date, each site has its own information systems department that manages and supports all users and resources at the respective site. Your company has decided to maintain this network management structure.

1. What domain model is the best choice for the new Windows NT network?

   A. Multiple master domains

   B. Single master domain

   C. Single domain

   D. Complete trust domains

2. In addition to the 1,600 users, it is estimated that the new Windows NT network requires 200 global groups, 55 local groups on domain controllers, and 1,150 computer accounts. The average global group has 35 members and the average local group has five members. If all this information were installed in a single SAM database, approximately how large would the database be?

   A. 1 MB

   B. 2.45 MB

   C. 4.4 MB

   D. 700 KB

3. A large number of your company's employees work at more than one of the wide-area sites that comprise the network. Generally, what directory services architecture is best suited for traveling users?

   A. Full-trust domains, so that the traveling users can have a logon ID for each site and still access resources at other sites.

   B. A single domain, so that each user has one logon ID, and all resources on the network are accessible.

   C. Full-trust domains, so that the user has one logon ID and can use any local domain controller for the logon process.

   D. None of the above.

4. The Widget company network consists of three domains: DM_Sales, DM_Mfg, and DM_Admin. At present, the three domains do not share resources. Users in the DM_Sales domain need to access some resources that belong to the DM_Mfg domain. How would you enable access to the resources in DM_Mfg for users in DM_Sales?

   A. Establish a two-way trust relationship between DM_Mfg and DM_Sales.

   B. Configure DM_Mfg to trust DM_Sales.

   C. Configure DM_Mfg to trust DM_Sales and DM_Sales to allow DM_Mfg to trust DM_Sales.

   D. Set up user accounts in the DM_Mfg domain with the same username and password as the corresponding accounts in DM_Sales.

5. When a trust relationship is broken by a failed network connection, you can easily reestablish the trust relationship (after the network connection is restored) by which of the following methods? Select the best answer.

   A. Reboot the domain controllers.

   B. Reestablish the network connection to restore the trust relationship.

C. Reestablish the network connection and reboot the Primary Domain Controller for each domain.

D. Reestablish the network connection, delete the trust relationship in both domains, and create a new trust relationship.

6. **What are the limitations of local user accounts? Select the best answer.**

    A. They cannot be used to access another domain.

    B. Their passwords cannot be synchronized.

    C. They do not support the interactive logon process.

    D. All of the above.

7. **Which of the following statements is true about the local Administrator account on a Windows NT domain controller?**

    A. It cannot be deleted.

    B. It is by default a member of the local Server Operators group.

    C. It cannot be renamed.

    D. None of the above.

8. **After a trust relationship has been established between two domains, why is it possible for users to access resources across domains?**

    A. Establishing the trust relationship merges the user account databases from the two domains.

    B. The logon services from the trusted domain pass the resource access request to the trusting domain's logon services, where the resource access permissions are authenticated.

    C. Duplicate logon IDs are created in the trusting domain's account database when you assign permissions.

    D. The trust relationship allows logon services from the trusting domain to access the trusted domain's account database.

9. **Which RAID levels are built in to Windows NT Server?**

    A. Levels 1, 2, and 3

    B. Levels 1, 2, and 5

    C. Levels 0, 1, and 5

    D. All levels of RAID fault-tolerance

10. **What is the maximum number of physical disks that Windows NT Server RAID 5 fault-tolerance supports?**

    A. There is no limit.

    B. 16.

    C. 32.

    D. 128.

11. **Which is the best Windows NT disk fault-tolerance configuration for read performance?**

    A. RAID Level 1

    B. Disk mirroring

    C. Disk striping

    D. Disk striping with parity

12. **What is the method by which Windows NT Server protects against writing data to a bad sector on its fault-tolerant volume of a hard disk?**

    A. RAID Level 5

    B. Hot swapping

    C. Sector sparing

    D. Hot fixing

13. **What is one reason why TCP/IP is the protocol of choice for most networks?**

    A. It allows connectivity between dissimilar networks and devices.

    B. TCP/IP is more easily installed and configured than other protocols.

    C. It is a self-encrypting protocol that provides secure communications.

    D. All the above.

14. **After you shut down a Windows NT Server that is a master browser, what must you do? Select the best response.**

    A. Do nothing; the network will elect a new master browser when the time limit on the downed browser expires.

    B. Promote a domain controller to master browser.

    C. Manually trigger a WINS replication for the entire network.

    D. None of the above.

15. **What switch is used with the Windows NT Server installation program to suppress the creation of floppy startup disks?**

    A. /B

    B. /N

    C. /NOBOOT

    D. /SI

16. **To promote a Windows NT member Server to domain controller, what must you do? Select the best answer.**

    A. Select the Domain Controller option from Add/Remove software in the Control Panel.

    B. Run the Windows NT installation program using the /DC switch.

    C. Reinstall the server and configure it as a domain controller during installation.

    D. Promote the server to domain controller by using Server Manager.

17. **You are the network administrator for a small network that consists of 12 workstations and a single Windows NT Server. Your boss asks you to set up an intranet Web site. What is required to install Internet Information Server?**

    A. Purchase Internet Information Server and install it on the current server.

    B. Install Internet Information Server from the Windows NT Server CD-ROM if you did not install it during the initial installation of the Windows NT Server software.

    C. Install Internet Information Server from the Windows NT Server CD-ROM only if the Windows NT Server is a domain controller.

D. Activate Internet Information Server, which is automatically included in the Windows NT Server installation process.

18. **The NETLOGON service is used to do what? Select the best answer.**

    A. Facilitate SAM database synchronization.

    B. Process logon requests.

    C. Facilitate pass-through authentication.

    D. All the above.

19. **To promote a Backup Domain Controller to a Primary Domain Controller, what must you do?**

    A. Reinstall Windows NT Server and specify the server as a PDC during installation.

    B. Choose the Primary Domain Controller option from the Networks applet in the Control Panel.

    C. Choose Promote to Primary Domain Controller in the File menu for Server Manager.

    D. Backup Domain Controllers cannot be manually promoted. This is handled automatically by Windows NT.

20. **What do you call a Windows NT Server that has more than one network adapter installed?**

    A. A routable server.

    B. A multihomed server.

    C. A proxy server.

    D. None of the above. A Windows NT Server is limited to a single network interface card.

21. **DHCP can be used on a Windows NT Network to do what? Select the best answer.**

    A. Set the default gateway for DHCP clients.

    B. Assign IP addresses to DHCP clients.

    C. Set the WINS server addresses for DHCP clients.

    D. All the above.

22. **255.255.255.0 is the default subnet mask for what IP address class?**

    A. Class A

    B. Class B

    C. Class C

    D. Class A or Class B, depending on the value of the first octet

23. **What happens when duplicate IP addresses are assigned to two Windows NT Workstations on the same network?**

    A. All network communications stop.

    B. When the second workstation is started, a warning message is issued, and the workstation does not connect to the network.

    C. DHCP automatically assigns a new, unique address to the second workstation that starts.

    D. WINS automatically translates communications to and from the second workstation started.

24. This is a scenario question. First you must review the scenario, then review the required and optional results. Following that is a solution. You must pick the best evaluation of that solution.

    Scenario:

    Alice has taken over as administrator of a small network. It consists of 150 users with two domains that fully trust each other. There are three file servers in Domain A, of which the Primary Domain Controller is one. In Domain B, the Primary Domain Controller is a print server and there is also an application server. No baseline has been created for the domain controllers of either domain.

    Required Result:
    A baseline must be created for each of the domain controllers.

    Optional Results:
    A baseline must be created for the application server.

    A baseline must be created for the print server.

    Proposed Solution:
    Alice uses Performance Monitor on each of the file servers and the application server each day, throughout the day, for two weeks. She uses the Log view so that a log file can be created and referenced at a later date.

    Evaluation of Proposed Solution:
    (Choose the most correct answer.)

    A. The required result is met, and both optional results are also met.

    B. The required result and one optional result is met.

    C. The required result is met, and neither optional result is met.

    D. The required result is not met, and one optional result is met.

    E. No result is met.

25. What is the purpose of a DHCP relay agent?

    A. To facilitate communication between WINS servers across routers

    B. To forward DHCP broadcasts to DHCP servers across routers.

    C. To redirect NetBIOS broadcasts to the domain master browser

    D. To provide communication between WINS-enabled hosts and WINS servers across routers

26. A multihomed Windows NT Server can be used in which capacities?

    A. As a NetBEUI router

    B. As an IPX router

    C. As an IP router

    D. As an IPX router, an IP router, or both

27. When configuring a Windows NT Server to connect to a NetWare 3.11 Server by using Ethernet, it is very likely that the correct frame will be of what type?

    A. 802.5

    B. Ethernet_SNAP

    C. 802.2

    D. 802.3

28. For development purposes, a Windows NT Server is installed on your network to

use both as a workstation and a test server for no more than three programmers. What server service optimization option should be selected for this server?

   A. Minimize Memory Used

   B. Balance

   C. Maximize Throughput for File Sharing

   D. Maximize Throughput for Network Applications

29. You can edit the Windows NT Server Registry by using which of the following? Select the best answer.

   A. Any text editor

   B. NOTEPAD.EXE

   C. REGEDT32.EXE

   D. REDIT.EXE

30. To better manage traffic on your network, you manually configure one of the Windows NT Servers to be the master browser. What should you know about manually configured master browsers?

   A. The Windows NT Server configured to be the master browser will remain the master browser until it is manually reconfigured.

   B. The Windows NT Server cannot be manually configured to act as a master browser.

   C. The Windows NT Server may lose its status as a master browser if it is downed or disconnected from the network.

   D. The Windows NT Server must be a domain controller to be a master browser.

31. The users on your company's network require different configurations. As a result, many users require a special logon script. You have just installed the second Windows NT Server on your network and configured it as a Backup Domain Controller. Because users will now be logging on to one of two domain controllers, how are the special logon scripts best managed?

   A. Place all logon scripts in the default logon script location, configure user profiles to use the default location for logon scripts, and configure the Windows NT directory replication service to replicate the logon script directory between the domain controllers.

   B. Leave all logon scripts on one domain controller, and then modify the profile for each user to access the logon script from only the domain controller that contains the scripts.

   C. Create a logon script for each user and place it in their respective home directories; change all user profiles to access logon scripts in home directories.

   D. Place all logon scripts in the default logon script directory on the Primary Domain Controller. Logon scripts are automatically replicated to all domain controllers in the domain.

32. To configure the Directory Replication service, you must use what utility?

A. Server Manager.

B. The Services applet in Control Panel.

C. Directory Replication service must be configured when Windows NT Server is installed.

D. Directory Replication Manager.

33. What Windows NT utility is used to monitor network activity?

    A. Performance Monitor

    B. Network Monitor

    C. Network Manager

    D. Windows Diagnostics

34. Which of the following are counter types used by Performance Monitor? Choose all that apply.

    A. Averaging

    B. Instantaneous

    C. Delayed

    D. Difference

35. Which of the following is required to configure a mirrored drive set on a Windows NT Server?

    A. A minimum of 4 GB of storage space.

    B. At least two physical disk drives.

    C. Disk volumes must use NTFS formatting.

    D. None of the above.

36. What Windows NT Server utility is used for disk fault-tolerance configuration?

    A. Server Manager

    B. Disk Manager

    C. Server Administrator

    D. Disk Administrator

37. Which of the following is one way to configure a printer on a Windows NT Server?

    A. Use the Printers applet in Control Panel.

    B. Use Printer Manager.

    C. Use Printer Administrator.

    D. None of the above.

38. This is a scenario question. First you must review the scenario, then review the required and optional results. Following that is a solution. You must pick the best evaluation of that solution. Note that questions 39, 40, and 41 also deal with the same scenario.

Scenario:
Satellites, Inc., has three locations: Headquarters, R&D, and Manufacturing. Users in Manufacturing use files at Headquarters and R&D in addition to files on their own servers. Users at the other locations access files only on local servers.

Required Results:
Centrally manage all user accounts.

Centrally manage access to all resources.

Users at Manufacturing must access resources at Headquarters and R&D.

Optional Results:
Users at Headquarters can access resources at Manufacturing.

Users at R&D can access resources at Manufacturing.

Proposed Solution:
Implement a single master domain model with the master domain at Headquarters. Add the Domain Users group from Headquarters to the local Users group on each server to which users need access.

Evaluation of Proposed Solution:
(Choose the most correct answer.)

A. The proposed solution produces the required results and produces both optional results.

B. The proposed solution produces the required results and produces only one optional result.

C. The proposed solution produces the required results but does not produce any optional results.

D. The proposed solution does not produce the required results.

39. This applies to the same scenario as number 38.

    Scenario:
    Satellites, Inc., has three locations: Headquarters, R&D, and Manufacturing. Users in Manufacturing use files at Headquarters and R&D in addition to files on their own servers. Users at the other locations access files only on local servers.

    Required Results:
    Headquarters manages all user accounts.

    Manufacturing must access resources at Headquarters and R&D.

    Optional Results:
    R&D can access resources at Manufacturing.

Headquarters can access resources at R&D.

Proposed Solution:
Implement a single domain model. Add the Domain Users group to the local Users group on any server that needs to be accessed by users.

Evaluation of Proposed Solution:
(Choose the most correct answer.)

A. The proposed solution produces the required results and produces both optional results.

B. The proposed solution produces the required results and produces only one optional result.

C. The proposed solution produces the required results but does not produce any optional results.

D. The proposed solution does not produce the required results.

40. This applies to the same scenario as number 38.

    Scenario:
    Satellites, Inc., has three locations: Headquarters, R&D, and Manufacturing. Users in Manufacturing use files at Headquarters and R&D in addition to files on their own servers. Users at the other locations access files only on local servers.

    Required Result:
    Users at Manufacturing must access resources at Headquarters and R&D.

    Optional Results:
    Administrators at each location can manage their own accounts.

    Access to resources can be managed from a central location.

Proposed Solution:
Implement a complete trust domain model. Create accounts for each user in the domain for their location. Add the Domain Users groups from each domain to the local Users group on each server to which users need access.

Evaluation of Proposed Solution:
(Choose the most correct answer.)

- A. The proposed solution produces the required result and produces both optional results.
- B. The proposed solution produces the required result and produces only one optional result.
- C. The proposed solution produces the required result but does not produce any optional results.
- D. The proposed solution does not produce the required result.

41. **This applies to the same scenario as number 38.**

    Scenario:
    Satellites, Inc., has three locations: Headquarters, R&D, and Manufacturing. Users in Manufacturing use files at Headquarters and R&D in addition to files on their own servers. Users at the other locations access files only on local servers.

    Required Result:
    Users at Manufacturing must access resources at Headquarters and R&D.

    Optional Results:
    Users at Headquarters can access resources at Manufacturing.

    Users at R&D can access resources at Manufacturing.

Proposed Solution:
Create a domain for each location. Create trust relationships in which Manufacturing trusts R&D, and Manufacturing and Headquarters trust each other with a two-way trust. Assign domain users from each domain to the local Users group where users need to access resources.

Evaluation of Proposed Solution:
(Choose the most correct answer.)

- A. The proposed solution produces the required result and produces both optional results.
- B. The proposed solution produces the required result and produces only one optional result.
- C. The proposed solution produces the required result but does not produce any optional results.
- D. The proposed solution does not produce the required result.

42. **Which of the following groups can lock out global user accounts in a Windows NT domain? Select the best answer.**

    - A. Domain Admins
    - B. Administrators
    - C. Account Operators
    - D. System

43. **A Windows NT logon script can be of which types? Select all that apply.**

    - A. *.BAT
    - B. *.CMD
    - C. *.EXE

D. *.SYS

E. All the above.

44. **Windows NT passwords must include which of the following character types? Select the best answer.**

    A. At least one non-alphanumeric character.

    B. At least one numeric character.

    C. At least one uppercase alpha character.

    D. None of the above.

45. **Which of the following statements about global groups are true? Choose all that apply.**

    A. Global groups can have local groups as members.

    B. Global groups can be accessed across domains.

    C. Global groups can be members of local groups.

    D. Members of local groups inherit file rights assigned to global groups.

46. **What Windows NT tool is used to create global groups?**

    A. Domain Administrator

    B. User Manager

    C. Server Manager

    D. User Manager for Domains

47. **What are the global groups created when you create a Windows NT domain?**

    A. Domain Admins, Domain Controllers, and Domain Guests

    B. Domain Admins, Domain Guests, and Domain Users

    C. Domain Administrators, Domain Users, and Everyone

    D. Domain Admins, Domain Guests, and Everyone

48. **This is a scenario question. First you must review the scenario, then review the required and optional results. Following that is a solution. You must pick the best evaluation of that solution. Note that questions 49, 50, and 51 also deal with the same scenario.**

    Scenario:
    Possum County has domains at each of its county offices in Concord, Martin, and Richmond. The domains have member servers in addition to domain controllers. Each of the users has a Windows NT workstation.

    Required Result:
    Server administrators in Concord need to configure domain controllers in all three domains.

    Optional Results:
    Server administrators in Concord can configure member servers in all three domains.

    Server administrators in Concord can configure Windows NT workstations in all three domains.

    Proposed Solution:
    The Martin and Richmond domains are configured to trust the Concord domain. The Server Operators group from the Concord domain is added to the Server Operators group in the Martin and Richmond domains.

    Evaluation of Proposed Solution:
    (Choose the most correct answer.)

A. The proposed solution produces the required result and produces both optional results.

B. The proposed solution produces the required result and produces only one optional result.

C. The proposed solution produces the required result but does not produce any optional results.

D. The proposed solution does not produce the required result.

49. **This applies to the same scenario as number 48.**

    Scenario:
    Possum County has domains at each of its county offices in Concord, Martin, and Richmond. The domains have member servers in addition to domain controllers. Each of the users has a Windows NT workstation.

    Required Result:
    Administrators for the Concord domain need to administer the Richmond and Martin domains.

    Optional Results:
    Administrators for the Concord domain can administer the member servers of the Richmond and Martin domains.

    Administrators for the Concord domain can administer the Windows NT workstations of the Richmond and Martin domains.

    Proposed Solution:
    The three domains are configured in a single master domain model with the Concord domain as the master domain. The Domain Admins group from the Concord domain is added to the Administrators group of the Martin and Richmond domains.

    Evaluation of Proposed Solution:
    (Choose the most correct answer.)

    A. The proposed solution produces the required result and produces both optional results.

    B. The proposed solution produces the required result and produces only one optional result.

    C. The proposed solution produces the required result but does not produce any optional results.

    D. The proposed solution does not produce the required result.

50. **This applies to the same scenario as number 48.**

    Scenario:
    Possum County has domains at each of its county offices in Concord, Martin, and Richmond. The domains have member servers in addition to domain controllers. Each of the users has a Windows NT workstation.

    Required Result:
    Administrators need to configure user accounts in any domain.

    Optional Results:
    Administrators can back up any Windows NT machine in any domain.

    Administrators can modify network settings on the member servers in any domain.

    Proposed Solution:
    The three domains are configured in a complete trust model. The Domain Admins group from each domain is added to the administrators group in the other domains and the administrators group on each Windows NT member server in each domain.

Evaluation of Proposed Solution:
(Choose the most correct answer.)

A. The proposed solution produces the required results and produces both optional results.

B. The proposed solution produces the required results and produces only one optional result.

C. The proposed solution produces the required results but does not produce any optional results.

D. The proposed solution does not produce the required results.

51. **This applies to the same scenario as number 48.**

    Scenario:
    Possum County has domains at each of its county offices in Concord, Martin, and Richmond. The domains have member servers in addition to domain controllers. Each of the users has a Windows NT workstation.

    Required Result:
    Administrators from the Concord domain need to administer member servers in the Richmond and Martin domains.

    Optional Results:
    Administrators from the Concord domain can manage domain accounts in the Richmond domain.

    Administrators from the Concord domain can back up domain controllers in the Martin domain.

    Proposed Solution:
    The three domains are configured in a complete trust domain model. Domain Admins from the Concord domain is added to the Account Operators group in the Richmond domain. The default group assignments are used for the Concord to Martin domain.

    Evaluation of Proposed Solution:
    (Choose the most correct answer.)

    A. The proposed solution produces the required result and produces both optional results.

    B. The proposed solution produces the required result and produces only one optional result.

    C. The proposed solution produces the required result but does not produce any optional results.

    D. The proposed solution does not produce the required result.

52. **Where are roaming user profiles stored on a Windows NT Server?**

    A. On the workstation's local hard drive.

    B. In the same directory as the Windows NT Registry.

    C. In the user's home directory as defined in the user account properties.

    D. In the directory specified by the Profile Path in the user account properties.

53. **What Windows NT utility do you use to set system policies for users?**

    A. Domain Administrator

    B. User Manager for Domains

    C. System Policy Editor

    D. Policy Editor for Domains

54. How do you change the update interval time on master and backup Windows NT browsers?

    A. Run WINS Manager, select the browser, and choose Configuration from the File menu.

    B. Modify the browser's Registry.

    C. Run Server Manager, select the browser, and choose the Browser option from the File menu.

    D. None of the above. The interval time for browsers cannot be changed from its default 12 minutes.

55. What is the purpose of the %systemroot%\System32\Autoexec.nt file?

    A. It runs as a batch command file when the Windows NT Server is initialized.

    B. It is used as the Autoexec.Bat file for DOS sessions.

    C. The boot process uses this file to locate the system partition.

    D. None of the above.

EXAM ANSWERS

1. **A.** The Multiple Master domain model is the best choice because management wants to retain distributed administration of users. (Planning.)

2. **B.** The SAM database size is calculated as follows:
   - Add 1,024 bytes (1 KB) per user in the account.
   - Add 512 bytes (0.5 KB) per local group on domain controllers plus 36 bytes per member for each group.
   - Add 512 bytes (0.5 KB) per global group plus 12 bytes per member for each group.
   - Add 512 bytes (0.5 KB) per computer account.

   Use this information to make the following calculations:

1,638,400 bytes	(1,600 users × 1,024 bytes)
+ 102,400 bytes	(200 global groups × 512 bytes)
+ 84,000 bytes	(200 global groups × 35 members × 12 bytes)
+ 28,160 bytes	(55 local groups × 512 bytes)
+ 9,900 bytes	(55 local groups × 5 members × 36 bytes)
+ 588,800 bytes	(1,150 computer accounts × 512 bytes)
=2,451,660 bytes = 2.45 MB. (Planning.)	

3. **B.** Single domain directory services are best suited for traveling users, so that each user has one logon ID, all resources on the network are accessible, and logon authentication is performed at the nearest domain controller. The single domain directory services architecture may not work well for networks that have few traveling users, but it is the best choice of the options offered when only traveling users are considered. (Installation and Configuration.)

4. **C.** To enable access to the resources in DM_Mfg for users in DM_Sales, use the User Manager for Domains utility to configure DM_Mfg to trust DM_Sales and to configure DM_Sales to allow DM_Mfg to trust DM_Sales. (Managing Resources.)

5. **A.** When a trust relationship breaks, it is easily reestablished by rebooting the domain controllers. (Managing Resources.)

6. **D.** All the listed issues are limitations of local user accounts. (Managing Resources.)

7. **A.** You cannot delete the local Administrator account on a Windows NT domain controller. (Managing Resources.)

8. **B.** After a trust relationship is established between two domains, users can access resources across domains because the trust relationship allows logon services from the trusted domain to pass through access requests to the trusting domain. (Managing Resources.)

9. **C.** RAID fault-tolerance levels 0, 1, and 5 are built in to Windows NT Server. (Installation and Configuration.)

10. **C.** Windows NT Server RAID fault-tolerance supports at most 32 disks. (Installation and Configuration.)

11. **D.** The best Windows NT disk fault-tolerance configuration for read performance is disk striping with parity. (Installation and Configuration.)

12. **C.** Sector sparing is the method by which Windows NT Server protects against writing data to a bad sector on its hard disk drive(s). (Installation and Configuration.)

13. **A.** TCP/IP is the protocol of choice for most networks because it is the network industry standard and allows connectivity between dissimilar networks and devices. (Connectivity.)

14. **A.** If you shut down a Windows NT Server that is a master browser, you do nothing; the network elects a new master browser when the time limit on the downed browser expires. (Managing Resources.)

15. **A.** Use the /B switch with the Windows NT Server installation program to suppress the creation of floppy startup disks. (Installation and Configuration.)

16. **C.** You must configure a Windows NT Server as a domain controller at installation time. To promote a member server to domain controller, you must reinstall Windows NT Server. (Installation and Configuration.)

17. **B.** Internet Information Server (IIS) ships with Windows NT Server. You can install IIS on any Windows NT Server (domain controller or not), and you have the option of installing IIS when you install Windows NT Server. (Installation and Configuration.)

18. **D.** The NETLOGON service facilitates SAM database synchronization, processes logon requests, and processes authentications for trusted domains (pass-through authentication). (Troubleshooting.)

19. **C.** You can promote a Backup Domain Controller to a Primary Domain Controller by starting Server Manager, selecting the target Backup Domain Controller, and choosing the Promote to Primary Domain Controller option in Server Manager's File menu. (Managing Resources.)

20. **B.** A multihomed server is a Windows NT Server that has more than one network adapter installed. (Connectivity.)

21. **D.** DHCP can set a number of configuration parameters on a DHCP client, including setting the default gateway, assigning an IP address to the client, and setting the IP address for the (usually nearest) WINS server. (Connectivity.)

22. **C.** By definition, a TCP/IP address that uses the first three octets for the network address is a Class C IP address. Note that any valid subnet mask may be used for any Class IP network address: The subnet mask in this question is the default Class C subnet mask. (Installation and Configuration.)

23. **B.** When a Windows NT Workstation starts up, it looks for a duplicate of its IP address on the network before connecting to the network. If the Windows NT Workstation finds a duplicate IP address, it issues a warning message, and it does not connect to the network. (Connectivity.)

24. **D.** The application server had a baseline created. Neither of the other results was achieved. (Monitoring and Optimization.)

25. **B.** DHCP relay agents are configured with the IP address(es) of one or more DHCP servers that are connected to another network segment. The agents capture client DHCP broadcasts and send them to the DHCP server. (Connectivity.)

26. **D.** NetBEUI is not routable. You can configure Windows NT Server to be both an IPX router and an IP router. Windows NT Server can also route both protocols simultaneously. Note that answers B and C are correct answers, but D is the *most* correct answer. (Installation and Configuration.)

27. **D.** 802.3 is the default frame type for Net Ware 3.11. (Installation and Configuration.)

28. **A.** Minimize Memory Used is the server optimization option that you should select for this server. Minimize Memory Used is the setting when fewer than 10 connections are guaranteed as the maximum. (Installation and Configuration.)

29. **C.** You can also use REGEDIT.EXE. (Troubleshooting.)

30. **C.** The Registry setting can change if the computer is rebooted, or if it is disconnected from the network long enough for the other browsers on the network to hold a master browser election. (Connectivity.)

31. **A.** Answers A, B, and C all work; however, A provides the *best* way to manage a messy situation. If logon scripts are replicated among domain controllers, any additional logon scripts or edits to existing logon scripts are replicated to other domain controllers. The logon scripts run regardless of which domain controller processes the logon. (Managing Resources.)

32. **A.** Configure the Directory Replication service by using Server Manager. (Installation and Configuration.)

33. **B.** You can use Network Monitor to view network activity in and out of a specific computer on a Windows NT network. (Monitoring and Optimization.)

34. **A - B - D.** The three types of counters used by Performance Monitor are Averaging, Instantaneous, and Difference. (Monitoring and Optimization.)

35. **B.** Disk Mirroring requires two physical drives and you can mirror any size disk. The boot partition can be mirrored. (Installation and Configuration.)

36. **D.** Use Disk Administrator to configure disk fault-tolerance. (Installation and Configuration.)

37. **A.** One way to configure a printer on a Windows NT Server is to use the Printers applet in Control Panel. (Managing Resources.)

38. **D.** Although the single master model enables centralized administration of accounts, it does not enable centralized administration of resources, which was one of the required results. (Planning.)

39. **A.** With the single domain model, administration is centralized. In a single domain, the location of users is not important, so if the Domain Users group is added to all the servers where access is needed, all users can access all required resources regardless of location. (Planning.)

40. **B.** The complete trust model lets all users access everything. It also allows decentralized account administration, but does not allow centralized resource administration. (Planning.)

41. **D.** The trust between R&D and Manufacturing is in the wrong direction for the required result to be met. (Planning.)

42. **D.** Only System can lock out accounts. Note that users with the appropriate permissions can disable user accounts. (Installation and Configuration.)

43. **A - B - C.** A Windows NT logon script can be either a batch file (`*.BAT`, `*.CMD`) or an executable (`*.EXE`). (Managing Resources.)

44. **D.** Although you can configure Windows NT password security to require any or all the character types listed, none are required by default. The Windows NT Server Resource Kit includes a toolset that can enable the character types feature, as well as other password security enhancement features. (Installation and Configuration.)

45. **B - C.** Global groups can be accessed across domains, and they can be members of local groups. (Managing Resources.)

46. **D.** User Manager for Domains is one tool you use to create global groups. (Managing Resources.)

47. **B.** When you create a Windows NT domain, the global groups Domain Admins, Domain Guests, and Domain Users are automatically created. Domain Controllers is not a standard group, and Everyone is a special group. (Installation and Configuration.)

48. **D.** The trust is correct, but Server Operators is the local group that cannot be copied across a trust and also cannot be assigned to another local group. (Planning.)

49. **C.** The trust is correct, but Domain Admins is added only to the administrators group in the domain, which allows domain administration but not administration of member servers or Windows NT workstations. (Planning.)

50. **B.** The complete trust model creates the proper trust relationships. Adding Domain Admins to the domain administrators group allows account administration. Adding Domain Admins to the member server administrators groups allows server configuration. However, nothing is added to groups on the Windows NT workstations. (Planning.)

51. **D.** The trusts will work but no group assignments are automatically made across a trust, so the required result is not produced. (Planning.)

52. **D.** Roaming user profiles are stored in the profile directory specified in the user account properties. (Installation and Configuration.)

53. **C.** You use the System Policy Editor to set system policies for users. (Managing Resources.)

54. **B.** The only way to change the update interval time for browsers is to manually modify the Registry. (Monitoring and Optimization.)

55. **B.** The `%systemroot%\system32\Autoexec.nt` runs at the start of a Windows NT DOS session. (Monitoring and Optimization.)

The Windows NT Server Enterprise exam is an adaptive test—meaning that the number of questions you must answer is indeterminate. The following describes how an adaptive test works:

- The test covers six categories: Planning, Installation and Configuration, Managing Resources, Connectivity, Monitoring and Optimization, and Troubleshooting. Test questions are associated with these categories.

- The testing system asks an extremely difficult question for one of the five test categories. If you answer correctly, the testing system asks you a few easier questions to pass the category.

- If you answer incorrectly, the testing system presents you with at least one less difficult question for the category. If you continue to incorrectly answer questions for the category, the questions become increasingly less difficult until the testing system determines that you do not have sufficient knowledge to pass the category.

- If you finally answer a question correctly, the testing system asks increasingly difficult questions for that category until you correctly answer a certain number of questions (the number is unknown to you or me).

You are not asked the questions in any particular order; they are distributed randomly. The testing system presents questions for all six categories in a seemingly random order. The passing score is 78.4 out of 100. The following are the two types of questions in the test:

- **Multiple-choice questions.** Select the correct answer.

Practice Exam 2

- **Scenario-based questions.** Select the response or best scenario from the scenario description.

It is suggested that you set a timer to track your progress while taking the practice exam, because the time restrictions on the tests are often the biggest obstacles to overcome. Begin the following practice exam after you set your timer.

1. **A user on your Windows NT network requires full access to all services, files, and directories on a Windows NT applications server. Which of the following actions is the best solution?**

   A. Assign the user to the Domain Admins group.

   B. Create a global group, add the user to the global group, and add the global group to the local Administrators group for the target file server.

   C. Grant the user full access to all files and directories on the target server.

   D. A and C.

   E. B and C.

2. **How can you create a Windows NT boot disk? Select the best answer.**

   A. Format a disk from within Windows NT, copy NTLDR, BOOT.INI, NTDETECT.COM, and NTBOOTDD.SYS (if required) to the disk.

   B. Run the FORMAT /S command from a DOS session.

   C. Run RDISK, and then delete the nonsystem files from the emergency repair disk.

   D. Copy all the files (including hidden and system files) from the root directory of the Windows NT system partition to a formatted floppy disk.

3. **Domain A trusts Domain B. Domain B trusts Domain C. Which of the following statements is true?**

   A. Domain A trusts Domain C.

   B. Domain C trusts Domain A.

   C. Domains A, B, and C have a full-trust relationship.

   D. None of the above.

4. **When establishing a trust relationship between two domains, which of the following is true?**

   A. The Administrator password is used to establish the communications link between the domains.

   B. After the trust relationship is established, the domain controllers generate a password to secure their communications link.

   C. After the trust relationship is established, it can break only if both domain controllers agree to break the trust relationship.

   D. None of the above.

5. **To assign administrative control to the global group Domain Admins when adding domain controllers to an existing domain, what should you do?**

   A. You should do nothing. Domain Admins is automatically added to the local group Administrators.

   B. You should add Domain Admins to the local group Administrators, and then delete the local (built-in) user Administrator.

   C. You should assign full permissions to Domain Admins and to all volumes on the server, and then add Domain Admins to the local (built-in) group Administrators.

   D. You should add Domain Admins to the local (built-in) group Users, and then assign the Administrate This Computer permissions to Users.

6. **Why is the NetBEUI protocol best-suited for large, segmented networks? Select the best answer.**

   A. It is efficient and easily routed.

   B. NetBEUI is the Internet standard protocol.

   C. It offers scalability.

   D. None of the above. NetBEUI is not well-suited for large, segmented networks.

7. **How do you exclude a Windows NT Server from functioning as a master browser?**

    A. Disable the Master Browser setting on the Browsing tab in Network Neighborhood properties.

    B. Set the Registry entry MaintainServerList to False.

    C. Set the IsBrowser setting in WIN.INI to 0.

    D. Do not use the NetBEUI protocol.

8. **What program can you use to install Windows NT Server?**

    A. WINNT.EXE

    B. WINNT32.EXE

    C. SETUP.EXE

    D. SETUP32.EXE

9. **What is the default installation directory for Windows NT Server?**

    A. \WINDOWS

    B. \WINNT on the system partition

    C. \WINNT on the first available NTFS volume

    D. \SYSTEM32

10. **It is a good idea to do which of the following after installing and configuring a Primary Domain Controller? Select the best answer.**

    A. Delete the local Administrator account.

    B. Delete the local group Administrators.

    C. Add the global group Domain Admins to the local group Administrators.

    D. None of the above.

11. **Windows NT network logon requests are processed by which of the following?**

    A. Primary Domain Controllers

    B. Backup Domain Controllers

    C. Both Primary and Backup Domain Controllers

    D. Any Windows NT Server that has an account on the domain

12. **What is the software interface that communicates between system hardware and Windows NT?**

    A. Hardware Interface Layer

    B. Hardware Abstraction Layer

    C. Windows Hardware Interface

    D. MPR

13. **How many browsers are on a Windows NT network?**

    A. There is a master browser and a backup browser.

    B. At least one master browser for each network segment and a domain master browser.

    C. One browser for each Windows NT Server on the network.

    D. One browser for each network segment.

14. **A TCP/IP subnet mask is used to do what? Select the best answer.**

    A. Define the host and network portions of an IP address.

B. Hide the IP address from non-domain resources.

C. Determine which DHCP clients must be renewed.

D. None of the above.

15. Which of the following is a difference between WINS and DNS?

    A. WINS is completely dynamic; DNS is a static service.

    B. WINS services hostnames; DNS handles NetBIOS names.

    C. DNS services hostnames; WINS handles NetBIOS names.

    D. DNS is a dynamic service; WINS is a static service.

16. Why must the DNS domain name be the same as the Windows NT domain name on a Windows NT network?

    A. WINS and DNS exchange information to translate NetBIOS names to Internet Names.

    B. The Windows NT domain name and the DNS name are not required to be the same on a Windows NT network.

    C. Microsoft Network clients use their assigned WINS servers to locate the nearest DNS server.

    D. Microsoft Network clients use their assigned DNS servers to locate the nearest WINS server.

17. You just installed a Windows NT member server on your multisegment TCP/IP network. You configure this new server as the first DHCP server on your network and configure workstations on several different segments as DHCP clients. Workstations not connected on the same segment as the DHCP server are unable to obtain an IP address from the DHCP server. Which of the following describes the possible reason that the workstations cannot connect to the DHCP server and the solution?

    A. The DHCP clients must be members of the same domain as the DHCP server. Add the workstations to the appropriate domain.

    B. The routers that connect the network segments are configured with BOOTP broadcasts disabled. Enable BOOTP broadcasts on the routers that connect the DHCP server's segment.

    C. The workstations do not know the IP address of the DHCP server. You must add the IP address of the DHCP server to the LMHOSTS file on each workstation.

    D. The workstations do not know the IP address of the DHCP server. You must configure the workstation to query its assigned WINS server for the IP address of the DHCP server.

18. You are the network administrator for a small (20-user) single-segment Windows NT network using NWLink protocol. Your boss asks you to create an additional segment on the network for a special development project. Four new Windows NT Workstations will connect to the additional segment. All network cabling is in place for the new segment. You have been instructed to create this new segment as inexpensively as possible.

Which of the following offers the best solution?

A. Add a network adapter to one of the new workstations and configure the workstation as a router.

B. Add a network adapter to the Windows NT Server and configure the server as a router.

C. Change the network protocol to TCP/IP, add a network adapter to the Windows NT Server, and configure the server as a router.

D. Purchase an inexpensive network bridge and connect the bridge between the two physical segments.

19. **What is the primary purpose of NWLink?**

A. To guarantee connectivity between domain controllers

B. To communicate between Windows NT and Windows 95 workstations

C. To facilitate communications with Novell NetWare hosts

D. None of the above

20. **The binding order of network services on a Windows NT Server can be important to network and server performance because the binding order determines which of the following? Select the best answer.**

A. The order in which Windows NT services network requests.

B. The order in which Windows NT services network clients.

C. The amount of memory used by protocol drivers.

D. The number of broadcasts that the server must issue.

21. **Your Windows NT Server has 64MB of RAM and a single 4GB hard drive. The hard drive is configured as a single FAT partition that serves as the system partition. You are installing another 4GB hard drive. After installing and partitioning the new disk drive, what must you do to add the additional disk space to the existing partition?**

A. You must extend the existing volume.

B. You must format the new disk drive as FAT, and then extend the existing volume.

C. You must convert the existing disk partition to NTFS file format, configure the new partition to NTFS file format, and then add the new partition to the existing volume as an extended volume.

D. You must reinstall Windows NT, defining both physical disk drives as a single volume.

22. **What utility do you use to extend a volume set?**

A. Server Manager

B. Disk Manager

C. Server Administrator

D. Disk Administrator

23. Which of the following is the most secure disk fault-tolerance supported by Windows NT Server?

    A. Disk duplexing

    B. Disk striping with parity

    C. Disk striping

    D. Sector swapping

24. Which of the following terms means to assign multiple printers to a single print queue?

    A. Printer sharing

    B. Printer pooling

    C. Printer polling

    D. Printer integration

25. What Windows NT Server utility do you use to create client startup disks?

    A. Network Client Administrator

    B. Disk Administrator

    C. Server Manager

    D. User Manager for Domains

26. What Windows NT Server tool creates local groups?

    A. User Manager

    B. User Manager for Domains

    C. NET.EXE

    D. All the above

27. User accounts that you use to back up disk drives on domain controllers should be members of what group?

    A. Domain Admins.

    B. Server Operators.

    C. Administrators.

    D. Backup Operators.

    E. None of the above.

28. Which one of the following functions can members of the local group Print Operators perform on a Windows NT member server?.

    A. Manage print jobs

    B. Create new printers

    C. Create print shares

    D. All the above

29. Your company's human resources department wants to place several documents on the network and make them available to users only on your single domain Windows NT network. These documents should be read/write access for the local group HRDept and read only access for all other users. How should you set the NTFS permissions for these files?

    A. You should assign Change permission for the local group HRDept and Read permission for the special group Everyone.

    B. You should assign Change permission for the local group HRDept and Read permission for the global group Domain Users.

    C. You should assign Full Control permission for the local group HRDept and Read permission for the Global group Domain Users.

D. You should create a local group on the target server, add the global group Domain Users to that local group, assign Read permission to the local group, and then assign Change permission to the local group HRDept.

30. **What special attribute does a user account known as a service account have?**

    A. A service account is a user account assigned the right to log on as a service.

    B. A service account is a Windows NT service that emulates a user account.

    C. A service account is a user account that is a member of the built-in local group Service Admins.

    D. Service accounts are system-level objects used by the special group System and are not accessible by any user accounts.

31. **You configured your Windows NT network so that all user profiles for Windows NT Workstations are stored on a shared network drive. A user modifies her desktop and then logs off the Windows NT Workstation. After logging off, she realizes that she was not connected to the network when she modified her desktop. Has she lost the changes that she made to her desktop?**

    A. No. A copy of the modified profile is saved on the Windows NT Workstation's local hard drive. When the Windows NT Workstation boots, the system automatically uses the newest user profile.

    B. Yes. If a Windows NT Workstation is configured to store profiles on a shared network drive, any changes made while the workstation is not connected to the network are lost.

    C. No. A copy of the modified profile is saved on the Windows NT Workstation's local hard drive. When the Windows NT Workstation boots, the system prompts the user to update the profile stored on the shared network drive.

    D. No. A copy of the modified profile saves to the shared network drive whether or not the user is logged on.

32. **This is a scenario question. First you must review the scenario, then review the required and optional results. Following that is a solution. You must pick the best evaluation of that solution.**

    Scenario:
    The Grabling Group has installed two Windows NT Server computers in its Vancouver office. It has set up the RESOURCE server as the primary file location. It also is functioning as the print server for the office.

    The BACKEND server is running Microsoft Exchange Server and SQL Server. It also is functioning as the PDC for the GRABLING domain. A consultant has been hired to configure these computers to optimize network performance.

    Required Result:
    The Grabling group wants to make sure its PDC is running efficiently, so the 100 users do not suffer any delays when authenticating with the network.

Optional Results:
The users need fast access to their data stores.

The Grabling group is planning to install a BDC next year and wants to make sure its user account database is protected.

Proposed Solution:
Configure the Server service of the BACKEND server to Maximize Throughput for Network Applications. Configure the RESOURCE server's Server service to be Balanced. Install a tape backup unit on the RESOURCE server. Configure NT Backup to back up the Registries of both the BACKEND and RESOURCE servers as well as all the data files on the BACKEND and RESOURCE servers.

Evaluation of Proposed Solution:
(Choose the most correct answer.)

- A. The required result and both optional results are met.
- B. The required result and only one optional result are met.
- C. Only the required results are met.
- D. None of the required or optional results are met.

33. This is a scenario question. First you must review the scenario, then review the required and optional results. Following that is a solution. You must pick the best evaluation of that solution.

    Scenario:
    Your office wants to enable users to access the office network from home. The office is connected to the Internet through a fractional T1 line.

    Required Result:
    The office has decided to provide only managers with dial-in access to the network.

    Optional Results:
    Because the network is being accessed from the homes of personnel, the office wants to encrypt all information transferred to and from the network.

    Due to the nature of the files the managers have access to on the network, it has been determined that call-back security will be implemented. The managers are to be called back at a predetermined phone number.

    Proposed Solution:
    Install a RAS Server that contains a digiboard on the local network. Set up four modems to enable the users to access the network. In User Manager for Domains, create a global group containing all the managers' accounts. In Remote Access Admin, assign the newly created global group the Dial-In permission. Set call-back security on the global group so the users can set the number to be called back at.

    Evaluation of Proposed Solution:
    (Choose the most correct answer.)

    - A. The required result and both optional results are met.
    - B. The required result and only one optional result are met.
    - C. Only the required result is met.
    - D. The required result is not met.

34. What is the name of the file in which Windows 95 policies are stored on a Windows NT network?

    - A. POLICY.CFG
    - B. NTCONFIG.POL
    - C. CONFIG.POL
    - D. WIN95.POL

35. When a Windows NT Workstation reads a user policy file, how does it store the information?

   A. The policy file is stored in a file on the local hard drive.

   B. The Windows NT Workstation does not store the information, but the workstation reads the policy file from the network each time Windows NT starts.

   C. The policy file is stored in the Default User directory.

   D. The information merges into the HKEY_CURRENT_USER subtree of the Windows NT Workstation Registry.

36. Assuming NTFS, which of the following file permissions can be assigned under the Special permission? Choose all correct answers.

   A. Read

   B. Take Ownership

   C. File Scan

   D. Add

37. Which of the following best describes NTFS file permissions?

   A. Mutually exclusive

   B. Hierarchically exclusive

   C. Cumulative

   D. Collective

38. Some data files are stored on a Windows NT Server in the (NTFS) directory C:\INVENTORY\DATA. These files are assigned Read permissions for local group Accounting and Change permissions for local group Management. They are moved to the (NTFS) directory C:\INVENTORY\SECRET, which is located on a different server. The target directory for these files has Read permissions for both Accounting and Management. What access permissions will Management have to these files after they move to the target directory? Select the best answer.

   A. Read

   B. Change

   C. Access Denied

   D. List

39. Some data files are stored on a Windows NT Server in the (NTFS) directory C:\INVENTORY\DATA. These files are assigned Read permissions for local group Accounting and Change permission for local group Management. They are moved to the (NTFS) directory C:\INVENTORY\SECRET, which is located on the same server. The target directory for the files has Read permissions for both Accounting and Management. What access permissions will Management have to these files after they move to the target directory? Select the best answer.

   A. Read

   B. Change

   C. Access Denied

   D. List

40. You suspect that one or more of the users on your Windows NT network are attempting to hack into unauthorized resources. What audit policy do you use to look for these users?

    A. File and Object Access: Look for failed attempts to access unauthorized resources.

    B. Process Tracking: Look for attempts to access unauthorized resources.

    C. Logon and Logoff: Look for excessive failed logon attempts.

    D. Use of User Rights: Look for failed attempts to perform a task.

41. What service do you use to provide printer access to Windows NT network printers for UNIX (IP) print requests?

    A. TCP/IP printing support

    B. LPD

    C. LPR

    D. UNIX Gateway for Windows NT

42. What utility do you use to manage and configure WINS on a Windows NT network?

    A. Server Manager

    B. WINS Manager

    C. WINS Administrator

    D. Protocol Manager

43. What command do you use to add routes to a multihomed Windows NT Server?

    A. ARP

    B. ROUTE

    C. RARP

    D. NET

44. What line protocols does Windows NT Remote Access Service support? Choose all correct answers.

    A. PPP

    B. PPTP

    C. SLIP

    D. TCP/IP

45. This is a scenario question. First you must review the scenario, then review the required and optional results. Following that is a solution. You must pick the best evaluation of that solution.

    Scenario:
    The Xavier group has offices in Boston, Montreal, and Seattle. Each office has its own domain, with the Boston domain functioning as the master domain in a Master Domain Model. Global groups have been created to represent the Boston users, the Montreal users, and the Seattle users. The resource domains each have their own printer resources that are shared throughout the entire enterprise.

    Required Result:
    Bob, Mary, and Jane, who comprise the Systems group, should be the only users with Full Control on all printers in the enterprise.

    Optional Results:
    The Xavier group wants all print servers to be capable of hosting jobs sent by UNIX computers.

    The Xavier group wants to provide printing support to all Macintosh clients in the enterprise.

Proposed Solution:
When a printer is installed, change the permissions on each print share to assign Bob, Mary, and Jane to manage all documents for the printer. Be sure to install the TCP/IP and AppleTalk Protocols on each print server to enable print support for UNIX and Macintosh clients.

Evaluation of Proposed Solution:
(Choose the most correct answer.)

- A. The required result and both optional results are met.
- B. The required result and only one optional result are met.
- C. Only the required result is met.
- D. None of the required or optional results are met.

46. Why is a multihomed Windows NT Server able to provide improved performance over a single-homed Windows NT server? Select the best answer.
    - A. It can process CPU requests quicker.
    - B. It can simultaneously process network requests from multiple subnets.
    - C. It can run more protocols on a single network.
    - D. There is no performance advantage to a multihomed server.

47. What tool would you use to view user connections on a Windows NT Server?
    - A. User Manager
    - B. Server Manager
    - C. NET.EXE
    - D. Windows Diagnostics

48. What Windows NT utility do you use to log system resource utilization?
    - A. Performance Monitor
    - B. Resource Manager
    - C. Windows Diagnostics
    - D. Task Manager

49. Which of the following Windows NT Server objects is not an object that you can monitor using Performance Monitor?
    - A. Paging file
    - B. Memory
    - C. Network adapter
    - D. Redirector

50. What Windows NT program do you use to initialize the physical disk counters for use with Performance Monitor?
    - A. NTFSCVT.EXE
    - B. DISKPERF.EXE
    - C. FDISK.EXE
    - D. NET.EXE

51. This is a scenario question. First you must review the scenario, then review the required and optional results. Following that is a solution. You must pick the best evaluation of that solution.

Scenario:
The Orion Organization has hired a consultant to assist with the deployment of 1,000 new computer systems, all of which will be running Windows NT 4 Workstation.

Required Result:
The IS Manager wants the installations to be completely automated and be consistent between computers.

Optional Results:
The workstations should be installed to different resource domains based on their geographic locations and should have the correct time zone settings.

All applications used in the Orion Organization should be included in the deployment process.

Proposed Solution:
Create an unattended script file for the installation process. Install all necessary software onto the first system using the unattended script file. Run the SYSDIFF utility to take a snapshot of all the software installed. Perform all remaining installations using the unattended script file and the SYSDIFF snapshot.

Evaluation of Proposed Solution:
(Choose the most correct answer.)

A. The required result and both optional results are met.

B. The required result and only one optional result are met.

C. Only the required result is met.

D. None of the required or optional results are met.

52. **What is the maximum length of a NetBIOS name?**

   A. 16 characters

   B. 15 characters

   C. 32 characters

   D. Unlimited, but you use only the first 15 characters

53. **Under what circumstances does a browser election take place? Select the best answer.**

   A. When a master browser announces that it is being shut down.

   B. When a client cannot find a master browser.

   C. When a domain controller is being initialized.

   D. All the above.

54. **What Windows NT utility do you use to create an emergency repair disk?**

   A. RDISK.EXE

   B. FDISK.EXE

   C. ERD.EXE

   D. NET.EXE

55. **A large number of your company's employees work at more than one of the wide-area sites that comprise the network. Generally, what directory services architecture is best suited for traveling users?**

   A. Full-trust domains, so that the traveling users can have a logon ID for each site and still access resources at other sites.

   B. A single domain, so that each user has one logon ID, and all resources on the network are accessible.

   C. Full-trust domains, so that the user has one logon ID and can use any local domain controller for the logon process.

   D. None of the above.

EXAM ANSWERS

1. **B.** Members of the Administrators local group have full access to the server's resources. (Managing Resources.)

2. **A.** To create a Windows NT boot disk, format a disk from within Windows NT, and then copy NTLDR, BOOT.INI, NTDETECT.COM, and NTBOOTDD.SYS (if required) to the disk. (Installation and Configuration.)

3. **D.** Domain trust relationships are non-transitive. (Planning.)

4. **B.** The two domains involved in a trust relationship establish a password-secured communication link. You must have administrative rights to set up a trust relationship, but you don't use the Administrator password. Either domain in a trust relationship can break the trust. (Managing Resources.)

5. **A.** The global group is automatically added to the local group Administrators after a Windows NT Server or Workstation joins a domain. (Installation and Configuration.)

6. **D.** NetBEUI is not routable—TCP/IP is the Internet standard—and NetBEUI offers only limited scalability. (Connectivity.)

7. **B.** You exclude a Windows NT Server from functioning as a master browser by setting the Registry entry MaintainServerList to False. (Installation and Configuration.)

8. **A - B.** Use both WINNT.EXE and WINNT32.EXE to install Windows NT Server. (Installation and Configuration.)

9. **B.** The default installation directory for Windows NT Server is \WINNT on the system partition. (Troubleshooting.)

10. **D.** Neither the built-in Administrator nor the local group Administrators can be deleted. The global group Domain Admins is automatically added to the local group Administrators when you install a domain controller. (Installation and Configuration.)

11. **C.** Both Primary and Backup Domain Controllers handle Windows NT network logon requests. (Troubleshooting.)

12. **B.** The software interface that communicates between system hardware and Windows NT is called the Hardware Abstraction Layer (HAL). (Troubleshooting.)

13. **B.** "At least" is the key phrase. You can have more than one browser per network segment, depending on the number of hosts on the segment. (Installation and Configuration.)

14. **A.** Use a TCP/IP subnet mask to define the host and network portions of an IP address. (Connectivity.)

15. **C.** You might answer A; however, remember that you can add static addresses to a WINS database. (Installation and Configuration.)

16. **B.** The Windows NT domain name and the DNS name do not have to be the same on a Windows NT network. (Installation and Configuration.)

17. **B.** DHCP clients look for a DHCP server via BOOTP broadcasts. (Installation and Configuration.)

18. **B.** Although C will work, B is the best solution because it requires only a single network adapter and a very limited configuration. Answer D seems to be a viable option except the bridges do not route; therefore, the network still is a single segment. (Connectivity.)

19. **C.** NWLink is an implementation of the Novell IPS/SPX protocol. It is used to facilitate communication between Windows NT and NetWare hosts. (Connectivity.)

20. **A.** The binding order of network services on a Windows NT Server determines the order in which the system services network requests. (Monitoring and Optimization.)

21. **D.** The system partition on a Windows NT Server is not extendible. To increase the size of the system partition, you must reinstall Windows NT defining both physical drives as a single volume. (Installation and Configuration.)

22. **D.** Use Disk Administrator to extend a volume set. (Installation and Configuration.)

23. **B.** Disk striping with parity is the most secure disk fault-tolerance supported by Windows NT Server. (Installation and Configuration.)

24. **B.** Assigning multiple printers to a single print queue is called printer pooling. (Managing Resources.)

25. **A.** Network Client Administrator creates client startup disks. (Managing Resources.)

26. **B.** User Manager is not a Windows NT Server tool. (Managing Resources.)

27. **D.** User accounts that you use to back up disk drives on domain controllers should be members of the local group Backup Operators. (Managing Resources.)

28. **D.** Print operators can manage print jobs, create new printers, and create print shares. (Managing Resources.)

29. **D.** Following the AGLP rule, you should create a local group on the target server, add the global group Domain Users (actual users that belong to the domain) to the local account, and then assign Read permission for the target files. Remembering that NTFS permissions are cumulative (except for No Access), when you assign Change permissions to the local group HRDept, users have Read/Write permissions to the target files. (Managing Resources.)

30. **A.** A service account is a user account that you assign the right to logon as a service. (Installation and Configuration.)

31. **C.** A copy of the modified profile is saved on the Windows NT Workstation's local hard drive. When the Windows NT Workstation boots, the system prompts the user to update the profile stored on the shared network drive. (Installation and Configuration.)

32. **C.** The RESOURCE server should have been set to Maximize Throughput for File and Print Sharing. In addition, Windows NT Backup can perform only a local Registry backup. Because the tape backup unit is located on the resource server, the NT account database will not be backed up in this scenario. (Troubleshooting.)

33. **D.** Dial-in permissions are granted to individual users, not groups. (Troubleshooting.)

34. **C.** Windows 95 policies are stored as CONFIG.POL. (Installation and Configuration.)

35. **D.** After a Windows NT Workstation reads a user policy file, the information merges into the HKEY_CURRENT_USER subtree of the Windows NT Workstation Registry. (Installation and Configuration.)

36. **A - B.** File Scan and Add are not valid NTFS permissions for creating Special Permissions. (Managing Resources.)

37. **C.** NTFS file permissions are cumulative. (Managing Resources.)

38. **A.** If a file is moved from one directory to another across NTFS volumes, the files inherit the permissions from the target directory. (Managing Resources.)

39. **B.** The files are moved to a directory on the same volume. When files move to a new location on the same NTFS volume, they retain their original permissions. (Managing Resources.)

40. **A.** File and Object Access: By looking for failed attempts to access unauthorized resources, you can identify attempts to access unauthorized resources. (Monitoring and Optimization.)

41. **B.** LPD (Line Printer Daemon) enables UNIX to access Windows NT printers; LPR enables the Windows NT network to access UNIX printers; and TCP/IP printing support is the LPD and LPR services. (Connectivity.)

42. **B.** Use WINS Manager to manage and configure WINS on a Windows NT network. (Installation and Configuration.)

43. **B.** You use the ROUTE command to add routes to a multihomed Windows NT Server. (Installation and Configuration.)

44. **A - B - C.** RAS supports TCP/IP, but TCP/IP is a network protocol, not a line protocol. (Connectivity.)

45. **D.** According to the requirements, Bob, Mary, and Jane require Full Control permissions, not Manage Documents permissions. This could have been achieved without granting excess permissions by making them members of the Print Operators local group in each of the three domains. (Troubleshooting)

46. **B.** A multihomed network server can process requests from multiple subnets simultaneously, instead of the network request having to pass through a router. (Connectivity.)

47. **B.** You use Server Manager to view user connections on a Windows NT Server. (Monitoring and Optimization.)

48. **A.** Use Performance Monitor to log system resource utilization. (Monitoring and Optimization.)

49. **C.** You cannot directly monitor network adapters by Performance Monitor. (Monitoring and Optimization.)

50. **B.** Use DISKPERF.EXE to initialize the physical disk counters for use with Performance Monitor. (Monitoring and Optimization.)

51. **D.** Although this solution appears to answer the required result, a uniqueness database file is required to do 1,000 installs. The UDF provides the unique settings required by each computer. Without the UDF, the computers would have to be renamed manually after the install is completed. In addition, the SYSDIFF procedure is performed incorrectly. The initial snapshot must be performed before the software is installed to the master template system. (Troubleshooting.)

52. **A.** You are limited to 15 characters by Windows NT because the system internally uses the 16th character. (Managing Resources.)

53. **D.** A browser election takes place when a master browser announces that it is being shut down, when a client cannot find a master browser, and when a domain controller is being installed. A browser election can also take place when a master browser fails to respond to other hosts on the network for a predetermined period of time (the default is 12 minutes). (Troubleshooting.)

54. **A.** You use RDISK.EXE to create an emergency repair disk. (Troubleshooting.)

55. **B.** The rationale for either A or C is incorrect. When operating in a full-trust domain environment, the user does not automatically have a logon ID for each site (site is synonymous with domain in this example), and logon requests are processed by the nearest domain controller that belongs to the user's domain, not simply the nearest domain controller. (Managing Resources.)

APPENDIX A

Exam Strategies

You must pass rigorous certification exams to become a Microsoft Certified Professional. These closed-book exams provide a valid and reliable measure of your technical proficiency and expertise. Developed in consultation with computer industry professionals who have on-the-job experience with Microsoft products in the workplace, the exams are conducted by two independent organizations. Sylvan Prometric offers the exams at more than 1,400 Authorized Prometric Testing Centers around the world. Virtual University Enterprises (VUE) testing centers offer exams as well.

To schedule an exam, call Sylvan Prometric Testing Centers at 800-755-EXAM (3926) or VUE at 888-837-8616.

This appendix is divided into two main sections. First, it describes the different certification options provided by Microsoft, and how you can achieve those certifications. The second portion highlights the different kinds of examinations and the best ways to prepare for those different exam and question styles.

TYPES OF CERTIFICATION

Currently Microsoft offers seven types of certification, based on specific areas of expertise:

- **Microsoft Certified Professional (MCP).** Qualified to provide installation, configuration, and support for users of at least one Microsoft desktop operating system, such as Windows NT Workstation. Candidates can take elective exams to develop areas of specialization. MCP is the base level of expertise.

- **Microsoft Certified Professional+Internet (MCP+Internet).** Qualified to plan security, install and configure server products, manage server resources, extend service to run CGI scripts or ISAPI scripts, monitor and analyze performance, and troubleshoot problems. Expertise is similar to that of an MCP, but with a focus on the Internet.

- **Microsoft Certified Professional+Site Building (MCP+Site Building).** Qualified to plan, build, maintain, and manage Web sites by using Microsoft technologies and products. The credential is appropriate for people who manage sophisticated, interactive Web sites that include database connectivity, multimedia, and searchable content.

- **Microsoft Certified Systems Engineer (MCSE).** Qualified to effectively plan, implement, maintain, and support information systems with Microsoft Windows NT and other Microsoft advanced systems and workgroup products, such as Microsoft Office and Microsoft BackOffice. MCSE is a second level of expertise.

- **Microsoft Certified Systems Engineer+ Internet (MCSE+Internet).** Qualified in the core MCSE areas, and also qualified to enhance, deploy, and manage sophisticated intranet and Internet solutions that include a browser, proxy server, host servers, database, and messaging and commerce components. An MCSE+Internet–certified professional is able to manage and analyze Web sites.

- **Microsoft Certified Solution Developer (MCSD).** Qualified to design and develop custom business solutions by using Microsoft development tools, technologies, and platforms, including Microsoft Office and Microsoft BackOffice. MCSD is a second level of expertise, with a focus on software development.

- **Microsoft Certified Trainer (MCT).** Instructionally and technically qualified by Microsoft to deliver Microsoft Education Courses at Microsoft-authorized sites. An MCT must be employed by a Microsoft Solution Provider Authorized Technical Education Center or a Microsoft Authorized Academic Training site.

▼ **NOTE**

For the most up-to-date information about each type of certification, visit the Microsoft Training and Certification Web site at http://www.microsoft.com/train_cert. You also can call or email the following sources:

- Microsoft Certified Professional Program: 800-636-7544

- mcp@msprograms.com

- Microsoft Online Institute (MOLI): 800-449-9333

CERTIFICATION REQUIREMENTS

The requirements for certification in each of the seven areas are detailed below. An asterisk after an exam indicates that the exam is slated for retirement.

How to Become a Microsoft Certified Professional

Passing any Microsoft exam (with the exception of Networking Essentials) is all you need to do to become certified as an MCP.

How to Become a Microsoft Certified Professional+Internet

You must pass the following exams to become an MCP specializing in Internet technology:

- Internetworking Microsoft TCP/IP on Microsoft Windows NT 4.0, #70-059

- Implementing and Supporting Microsoft Windows NT Server 4.0, #70-067

- Implementing and Supporting Microsoft Internet Information Server 3.0 and Microsoft Index Server 1.1, #70-077

  OR Implementing and Supporting Microsoft Internet Information Server 4.0, #70-087

How to Become a Microsoft Certified Professional+Site Building

You need to pass two of the following exams in order to be certified as an MCP+Site Building:

- Designing and Implementing Web Sites with Microsoft FrontPage 98, #70-055

CERTIFICATION REQUIREMENTS 417

- Designing and Implementing Commerce Solutions with Microsoft Site Server 3.0, Commerce Edition, #70-057
- Designing and Implementing Web Solutions with Microsoft Visual InterDev 6.0, #70-152

How to Become a Microsoft Certified Systems Engineer

You must pass four operating system exams and two elective exams to become an MCSE. The MCSE certification path is divided into two tracks: the Windows NT 3.51 track and the Windows NT 4.0 track.

The following lists show the core requirements (four operating system exams) for both the Windows NT 3.51 and 4.0 tracks, and the elective courses (two exams) you can take for either track.

The four Windows NT 3.51 Track Core Requirements for MCSE certification are as follows:

- Implementing and Supporting Microsoft Windows NT Server 3.51, #70-043*
- Implementing and Supporting Microsoft Windows NT Workstation 3.51, #70-042*
- Microsoft Windows 3.1, #70-030*

  OR Microsoft Windows for Workgroups 3.11, #70-048*

  OR Implementing and Supporting Microsoft Windows 95, #70-064

  OR Implementing and Supporting Microsoft Windows 98, #70-098

- Networking Essentials, #70-058

The four Windows NT 4.0 Track Core Requirements for MCSE certification are as follows:

- Implementing and Supporting Microsoft Windows NT Server 4.0, #70-067
- Implementing and Supporting Microsoft Windows NT Server 4.0 in the Enterprise, #70-068
- Microsoft Windows 3.1, #70-030*

  OR Microsoft Windows for Workgroups 3.11, #70-048*

  OR Implementing and Supporting Microsoft Windows 95, #70-064

  OR Implementing and Supporting Microsoft Windows NT Workstation 4.0, #70-073

  OR Implementing and Supporting Microsoft Windows 98, #70-098

- Networking Essentials, #70-058

For both the Windows NT 3.51 and the 4.0 tracks, you must pass two of the following elective exams for MCSE certification:

- Implementing and Supporting Microsoft SNA Server 3.0, #70-013

  OR Implementing and Supporting Microsoft SNA Server 4.0, #70-085

- Implementing and Supporting Microsoft Systems Management Server 1.0, #70-014*

  OR Implementing and Supporting Microsoft Systems Management Server 1.2, #70-018

  OR Implementing and Supporting Microsoft Systems Management Server 2.0, #70-086

- Microsoft SQL Server 4.2 Database Implementation, #70-021

  OR Implementing a Database Design on Microsoft SQL Server 6.5, #70-027

  OR Implementing a Database Design on Microsoft SQL Server 7.0, #70-029

- Microsoft SQL Server 4.2 Database Administration for Microsoft Windows NT, #70-022

  OR System Administration for Microsoft SQL Server 6.5 (or 6.0), #70-026

  OR System Administration for Microsoft SQL Server 7.0, #70-028

- Microsoft Mail for PC Networks 3.2-Enterprise, #70-037

- Internetworking with Microsoft TCP/IP on Microsoft Windows NT (3.5-3.51), #70-053

  OR Internetworking with Microsoft TCP/IP on Microsoft Windows NT 4.0, #70-059

- Implementing and Supporting Microsoft Exchange Server 4.0, #70-075*

  OR Implementing and Supporting Microsoft Exchange Server 5.0, #70-076

  OR Implementing and Supporting Microsoft Exchange Server 5.5, #70-081

- Implementing and Supporting Microsoft Internet Information Server 3.0 and Microsoft Index Server 1.1, #70-077

  OR Implementing and Supporting Microsoft Internet Information Server 4.0, #70-087

- Implementing and Supporting Microsoft Proxy Server 1.0, #70-078

  OR Implementing and Supporting Microsoft Proxy Server 2.0, #70-088

- Implementing and Supporting Microsoft Internet Explorer 4.0 by Using the Internet Explorer Resource Kit, #70-079

How to Become a Microsoft Certified Systems Engineer+ Internet

You must pass seven operating system exams and two elective exams to become an MCSE specializing in Internet technology.

The seven MCSE+Internet core exams required for certification are as follows:

- Networking Essentials, #70-058

- Internetworking with Microsoft TCP/IP on Microsoft Windows NT 4.0, #70-059

- Implementing and Supporting Microsoft Windows 95, #70-064

  OR Implementing and Supporting Microsoft Windows NT Workstation 4.0, #70-073

  OR Implementing and Supporting Microsoft Windows 98, #70-098

- Implementing and Supporting Microsoft Windows NT Server 4.0, #70-067

- Implementing and Supporting Microsoft Windows NT Server 4.0 in the Enterprise, #70-068

- Implementing and Supporting Microsoft Internet Information Server 3.0 and Microsoft Index Server 1.1, #70-077

  OR Implementing and Supporting Microsoft Internet Information Server 4.0, #70-087

- Implementing and Supporting Microsoft Internet Explorer 4.0 by Using the Internet Explorer Resource Kit, #70-079

You must also pass two of the following elective exams for MCSE+Internet certification:

- System Administration for Microsoft SQL Server 6.5, #70-026
- Implementing a Database Design on Microsoft SQL Server 6.5, #70-027
- Implementing and Supporting Web Sites Using Microsoft Site Server 3.0, # 70-056
- Implementing and Supporting Microsoft Exchange Server 5.0, #70-076

  OR Implementing and Supporting Microsoft Exchange Server 5.5, #70-081

- Implementing and Supporting Microsoft Proxy Server 1.0, #70-078

  OR Implementing and Supporting Microsoft Proxy Server 2.0, #70-088

- Implementing and Supporting Microsoft SNA Server 4.0, #70-085

How to Become a Microsoft Certified Solution Developer

The MCSD certification is undergoing substantial revision. Listed next are the requirements for the new track (available fourth quarter 1998), as well as the old.

For the new track, you must pass three core exams and one elective exam.

The core exams include the following:

Desktop Applications Development (1 required)

- Designing and Implementing Desktop Applications with Microsoft Visual C++ 6.0, #70-016

  OR Designing and Implementing Desktop Applications with Microsoft Visual Basic 6.0, #70-176

Distributed Applications Development (1 required)

- Designing and Implementing Distributed Applications with Microsoft Visual C++ 6.0, #70-015

  OR Designing and Implementing Distributed Applications with Microsoft Visual Basic 6.0, #70-175

Solution Architecture (required)

- Analyzing Requirements and Defining Solution Architectures, #70-100

Elective Exams

You must also pass one of the following elective exams:

- Designing and Implementing Distributed Applications with Microsoft Visual C++ 6.0, #70-015

  OR Designing and Implementing Desktop Applications with Microsoft Visual C++ 6.0, #70-016

  OR Microsoft SQL Server 4.2 Database Implementation, #70-021*

- Implementing a Database Design on Microsoft SQL Server 6.5, #70-027

  OR Implementing a Database Design on Microsoft SQL Server 7.0, #70-029

- Developing Applications with C++ Using the Microsoft Foundation Class Library, #70-024

- Implementing OLE in Microsoft Foundation Class Applications, #70-025

- Designing and Implementing Web Sites with Microsoft FrontPage 98, #70-055

- Designing and Implementing Commerce Solutions with Microsoft Site Server 3.0, Commerce Edition, #70-057

- Programming with Microsoft Visual Basic 4.0, #70-065

  OR Developing Applications with Microsoft Visual Basic 5.0, #70-165

  OR Designing and Implementing Distributed Applications with Microsoft Visual Basic 6.0, #70-175

  OR Designing and Implementing Desktop Applications with Microsoft Visual Basic 6.0, #70-176

- Microsoft Access for Windows 95 and the Microsoft Access Development Toolkit, #70-069

- Designing and Implementing Solutions with Microsoft Office (Code-named Office 9) and Microsoft Visual Basic for Applications, #70-091

- Designing and Implementing Web Solutions with Microsoft Visual InterDev 6.0, #70-152

Former MCSD Track

For the old track, you must pass two core technology exams and two elective exams for MCSD certification. The following lists show the required technology exams and elective exams needed to become an MCSD.

You must pass the following two core technology exams to qualify for MCSD certification:

- Microsoft Windows Architecture I, #70-160*
- Microsoft Windows Architecture II, #70-161*

You must also pass two of the following elective exams to become an MSCD:

- Designing and Implementing Distributed Applications with Microsoft Visual C++ 6.0, #70-015

- Designing and Implementing Desktop Applications with Microsoft Visual C++ 6.0, #70-016

- Microsoft SQL Server 4.2 Database Implementation, #70-021*

  OR Implementing a Database Design on Microsoft SQL Server 6.5, #70-027

  OR Implementing a Database Design on Microsoft SQL Server 7.0, #70-029

- Developing Applications with C++ Using the Microsoft Foundation Class Library, #70-024

- Implementing OLE in Microsoft Foundation Class Applications, #70-025

- Programming with Microsoft Visual Basic 4.0, #70-065

- *OR* Developing Applications with Microsoft Visual Basic 5.0, #70-165
- *OR* Designing and Implementing Distributed Applications with Microsoft Visual Basic 6.0, #70-175
- *OR* Designing and Implementing Desktop Applications with Microsoft Visual Basic 6.0, #70-176
- Microsoft Access 2.0 for Windows-Application Development, #70-051
- *OR* Microsoft Access for Windows 95 and the Microsoft Access Development Toolkit, #70-069
- Developing Applications with Microsoft Excel 5.0 Using Visual Basic for Applications, #70-052
- Programming in Microsoft Visual FoxPro 3.0 for Windows, #70-054
- Designing and Implementing Web Sites with Microsoft FrontPage 98, #70-055
- Designing and Implementing Commerce Solutions with Microsoft Site Server 3.0, Commerce Edition, #70-057
- Designing and Implementing Solutions with Microsoft Office (Code-named Office 9) and Microsoft Visual Basic for Applications, #70-091
- Designing and Implementing Web Solutions with Microsoft Visual InterDev 6.0, #70-152

Becoming a Microsoft Certified Trainer

To understand the requirements and process for becoming an MCT, you need to obtain the Microsoft Certified Trainer Guide document from the following site:

    http://www.microsoft.com/train_cert/mct/

At this site, you can read the document as Web pages or display and download it as a Word file. The MCT Guide explains the four-step process of becoming an MCT. The general steps for the MCT certification are as follows:

1. Complete and mail a Microsoft Certified Trainer application to Microsoft. You must include proof of your skills for presenting instructional material. The options for doing so are described in the MCT Guide.

2. Obtain and study the Microsoft Trainer Kit for the Microsoft Official Curricula (MOC) courses for which you want to be certified. Microsoft Trainer Kits can be ordered by calling 800-688-0496 in North America. Interested parties in other regions should review the MCT Guide for information on how to order a Trainer Kit.

3. Take the Microsoft certification exam for the product about which you want to be certified to teach.

4. Attend the MOC course for the course for which you want to be certified. This is done so you can understand how the course is structured, how labs are completed, and how the course flows.

> ✱ **WARNING**
>
> You should consider the preceding steps a general overview of the MCT certification process. The precise steps that you need to take are described in detail on the site mentioned earlier. Do not misinterpret the preceding steps as the exact process you need to undergo.

If you are interested in becoming an MCT, you can receive more information by visiting the Microsoft Certified Training site at `http://www.microsoft.com/train_cert/mct/` or by calling 800-688-0496.

STUDY AND EXAM PREPARATION TIPS

This part of the appendix provides you with some general guidelines for preparing for the exam. It is organized into three sections. The first section, "Study Tips," addresses your pre-exam preparation activities, covering general study tips. This is followed by "Exam Prep Tips," an extended look at the Microsoft Certification exams, including a number of specific tips that apply to the Microsoft exam formats. Finally, "Putting It All Together" discusses changes in Microsoft's testing policies and how they might affect you.

To better understand the nature of preparation for the test, it is important to understand learning as a process. You probably are aware of how you best learn new material. You may find that outlining works best for you, or you may need to see things as a visual learner. Whatever your learning style, test preparation takes place over time. Although it is obvious that you can't start studying for these exams the night before you take them, it is very important to understand that learning is a developmental process. Understanding it as a process helps you focus on what you know and what you have yet to learn.

Thinking about how you learn should help you to recognize that learning takes place when you are able to match new information to old. You have some previous experience with computers and networking, and now you are preparing for this certification exam. Using this book, software, and supplementary materials will not just add incrementally to what you know. As you study, you actually change the organization of your knowledge as you integrate this new information into your existing knowledge base. This will lead you to a more comprehensive understanding of the tasks and concepts outlined in the objectives and of computing in general. Again, this happens as an iterative process rather than a singular event. Keep this model of learning in mind as you prepare for the exam, and you will make better decisions about what to study and how much more studying you need to do.

Study Tips

There are many ways to approach studying, just as there are many different types of material to study. However, the tips that follow should prepare you well for the type of material covered on the certification exams.

Study Strategies

Individuals vary in the ways they learn information. Some basic principles of learning apply to everyone, however; you should adopt some study strategies that take advantage of these principles. One of these principles is that learning can be broken into various depths. Recognition (of terms, for example) exemplifies a more surface level of learning—you rely on a prompt of some sort to elicit recall. Comprehension or understanding (of the concepts behind the terms, for instance) represents a deeper level of learning. The ability to analyze a concept and apply your understanding of it in a new way or novel setting represents an even further depth of learning.

Your learning strategy should enable you to understand the material at a level or two deeper than mere recognition. This will help you to do well on the exam(s). You will know the material so thoroughly that you can easily handle the recognition-level types of questions used in multiple-choice testing. You will also be able to apply your knowledge to solve novel problems.

Macro and Micro Study Strategies

One strategy that can lead to this deeper learning includes preparing an outline that covers all the objectives and subobjectives for the particular exam you are working on. You should delve a bit further into the material and include a level or two of detail beyond the stated objectives and subobjectives for the exam. Then flesh out the outline by coming up with a statement of definition or a summary for each point in the outline.

This outline provides two approaches to studying. First, you can study the outline by focusing on the organization of the material. Work your way through the points and subpoints of your outline with the goal of learning how they relate to one another. For example, be sure you understand how each of the main objective areas is similar to and different from another. Then do the same thing with the subobjectives; be sure you know which subobjectives pertain to each objective area and how they relate to one another.

Next, you can work through the outline, focusing on learning the details. Memorize and understand terms and their definitions, facts, rules and strategies, advantages and disadvantages, and so on. In this pass through the outline, attempt to learn detail rather than the big picture (the organizational information that you worked on in the first pass through the outline).

Research has shown that attempting to assimilate both types of information at the same time seems to interfere with the overall learning process. Separate your studying into these two approaches, and you will perform better on the exam than if you attempt to study the material in a more conventional manner.

Active Study Strategies

In addition, the process of writing down and defining the objectives, subobjectives, terms, facts, and definitions promotes a more active learning strategy than merely reading the material. In human information-processing terms, writing forces you to engage in more active encoding of the information. Simply reading over it constitutes more passive processing.

Next, determine whether you can apply the information you have learned by attempting to create examples and scenarios of your own. Think about how or where you could apply the concepts you are learning. Again, write down this information to process the facts and concepts in a more active fashion.

The hands-on nature of the step-by-step tutorials and exercises at the ends of the chapters provide further active learning opportunities that will reinforce concepts as well.

Common-sense Strategies

Finally, you should follow commonsense practices in studying. Study when you are alert, reduce or eliminate distractions, take breaks when you become fatigued, and so on.

Pre-testing Yourself

Pre-testing allows you to assess how well you are learning. One of the most important aspects of learning is what has been called meta-learning. *Meta-learning* has to do with realizing when you know something well or when you need to study more. In other words, you recognize how well or how poorly you have learned the material you are studying. For most people, this can be difficult to assess objectively on their own. Practice tests are useful in that they reveal more objectively what you have learned and what you have not learned. You should use this information to guide review and further studying. Developmental learning takes place as you cycle through studying, assessing how well you have learned, reviewing, assessing again, until you feel you are ready to take the exam.

You may have noticed the practice exams included in this book. Use them as part of this process.

Exam Prep Tips

Having mastered the subject matter, your final preparatory step is to understand how the exam will be presented. Make no mistake about it—a Microsoft Certified Professional (MCP) exam will challenge both your knowledge and test-taking skills! This section starts with the basics of exam design, reviews a new type of exam format, and concludes with hints that are targeted to each of the exam formats.

The MCP Exams

Every MCP exam is released in one of two basic formats. What's being called exam format here is really little more than a combination of the overall exam structure and the presentation method for exam questions.

Each exam format utilizes the same types of questions. These types or styles of questions include multiple-rating (or scenario-based) questions, traditional multiple-choice questions, and simulation-based questions. It's important to understand the types of questions you will be presented with and the actions required to properly answer them.

Understanding the exam formats is key to good preparation because the format determines the number of questions presented, the difficulty of those questions, and the amount of time allowed to complete the exam.

Exam Formats

There are two basic formats for the MCP exams: the traditional fixed-form exam and the adaptive form. As its name implies, the fixed-form exam presents a fixed set of questions during the exam session. The adaptive format, however, uses only a subset of questions drawn from a larger pool during any given exam session.

Fixed-form

A fixed-form, computerized exam is based on a fixed set of exam questions. The individual questions are presented in random order during a test session. If you take the same exam more than once, you won't necessarily see the exact same questions. This is because two to three final forms are typically assembled for every fixed-form exam Microsoft releases. These are usually labeled Forms A, B, and C.

The final forms of a fixed-form exam are identical in terms of content coverage, number of questions, and allotted time, but the questions themselves are different. You may have noticed, however, that some of the same questions appear on, or rather are shared across, different final forms. When questions are shared across multiple final forms of an exam, the percentage of sharing is generally small. Many final forms share no questions, but some older exams may have a ten to fifteen percent duplication of exam questions on the final exam forms.

Fixed-form exams also have a fixed time limit in which you must complete the exam.

Finally, the score you achieve on a fixed-form exam, which is always reported for MCP exams on a scale of 0 to 1000, is based on the number of questions you answer correctly. The exam passing score is the same for all final forms of a given fixed-form exam.

The typical format for the fixed-form exam is as follows:

- 50–60 questions
- 75–90 minute testing time
- Question review allowed, including the opportunity to change your answers

Adaptive Form

An adaptive form exam has the same appearance as a fixed-form exam, but differs in both how questions are selected for presentation and how many questions actually are presented. Although the statistics of adaptive testing are fairly complex, the process is concerned with determining your level of skill or ability with the exam subject matter. This ability assessment begins by presenting questions of varying levels of difficulty and ascertaining at what difficulty level you can reliably answer them. Finally, the ability assessment determines if that ability level is above or below the level required to pass that exam.

Examinees at different levels of ability will then see quite different sets of questions. Those who demonstrate little expertise with the subject matter will continue to be presented with relatively easy questions. Examinees who demonstrate a higher level of expertise will be presented progressively more difficult questions. Both individuals may answer the same number of questions correctly, but because the exam-taker with the higher level of expertise can correctly answer more difficult questions, he or she will receive a higher score, and is more likely to pass the exam.

The typical design for the adaptive form exam is as follows:

- 20–25 questions
- 90-minute testing time, although this is likely to be reduced to 45–60 minutes in the near future
- Question review not allowed, providing no opportunity to change your answers

Your first adaptive exam will be unlike any other testing experience you have had. In fact, many examinees have difficulty accepting the adaptive testing process because they feel that they are not provided the opportunity to adequately demonstrate their full expertise.

You can take consolation in the fact that adaptive exams are painstakingly put together after months of data gathering and analysis and are just as valid as a fixed-form exam. The rigor introduced through the adaptive testing methodology means that there is nothing arbitrary about what you'll see! It is also a more efficient means of testing, requiring less time to conduct and complete.

As you can see from Figure A.1, there are a number of statistical measures that drive the adaptive examination process. The most immediately relevant to you is the ability estimate. Accompanying this test statistic are the standard error of measurement, the item characteristic curve, and the test information curve.

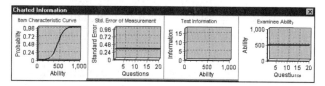

FIGURE A.1
Microsoft's Adaptive Testing Demonstration Program.

The standard error, which is the key factor in determining when an adaptive exam will terminate, reflects the degree of error in the exam ability estimate. The item characteristic curve reflects the probability of a correct response relative to examinee ability. Finally, the test information statistic provides a measure of the information contained in the set of questions the examinee has answered, again relative to the ability level of the individual examinee.

When you begin an adaptive exam, the standard error has already been assigned a target value below which it must drop for the exam to conclude. This target value reflects a particular level of statistical confidence in the process. The examinee ability is initially set to the mean possible exam score: 500 for MCP exams.

As the adaptive exam progresses, questions of varying difficulty are presented. Based on your pattern of responses to these questions, the ability estimate is recalculated. Simultaneously, the standard error estimate is refined from its first estimated value of one toward the target value. When the standard error reaches its target value, the exam terminates. Thus, the more consistently you answer questions of the same degree of difficulty, the more quickly the standard error estimate drops, and the fewer questions you will end up seeing during the exam session. This situation is depicted in Figure A.2.

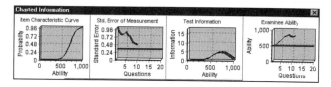

FIGURE A.2
The changing statistics in an adaptive exam.

As you might suspect, one good piece of advice for taking an adaptive exam is to treat every exam question as if it were the most important. The adaptive scoring algorithm is attempting to discover a pattern of responses that reflects some level of proficiency with the subject matter. Incorrect responses almost guarantee that additional questions must be answered (unless, of course, you get every question wrong). This is because the scoring algorithm must adjust to information that is not consistent with the emerging pattern.

New Question Types

A variety of question types can appear on MCP exams. Examples of multiple-choice questions and scenario-based questions appear throughout this book. They appear in the Top Score software as well. Simulation-based questions are new to the MCP exam series.

Simulation Questions

Simulation-based questions reproduce the look and feel of key Microsoft product features for the purpose of testing. The simulation software used in MCP exams has been designed to look and act, as much as possible, just like the actual product. Consequently, answering simulation questions in an MCP exam entails completing one or more tasks just as if you were using the product itself.

The format of a typical Microsoft simulation question is straightforward. It presents a brief scenario or problem statement along with one or more tasks that must be completed to solve the problem. An example of a simulation question for MCP exams is shown in the following section.

A Typical Simulation Question

It sounds obvious, but the first step when you encounter a simulation is to carefully read the question (see Figure A.3). Do not go straight to the simulation application! Assess the problem being presented and identify the conditions that make up the problem scenario. Note the tasks that must be performed or outcomes that must be achieved to answer the question, and review any instructions about how to proceed.

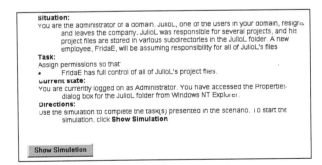

FIGURE A.3
Typical MCP exam simulation question with directions.

The next step is to launch the simulator. Click the Show Simulation button to see a feature of the product, such as the dialog box shown in Figure A.4. The simulation application partially covers the question text on many test center machines. Feel free to reposition the simulation or to move between the question text screen and the simulation using hot keys, point-and-click navigation, or even by clicking the simulation launch button again.

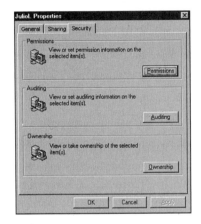

FIGURE A.4
Launching the simulation application.

It is important to understand that your answer to the simulation question is not recorded until you move on to the next exam question. This gives you the added capability to close and reopen the simulation application (using the launch button) on the same question without losing any partial answer you may have made.

The third step is to use the simulator as you would the actual product to solve the problem or perform the defined tasks. Again, the simulation software is designed to function, within reason, just as the product does. But don't expect the simulation to reproduce product behavior perfectly.

Most importantly, do not allow yourself to become flustered if the simulation does not look or act exactly like the product. Figure A.5 shows the solution to the example simulation problem.

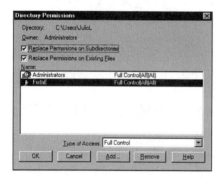

FIGURE A.5
The solution to the simulation example.

There are two final points that will help you tackle simulation questions. First, respond only to what is being asked in the question. Do not solve problems that you are not asked to solve. Second, accept what is being asked of you. You may not entirely agree with conditions in the problem statement, the quality of the desired solution, or the sufficiency of defined tasks to adequately solve the problem. Always remember that you are being tested on your ability to solve the problem as it has been presented.

The solution to the simulation problem shown in Figure A.5 perfectly illustrates both of these points. As you'll recall from the question scenario (refer to Figure aA3), you were asked to assign appropriate permissions to a new user, FridaE. You were not instructed to make any other changes in permissions. Thus, if you had modified or removed Administrators permissions, this item would have been scored as incorrect on an MCP exam.

Putting It All Together

Given all these different pieces of information, the task is now to assemble a set of tips that will help you successfully tackle the different types of MCP exams.

More Pre-exam Preparation Tips

Generic exam preparation advice is always useful. Tips include the following:

- Become familiar with the product. Hands-on experience is one of the keys to success on any MCP exam. Review the exercises and the step-by-step activities in the book.

- Review the current exam preparation guide on the Microsoft MCP Web site. The documentation Microsoft makes publicly available over the Web identifies the skills every exam is intended to test.

- Memorize foundational technical detail as appropriate. Remember that MCP exams are generally heavy on problem solving and application of knowledge rather than just questions that only require rote memorization.

- Take any of the available practice tests. We recommend the ones included in this book and the ones you can create using New Riders' exclusive Top Score Test Simulation software suite, available through your local bookstore or software distributor. Although these are fixed-format exams, they provide practice that is valuable for preparing for an adaptive exam. Because of the interactive nature of adaptive testing, it is not possible to provide examples of the adaptive format in the included practice exams. However, fixed-format exams do provide the same types of questions as found on adaptive exams and are the most effective way to prepare for either type of exam. As a supplement to the material bound with this book, also try the free practice tests available on the Microsoft MCP Web site.

- Look on the Microsoft MCP Web site for samples and demonstration items. These tend to be particularly valuable for one significant reason: They allow you to become familiar with any new testing technologies before you encounter them on an MCP exam.

During the Exam Session

Similarly, the generic exam-taking advice you've heard for years applies when taking an MCP exam:

- Take a deep breath and try to relax when you first sit down for your exam session. It is very important to control the pressure you may (naturally) feel when taking exams.

- You will be provided scratch paper. Take a moment to write down any factual information and technical detail that you've committed to short-term memory.

- Carefully read all information and instruction screens. These displays have been put together to give you information relevant to the exam you are taking.

- Accept the Non-Disclosure Agreement and preliminary survey as part of the examination process. Complete them accurately and quickly move on.

- Read the exam questions carefully. Reread each question to identify all relevant detail.

- Tackle the questions in the order they are presented. Skipping around won't build your confidence; the clock is always counting down.

- Don't rush, but similarly, don't linger on difficult questions. The questions vary in degree of difficulty. Don't let yourself be flustered by a particularly difficult or verbose question.

Fixed-form Exams

Building from this basic preparation and test-taking advice, you also need to consider the challenges presented by the different exam designs. Because a fixed-form exam is composed of a fixed, finite set of questions, add these tips to your strategy for taking a fixed-form exam:

- Note the time allotted and the number of questions appearing on the exam you are taking. Make a rough calculation of how many minutes you can spend on each question and use this to pace yourself through the exam.

- Take advantage of the fact that you can return to and review skipped or previously answered questions. Mark the questions you can't answer confidently, noting the relative difficulty of each question on the scratch paper provided. When you reach the end of the exam, return to the more difficult questions.

- If there is session time remaining after you have completed all questions (and you aren't too fatigued!), review your answers. Pay particular attention to questions that seem to have a lot of detail or that required graphics.

- As for changing your answers, the rule of thumb here is *don't*! If you read the question carefully and completely, and you felt like you knew the right answer, you probably did. Don't second-guess yourself. If, as you check your answers, one stands out as clearly marked incorrectly, however, you should change it in that instance. If you are at all unsure, go with your first impression.

Adaptive Exams

If you are planning to take an adaptive exam, keep these additional tips in mind:

- Read and answer every question with great care. When reading a question, identify every relevant detail, requirement, or task that must be performed and double-check your answer to be sure you have addressed every one of them.

- If you cannot answer a question, use the process of elimination to reduce the set of potential answers, then take your best guess. Stupid mistakes invariably mean additional questions will be presented.

- Forget about reviewing questions and changing your answers. After you leave a question, whether you've answered it or not, you cannot return to it. Do not skip a question, either; if you do, it's counted as incorrect!

Simulation Questions

You may encounter simulation questions on either the fixed-form or adaptive form exam. If you do, keep these tips in mind:

- Avoid changing any simulation settings that don't pertain directly to the problem solution. Solve the problem you are being asked to solve, and nothing more.

- Assume default settings when related information has not been provided. If something has not been mentioned or defined, it is a non-critical detail that does not factor in to the correct solution.

- Be sure your entries are syntactically correct, paying particular attention to your spelling. Enter relevant information just as the product would require it.

- Close all simulation application windows after completing the simulation tasks. The testing system software is designed to trap errors that could result when using the simulation application, but trust yourself over the testing software.

- If simulations are part of a fixed-form exam, you can return to skipped or previously answered questions and review your answers. However, if you choose to change your answer to a simulation question, or even attempt to review the settings you've made in the simulation application, your previous response to that simulation question will be deleted. If simulations are part of an adaptive exam, you cannot return to previous questions.

FINAL CONSIDERATIONS

There are a number of changes in the MCP program that will impact how frequently you can repeat an exam and what you will see when you do.

- Microsoft has instituted a new exam retake policy. This new rule is "two and two, then one and two." That is, you can attempt any exam two times with no restrictions on the time between attempts. But after the second attempt, you must wait two weeks before you can attempt that exam again. After that, you will be required to wait two weeks between any subsequent attempts. Plan to pass the exam in two attempts, or plan to increase your time horizon for receiving an MCP credential.

- New questions are being seeded into the MCP exams. After performance data has been gathered on new questions, they will replace older questions on all exam forms. This means that the questions appearing on exams are regularly changing.

- Many of the current MCP exams will be republished in adaptive format in the coming months. Prepare yourself for this significant change in testing format; it is entirely likely that this will become the new preferred MCP exam format.

These changes mean that the brute-force strategies for passing MCP exams may soon completely lose their viability. So if you don't pass an exam on the first or second attempt, it is entirely possible that the exam will change significantly in form. It could be updated to adaptive form from fixed-form or have a different set of questions or question types.

The intention of Microsoft is clearly not to make the exams more difficult by introducing unwanted change. Their intent is to create and maintain valid measures of the technical skills and knowledge associated with the different MCP credentials. Preparing for an MCP exam has always involved not only studying the subject matter, but also planning for the testing experience itself. With these changes, this is now more true than ever.

APPENDIX B

Glossary

A

Access Token A Windows NT object describing a user account and group memberships. This object is provided by the Local Security Authority upon successful logon and validation and is attached to all user processes.

Account Lockout A Windows NT Server security feature that locks a user account if a number of failed logon attempts occurs within a specified amount of time, based on account policy lockout settings. (Locked accounts cannot log on.)

Account Policy A setting that controls the way passwords must be used by all user accounts of a domain or of an individual computer. Specifics include minimum password length, how often a user must change his or her password, and how often users can reuse old passwords. Account policy can be set for all user accounts in a domain when administering a domain, and for all user accounts of a single workstation or member server when administering a computer.

Active Partition The disk partition that has been designated as being bootable. Although an NT system can have up to four partitions that are capable of booting, only one can be active at any one time.

Address Resolution Protocol (ARP) The protocol within TCP/IP that determines whether a packet's source and destination addresses are in the Data-Link Control (DLC) or Internet Protocol (IP) format. ARP is necessary for proper packet routing on a TCP/IP network.

Administrative Share A network share that is created and maintained by the Windows NT operating systems. Administrative shares are hidden and accessible only by users in the local Administrators account. All disk partitions have Administrative shares associated with them. For example, C$ is the share for the C drive.

AGLPAccounts/Global/Local/Permissions The "best practice" process for applying permissions to user accounts and groups in a Windows NT domain.

Alert View A view in the Performance Monitor in which thresholds for counters are set and then actions are taken when those thresholds are crossed.

API (Application Programming Interface) A standard used to communicate between software applications. API calls are used to transfer information between programs.

Application Log A server log accessible from the Event Viewer. This log records messages, warnings, and errors generated by applications running on your NT Server or Workstation.

ARC-path (Advanced RISC Computing path) An industry-standard method of identifying the physical location of a partition on a hard drive. ARC-paths are used in the BOOT.INI file to identify the location of NT boot files.

B

Backup Browser A computer chosen by an election process to maintain a list of resources on a network. These computers have browse clients directed to them by a master browser when a request for resources is made on a network.

Backup Domain Controller (BDC) In a Windows NT Server domain, a computer running Windows NT Server that receives a copy of the domain's directory database, which contains all account and security policy information for the domain. The copy is synchronized periodically and automatically, with the master copy on the primary domain controller (PDC). BDCs also authenticate user logons and can be promoted to function as PDCs as needed. Multiple BDCs can exist on a domain. See also *member server; PDC.*

Baseline A collection of the measurements of resources on your system that have been taken at normal usage of the system. This measurement is then used to compare to any changes to the system.

Binding A process that establishes the communication channel between a protocol driver (such as TCP/IP) and a network card.

Blue Screen Stop Error The resulting screen after a system crash. The blue screen is comprised of event error codes and hexadecimal data.

Boot Partition The volume, formatted for either an NTFS or FAT file system, that has the Windows NT operating system and its support files. The boot partition can be (but does not have to be) the same as the system partition. See also *FAT; NTFS; partition.*

BOOT.INI A file, located on the system partition of an NT Server or Workstation, responsible for pointing the boot process to the correct boot files for the operating system chosen in the boot menu.

BOOTSECT.DOS A file, located on the system partition, containing information required to boot an NT System to MS-DOS if a user requests it.

Bottleneck A system resource that is the limiting factor in the speed of processing. All systems have a bottleneck of some sort; the question is whether the bottleneck is significant in the context in which a server finds itself.

Broadcast Frame Transmission of a message intended for all network recipients.

Browser Called the Computer Browser service, the browser maintains an up-to-date list of computers, and provides the list to applications when requested. This list is kept up to date by consulting with a master or backup browser on the network. The browser provides the computer lists displayed in the Network Neighborhood, Select Computer, and Select Domain dialog boxes, and (for Windows NT Server only) the Server Manager window.

C

CACLS (Change the Access Control Lists) A command-line utility that can be used to modify the access control lists.

Call Back A security feature, enabled in the configuration of a RAS server, that requires that a RAS server call a client at a specific phone number (system or user-configured) when a client has initiated a RAS connection to the server. This feature is used either to transfer the bulk of long-distance charges to the server rather than the user, or to ensure that a user is authentic by being at a specific location rather than a hacker trying to gain unauthorized access to a network through RAS.

Chart View A view in the Performance Monitor in which a dynamically updated line graph or histogram is displayed for the counters selected in the view configuration.

Client Access License A license, required by all users connecting to an NT server, which provides legal access to NT server resources.

Client Administration Tools A set of applications that allows for the administration of an NT Domain Controller from a Windows 95 or Windows NT Workstation, or Windows NT Server computer. The Client Administration Tools provide the most commonly used administration tools but do not provide complete administration functionality.

Client Services for NetWare (CSNW) Services included with Windows NT Workstation, enabling workstations to make direct connections to file and printer resources at NetWare servers running NetWare 2.x or later.

COMPACT.EXE A command-line utility used to compress files on NTFS volumes. To see command-line options, type **compact /?** at the command prompt. By right-clicking any file or folder on an NTFS volume in Windows NT Explorer and clicking Properties to compress or uncompress the files, you can also access this utility.

Control Panel A folder containing a number of applets (applications) that help you configure and monitor your system running Windows NT. This includes configuring hardware, software, network configurations, service startup parameters, and system properties.

CONVERT.EXE A command-line utility used to convert an NT volume from FAT to NTFS. The command syntax is CONVERT <drive letter>: /fs:NTFS; an example of a command is CONVERT C: /fs:NTFS.

Counter A specific component of a Performance Monitor object that has a displayable value. For example, for the object Memory, one counter is Available Bytes.

D, E

Default Gateway In TCP/IP, the intermediate network device on the local network that has knowledge of the network IDs of the other networks in the Internet so that it can forward the packets to other gateways until the packet is eventually delivered to a gateway connected to the specified destination.

DETECT (Discover, Explore, Track, Execute, Check, Tie-Up) A recommended troubleshooting method for approaching Windows NT problems.

Differential Backup A backup method that backs up all files without their archive attribute set but does not set the archive attribute of those files it backs up.

Directory Replication The copying of a master set of directories from a server (called an export server) to specified servers or workstations (called import computers) in the same or other domains.

Replication simplifies the task of maintaining identical sets of directories and files on multiple computers, because only a single master copy of the data must be maintained. Files are replicated when they are added to an exported directory and every time a change is saved to the file.

Directory Service Manager for NetWare (DSMN)   An NT add-on that provides directory synchronization between an NT network and a NetWare network.

Directory Services   The network and specifically the account and security database used to combine your network into an organized structure. There are numerous implementations of directory services, and in previous versions of Windows NT, Microsoft referred to them as simply the domain models.

Directory Synchronization   A process for automatically transferring the account database, containing all user and security information, from the Primary Domain Controllers to all Backup Domain Controllers in your Windows NT environment.

Disk Administrator   An administration program that enables an NT administrator to create, format, and maintain hard drive partitions, volumes, and fault-tolerant mechanisms.

Disk Duplexing   A mirror set created with two hard drives controlled by separate disk controller cards. Disk duplexing provides more fault tolerance than standard mirror sets because it ensures that a controller card failure will not bring down the mirror set.

Disk Mirroring   A fault-tolerant mechanism that provides a fully redundant, or *shadow*, copy of data (mirror set). Mirror sets provide an identical twin for a selected disk; all data written to the primary disk is also written to the shadow, or mirror, disk. This enables you to have instant access to another disk with a redundant copy of the information on a failed disk.

Disk Striping with Parity   A method of data protection in which data is striped in large blocks across all the disks in an array. The parity information provides data redundancy.

DISKPERF   A utility used to enable the hard disk counters in the Performance Monitor.

Domain   In Windows NT, a collection of computers defined by the administrator of a Windows NT Server network that share a common directory database. A domain provides access to the centralized user accounts and group accounts maintained by the domain administrator. Each domain has a unique name.

Domain Master Browser   A kind of network name server that keeps a browse list of all the servers and domains on the network. The Domain Master browser for a domain is always the Primary Domain Controller.

Domain Name Service (DNS)   A static, hierarchical name service for TCP/IP hosts. The network administrator configures the DNS with a list of host names and IP addresses, allowing users of workstations configured to query the DNS to specify remote systems by host names rather than IP addresses. For example, a workstation configured to use DNS name resolution could use the command `ping remotehost` rather than `ping 1.2.3.4` if the mapping for the system named remotehost was contained in the DNS database.

Dynamic Host Configuration Protocol (DHCP) A protocol that offers dynamic configuration of IP addresses and related information through the DHCP server service running on an NT Server. DHCP provides safe, reliable, and simple TCP/IP network configuration, prevents address conflicts, and helps conserve the use of IP addresses through centralized management of address allocation.

Emergency Repair Disk   A disk containing configuration information for a specific NT Server or Workstation. This disk is created and updated using the RDISK utility and can be used with the three NT setup disks to recover from many NT system failures resulting from file and/or Registry corruption.

Event Viewer   An administrative utility used to look at event logs. Three logs are provided to the Event Viewer: system, security, and application.

Export Computer   In directory replication, a server from which a master set of directories is exported to specified servers or workstations (called import computers) in the same or other domains.

Extended Partition   Created from free space on a hard disk, an extended partition can be subpartitioned into zero or more logical drives. Only one of the four partitions allowed per physical disk can be an extended partition, and no primary partition needs to be present to create an extended partition.

F

FAT (File Allocation Table)   A table or list maintained by some operating systems to keep track of the status of various segments of disk space used for file storage. Also referred to as the FAT file system, this method is used to format hard drives in DOS, Windows 95, and OS/2, and can be used in Windows NT.

FAT32   A variation of FAT that provides for more efficient file storage. This FAT variation is available only on Windows 95 and Windows 98 and is not readable by Windows NT.

Fault Tolerance   Ensuring data integrity when hardware failures occur. In Windows NT, the FTDISK.SYS driver provides fault tolerance. In Disk Administrator, fault tolerance is provided using mirror sets, stripe sets with parity, and volume sets.

Fault-Tolerant Boot Disk   A disk that contains the files required by NT to begin the boot and to point to the boot partition. The files required for an Intel system are BOOT.INI, NTDETECT.COM, NTLDR, and NTBOOTDD.SYS (if the hard drive is SCSI with BIOS disabled).

File and Print Services for NetWare (FPNW)   A service installed on an NT server that enables NetWare clients to access an NT server for the purposes of reading files and printing to NT-controlled printers. For this service to work, the NT Server must have NWLink installed on it.

Filename Alias   An 8.3-compatible short name given to a long filename created on an NT computer to allow MS-DOS and Windows 3.x clients to read files.

Frame   The addressing and protocol information, as well as the data sent from one computer or host (routers, bridges, and so on) to another. There are three types of frames: broadcast, multicast, and directed.

Frame Type   The type of network package generated on a network. In NT configuration, this term refers to the type of network packages sent by a NetWare server that an NT client is configured to accept.

FTP (File Transfer Protocol)   FTP is the TCP/IP protocol for file transfer.

Full Backup   A method that backs up all files and then sets the archive attribute of those files it backs up. Sometimes referred to as a *normal backup*.

G

Gateway Services for NetWare (GSNW) Included with Windows NT Server, these services enable a computer running Windows NT Server to connect to NetWare servers. Creating a gateway enables computers running only Microsoft client software to access NetWare resources through the gateway.

Global Group For Windows NT Server, a group that can be used in its own domain, member servers, and workstations of the domain, and trusting domains. In all those places, the group can be granted rights and permissions and can become a member of local groups. However, the group can contain only user accounts from its own domain. Global groups provide a way to create handy sets of users from inside the domain, available for use both in and out of the domain.

Global groups cannot be created or maintained on computers running Windows NT Workstation. However, for Windows NT Workstation computers that participate in a domain, domain global groups can be granted rights and permissions at those workstations, and can become members of local groups at those workstations.

Gopher The Internet Gopher is a distributed document-delivery system.

Group Account A collection of user accounts. Giving a user account membership in a group gives that user all the rights and permissions granted to the group.

H

Hardware Compatibility List (HCL) The Windows NT Hardware Compatibility List lists the devices supported by Windows NT. The latest version of the HCL can be downloaded from the Microsoft web page (www.microsoft.com) on the Internet.

Hidden Share A network share that is configured not to show up in browse lists, but to which you can connect explicitly if you know the share name. You can create hidden shares by appending a dollar sign ($) to the end of a share name, as in SECRET$. All Administrative shares are hidden shares.

Hive A section of the Registry that appears as a file on your hard disk. The Registry subtree is divided into hives (named for their resemblance to the cellular structure of a beehive). A hive is a discrete body of keys, subkeys, and values that is rooted at the top of the Registry hierarchy. A hive is backed by a single file and a .log file that are in the %SystemRoot%\system32\config or %SystemRoot%\profiles\username folder. By default, most hive files (Default, SAM, Security, and System) are stored in the %SystemRoot%\system32\config folder. The %SystemRoot%\profiles folder contains the user profile for each user of the computer. Because a hive is a file, it can be moved from one system to another, but can be edited only using Registry Editor.

HKEY_LOCAL_MACHINE A Registry subtree that maintains all the configuration information for the local machine, including hardware settings and software installed.

Host Name The name assigned to any computer or service that can be accessed through the TCP/IP protocol. *Host name* is a commonly used term in the Internet community.

HTTP (Hypertext Transfer Protocol) A standard used for accessing web pages.

I, J, K

ICMP (Internet Control Message Protocol) The protocol used to handle errors and control messages at the IP layer. ICMP is actually part of the IP protocol.

IIS (Internet Information Server) The Internet components that are integrated into Windows NT Server 4.0. This service enables your Windows NT system to function as an Internet server using the HTTP, FTP, or Gopher services.

Import Computer In directory replication, the server or workstation that receives copies of the master set of directories from an export server.

Incremental Backup A backup method that backs up all files that do not have their archive attributes set and which sets the archive attributes of those files it backs up.

Installation Disk Set A set of disks that contain a minimal configuration of Windows NT used to initiate Windows NT installation and repair.

IP (Internet Protocol) IP is part of the TCP/IP suite. It is a network-layer protocol that governs packet forwarding.

IP Address An address used to identify a node on a network and to specify routing information. Each node on the network must be assigned a unique IP address, which is made up of the network ID plus a unique host ID assigned by the network administrator. This address is typically represented in dotted-decimal notation, with the decimal value of each octet separated by a period (for example, 138.57.7.27). In Windows NT, the IP address can be configured statically on the client or configured dynamically through DHCP.

IPC (Interprocess Communication) The exchange of information between processes through a secured message channel.

IPConfig A command-line utility that is used to determine the current TCP/IP configuration of a local computer. It is also used to request a new TCP/IP address from a DHCP server through the use of the /RELEASE and /RENEW switches. The /ALL switch displays a complete list of TCP/IP configurations.

IPX/SPX Transport protocols used in Novell NetWare networks. Windows NT implements IPX through NWLink.

L

LastKnownGood A set of Registry settings that records the hardware configuration of a Windows NT computer at last successful login. LastKnownGood can be used to recover from incorrect hardware setup as long as logon does not occur between when the configuration was changed and the LastKnownGood was invoked.

License Manager An administrative utility that enables you to track the purchase of Client Access Licenses for an NT Server and/or Domain.

Licensing Mode An indicator of the kind of licensing being used on a Windows NT Server. The choices are Per Server and Per Seat.

Local Group For Windows NT Workstation, a group that can be granted permissions and rights only for its own workstation. However, the group can contain user accounts from its own computer and (if the workstation participates in a domain) user accounts and global groups both from its own domain and from trusted domains.

For Windows NT Server, a group that can be granted permissions and rights only for the domain controllers of its own domain. However, the group can contain user accounts and global groups both from its own domain and from trusted domains.

Local groups provide a way to create handy sets of users from both inside and outside the domain, to be used only at domain controllers of the domain.

Local Profile   A profile stored on a local machine that is accessible only to a user who logs on to a Windows NT computer locally.

Local Security Authority (LSA)   The Windows NT process responsible for directing logon requests to the local Security Accounts Manager (SAM) or to the SAM of a domain controller through the NetLogon service. The LSA is responsible for generating an Access Token after a user logon has been validated.

Log View   A view in the Performance Monitor in which the configuration of a log is determined. Logs have no dynamic information; however, the resulting file can be analyzed using any of the other Performance Monitor views.

Logical Drive   A subpartition of an extended partition on a hard disk.

Logon Script   These are files containing commands that are used to set up a user's environment when connecting to the network.

M

MAC (Media Access Control) Address   The hardware address of a device that is connected to a network. For example, the hardware address of an Ethernet card is referred to as the MAC address.

Mandatory Profile   A profile that is downloaded to the user's desktop each time he logs on. A mandatory user profile is created by an administrator and assigned to one or more users to create consistent or job-specific user profiles. A profile cannot be changed by the user and remains the same from one logon session to the next.

Master Boot Record (MBR)   The place on the disk that the initial computer startup is directed to go to initiate operating system boot. The MBR is located on the primary partition.

Master Browser   A kind of network name server that keeps a browse list of all the servers and domains on the network. Also referred to as *browse master*.

Member Server   A computer that runs Windows NT Server but is not a Primary Domain Controller (PDC) or Backup Domain Controller (BDC) of a Windows NT domain. Member servers do not receive copies of the directory database.

Migration Tool for NetWare   A tool included with Windows NT that enables you to transfer user and group accounts, volumes, folders, and files easily from a NetWare server to a computer running Windows NT Server.

Multi-Boot   A computer that runs two or more operating systems. For example, Windows 95, MS-DOS, and Windows NT operating systems can be installed on the same computer. When the computer is started, any one of the operating systems can be selected. Also known as *dual-boot*.

Multicast Packet   A single packet that is copied to a specific subset of network addresses. In contrast, broadcast packets are sent to all stations in a network.

Multilink Protocol A protocol that combines multiple physical links into a logical bundle. This aggregate link increases your bandwidth.

Multiprotocol Routing Enabling one computer system to route the packets from dissimilar networking protocols.

N, O

Net Logon For Windows NT Server, a feature that performs authentication of domain logons, and keeps the domain's directory database synchronized between the Primary Domain Controller (PDC) and the other Backup Domain Controllers (BDCs) of the domain.

NetBEUI (NetBIOS Extended User Interface) A network protocol usually used in small, department-size local area networks (LANs) of 1 to 200 clients. It is nonroutable and therefore not a preferred wide area network (WAN) protocol.

NetBIOS (Network Basic Input/Output System) A standard network interface for IBM PCs. NetBIOS is used for locating named resources on a network.

Network Adapter An expansion card or other device used to connect a computer to a LAN. Also called a *network card, network adapter card, adapter card,* or *network interface card (NIC)*.

Network Monitor An administrative utility installed on a Windows NT computer when the Network Monitor Tools and Agent service is installed. The network monitor provided with Windows NT enables you to capture and analyze network traffic coming into and going out of the local network card. The SMS version of Network Monitor runs in promiscuous mode that allows monitoring of traffic on the local network.

Network Protocols Communication "languages" that enable networked computer and devices to communicate with each other. Common network protocols are TCP/IP, NetBEUI, NWLink, and DLC (used for communicating with networked printers, such as HP DirectJet).

Network Services A process that performs a specific network system function and often provides an application programming interface (API) for other processes to call. Windows NT services are RPC-enabled, meaning that their API routines can be called from remote computers.

Non-Browser A computer that is configured never to participate in browser elections and therefore can never become a master or backup browser.

Normal Backup A method that backs up all files and then sets the archive attribute of those files it backs up. Sometimes referred to as a *full backup.*

NTBOOTDD.SYS The driver for a SCSI boot device that does not have its BIOS enabled. NTBOOTDD.SYS is found on an NT system partition and is also required to create a fault-tolerant boot disk.

NTCONFIG.POL A file that defines a Windows NT system policy.

NTDETECT.COM The program in the Windows NT boot process responsible for generating a list of hardware devices. This list is later used to populate part of the HKEY_LOCAL_MACHINE subtree in the Registry.

NTFS An advanced file system designed for use specifically within the Windows NT operating system. It supports file system recovery, extremely large storage media, long filenames, and various features for the POSIX subsystem. It also supports object-oriented applications by treating all files as objects with user-defined and system-defined attributes.

NTFS Compression A compression type supported only on an NTFS volume. This supports file-level compression and is dynamic.

NTFS Permissions Local permissions on NTFS volumes that allow for the restriction of both local and network access to files and folders.

NTHQ A program that executes from a disk that enables you to have hardware on a computer automatically checked against the HCL for NT compatibility.

NTLDR The program responsible for booting an NT system. It is invoked when an NT computer is started and is responsible for displaying the boot menu (from the BOOT.INI file) and for starting the NTDETECT.COM program.

NTOSKRNL.EXE The program responsible for maintaining the core of the NT operating system. When NTLDR has completed the boot process, control of NT is handed over to the NTOSKRNL.

NWCONV The utility used within Windows NT to convert NetWare user and group information and file information from a Novell server into a Windows NT domain.

NWLink A standard network protocol that supports routing and can support NetWare client-server applications, where NetWare-aware Sockets-based applications communicate with IPX\SPX Sockets-based applications.

Object A specific system category for which counters can be observed in Performance Monitor. Objects whose counters are frequently monitored are Memory, Processor, Network, and PhysicalDisk.

Octet An octet is eight bits. In networking, the term *octet* is often used in place of *byte* because TCP/IP uses multiple octets in the addressing.

OSLOADER.EXE The program on a RISC–based machine responsible for the function of the NTLDR on an Intel-based machine.

P

Partition A portion of a physical disk that functions as though it were a physically separate unit.

Per-Client Licensing Mode A Windows NT licensing mode that allocates server access on a per-person basis, not on a per-connection basis. Using a per-client license, a user can connect to many Windows NT servers simultaneously.

Per-Server Licensing Mode A Windows NT licensing mode that allocates server access on a per-connection basis. This licensing mode allocates a certain number of simultaneous connections to a server, and when that number of connections is reached, no more users are allowed to access the server.

Performance Monitor An administrative application used to monitor object counters on a Windows NT computer to determine bottlenecks in the system and to increase overall efficiency.

Persistent Connection A network connection from a client to a server that is automatically reestablished when disconnected.

PING A command used to verify connections to one or more remote hosts. The PING utility uses the ICMP echo request and echo reply packets to determine whether a particular IP system on a network is functional. The PING utility is useful for diagnosing IP network or router failures.

Point-to-Point Protocol (PPP) A set of industry-standard framing and authentication protocols that is part of Windows NT RAS to ensure interoperability with third-party remote access software. PPP negotiates configuration parameters for multiple layers of the OSI model.

Point-to-Point Tunneling Protocol (PPTP)   A new networking technology that supports multi-protocol virtual private networks (VPNs), enabling remote users to access corporate networks securely across the Internet by dialing into an Internet service provider (ISP) or by connecting directly to the Internet.

Potential Browser   A computer that is not currenly functioning as a browser on a network but which could, if needed, become one.

Primary Domain Controller (PDC)   In a Windows NT Server domain, the computer running Windows NT Server that authenticates domain logons and maintains the directory database for a domain. The PDC tracks changes made to accounts of all computers on a domain. It is the only computer to receive these changes directly. A domain has only one PDC.

Primary Partition   A partition is a portion of a physical disk that can be marked for use by an operating system. There can be up to four primary partitions (or up to three, if there is an extended partition) per physical disk. A primary partition cannot be subpartitioned.

Print Device   The actual hardware device that produces printed output.

Printer   The software interface between the operating system and the print device. The printer defines where the document will go before it reaches the print device (to a local port, to a file, or to a remote print share), when it will go, and various other aspects of the printing process.

Printer Driver   A program that converts graphics commands into a specific printer language, such as PostScript or PCL.

Printer Pool   Two or more identical print devices associated with one printer.

Protocols   See *Network Protocols*.

PSTN (Public Switched Telephone Network)   This is the network put in place and used by your phone company. You can use PSTN to connect RAS from one locale to another (through an ordinary phone line).

R

RAID (Redundant Array of Inexpensive Disks)   RAID is a standard used for allowing fault tolerance for your computer systems disk drives. Windows NT supports RAID 1 and RAID 5. RAID 1 is disk mirroring, in which all data is duplicated across two drives. In RAID 5, the controllers write data a segment at a time and interleave parity among the segments. (A segment is a selectable number of blocks.) RAID 5 does not use a dedicated parity disk.

RDISK.EXE   A program used to create and update Emergency Repair Disks and the /REPAIR folder on an NT system.

REGEDIT.EXE   One of two Registry editors available in Windows NT. This one has the same interface as the Registry editor available in Windows 95 and provides key value searching.

REGEDT32.EXE   One of two Registry editors available in Windows NT. This one has a cascaded subtree interface and enables you to set Registry security.

Regenerate   To rebuild a replaced hard drive in a stripe set with parity after hard drive failure. This process can be initiated from the Disk Administrator.

Registry   Windows NT's database repository for information about a computer's configuration. It is organized in a hierarchical structure, and is comprised of subtrees and their keys, hives, and value entries.

Registry Key   A specific Registry entry that has a configurable value.

Registry Tree   A collection of similar Registry keys. HKEY_LOCAL_MACHINE is an example of a Registry tree.

Remote Access Service (RAS)   A service that provides remote networking for telecommuters, mobile workers, and system administrators who monitor and manage servers at multiple branch offices. Users with RAS on a Windows NT computer can dial in to access their networks remotely for services such as file and printer sharing, electronic mail, scheduling, and SQL database access.

Remote Procedure Call (RPC)   A common communication standard that enables processes to interact and communicate through a secured channel.

Report View   A view in Performance Monitor that displays current counter values in a single-page format.

Reporting Interval   In Performance Monitor, the interval at which a new set of statistical information is processed and delivered to the view or views currently operating.

Response Probe   A utility used to apply a controlled stress on a system and monitor the response. This tool is useful for determining a resource's capacity before placing it in a "live" production environment.

Roaming Profile   A profile that is enabled when an administrator enters a user profile path into the user account. The first time the user logs off, the local user profile is copied to that location. Thereafter, the server copy of the user profile is downloaded each time the user logs on (if it is more current than the local copy) and is updated each time the user logs off.

S

SCSI (Small Computer System Interface)   A standard high-speed parallel interface defined by the American National Standards Institute (ANSI).

SCSI Adapter   An adapter used for connecting microcomputers to peripheral devices such as hard disks and printers, and to other computers and local area networks.

Security Accounts Manager (SAM)   The Windows NT process responsible for querying the directory database to locate a specific user name and password combination when a user attempts to log on.

Security Log   A log that records security events and can be viewed through the Event Viewer. This log helps track changes to the security system and identify any possible breaches of security. For example, depending on the Audit settings in User Manager or User Manager for Domains, the security log might record attempts to log on the local computer. The security log contains both valid and invalid logon attempts as well as events related to resource use (such as creating, opening, or deleting files).

Serial Line Interface Protocol (SLIP)   An older industry standard that is part of Windows NT

RAS to ensure interoperability with third-party remote access software. Windows NT supports SLIP as a client but not as a server; that is, an NT machine can connect to a SLIP server but cannot itself be a SLIP server.

Server Message Block (SMB) A file-sharing protocol designed to enable systems to transparently access files that reside on remote systems.

Service A process that performs a specific system function and often provides an application programming interface (API) for other processes to call. Windows NT services are RPC-enabled, meaning that their API routines can be called from remote computers.

Share Permissions A set of permissions controlling access to a network share when that access is attempted over the network. Share permissions do not apply to local users of a system and can be applied only at the folder level.

Sharing The process of making a resource available on the network. This resource can be a drive, a folder, or a printer.

/SOS A BOOT.INI switch indicating that, on NT Server or Workstation boot, the list of drivers loading should be displayed. This switch is used for troubleshooting and is normally configured as part of the [VGA] boot option.

Spooler Software that accepts documents sent by a user to be printed, and then stores those documents and sends them, one by one, to an available printer.

Stand-Alone Server A Windows NT server that participates as part of a workgroup and not as a part of a domain.

Stripe Set The saving of data across identical partitions on different drives. A stripe set does not provide fault tolerance.

Subnet Mask A 32-bit value that enables the recipient of IP packets to distinguish the network ID portion of the IP address from the host ID.

System Groups One or more groups maintained by Windows NT for special purposes. The Everyone group is an example of a system group; it cannot be changed because its membership is defined and maintained by Windows NT.

System Log A log that contains events logged by the Windows NT components and that can be looked at through Event Viewer. For example, the failure of a driver or other system component to load during startup is recorded in the system log.

System Partition The volume that has the hardware-specific files needed to load Windows NT.

System Policy A policy created with the System Policy Editor to control user work environments and actions, and to enforce system configuration for Windows NT clients. System policy can be implemented for specific users, groups, or computers, or for all users. System policy for users overwrites settings in the current user area of the Registry, and system policy for computers overwrites the current local machine area of the Registry. If you have clients who are using Windows 95, separate system policies must be created for them on a Windows 95 system because Windows NT system policies are not compatible with Windows 95.

T

Take Ownership The process by which the ownership of a resource is transferred from one user to another. By default, administrators can take ownership of any NT resource.

Task Manager A utility integrated within Windows NT that enables you to monitor processes and applications on your system. You can also use the task manager to view processor and memory statistics.

TCP (Transmission Control Protocol) A protocol that provides end-to-end, connection-oriented, reliable transport layer (layer 4) functions over IP-controlled networks. TCP performs the following functions: flow control between two systems, acknowledgments of packets received, and end-to-end sequencing of packets. The protocol uses IP for delivery. TCP was originally developed by the Department of Defense to support interworking of dissimilar computers across a network.

TCP/IP (Transmission Control Protocol/Internet Protocol) A set of networking protocols that provide communications across interconnected networks made up of computers with diverse hardware architectures and various operating systems. TCP/IP includes standards for how computers communicate and conventions for connecting networks and routing traffic.

Telephony API (TAPI) Used by programs to make data/fax/voice calls, including the Windows NT applets HyperTerminal, Dial-Up Networking, Phone Dialer, and other Win32 communications applications written for Windows NT.

Thread The object of a process that is responsible for executing code segments.

Tracert A TCP/IP troubleshooting utility used to trace the route from one host to another. You can use this utility to locate the source of a transmission breakdown between TCP/IP hosts.

Trust Relationship A secured communication channel between Windows NT server domains, allowing for the sharing of user account database information. A trust relationship is used to establish the connections between domains in the Windows NT domain models.

U, V

UDP (User Datagram Protocol) A protocol that is part of the TCP/IP protocol suite and provides a means for applications to access the connectionless features of IP. UDP operates at layer 4 of the OSI reference model and provides for the exchange of datagrams without acknowledgments or guaranteed delivery.

UNC (Universal Naming Convention) name A full Windows NT name of a resource on a network. It conforms to the *servername**sharename* syntax, where *servername* is the server's name and *sharename* is the name of the shared resource. UNC names of directories or files can also include the directory path under the share name, with the following syntax:

*servername**sharename**directory**filename*

UPS (Uninterruptible Power Supply) A battery-operated power supply connected to a computer to keep the system running during a power failure.

User Account An identifier that consists of all the information that defines a user to Windows NT. This includes such things as the user name and password required for the user to log on, the groups in which the user account has membership, and the rights and permissions the user has for using the system and accessing its resources. For Windows NT Workstation, user accounts are managed with User Manager. For Windows NT Server, user accounts are managed with User Manager for Domains.

User Manager for Domains A Windows NT Server tool used to manage security for a domain or an individual computer. The tool administers user accounts, groups, and security policies.

User Profiles Profiles that save configuration information that can be retained on a user-by-user basis. This information includes all the per-user settings of the Windows NT environment, such as the desktop arrangement, personal program groups and the program items in those groups, screen colors, screen savers, network connections, printer connections, mouse settings, window size and position, and more. When a user logs on, the user's profile is loaded and the user's Windows NT environment is configured according to that profile.

User Rights Access permissions that allow the users and/or groups to perform specific functions and tasks on the Windows NT system.

Volume Set A combination of partitions on a physical disk that appears as one logical drive.

W, X, Y, Z

Windows Internet Name Service (WINS) A name-resolution service that resolves Windows NT networking computer names to IP addresses in a routed environment. A WINS server handles name registrations, queries, and releases.

WinLogon The Windows NT process that initiates login by presenting the logon dialog box to a user.

WINNT.EXE The program used to install Windows NT from a non-NT platform.

WINNT32.EXE The program used to install or upgrade Windows NT from an NT platform.

Workgroup For Windows NT, a collection of computers that are grouped for viewing purposes. Each workgroup is identified by a unique name.

APPENDIX C

Fast Facts

The fast facts listed in this section are designed as a refresher of key points and topics required to succeed on the Windows NT Server 4.0 in the Enterprise exam. By using these summaries of key points, you can spend an hour before your exam to refresh key topics, and ensure that you have a solid understanding of the objectives and information required for you to succeed in each major area of the exam.

The following are the main categories Microsoft uses to arrange the objectives:

- Planning
- Installation and configuration
- Managing resources
- Connectivity
- Monitoring and optimization
- Troubleshooting

For each of these main sections, or categories, the assigned objectives are reviewed, and following each objective, review material is offered.

PLANNING

Objective Planning 1—Plan the implementation of a directory services architecture. Considerations include the following:

- Selecting the appropriate domain model
- Supporting a single logon account
- Enabling users to access resources in different domains

The main goals of directory services are the following:

- One user, one account
- Universal resource access
- Centralized administration
- Directory synchronization

To ensure that you are selecting the best plan for your network, always address each of the goals of directory services.

The requirements for setting up a trust are as follows:

- The trust relationship can be established only between Windows NT Server domains.
- The domains must be able to make an RPC connection. To establish an RPC connection, you must ensure that a network connection exists between the domain controllers of all participating domains.
- The trust relationship must be set up by a user with administrator access.
- You should determine the number and type of trusts before the implementation.
- You must decide where to place the user accounts because that is the trusted domain.

Trust relationships enable communication between domains. The trusts must be organized, however, to achieve the original goal of directory services. Windows NT domains can be organized into one of four different domain models:

- The single domain model
- The single master domain model
- The multiple master domain model
- The complete trust model

Table C.1 summarizes the advantages and disadvantages of the domain models.

TABLE C.1 PROFILING THE DOMAIN MODELS

Domain Model	Advantages	Disadvantages
Single domain model	Centralized administration.	Limited to 40,000 user accounts. No trust relationships. No distribution of resources.
Single master domain model	Centralized administration. Distributed resources.	Limited to 40,000 user accounts.
Multiple master domain model	Unlimited number of user accounts; each master domain can host 40,000 user accounts. Distributed resources. Complex trust relationships.	No centralized administration of user accounts.
Complete trust model	Unlimited number of user accounts; each domain can host 40,000 user accounts. Complex trust relationships.	No centralized administration of user accounts.

Objective Planning 2—Plan the disk drive configuration for various requirements. Requirements include choosing a fault-tolerance method.

Windows NT Server 4 supports the following fault-tolerance solutions:

- RAID Level 0 (disk striping)
- RAID Level 1 (disk mirroring)
- RAID Level 5 (disk striping with parity)

A comparison of the three fault-tolerance options might help to summarize the information and to ensure that you have a strong understanding of the options available in Windows NT Server 4.0 (see Table C.2).

TABLE C.2 SUMMARY OF FAULT-TOLERANCE OPTIONS IN WINDOWS NT SERVER 4

Disk Striping	Disk Mirroring/ Disk Duplexing	Disk Striping with Parity
No fault tolerance	Complete disk duplication.	Data regeneration from stored parity information.
Minimum of two physical disks, maximum of 32 disks	Two physical disks.	Minimum of three physical disks, maximum of 32 disks.
100% available disk utilization	50% available disk utilization.	Dedicates the equivalent of one disk's space in the set for parity information. The more disks, the higher the utilization.
Cannot include a system/boot partition	Includes all partition types.	Cannot include a system/boot partition.
Excellent read/write performance	Moderate read/write performance.	Excellent read and moderate write performance.

Objective Planning 3—Choose a protocol for various situations. The protocols include the following:

- TCP/IP
- TCP/IP with DHCP and WINS

- NWLink IPX/SPX-compatible Transport Protocol
- Data Link Control (DLC)
- AppleTalk

Windows NT Server 4 comes bundled with several protocols that can be used for interconnectivity with other systems and for use within a Windows NT environment. You examine the various protocols, then try to define when each protocol best fits your network needs. The protocols discussed to prepare you for the enterprise exam are the following:

- **NetBEUI.** The NetBEUI protocol is the easiest to implement and has wide support across platforms. The protocol uses NetBIOS broadcasts to locate other computers on the network. This process of locating other computers requires additional network traffic and can slow down your entire network. Because NetBEUI uses broadcasts to locate computers, it is not routable; in other words, you cannot access computers that are not on your physical network. Most Microsoft and IBM OS/2 clients support this protocol. NetBEUI is best suited to small networks with no requirements for routing the information to remote networks or to the Internet.

- **TCP/IP.** Transmission Control Protocol/Internet Protocol, or TCP/IP, is the most common protocol—more specifically, it is the most common suite of protocols. TCP/IP is an industry-standard protocol that is supported by most network operating systems. Because of this acceptance throughout the industry, TCP/IP enables your Windows NT system to connect to other systems with a common communication protocol.

The following are advantages of using TCP/IP in a Windows NT environment:

- The capability to connect dissimilar systems
- The capability to use numerous standard connectivity utilities, including File Transfer Protocol (FTP), Telnet, and PING
- Access to the Internet

If your Windows NT system is using TCP/IP as a connection protocol, it can communicate with many non-Microsoft systems. Some of the systems it can communicate with are the following:

- Any Internet-connected system
- UNIX systems
- IBM mainframe systems
- DEC Pathworks
- TCP/IP-supported printers directly connected to the network

- **NWLink IPX/SPX-compatible.** The IPX protocol has been used within the NetWare environment for years. By developing an IPX-compatible protocol, Microsoft enables Windows NT systems to communicate with NetWare systems.

NWLink is best-suited to networks requiring communication with existing NetWare servers and for existing NetWare clients.

Other utilities must be installed, however, to enable the Windows NT Server system to gain access into the NetWare security. Gateway Services for NetWare/Client Services for NetWare (GSNW/CSNW) must be installed on the Windows NT server to enable the computer to be logged on to a NetWare system. GSNW functions as a NetWare client, but it also can share the connection to the Novell box with users from the Windows NT system. This capability enables a controlled NetWare connection for file and print sharing on the NetWare box, without requiring the configuration of each NT client with a duplicate network redirector or client.

- **DataLink Control.** The DLC protocol was originally used for connectivity in an IBM mainframe environment, and maintains support for existing legacy systems and mainframes. The DLC protocol is also used for connections to some network printers.

- **AppleTalk.** Windows NT Server can configure the AppleTalk protocol to enable connectivity with Apple Macintosh systems. This protocol is installed with the Services for the Macintosh included with your Windows NT Server CD-ROM. The AppleTalk protocol enables Macintosh computers on your network to access files and printers set up on the Windows NT server. It also enables your Windows NT clients to print to Apple Macintosh printers.

The AppleTalk protocol is best suited to connectivity with the Apple Macintosh.

INSTALLATION AND CONFIGURATION

Objective Installation and Configuration 1— Install Windows NT Server to perform various server roles. Server roles include the following:

- Primary Domain Controller
- Backup Domain Controller
- Member server

The following are different server roles into which Windows NT Server can be installed:

- **Primary Domain Controller.** The Primary Domain Controller (PDC) is the first domain controller installed into a domain. As the first computer in the domain, the PDC creates the domain. This fact is important to understand because it establishes the rationale for needing a PDC in the environment. Each domain can contain only one PDC. All other domain controllers in the domain are installed as Backup Domain Controllers. The PDC handles user requests and logon validation, and it offers all the standard Windows NT Server functionality. The PDC contains the original copy of the Security Accounts Manager (SAM), which contains all user accounts and security permissions for your domain.

- **Backup Domain Controller.** The Backup Domain Controller (BDC) is an additional domain controller used to handle logon requests by users in the network. To handle the logon requests, the BDC must have a complete copy of the domain database, or SAM. The BDC also runs the Net Logon service; however, the Net Logon service in a BDC functions a little differently than in a PDC. In the PDC, the Net Logon service handles synchronization of the SAM database to all the BDCs.

- **Member server.** In both of the domain controllers, PDC or BDC, the computer has an additional function. The domain controllers handle logon requests and ensure that the SAM is synchronized throughout the domain. These functions add overhead to the system. A computer that handles the server functionality you require without the overhead of handling logon validation is called a *member server*. A member server is a part of the domain, but it does not need a copy of the SAM database and does not handle logon requests. The main function of a member server is to share resources.

After you have installed your computer into a specific server role, you might decide to change the role of the server. This can be a relatively easy task if you are changing a PDC to a BDC, or vice versa. If you want to change a domain controller to a member server or member server to a domain controller; however, you must reinstall into the required server role. A member server has a local database that does not participate in domain synchronization. In changing roles, a member server must be reinstalled to ensure that the account database and the appropriate services are installed.

Objective Installation and Configuration 2—Configure protocols and protocol bindings. Protocols include the following:

- TCP/IP
- TCP/IP with DHCP and WINS
- NWLink IPX/SPX-compatible Transport Protocol
- DLC
- AppleTalk

You install a new protocol in Windows NT Server through the Network Properties dialog box.

Following are the protocols, and the configuration options available with each:

▼ NOTE

Notice that NetBEUI is not discussed. This list does not include the NetBEUI protocol because there are no configuration options available for this protocol.

- **TCP/IP.** The following tabs are available for configuration in the Microsoft TCP/IP Properties dialog box:
    - **IP Address.** The IP Address tab enables you to configure the IP address, the subnet mask, and the default gateway. You also can enable the system to allocate IP address information automatically through the use of the DHCP server.

    An IP address is a 32-bit address that is broken into four octets and used to identify your network adapter card as a TCP/IP host. Each IP address must be a unique address. If you have any IP address conflicts on your computer, you cannot use the TCP/IP protocol.

    Your IP address is then grouped into a subnet. The process you use to subnet your network is to assign a subnet mask. A *subnet mask* is used to identify the computers local to your network. Any address outside your subnet is accessed through the default gateway, also called the *router*. The default gateway is the address of the router that handles all routing of your TCP/IP information to computers, or hosts, outside your subnet.

    - **DNS.** The DNS tab shows you the options available for configuring your TCP/IP protocol to use a DNS server. The Domain Name System (DNS)

server translates TCP/IP host names of remote computers into IP addresses. Remember that an IP address is a unique address for each computer. The DNS server contains a database of all the computers you can access by host name. This database is used when you access a Web page on the Internet. Working with the naming scheme is easier than using the IP address of the computer.

- **WINS Address.** The WINS Address tab enables you to configure your primary and secondary Windows Internet Names Services (WINS) server addresses. WINS is used to reduce the number of NetBIOS broadcast messages sent across the network to locate a computer. By using a WINS server, you keep the names of computers on your network in a WINS database. The WINS database is dynamic.

  In configuring your WINS servers, you can enter your primary WINS server and a secondary WINS server. Your system searches the primary WINS server database first, then the secondary database if no match was found in the primary one.

- **DHCP Relay.** The DHCP relay agent is used to find your DHCP servers across routers. DHCP addresses are handed out by the DHCP servers. The client request, however, is made with a broadcast message. Broadcast messages do not cross routers; therefore, this protocol might place some restrictions on your systems. The solution is to use a DHCP relay agent to assist the clients in finding the DHCP server across a router.

  In configuring your DHCP relay agent, you can specify the seconds threshold and the maximum number of hops to use in searching for the DHCP servers. At the bottom of the tab, you can enter the IP addresses of the DHCP servers you want to use.

- **Routing.** In an environment in which multiple subnets are used, you can configure your Windows NT Server as a multihomed system. In other words, you can install multiple network adapters, each connecting to a different subnet. If you enable the Enable IP Forwarding option, your computer acts as a router, forwarding the packets through the network cards in the multihomed system to the other subnet.

- **NWLINK IPX/SPX-compatible.** The configuration of the NWLink protocol is simple in comparison to the TCP/IP protocol. It is this simplicity that makes it a popular protocol to use.

  The NWLink IPX/SPX Properties dialog box has two tabs:

  - **General.** On the General tab, you have the option to assign an internal network number. This eight-digit hexadecimal number format is used by some programs with services that can be accessed by NetWare clients.

You also have the option to select a frame type for your NWLink protocol. The frame type you select must match the frame type of the remote computer with which you need to communicate. By default, Windows NT Server uses the Auto Frame Type Detection setting, which scans the network and loads the first frame type it encounters.

- **Routing.** The Routing tab of the NWLink IPX/SPX Properties dialog box is used to enable or disable the Routing Information Protocol (RIP). If you enable RIP routing over IPX, your Windows NT Server can act as an IPX router.

- **DLC.** The configuration of DLC is done through Registry parameters. The DLC protocol is configured based on three timers:

    - **T1.** The response timer.
    - **T2.** The acknowledgment delay timer.
    - **Ti.** The inactivity timer.

    The Registry contains the entries that can be modified to configure DLC. You can find the entries at `HKEY_LOCAL_MACHINE\SYSTEM\CurrentControlSet\Services\DLC\Parameters\ELNKIII adapter name`.

- **AppleTalk.** To install the AppleTalk protocol, you install Services for Macintosh.

Table C.3 reviews the protocols that you can configure for your NT Enterprise (including the subcomponents—tabs—of each protocol).

TABLE C.3 PROTOCOLS TO CONFIGURE

Protocol	Subcomponent (Tab)
TCP/IP	IP Address DNS WINS Address DHCP Relay Routing
NWLink IPX/SPX-compatible	General Routing
AppleTalk	General Routing

The binding order is the sequence your computer uses to select which protocol to use for network communications. Each protocol is listed for each network-based service, protocol, and adapter available.

The Bindings tab contains an option, Show Bindings for, that can be used to select the service, adapter, or protocol you want to modify in the binding order. By clicking the appropriate button, you can enable or disable each binding, or move up or down in the binding order.

Objective Installation and Configuration 3—Configure Windows NT Server core services. Services include the following:

- Directory Replicator
- Computer Browser

In this objective, you look at configuring some of the core services in the Windows NT Server. These services are the following:

- **Server service.** The Server service answers network requests. By configuring Server service, you can change the way your server responds and, in a sense, the role it plays in your network environment. To configure Server service, you must open the Network dialog box. To do this, double-click the

Network icon in the Control Panel. Select the Services tab. In the Server dialog box, you have four optimization settings. Each of these settings modifies memory management based on the role the server is playing. These options are the following:

- **Minimize Memory Used.** The Minimize Memory Used setting is used when your Windows NT Server system is accessed by less than 10 users.

  This setting allocates memory so a maximum of 10 network connections can be properly maintained. By restricting the memory for network connections, you make more memory available at the local or desktop level.

- **Balance.** The Balance setting can be used for a maximum of 64 network connections. This setting is the default when using NetBEUI software. Like the Minimize setting, Balance is best used for a relatively low number of users connecting to a server that also can be used as a desktop computer.

- **Maximize Throughput for File Sharing.** The Maximize Throughput for File Sharing setting allocates the maximum amount of memory available for network connections. This setting is excellent for large networks in which the server is being accessed for file and print sharing.

- **Maximize Throughput for Network Applications.** If you are running distributed applications, such as SQL Server or Exchange Server, the network applications do their own memory caching. Therefore, you want your system to enable the applications to manage the memory. You accomplish this by using the Maximize Throughput for Network Applications setting. This setting also is used for very large networks.

- **Computer Browser service.** The Computer Browser service is responsible for maintaining the list of computers on the network. The browse list contains all the computers located on the physical network. As a Windows NT Server, your system plays a big role in the browsing of a network. The Windows NT Server acts as a master browser or backup browser.

  The selection of browsers is through an election. The election is called by any client computer or when a preferred master browser computer starts up. The election is based on broadcast messages. Every computer has the opportunity to nominate itself, and the computer with the highest settings wins the election.

  The election criteria are based on three things:

  - The operating system (Windows NT Server, Windows NT Workstation, Windows 95, Windows for Workgroups)
  - The version of the operating system (NT 4.0, NT 3.51, NT 3.5)
  - The current role of the computer (master browser, backup browser, potential browser)

- **Directory Replicator service.** You can configure the Directory Replicator service to synchronize an entire directory structure across multiple servers.

In configuring the directory service, you must select the export server and all the import servers. The export server is the computer that holds the original copy of the directory structure and files. Each import server receives a complete copy of the export server's directory structure. The Directory Replicator service monitors the directory structure on the export server. If the contents of the directory change, the changes are copied to all the import servers. The file copying and directory monitoring is completed by a special service account you create. You must configure the Directory Replicator service to use this service account. The following access is required for your Directory Replicator service account:

- The account should be a member of the Backup Operators and Replicators groups.
- There should be no time or logon restrictions for the account.
- The Password Never Expires option should be selected.
- The User Must Change Password at Next Logon option should be turned off.

When configuring the export server, you have the option to specify the export directory. The default export directory is `C:\WINNT\system32\repl\export\`.

In the Import Directories section of the Directory Replication dialog box, you can select the import directory. The default import directory is `C:\WINNT\system32\repl\import`.

Remember that the default directory for executing logon scripts in a Windows NT system is `C:\WINNT\system32\repl\import\scripts`.

Objective Installation and Configuration 4—Configure hard disks to meet various requirements. Requirements include the following:

- Providing duplication
- Improving performance

All hard disk configuration can be done by using the Disk Administrator tool. The different disk configurations you need to understand for the enterprise exam are the following:

- **Stripe set.** A stripe set gives you improved disk read and write performance; however, it supplies no fault-tolerance. A minimum of two disks is required, and the configuration can stripe up to 32 physical disks. A stripe set cannot include the system partition.
- **Volume set.** A volume set enables you to extend partitions beyond one physical disk; however, it supplies no fault-tolerance. To extend a volume set, you must use the NTFS file system.
- **Disk mirroring.** A mirror set uses two physical disks and provides full data duplication. Often referred to as RAID level 1, disk mirroring is a useful solution to assigning duplication to the system partition, as well as any other disks that might be in the system.
- **Stripe set with parity.** A stripe set with parity enables fault-tolerance in your system. A minimum of three physical disks is required, and a maximum of 32 physical disks can be included in a stripe set with parity. A stripe set with parity cannot include the system partition of your Windows NT system.

The solution that supplies the best duplication and optimization mix is the stripe set with parity.

Objective Installation and Configuration 5—Configure printers. Tasks include the following:

- Adding and configuring a printer
- Implementing a printer pool
- Setting print priorities

The installation of a printer is a fairly simplistic procedure and is not tested heavily on the exam; however, the printer pool is a key point. The items to remember about printer pools are as follows:

- All printers in a printer pool must be able to function using the same printer driver.
- A printer pool can have a maximum of eight printers in the pool.

Objective Installation and Configuration 6—Configure a Windows NT Server computer for various types of client computers. Client computer types include the following:

- Windows NT Workstation
- Windows 95
- Macintosh

The Network Client Administrator is found in the Administrative Tools group. You can use the Network Client Administrator program to do the following:

- **Make a Network Installation Startup Disk.** This option creates an MS-DOS boot disk that contains commands required to connect to a network server and that automatically installs Windows NT Workstation, Windows 95, or the DOS network clients.

- **Make an Installation Disk Set.** This option enables the creation of installation disks for the DOS network client, LAN Manager 2.2c for DOS, or LAN Manager 2.2c for OS/2.

- **Copy Client-based Network Administration Tools.** This option enables you to share the network administration tools with client computers. The client computers that can use the network administration tools are Windows NT Workstation and Windows 95 computers.

- **View Remoteboot Client Information.** This option enables you to view the remoteboot client information. To install remoteboot, go to the Services tab of the Network dialog box.

When installing a client computer, you must ensure that your Windows NT system is prepared for and configured for the client. The Windows clients can connect to the Windows NT server without any configuration required on the server; however, some configuration is required on the client computers. For the Apple Macintosh client, the NT server must install the services for the Macintosh, which includes the AppleTalk protocol. This protocol enables the seamless connection between the Windows NT system and the Apple clients.

Managing Resources

Objective Managing Resources 1—Manage user and group accounts. Considerations include the following:

- Managing Windows NT user accounts
- Managing Windows NT user rights

- Managing Windows NT groups
- Administering account policies
- Auditing changes to the user account database

AGLP stands for Accounts/Global Groups/Local Groups/Permissions. When you want to assign permissions to any resource, you should follow a few simple rules. All user accounts are placed into global groups, and global groups get assigned into local groups. The local groups have the resources and permissions assigned to them.

When you are working with groups across trust relationships, the following guidelines are useful:

- Always gather users into global groups. Remember that global groups can contain only user accounts from the same domain. You might have to create the same named global group in multiple domains.
- If you have multiple account domains, use the same name for a global group that has the same types of members. Remember that when multiple domains are involved, the group name is referred to as *DOMAIN\GROUP*.
- Before the global groups are created, determine whether an existing local group meets your needs. There is no sense in creating duplicate local groups.
- Remember that the local group must be created where the resource is located. If the resource is on a Domain Controller, create the local group in the Domain Account Database. If the resource is on a Windows NT Workstation or Windows NT Member Server, you must create the group in that system's local account database.
- Be sure to set the permissions for a resource before you make the global groups a member of the local group assigned to the resource. That way, you set the security for the resource.

Objective Managing Resources 2—Create and manage policies and profiles for various situations. Policies and profiles include the following:

- Local user profiles
- Roaming user profiles
- System policies

You can configure system policies to do the following:

- Implement defaults for hardware configuration for all computers using the profile or for a specific machine.
- Restrict the changing of specific parameters that affect the hardware configuration of the participating system.
- Set defaults for all users in the areas of their personal settings that the users can configure.
- Restrict users from changing specific areas of their configuration to prevent tampering with the system. An example is disabling all Registry editing tools for a specific user.
- Apply all defaults and restrictions on a group level, rather than just a user level.

Some common implementations of user profiles are the following:

- Locking down display properties to prevent users from changing the resolution of their monitor. Display properties can be locked down as a whole or on each individual property page of display properties.

You adjust this setting by clicking the Control Panel, Display, Restrict Display option of the Default User Properties dialog box.

- Setting a default color scheme or wallpaper. You can do this by clicking the Desktop option of the Default User Properties dialog box.

- If you want to restrict access to portions of the Start menu or desktop, you can do this by clicking the Shell, Restrictions option of the Default User Properties dialog box.

- If you need to limit the applications that the user can run at a workstation, you can do so by clicking the System, Restrictions option of the Default User Properties dialog box. You can also use this option to prevent the user from modifying the Registry.

- You can prevent users from mapping or disconnecting network drives by clicking the Windows NT Shell, Restrictions option of the Default User Properties dialog box.

Profiles and policies can be very powerful tools to assist in the administrative tasks in your environment. The following list reviews each of the main topics covered in this objective:

- **Roaming profiles.** The user portion of the Registry is downloaded from a central location, allowing the user settings to follow the user anywhere within the network environment.

- **Local profiles.** The user settings are stored at each workstation and are not copied to other computers. Each workstation that you use will have different desktop and user settings.

- **System policies.** System policies enable the administrator to restrict user configuration changes on systems. This enables the administrator to maintain the settings of the desktop of systems without the worry that a user can modify them.

- **Computer policies.** Computer policies allow the lockdown of common machine settings that affect all users of that computer.

Objective Managing Resources 3—Administer remote servers from various types of client computers. Client computer types include the following:

- Windows 95
- Windows NT Workstation

This objective focuses on the remote administration tools available for your Windows NT Server. The following list summarizes the key tools:

- **Remote Administration Tools for Windows 95.** Allows User Manager, Server manager, Event Viewer, and NTFS file permissions to be executed from the Windows 95 computer.

- **Remote Administration for Windows NT.** Allows User Manager, Server Manager, DHCP Manager, System Policy Editor, Remote Access Admin, Remote Boot Manager, WINS Manager, and NTFS file permissions to be executed from a Windows NT machine.

- **Web-based Administration.** Allows for common tasks to be completed through an Internet connection into the Windows NT Server.

Objective Managing Resources 4—Manage disk resources. Tasks include the following:

- Creating and sharing resources
- Implementing permissions and security
- Establishing file auditing

Windows NT has two levels of security for protecting your disk resources:

- Share permissions
- NTFS permissions

NTFS permissions enable you to assign more comprehensive security to your computer system. NTFS permissions can protect you at the file level. Share permissions, on the other hand, can be applied only to the folder level. NTFS permissions can affect users logged on locally or across the network to the system where the NTFS permissions are applied. Share permissions are in effect only when the user connects to the resource through the network.

The combination of Windows NT share permissions and NTFS permissions determines the ultimate access a user has to a resource on the server's disk. When share permissions and NTFS permissions are combined, no preference is given to one or the other. The key factor is which of the two effective permissions is the most restrictive.

For the exam, remember the following tips relating to managing resources:

- Users can be assigned only to global groups in the same domain.
- Only global groups from trusted domains can become members of local groups in trusting domains.
- NTFS permissions are assigned only to local groups in all correct test answers.

- Only NTFS permissions give you file-level security.

CONNECTIVITY

Objective Connectivity 1—Configure Windows NT Server for interoperability with NetWare servers by using various tools. The tools include the following:

- Gateway Service for NetWare
- Migration Tool for NetWare

Gateway Service for NetWare (GSNW) performs the following functions:

- GSNW enables Windows NT Servers to access NetWare file and print resources.
- GSNW enables the Windows NT Servers to act as a gateway to the NetWare file and print resources. The Windows NT Server enables users to borrow the connection to the NetWare server by setting it up as a shared connection.

The Migration Tool for NetWare (NWCONV) transfers file and folder information and user and group account information from a NetWare server to a Windows NT domain controller. The Migration Tool can preserve the folder and file permissions if it is being transferred to an NTFS partition.

Connectivity between Windows NT and a NetWare server requires the use of GSNW. If the user and file information from NetWare is to be transferred to a Windows NT Server, the NetWare conversion utility, NWCONV, is used for this task. The following list summarizes the main points in this section on NetWare connectivity:

- GSNW can be used as a gateway between Windows NT clients and a NetWare server.
- GSNW acts as a NetWare client to the Windows NT Server, allowing the NT server to have a connection to the NetWare server.
- GSNW is a service in Windows NT, and is installed using the Control Panel.
- For GSNW to be used as a gateway into a NetWare server, a gateway user account must be created and placed in a NetWare group called NTGATEWAY.
- In configuring the GSNW as a gateway, you can assign permissions to the gateway share by accessing the GSNW icon in the Control Panel.
- For GSNW to be functional, the NWLINK IPX/SPX protocol must be installed and configured.
- To convert user and file information from a NetWare server to a Windows NT server, you can use the NWCONV.EXE utility.
- NWCONV requires that GSNW be installed prior to any conversion being carried out.
- To maintain the NetWare folder- and file-level permissions in the NWCONV utility, you must convert to an NTFS partition on the Windows NT system.

Objective Connectivity 2—Install and configure multiprotocol routing to serve various functions. Functions include the following:

- Internet router
- BOOTP/DHCP Relay Agent
- IPX router

Multiprotocol routing gives you flexibility in the connection method used by your clients, and in maintaining security. Check out the following:

- **Internet router.** Setting up Windows NT as an Internet router is as simple as installing two network adapters in the system, then enabling IP routing in the TCP/IP protocol configuration. This option enables Windows NT to act as a static router. Note that Windows NT cannot exchange Routing Information Protocol (RIP) routing packets with other IP RIP routers unless the RIP routing software is installed.

- **IPX router.** You enable the IPX router by installing the IPX RIP router software by choosing Control Panel, Networks, Services.

  After installing the IPX RIP router, Windows NT can route IPX packets over the network adapters installed. Windows NT uses the RIP to exchange its routing table information with other RIP routers.

The inclusion of the industry-standard protocols and tools to simplify the configuration and extension of your NT network into other environments makes this operating system a very powerful piece of your heterogeneous environment. The following are the main factors to focus on for this objective:

- A strong understanding of the functionality of each of the Windows NT protocols—with a strong slant toward TCP/IP and the configuration options available. Understanding and configuration of the DHCP server are also tested on this exam.

- The services used to resolve the IP addresses and names of hosts in a TCP/IP environment. DNS service, WINS Service, the Hosts file, and the `LMHosts` files are among the services tested.

- The routing mechanisms available in Windows NT. These mechanisms are powerful, and largely unknown to the vast majority of NT administrators. Ensure that you review the configuration and functionality of Internet or IP routing, as well as the IPX routing tools available.

Objective Connectivity 3—Install and configure Internet Information Server.

Objective Connectivity 4—Install and configure Internet services. Services include the following:

- The World Wide Web
- DNS
- Intranets

Internet Information Server (IIS) uses Hypertext Transfer Protocol (HTTP), File Transfer Protocol (FTP), and the Gopher service to provide Internet publishing services to your Windows NT Server computer.

IIS provides a graphical administration tool called the Internet Service Manager. With this tool, you can centrally manage, control, and monitor the Internet services in your Windows NT network. The Internet Service Manager uses the built-in Windows NT security model, so it offers a secure method of remotely administering your web sites and other Internet services.

IIS is an integrated component in Windows NT Server 4.0. The IIS services are installed using the Control Panel, Networks icon or during the installation phase. The following list summarizes the key points in installing and configuring IIS:

- The three Internet services included in IIS are HTTP, FTP, and Gopher.

- HTTP is used to host Web pages from your Windows NT server system.

- FTP is a protocol used for transferring files across the Internet by using the TCP/IP protocol.

- Gopher is used to create a set of hierarchical links to other computers or to annotate files or folders.

- The Internet Service Manager is the utility used to manage and configure your Internet services in IIS.

- The Internet Service Manager has three views that you can use to view your services. The three views are Report view, Servers view, and Services view.

Objective Connectivity 5—Install and configure Remote Access Service (RAS). Configuration options include the following:

- Configuring RAS communications
- Configuring RAS protocols
- Configuring RAS security

RAS supports the Serial Line Internet Protocol (SLIP) and Point-to-Point Protocol (PPP) line protocols, and the NetBEUI, TCP/IP, and IPX network protocols.

RAS can connect to a remote computer using any of the following media:

- **Public Switched Telephone Network (PSTN).** (PSTN is also known simply as the phone company.) RAS can connect using a modem through an ordinary phone line.

- **X.25.** A packet-switched network. Computers access the network through a Packet Assembler Disassembler (PAD) device. X.25 supports dial-up or direct connections.

- **Null modem cable.** A cable that connects two computers directly. The computers then communicate using their modems (rather than network adapter cards).

- **ISDN.** A digital line that provides faster communication and more bandwidth than a normal phone line. (It also costs more, which is why not everybody has it.) A computer must have a special ISDN card to access an ISDN line.

RAS is designed for security. The following are some of RAS's security features:

- **Auditing.** RAS can leave an audit trail, enabling you to see who logged on when and what authentication they provided.

- **Callback security.** You can enable the RAS server to use callback (hang up all incoming calls and call the caller back), and you can limit callback numbers to prearranged sites that you know are safe.

- **Encryption.** RAS can encrypt logon information, or it can encrypt all data crossing the connection.

- **Security hosts.** In case Windows NT is not safe enough, you can add an extra dose of security by using a third-party intermediary security host—a computer that stands between the RAS client and the RAS server and requires an extra round of authentication.

- **PPTP filtering.** You can tell Windows NT to filter out all packets except ultra-safe Point-to-Point Tunneling Protocol (PPTP) packets.

RAS can be a very powerful and useful tool in enabling you to extend the reaches of your network to remote and traveling users. The following list summarizes main points for RAS in preparation for the exam:

- RAS supports SLIP and PPP line protocols.

- With PPP, RAS can support NetBEUI, NWLINK, and TCP/IP across the communication line.

- RAS uses the following media to communicate with remote systems: PSTN, X.25, Null Modem cable, and ISDN.

- The RAS security features available are auditing, callback security, encryption, and PPTP filtering.

- To install RAS, click the Network icon in the Control Panel.

Monitoring and Optimization

Objective Monitoring and Optimization 1—Establish a baseline for measuring system performance. Tasks include creating a database of measurement data.

You can use numerous database utilities to analyze the data collected. The following are some of the databases that Microsoft provides:

- Performance Monitor
- Microsoft Excel
- Microsoft Access
- Microsoft FoxPro
- Microsoft SQL Server

The following list summarizes the key items to focus on when you are analyzing your computer and network:

- Establish a baseline measurement of your system when functioning at its normal level. Later, you can use the baseline in comparative analysis.
- Establish a database to maintain the baseline results and any subsequent analysis results on the system, to compare trends and identify potential pitfalls in your system.
- The main resources to monitor are memory, the processor, the disks, and the network.

The following list summarizes the tools used to monitor your NT server that are available and are built-in to Windows NT Server 4.0:

- Server Manager
- Windows NT Diagnostics
- Response Probe
- Performance Monitor
- Network Monitor

Objective Monitoring and Optimization 2—Monitor performance of various functions by using Performance Monitor. Functions include the following:

- Processor
- Memory
- Disk
- Network

To summarize the main views used within Performance Monitor, review the following list:

- **Chart view.** This view is very useful for viewing the objects and counters in a real-time mode. This mode enables you to view the data in a graphical format. You can also use the chart view to view the contents of a log file.
- **Log view.** This view enables you to set all the options required for creating a log of your system resources or objects. After this log is created, you can view it by using the chart view.
- **Alert view.** Use the alert view to configure warnings or alerts of your system resources or objects. In this view, you can configure threshold levels for counters and can then launch an action based on the threshold values being exceeded.
- **Report view.** The report view enables you to view the object and counters as an averaged value. This view is useful for comparing the values of multiple systems that are configured similarly.

When monitoring the disk, remember to activate the disk counters using the command `diskperf -y`. If you do not enter this command, you can select Counter but will not see any activity displayed. In the case of a software RAID system, start `diskperf` with the `-ye` option.

When you want to monitor TCP/IP counters, make sure that SNMP is installed. Without the SNMP service installed, the TCP/IP counters are not available.

Performance Monitor is a graphical utility that you can use for monitoring and analyzing your system resources within Windows NT. You can enable objects and counters within Performance Monitor; it is these elements that enable the logging and viewing of system data.

In preparing you for this objective, this section introduces numerous objects and counters that you use with Performance Monitor. To prepare for the exam, you need to understand the following key topics:

- The four views available in Performance Monitor are the Report view, the Log view, the Chart view, and the Alert view.
- The main resources to monitor in any system are the disk, the memory, the network, and the processor.
- Each of the main resources are grouped as separate objects, and within each object are counters. A counter is the type of data available from a type of resource or object. Each counter might also have multiple instances. An instance is available if multiple components in a counter are listed.
- To enable the disk counters to be active, you must run the DISKPERF utility.

Objective Monitoring and Optimization 3—Monitor network traffic by using Network Monitor. Tasks include the following:

- Collecting data
- Presenting data
- Filtering data

Network Monitor is a network packet analyzer that comes with Windows NT Server 4.0. Actually two versions of Network Monitor are available from Microsoft. The first version comes with Windows NT Server 4.0 (simple version). This version can monitor the packets (frames) sent or received by a Windows NT Server 4.0 computer. The second version comes with Microsoft Systems Management Server (full version). This version can monitor all traffic on the network.

By fully understanding the various components found while analyzing traffic, you will be more successful in locating potential network bottlenecks and offering relevant optimization recommendations. The main components that need to be monitored with your network traffic analysis are the following:

- Locate and classify each service. Analyze the amount of traffic generated from each individual service, the frequency of the traffic, and the overall effect the traffic has on the network segment.
- Understand the three different types of frames: broadcast, multicast, and directed.
- Review the contents of a frame and ensure that you can find the destination address, source address, and data located in each frame.

The following points summarize the key items to understand in building a strong level of knowledge in using Network Monitor as a monitoring tool.

- Two versions of Network Monitor are available: the scaled-down version that is built in to the Windows NT Server operating system, and the full version that is a component of Microsoft Systems Management Server.

- The Network Monitor windows consist of four sections: Graph, Session Statistics, Station Statistics, and Total Statistics.
- After Network Monitor captures some data, you use the display window of Network Monitor to view the frames. The three sections of the display window are the Summary pane, the Detail pane, and the Hexadecimal pane.

Objective Monitoring and Optimization 4—Identify performance bottlenecks.

Objective Monitoring and Optimization 5—Optimize performance for various results. Results include the following:

- Controlling network traffic
- Controlling the server load

To optimize the logon traffic in your Windows NT network, you should consider four main points:

- Determine the hardware required to increase performance.
- Configure the domain controllers to increase the number of logon validations.
- Determine the number of domain controllers needed.
- Determine the best location for each of the domain controllers.

The following are a few good points to follow in optimizing file-session traffic:

- Remove any excess protocols that are loaded.
- Reduce the number of wide area network (WAN) links required for file transfer.

The following are three points to consider when attempting to optimize server browser traffic:

- Reduce the number of protocols.
- Reduce the number of entries in the browse list.
- Increase the amount of time between browser updates.

Trust relationships generate a large amount of network traffic. In optimizing your system, attempt to keep the number of trusts very low.

TROUBLESHOOTING

Objective Troubleshooting 1—Choose the appropriate course of action to take to resolve installation failures.

Troubleshooting a Windows NT system requires that you have a strong understanding of the processes and tools available to you. To be an effective troubleshooter, first and foremost you must have experience. The following is a list of some common installation problems:

- Hard disk problems
- Unsupported CD-ROMs
- Network adapter problems and conflicts
- Naming problems (each computer must be uniquely named, following the NetBIOS naming conventions)

Always use the hardware compatibility list to ensure that your components are supported by Windows NT.

Objective Troubleshooting 2—Choose the appropriate course of action to take to resolve boot failures.

For startup errors, try the following:

- Check for missing files that are involved in the boot process, including `NTLDR`, `NTDETECT.COM`, `BOOT.INI`, `NTOSKRNL.EXE`, and `OSLOADER (RISC)`.
- Modify `BOOT.INI` for options.
- Create an NT boot disk for bypassing the boot process from the hard disk.
- Use the LastKnownGood option to roll back to the last working set of your Registry settings.

Objective Troubleshooting 3—Choose the appropriate course of action to take to resolve configuration errors. Tasks include the following:

- Backing up and restoring the Registry
- Editing the Registry

You can resolve many problems that you encounter within Windows NT by configuring the Registry. However, before you make any Registry configurations, you must have a strong understanding of the keys within the Registry and always back up the Registry prior to making any modifications to ensure a smooth rollback if additional problems occur. The following are the main tools used to modify the Registry:

- REGEDT32
- REGEDIT

For configuration problems, remember the following:

- Using the Registry for configuration and troubleshooting can cause additional problems if you do not maintain a full understanding of the Registry.
- Always back up the Registry prior to editing the contents.
- You can back up and restore the local Registry by using REGEDT32.

Objective Troubleshooting 4—Choose the appropriate course of action to take to resolve printer problems.

For troubleshooting printers, you should do the following:

- Understand and review the overview of the printing process.
- Understand the files involved in the printing process.
- As a first step in troubleshooting a printer, always verify that the printer is turned on and is online.
- Note that the most common errors associated with a printer are an invalid printer driver or incorrect resource permissions set for a user.

Objective Troubleshooting 5—Choose the appropriate course of action to take to resolve RAS problems.

The following is a list of some of the problems that you might encounter with RAS:

- You must ensure that the protocol you are requesting from the RAS client is available on the RAS server. There must be at least one common protocol or the connection will fail.
- If you are using NetBEUI, ensure that the name you are using on the RAS client is not in use on the network to which you are attempting to connect.

- If you are attempting to connect using TCP/IP, you must configure the RAS server to provide you with an address.

You can use the Remote Access Admin tool to monitor the ports as well as the active connections of your RAS server.

Numerous RAS settings can cause some problems with your RAS connections. Ensure that you understand the installation process, as well as any configuration settings required to enable your RAS server. You can avoid some of the common problems that can occur by doing the following:

- Ensuring that the modem and communication mediums are configured and functional prior to installing RAS. It can be very difficult to modify settings after the installation, so it is recommended to have all hardware tested and working first.
- Verifying that dial-in permissions have been enabled for the required users. This small task is commonly forgotten in your RAS configuration.

Objective Troubleshooting 6—Choose the appropriate course of action to take to resolve connectivity problems.

To test and verify your TCP/IP settings, you can use the following utilities:

- IPCONFIG
- PING

The most effective method for troubleshooting connectivity is to understand thoroughly the installation and configuration options of each of the network protocols. If you understand the options available, you can narrow down the possible problem areas very quickly. Also ensure that you use utilities such as IPCONFIG and PING to test your connections.

Objective Troubleshooting 7—Choose the appropriate course of action to take to resolve resource access and permission problems.

You should keep in mind two main issues about permissions:

- The default permissions for both share and NTFS give the Windows NT group Everyone full control over the files and folders. Whenever you format a drive as NTFS or first share a folder, you should remove these permissions. The Everyone group contains everyone, including guests and any other user who, for one reason or another, can connect to your system.
- The NTFS folder permission delete takes precedence over any file permissions. In all other cases, the file permissions take precedence over the folder permissions.

Objective Troubleshooting 8—Choose the appropriate course of action to take to resolve fault-tolerance failures. Fault-tolerance methods include the following:

- Tape backup
- Mirroring
- Stripe set with parity

In using the NTBACKUP tool, the primary thing that you need to do is to determine the frequency and type of backup that you will do. There are three main types of backups that you might want to perform:

- **Full.** This backs up all the files that you mark, and marks the files as having been backed up. This is the longest of the backups because it transfers the most data.

- **Differential.** This backs up all the files that have changed since the last backup. A differential backup does not mark the files as being backed up. As time passes since the last full backup, the differentials become increasingly larger. However, you need only reload the full backup and the differential to return to the position of the last backup.

- **Incremental.** This backs up any files that have changed since the last backup, and then marks them as having been backed up. If your system crashes, you need to start by loading a full backup and then each incremental backup since that full backup.

If you are mirroring the system partition, the disks and partitions should be absolutely identical. Otherwise, the MBR/DBR (master boot record/disk boot record) that contains the driver information will not be correct.

Although ARC naming looks complicated, it is really rather simple. The name is in four parts, of which you use three. The syntax is as follows:

`multi/scsi(#)disk(#)rdisk(#)partition(#)`

The following list outlines the parts of the name:

- *multi/scsi.* You use either *multi* or *scsi*—not both. Use *multi* in all cases except when using a SCSI controller that cannot handle int13 (hard disk access) BIOS routines. Such cases are uncommon. The number is the logical number of the controller with the first controller being *0*, the second being *1*, and so forth.

- *disk.* When you use a SCSI disk, you use the *disk* parameter to indicate which of the drives on the controller is the drive you are talking about. Again, the numbers start at *0* for the first drive and then increase for each subsequent drive.

- *rdisk.* Use this parameter for the other controllers in the same way as you use the *disk* parameter for *scsi*.

- *partition.* This is the partition on the disk that you are pointing at. The first partition is *1*, the second is *2*, and so forth. Remember that you can have up to four primary partitions, or three primary and one extended. The extended partition is always the last one, and the first logical drive in the partition will have the partition's number. Other drives in the extended partition each continue to add one.

Breaking a Mirror Set

The boot floppy will get the operating system up and running. You should immediately back up the mirrored copy of the mirror set. To back up the drive, you must break your mirror set. To do this, perform the tasks outlined in the following steps.

1. Run the Disk Administrator.

2. From the Disk Administrator, click the remaining fragment of the mirrored set.

3. Choose Fault Tolerance, Break Mirror set from the menu.

At the end of these three steps, you should notice that the mirror set has been broken, and you can now back up the drive.

Regenerating a Stripe Set with Parity

Fixing a stripe set with parity is simple. Perform the tasks outlined in the following steps to regenerate your stripe set with parity.

1. Physically replace the faulty disk drive.
2. Start the Disk Administrator.
3. Select the stripe set with parity that you need to repair and then Ctrl+click the free space of the drive you added to fix the stripe set.
4. Choose Fault Tolerant, Regenerate. Note that this process can take some time, although it takes less time than restoring from tape.

The drives regenerate all the required data from the parity bits and the data bits, and on completion your stripe set with parity is completely functional.

Following is a list of typical issues you'll have to deal with when encountering troubleshooting concerns.

- **Share permissions.** A common problem when troubleshooting share resources is in the share permissions. Ensure that the minimum functional permissions have been assigned. Always remove the Everyone group from having full control of a share.
- **Combining NTFS and share permissions.** When combining these permissions, remember that NT uses the most restrictive of the permissions when combining. As a rule, use the NTFS permissions as the highest level of permissions, and use the share permissions mainly for access to the folder or share.
- **Tape backups.** In any system that you are using, ensure that you have a good backup strategy. Any component in your system can be faulty, and it is your responsibility to have a recovery plan in case of emergencies.
- **Disk mirroring.** If you are implementing disk mirroring in your system, ensure that you have created a fault-tolerant boot disk that you can use in case of drive failure. By having this disk preconfigured and handy, you can break the mirror set and replace the drive with very little downtime for your server.
- **Stripe set with parity.** This system automatically regenerates data if a drive is faulty. Although your system performance will dramatically decline, it is still a functional box and you risk no possibility of losing any data. If you find that a drive in your stripe set is faulty, replace the drive and use the regenerate command from the Disk Administrator.

Objective Troubleshooting 9—Perform advanced problem resolution. Tasks include the following:

- Diagnosing and interpreting a blue screen
- Configuring a memory dump
- Using the event log service

Three utilities come with Windows NT that enable you to work with the memory dump files that are created. You can find all of these utilities on the Windows NT Server CD-ROM. Each utility can be a very helpful tool. The following list briefly describes these utilities:

- **DUMPCHK.** This utility checks that the dump file is in order by verifying all the addresses and listing the errors and system information.
- **DUMPEXAM.** This creates a text file that can provide the same information that was on the blue screen at the time the stop error occurred. You need the symbol files and the kernel debugger extensions as well as IMAGEHLP.DLL to run DUMPEXAM.

- **DUMPFLOP.** This utility backs up the dump file to a series of floppies so that you can send them to Microsoft.

The following list summarizes the key points required for this objective:

- The Event Viewer is a very powerful troubleshooting tool. The three logs that can be viewed through the Event Viewer are the System log, the Application log, and the Security log.

- Cross-reference the events in the Event Viewer with knowledge base articles found on Microsoft TechNet for troubleshooting help.

- Interpreting blue screens can be very difficult. Use memory dump files and the following utilities to view your memory dumps to help you isolate the problems:
  - DUMPCHK
  - DUMPEXAM
  - DUMPFLOP

- If the problem persists, you might have to use the kernel debugger included on the NT Server CD-ROM in the \Support\debug folder.

- You can use the kernel debugger to monitor a remote machine through a null modem, or by using the RAS service into a machine that is connected to the problematic computer through a null modem.

Index

SYMBOLS

%Disk Read Time counter (Performance Monitor), 239
%Disk Time counter (Performance Monitor), 239, 261
%Network Utilization counter (Performance Monitor), 239
%Processor Time counter (Performance Monitor), 263
%User Time counter (Performance Monitor), 263
%Write Time counter (Performance Monitor), 239
100% fault tolerance option, 33

A

ability estimate (adaptive form exams), 426
absolute values (Performance Monitor), 235
Access Control Entries, *see* ACEs
Access Control Lists, *see* ACLs
access restrictions, system policies, 137
account operators in local groups, trust relationships, 19
Account-Global Groups-Local Groups-Permissions (AGLP) methodology, 353, 459
accounts
   Directory Replication, 77
   disabling, 116
   groups
     contrasting, 119
   global groups, *see* global groups
   trust relationships, 123
   lock outs, 116
   managing users and groups, 458-459
   Migration Tool for NetWare, 175
   multiple master domain models, 6, 14
   policies, 113
   rights, 121
   SAM (Security Account Manager), 17
   templates, 114
   user accounts, 112
     database, auditing, 124
     passwords, 115
     user properties, 115
ACEs (Access Control Entries), 161
acknowledgment delay timer (DataLink Control protocol), 455
ACLs (Access Control Lists), 161
active learning study strategy, 423
adaptive form exams
   ability estimate, 426
   statistics
     item characteristic curve, 426
     standard error, 426
     test information, 426
   tips for taking, 426, 430
Add & Read permission (NTFS), 158
Add Printer Wizard, 95
Add to dialog box, 236
Add/Remove Programs application (Control Panel), 139

Administrative Tools
    DHCP Manager, 184
    Disk Administrator
        stripe sets, 84
        volume sets, 83
    DNS Manager application, 200
    Network Client Administrator, 50
        Windows 95, 105
        Workstation, 105
administrators in local groups, trust relationships, 19
Advanced RISC Computing (ARC) names, components, 295
Alert view (Performance Monitor), 234, 465
analyzing systems (Performance Monitor)
    application servers, 240, 244
    domain servers, 244
    file servers, 239, 244
    print servers, 239, 244
answering simulation questions, 427-430
AppleTalk protocol, 48, 452
    configurations, 64, 455
Application Event Log, 277
application servers (Performance Monitor), 240, 244
applications
    automating system policies, 136
    configurations (Server service), 72
    DNS Manager application, 200
    installation via SYSDIFF utility, 286-287
    Network Client Administrator configurations, 50
    REGEDT32 tool, 73
ARC (Advanced RISC Computing) names
    disk, 470
    multi/scsi, 470
    partition, 470
    rdisk, 470
architectures, domain models, 1
assigning permissons to printers, 319-320
auditing
    files, 162
        copying, 160
        deleting, 162
    Generate Security Audits right, 122
    logons, 163
    Manage Auditing and Security Log right, 122
    RAS (Remote Access Service), 212, 464
authentication, RAS (Remote Access Service), 212
Authentication dialog box, 136
Available Bytes counter (Performance Monitor), 264
averaging counters (Performance Monitor), 235
Avg. Disk Bytes/Transfer counter (Performance Monitor), 239

B

backing up
    DHCP databases, 184
    Registry, RDISK command, 299-301, 309-310
backup browser (Computer Browser service), 74
Backup Domain Controller, *see* BDC
backup operators in local groups, trust relationships, 19
backups
    differential, 470
    full, 470
    incremental, 470
balance (Server service)
    configurations, 72
    core services, 456
baselines, 219
    creating (Performance Monitor), 225
BDC (Backup Domain Controller)
    communication failures with PDC, 282-283
    remote authentication, 340
    server roles, 452
binding order
    configurations, 65
    protocols, 455
blue screen STOP errors, 298
boot disks, creating for RISC system, 297-298
boot failures, troubleshooting, 467-468
boot sector viruses, repairing, 288-289

BOOT.INI file
    ARC names, 295
    debugging options, 296-297
    Intel platform, 293
bottlenecks, 220, 244, 260
    disks, 260
    network traffic, 266, 467
    performance monitoring, 467
    processors, 262
breaking mirror sets, 359, 470
browse list (Computer Browser service), 74
Bytes Sent/sec counter (Performance Monitor), 266
Bytes Total/sec counter (Performance Monitor), 266

C

cabling
    ISDN-RAS connection, 211
    null modem, 211, 376
cache object (Performance Monitor), 237
Call-back security (RAS Server), 212, 327-328, 464
Capture menu commands
    Display Captured Data, 249
    Start, 248
    Stop, 248
Capture window (Network Monitor), 248-250
CD-ROM, as non-supported drive on HCL, 284
centralized network administration
    multiple master domain models, 13
    single domain models, 12
    single master domain models, 15
certification requirements
    Microsoft Certified Professional (MCP), 415-416
    Microsoft Certified Professional+Internet (MCP+Internet), 415-416
    Microsoft Certified Professional+Site Building (MCP+Site Building), 415-416
    Microsoft Certified Solution Developer (MCSD), 416, 419-421
    Microsoft Certified Systems Engineer (MCSE), 415
        Windows NT 3.51 and 4.0, 417-418
    Microsoft Certified Systems Engineer+Internet (MCSE+Internet), 416, 418-419
    Microsoft Certified Trainer (MCT), 416, 421-422
Change permission (NTFS), 158
    event, 163
    shares, 153
Chart view (Performance Monitor), 234, 465
child objects (Performance Monitor), 236
classifying services (Network Monitor), 252
Client for Microsoft Networks, 453
Client for NetWare Networks, 453-454
Client Services for NetWare, 40, 338-339
client-to-server traffic (Network Monitor), 255
clients
    computers, configuring, 458-460
    configurations, 50
        Macintosh, 103, 106
        Windows 95, 105
        Workstation, 105
    logons (Network Monitor), 247
color schemes, default settings, system policies, 137
commands
    Capture menu
        Display Captured Data, 249
        Start, 248
        Stop, 248
    diskperf, 261
    Fault Tolerance menu
        Break Mirror, 86
        Create Stripe Set with Parity, 85
        Establish Mirror, 86
    IPCONFIG, 341
    NETSTAT, 340-341
    Partition menu
        Create Volume Set, 83
        Extend Volume Set, 83
    Policies menu, Trust Relationships, 8
    RDISK, 299-301
    TRACERT, 340
    User menu
        Copy, 114
        New Global Group, 119
    WINNT/OX, 299

Committed Bytes counter (Performance Monitor), 264
complete trust domain models, 9, 20
Computer Browser service
  configurations, 74
  core services, 456
computers
  policies, 135, 460
  role of, 282
configuration summary (Fast Facts section), 453-462
configurations
  bindings, 65
  clients, 50
    Macintosh, 103, 106
    Windows 95, 105
    Workstation, 105
  Computer Browser service, 74
  Directory Replication accounts, 77
  hard disks, 50
    disk mirroring, 86
    stripe sets, 84
    stripe sets with parity, 85
    volume sets, 83
  printers, 50
    installation, 95
    network connections, 96
    pooling, 94
  protocols
    AppleTalk, 64
    NWLink IPX/SPX, 66
  Server service, 70
    balance, 72
    file sharing, 72
    memory, 71
    network applications, 72
  Workstation service, 73
configuring
  core services
    Computer Browser service, 456
    Directory Replicator service, 456-457
    Server service, 455
  hard disks, 457-458
    disk mirroring, 457
    stripe set, 457
    stripe set with parity, 457
    volume set, 457
  Internet Information Server, 463
  NWLINK, 454-455
  policies, 459
  printers, 458
  profiles, 459-460
  protocols, 453-455
    AppleTalk, 455
    DataLink Control, 455
    NWLINK IPX/SPX-compatible, 454
    TCP/IP, 453
  Remote Access Service (RAS), 463
  system policies
    computer policies, 135
    group policies, 138
    user policies, 136
  TCP/IP
    DHCP relay agent, 454
    DNS, 453
    IP Address, 453
    routing, 454
    WINS Address, 454
connectivity
  DNS, 200
  frame type incompatibility, 339
  Gateway Service for NetWare, 461
  Internet Information Server, 166, 463
  Internet Information Server, see IIS, 166
  Internet services, 463
  Migration Tool for NetWare, 461
  multiprotocol routing, 462-463
  NetWare, 461-462
  potential problems, 276
  printer configurations, 96
  Remote Access Service (RAS), 463-464
  routers, 166
  TCP/IP (Transmission Control Protocol/Internet Protocol), 46
  troubleshooting, 469
Control Panel
  Add/Remove Programs application, 139
  Network application, RAS, 209

Services application, 70
Telephony application, 210
Copy command (User menu), 114
copying files
auditing, 160
permission issues, 350-351
core services
Computer Browser service, 456
Directory Replicator service, 456-457
Server service
Balance, 456
configuring, 455-456
Windows NT Server, 455-457
counters (Performance Monitor), 234
CRASHDUMP utility, 372-373
Create Stripe Set with Parity command (Fault Tolerance), 85
Create Volume Set command (Partition menu), 83
creating
boot disks for RISC system, 297-298
startup disks with WINNT/OX command, 299

D

databases
DHCP Server Service, backing up, 184
SAM Account Database, user rights, 121
user accounts, auditing, 124
DataLink Control (DLC) protocol, 452
acknowledgment delay timer, 455
inactivity timer, 455
response timer, 455
debugging
BOOT.INI file, 296-297
capabilities, enabling, 296-297
Event Viewer, 377-378
kernel debuggers, 370-371
preparations, 375
resources
Microsoft Knowledge Base, 380
Microsoft TechNet, 380

default gateways (IP addresses), 62
defaults
Migration Tool for NetWare, 176
system policies, 133-134
deleting
files, auditing, 162-163
print jobs, 316-317
descriptions in user accounts, 115
Detail pane (Network Monitor), 250
devices (network), start order, 294
DHCP (Dynamic Host Configuration Protocol), 43
DNS Service information, 201
Network Monitor, 219
RAS installation, 208
relay agents, configuring, 66, 454
Server Service, 184
databases, backing up, 184
Manager, 184
relays, 185
scope, 184
Dial-Up Networking, roaming profiles, 329
dialog boxes
Add to, 236
Authentication, 136
Logon Banner, 136
Network, 70
Network Configuration, 207
Network Properties, 206
New Global Group, 119
NWLink IPX/SPX Properties, 66
RAS Server IPX Configuration, 208
RAS Server NetBEUI, 207
RAS Server TCP/IP Configuration, 208
Remote Access Setup, 207
Select Network Service, 206
Server, 70
Trust Relationships, 8
User and Group Options, 175
User Properties, 115
difference counters (Performance Monitor), 235
differential backups, 470

directories
    Backup Files and Directories right, 121
    Restore Files and Directories right, 123
    services, domain models, 1
Directory Replication service
    accounts, 77
    installation
        export server, 76
        import server, 79
Directory Replicator (Network Monitor), 219
    core services, configuring, 456-457
directory services
    architecture planning, 449
    goals, 449
    trust relationships, 449
disabling accounts, 116
Disk Administrator, 457
    stripe sets, 84
    volume sets, 83
disk arrays, 31
Disk Bytes counter (Performance Monitor), 261
disk duplexing, 86, 358, 361
disk mirroring (RAID 1), 86, 358
    disk failure recovery, 364
    hard disks, configuring, 457
    mirror sets, breaking, 359
    troubleshooting, 471
Disk Queue counter (Performance Monitor), 261
disk resources
    managing, 461
    security
        NTFS permissions, 461
        protecting, 461
        share permissions, 461
disk striping (RAID Level 0), 360, 450
    disk failure recovery, 361-363
disk striping with parity (RAID Level 5), 450
diskperf command (Performance Monitor) 261
disks
    ARC naming, 470
    bottlenecks, 260
    drive configurations, 450
    mirroring (RAID level 1), 28, 32
    performance optimization, 243, 273
    security, 108, 152, 156
        share permissions, 152
    striping (RAID 0), 32
    striping with parity (RAID 5), 29, 32
Display Captured Data command (Capture menu), 249
display properties, locking, 137
DNS (Domain Name System), 200
    configuring, 200
    Manager application, 200
    Network Monitor, 219
    Search Order, 201
    TCP/IP (Transmission Control Protocol/Internet Protocol), 43, 45, 453
Domain Controller (Windows NT), 133
    single domain models, 12
    System Policy Editor, 133
    Web Administration tools, installation, 145
domains
    complete trust, 9, 20
    logging on, 450
    models
        advantages, 450
        disadvantages, 450
    multiple, masters, 13, 19
    planning summary, 450
    single, 12, 19
    trust relationships, 19, 352, 450
        permissions, 7
        setting up, 8
        trusted/trusting comparison, 10
downloading print drivers, 317
drivers (network), start order, 294
DriveSpace 3.0, monitoring/optimization summary, 463
DUMPCHK utility, 471
DUMPEXAM utility, 373-374, 471
DUMPFLOP utility, 374, 472
duplex printing, enabling, 320
duplexing disks, 31, 86
Dynamic Host Configuration Protocol, *see* DHCP

E

editing Registry (REGEDT32 tool), 307-308
elections (Computer Browser service), 75
emergency repair process, user account status, 301-302
enabling debugging capabilities, 296-297
encryption (Remote Access Service), 212, 464
Establish Mirror command (Fault Tolerance menu), 86
Ethernet (Performance Monitor), 243
event logs
　Application, 277
　filtering, 377-378
　RAS activity, viewing, 330
　Security, 277
　System Event, 277
Event Viewer, 144
　logs
　　filtering, 377-378
　　types, 377-378
　Security Log, auditing, 163
　STOP errors, 376-378
　tools, 472
exams
　formats
　　adaptive form, 425-426
　　fixed form, 424-425
　preparation, 422
　retaking, 430-431
　simulation questions, 427
　tips for taking, 424-430
execution files
　NWCONV.EXE, 174
　REGEDT32.exe, 73
expiration of passwords, controlling, 116
export server installation (Directory Replication service), 76

F

Fast Facts section
　configuration summary, 453-462
　connectivity summary, 465-470
　monitoring/optimization summary, 470-472
　planning summary, 449-453
　resource management summary, 462-465
fault tolerance, 2
　disk duplexing, 358, 361
　disk mirroring, 86, 277, 358-359
　disk striping with parity, 360
　failures, troubleshooting, 469-471
　sector sparing, 27
　stripe sets, 84-85
　volume sets, 83
Fault Tolerance menu commands
　Break Mirror, 86
　Create Stripe Set with Parity, 85
　Establish Mirror, 86
File and Print Services for NetWare, 144
file servers (Performance Monitor), 239, 244
file sharing, 72
files
　auditing, 162
　　copying, 160
　　deleting, 162
　Client Services for NetWare, 338
　NTFS permissions, 159
　permission issues, 348-351
　Restore Files and Directories rights, 123
　sharing (Server service), 72
Files Open counter (Performance Monitor), 239
filtering
　logs (Event Viewer), 377-378
　RAS (Remote Access Service), 213
filters (Network Monitor), 249
fixed-form exams, 424-425
　tips, 429-430
folders, auditing, 162
frames
　auto-detect versus default, 339
　NWLink IPX/SPX protocol, 66

full backups, 470
Full Control permission, 158
    shares, 153
Fully Qualified Domain Names (FQDN), 200

G

Gateway Services for NetWare, 170, 461
gateways (IP addresses), 62
global groups, 459
    creating, 119
    local groups, contrasting, 119
    multiple master domain models, 6, 14
    SAM (Security Account Manager), 17
    trust relationships, 123
Gopher (Internet Information Server), 192
Graph window (Network Monitor), 249
group policies, 138
groups
    contrasting, 119
    global groups, creating, 119
    multiple master domain models, 6, 14
    policies, 138
    trust relationships, 123, 459
guests in local groups, trust relationships, 19

H

hard disks, 50
    configuring, 457-458
    disk mirroring, configuring, 86, 457
    minimum NT requirements, 284-285
    stripe set with parity configurations, 85, 457
    stripe set configurations, 84, 457
    volume set configurations, 83, 457
hardware
    minimum NT requirements, 284-285
    Network Monitor, 250
Hardware Compatibility List (HCL)
    NT installation, 284-285
    printers, 95

Hexadecimal pane (Network Monitor), 250
HKEY_LOCAL_MACHINE subkey (Registry), 294
host computers
    kernel debuggers, 369
    RAS security, 212

I - K

IDE/EIDE drives versus SCSI drives, 288-289
implementing kernel debuggers, 375
import server installation (Directory Replication service), 79
inactivity timer (DataLink Control protocol), 455
incremental backups, 470
installations
    Directory Replication
        export server, 76
        import server, 79
    failures, troubleshooting, 467
    Network Monitor
        hardware, 250
        software, 250
    printers, 95
    Web Administration tools, 146
installing
    applications via SYSDIFF utility, 286-287
    BDC, troubleshooting, 282
    computers, role of, 282
    IDE/EIDE drives, 288-289
    modems, 326
    NT Server
        Hardware Compatibililty List (HCL), 284
        minimum requirements, 284-285
        server roles, 452-453
    print drivers, 317
    SCSI drives, 288-289
    video drivers, troubleshooting, 283
instantaneous counters (Performance Monitor), 235
Intel platform
    emergency repair process, 301-302
    mandatory NT files
        BOOT.INI, 293

NTBOOTDD.SYS, 293
NTDETECT.COM, 293
NTLDR, 293
Internet
DNS, configuring, 200
multiprotocol routing, 462
protocols, 42, 47
router, 181
services, 463
Internet Information Server, 166
configuring, 463
connectivity, 463
Gopher service, 192
installing, 190
Internet Service Manager, 193
Internet Service Manager, 193, 463
Interrupts/sec processor counter (Performance Monitor), 263
IP addresses
auto-assignment by RAS Server, 326-327
TCP/IP, configuring, 453
IPCONFIG command, 341
IPX
RAS installation, 208
router, 186, 462
IPX/SPX, configuration summary, 455
ISDN connections, RAS Server, 211, 464
kernel debuggers
automated, 370-371
commands, 371
preparation for use, 375
remote usage, 369-371
switches, 370-371
use on STOP errors, 372

L

LastKnownGood configuration
blue screen STOP errors, 298
save process, 294
learning methods
comprehension, 423
meta-learning, 424

List permission (NTFS), 158
local groups, 459
SAM (Security Account Manager), 17
trust relationships, 123
versus global groups, 119
local profiles, 460
lock outs on accounts, 116
locking display properties, system policies, 137
Log view (Performance Monitor), 234, 465
baselines, creating, 228
Logging Property page (WWW services), 198-199
LogicalDisk object (Performance Monitor), 237, 260
login scripts, user account profiles, 117
Logon Banner dialog box, 136
Logon servers (Network Monitor), 247
Logon Total counter (Performance Monitor), 266
Logon/sec counter (Performance Monitor), 266
logons
auditing, 163
Network Monitor, 247
System policies, 138

M

Macintosh
AppleTalk protocol, 48
client configurations, 103, 106
NT printers, Services for Macintosh, 318-319
Maintenance Wizard 463
managing
disk resources, 461
policies, 459-460
profiles, 459-460
resources, 107
user and group accounts, 458-459
mapping system policies, 137
master boot record/disk boot record (MBR/DBR), 470
master browsers, 74
master domain models
multiple, 13, 19
single, 14, 19

MBR/DBR (master boot record/disk boot record), 470
MCP, *see* Microsoft Certified Professional
MCP+Internet, *see* Microsoft Certified Professional+Internet
MCP+Site Building, *see* Microsoft Certified Professional+Site Building
MCSD, *see* Microsoft Certified Solution Developer
MCSE, *see* Microsoft Certified Systems Engineer
MCSE+Internet, *see* Microsoft Certified Systems Engineer+Internet
MCT, *see* Microsoft Certified Trainer
member servers, 59, 452
   selection of, 282
memory
   configurations (Server service), 71
   dump files, 471
   optimizing (Performance Monitor), 243
Memory object (Performance Monitor), 237
meta-learning, 424
Microsoft Certified Professional (MCP) certification requirements, 415-416
Microsoft Certified Professional+Internet (MCP+Internet) certification requirements, 416
Microsoft Certified Professional+Site Building (MCP+Site Building) certification requirements, 416
Microsoft Certified Solution Developer (MCSD)
   certification requirements, 416
      new track, 419-420
      old track, 420-421
Microsoft Certified Systems Engineer (MCSE) certification requirements, 415-417
   Windows 3.1, 417-418
   Windows NT 3.51, 417
   Windows NT 4.0, 417
Microsoft Certified Systems Engineer+Internet (MCSE+Internet) certification requirements, 416, 418-419
Microsoft Certified Trainer (MCT) certification requirements, 416, 421-422
Microsoft Certified Training Web site, 421-422
Microsoft Knowledge Base, 380

Microsoft TechNet, 380
Migration Tool for NetWare, 174, 461
   accounts, 175
   connectivity, 461
   defaults, 176
   passwords, 175
mirror sets
   breaking, 359, 470
   failures, recovery, 364
models (domains)
   complete trust, 9, 20
   multiple master, 13, 19
   single, 12, 19
   single master, 14, 19
modems
   drivers, 326
   installing, 326
   null modem cable, RAS connection, 211
monitoring performance
   baselines, 219, 225
   bottlenecks, 220, 260
      disks, 260
      network, 266
      processors, 262
   diskperf commands, 261
   Network Monitor, 220, 252, 466-467
   Performance Monitor, 242, 465-466
      counters, 234
      disks, 243
      instances, 236
      memory, 243
      networks, 243
      objects, 236
      processors, 243
monitoring/optimization summary (Fast Facts section), 470-472
moving files, permission issues, 350-351
multi/scsi ARC naming, 470
multidomain environments, security problems, 277
multilinking, 213
   RAS Server, 330
multiple domain models, 13, 19

multiple protocol routing
    connectivity, 462-463
    DHCP Server Service, 184
    Internet router, 181, 462
    IPX router, 186, 462

N - O

naming user accounts
    Full Name, 115
    Migration Tool for NetWare, 175
    username, 115
NetBEUI, 40, 47, 451
    advantages/disadvantages, 337
    configuration summary, 455
    RAS installation, 207
Net Logon (Network Monitor), 219
NETSTAT command, port usage, 340-341
NetWare, 165
    connectivity, 461-462
    conversion utility, 461
    Gateway Service for NetWare, 461
    Migration Tool, 174
        accounts, 175
        passwords, 175
    Migration Tool for NetWare, 461
    NWLink, 39, 43, 47
network adapters, IPCONFIG command, 341
Network Bytes Sent/sec counter (Performance Monitor), 266
Network Client Administrator, 458
    configurations, 50
        Windows 95, 105
        Workstation, 105
    Copy Client-based Network Administration Tools, 458
    Make a Network Installation Startup Disk, 458
    Make and Installation Disk Set, 458
    View Remoteboot Client Information, 458
Network Configuration dialog box, 207
Network dialog box, 70

Network Monitor, 220
    capturing data, 248
        filters, 249
        panes, 250
    installation
        hardware, 250
        software, 250
    monitoring, 466-467
    network traffic, 466
    traffic, 252
    windows, 248
Network Properties dialog box, 206
Network Total/sec counter (Performance Monitor), 266
networks
    applications (Server service), 72
    bottlenecks, 266, 467
    mapping system policies, 137
    performance optimization, 243, 271
    printer configurations, 96
    RAS (Remote Access Service), 166
        configuring, 209
        installation, 206
        security, 212
    traffic
        bottlenecks, 467
        Network Monitor, 466
New Global Group command (User menu), 119
New Global Group dialog box, 119
No Access permission (NTFS), 158
    shares, 154
no fault-tolerance options, 33
Non paged RAM (performance monitoring), 264
non-transitive trust relationships, 8
NTBOOTDD.SYS file (Intel platform), 293
NTDETECT.COM file (Intel platform), 293
NTFS permissions
    files, 159
    rights, 174
    security, disk resources, 461
NTLDR file (Intel platform), 293
null modem cabling, 376
    Remote Access Network (RAS), 211, 464

NWCONV (NetWare conversion utility), 174, 461
NWLink, 39, 43, 47, 451-452
  functions, 337-338
  Microsoft version of IPX/SPX, 337-338
  routing, 455
NWLink IPX/SPX Properties dialog box, 66
objects (Performance Monitor), 236
one hundred percent (100%) fault-tolerance option, 33
one-way trust relationships, 18
operators in local groups, trust relationships, 19
optimizing performance, 221
  disks, 273
  networks, 271

P

paged RAM (performance monitoring), 264
Pages/sec counter (Performance Monitor), 264
Paging File object (Performance Monitor), 237
panes (Network Monitor), 250
parent objects (Performance Monitor), 236
parity configurations, 85
Partition menu commands
  Create Volume Set, 83
  Extend Volume Set, 83
partitions, ARC naming, 470
passwords
  account policies, 113
  Migration Tool for NetWare, 175
  resource management summary, 458
  user accounts, 115
PDC (Primary Domain Controller), 452
  communication failures with BDC, 282-283
  server roles, 452
  single domain models, 12
performance
  bottlenecks, 467
  monitoring, 467
  Profile System Performance right, 123

Performance Monitor, 242, 465
  alert view, 465
  baselines, creating, 225
  bottlenecks, 220, 260
    disks, 260
    network, 266
    processors, 262
  chart view, 465
  counters, 234
  diskperf commands, 261
  disks, 243
  instances, 236
  log view, 465
  memory, 243
  monitoring, 465-466
  networks, 243
  objects, 236
  processors, 243
  report view, 465
  system analysis
    application servers, 240, 244
    domain servers, 244
    file servers, 239, 244
    print servers, 239, 244
permissions
  Change, 348-349
  default settings, 348-349
  files
    copying, 350-351
    moving, 350-351
  Full Control, 348-349
  No Access, 348-349
  potential problems, 277
  print devices, 319-320
  Read, 348-349
  share, 152
  troubleshooting, 469
  trust relationships, 7
PhysicalDisk object (Performance Monitor), 237, 260

planning
	directory services
		architecture, 449
		domain models, 1
	disk drive configurations, 450
	fault tolerance, 2, 27
	protocols, 2, 34, 39
		NetBEUI, 40, 47
		NWLink, 39, 43, 47
planning summary (Fast Facts section), 449-453
Point-to-Point Protocol (PPP), 215
policies
	accounts, 113
	computers, 460
	configuring, 459
	managing, 459-460
	System, 128
		computer policies, 135
		creating, 134
		group policies, 138
		logon process, 138
		System Policy Editor, 133
		user policies, 136
		Windows 95, 139
	systems, 460
Policies menu commands, Trust Relationships, 8
Pool Nonpaged Bytes counter (Performance Monitor), 264
pooling printers, 94
ports
	RAS (Remote Access Service), configuring, 209
	usage of, NETSTAT command, 340-341
PPP (Point-to-Point Protocol), 215
PPTP (Point-to-Point Tunneling) filtering
	security, Remote Access Service (RAS), 215, 464
	Virtual Private Networks (VPNs), 327
pre-exam preparation tips, 428-429
preparation for exam, 422
print devices, 276
	permissions, 319-320
print drivers
	downloading, 317
	installing, 317

print jobs, 276
	deleting, 316-317
	redirecting, 321
print operators in local groups, trust relationships, 19
print queues, 276
print spoolers, 276
printer pools, 458
printers
	Client Services for NetWare, 338
	configuration summary, 456-458
		network connections, 96
		pooling, 94
	devices, 276
	drivers, installing, 317
	duplex option, 320
	installations, 95
	jobs, 276
		deleting, 316-317
		redirecting, 321
	Macintosh clients on NT printers (Services for Macintosh), 318-319
	permissions, assigning, 319-320
	spoolers, 276
	troubleshooting, 468
	UNIX capability (TCP/IP Printing service), 316
Processor object (Performance Monitor), 237
processors
	bottlenecks, 262
	optimizing, 243
profiles
	configuring, 459-460
	local, 460
	managing, 459-460
	roaming, 460
	users
		comparing, 129
		roaming, 130
properties (WWW Services)
	Advanced Property page, 199
	Logging Property page, 198
	Services Property page, 198
	user accounts, 115

protecting disk resources, 461
protocols, 2, 450-451
    AppleTalk, 48, 452
        configuring, 455
    binding order, 453-455
    configurations
        AppleTalk, 64
        NWLink IPX/SPX, 66
    configuring, 453-455
    DataLink Control (DLC), 452-455
    FTP (Internet Information Server), 192
    Gopher (Internet Information Server), 192
    HTTP (Internet Information Server), 191
    NetBEUI, 40, 47, 451
        advantages/disadvantages, 337
    NWLink, 39, 43, 47, 451-452
    RIP (Routing Information Protocol), 181
    routing
        DHCP Server Service, 184
        Internet router, 181
        IPX, 186
    selecting, 34, 39
    TCP/IP (Transmission Control Protocols/Internet Protocol), 451
        configuring, 453
        connectivity, 46
        services, 43
Proxy Server, integration summary, 461
Public Switched Telephone Network (PSTN), 211, 464

Q - R

Queue Length counter (Performance Monitor), 263
RAID Level 0 (disk striping), 450
RAID Level 1 (disk mirroring), 277, 450
RAID Level 5 (disk striping with parity), 277, 450
RAM (random access memory), performance monitoring, 264
RAS (Remote Access Service)
    configuring, 463
    connectivity, 463-464
    event logs, viewing, 330
    ISDN, 464
    Multilink, 213
    null modem cable, 464
    overview, 276
    security, 212
        auditing, 464
        callback security, 464
        encryption, 464
        PPTP (Point-to-Point Tunneling) filtering, 464
        security hosts, 464
    troubleshooting, 468-469
    X.25, 464
RAS Server
    call-back security, 327-328
    IP addresses, auto-assignment, 326-327
    multilink, 330
    Remote Access Auto-Dial Manager, 330
    roaming profiles, 329
    Virtual Private Networks (VPNs), 327
RAS Server IPX Configuration dialog box, 208
RAS Server NetBEUI dialog box, 207
RAS Server TCP/IP Configuration dialog box, 208
RDISK tool
    ARC naming, 470
    function, 309-310
    Registry backup, 299-301
Read event, file auditing, 163
Read permission (NTFS), 158
    shares, 153
recovery disks
    necessary files, 300-301
    updates, 300-301
redirecting print jobs, 321
Redirector object (Performance Monitor), 237
Redundant Array of Inexpensive Disks, *see* RAID
REGEDT32 tool, 73
    edit functions, 307-308
    function, 310-311
regenerating stripe set with parity, 471

Registry
    backing up, 299-301, 459
    data types
        REG_BINARY, 308-309
        REG_DWORD, 308-309
        REG_EXPAND_SZ, 308-309
        REG_SZ, 308-309
    entries, researching, 306
    functions, 276, 306
    HKEY_LOCAL_MACHINE subkey, 294
    organization of, 276 306
    RDISK tool, 309-310
    REGEDT32 tool
        editing, 307-308
        function, 310-311
    System policies, 128
        computer policies, 135
        creating, 134
        group policies, 138
        logon process, 138
        System Policy Editor, 133
        user policies, 136
        Windows 95, 139
    troubleshooting, 468
    Workstation service, 73
REG_BINARY (Registry data type), 308-309
REG_DWORD (Registry data type), 308-309
REG_EXPAND_SZ (Registry data type), 308-309
REG_SZ (Registry data type), 308-309
relative values (Performance Monitor), 235
relay agents (DHCP), 66, 185
Remote Access Auto-Dial Manager, 330
Remote Access Setup dialog box, 207
remote administration tools, 460
    Web Administration tools, 145
    Windows 95, 143
    Windows NT, 144
repairing boot sector viruses, 288-289
replication (Directory Replication service)
    accounts, 77
    configurations, 77
replicators in local groups, trust relationships, 19
Report view (Performance Monitor), 234, 465

requirements
    MCP certification, 416
    MCP+Internet certification, 416
    MCP+Site Building certification, 416
    MCSD certification, 419-421
    MCSE certification, 417-418
    MCSE+Internet certification, 418-419
    MCT certification, 421-422
    Windows 95 clients, 101, 105
resource domains, 10
resource management, 107
    files, auditing, 162
    groups
        contrasting, 119
        trust relationships, 123
    logons, auditing, 163
    permissions, 152
    policies, 113
    Remote Administration Tools
        Windows 95, 143
        Windows NT, 144
    rights of users, 121
    system policies, 128
        computer policies, 135
        creating, 134
        group policies, 138
        logon process, 138
        System Policy Editor, 133
        user policies, 136
        Windows 95, 139
    troubleshooting, 469
    user accounts, 112
        database, auditing, 124
        user properties, 115
    user profiles
        comparing, 129
        roaming, 130
    Web Administration tools, 145
resource management summary (Fast Facts section), 462-465
response timer (DataLink Control protocol), 455
restricting access, system policies, 137
retaking exams, 430-431

rights
    NTFS, 174
    users, 121
RIP (Routing Information Protocol), 181
RISC system, boot disks, creating, 297-298
roaming profiles, 460
    configuring, 130
    Dial-Up Networking, 329
    Windows 95, 131
routers, 453
    DHCP Server Service, 184
    Internet, 181
    IPX, 186
        configurations, 455
    NetBEUI, 40, 42, 47
    TCP/IP (Transmission Control Protocol/Internet Protocol), 47
        configurations, 63, 454
Routing Information Protocol (RIP), 181
RPCs (remote procedure calls)
    trust relationships
        permissions, 7
        setting up, 8
        trusted/trusting comparison, 10

S

SAM (Security Account Manager), 452
    single domain models, 12
    user rights, 121
scaling multiple master domain models, 13
ScanDisk, monitoring/optimization summary, 463
scopes, DHCP Server Service, 184
SCSI drives versus IDE/EIDE drives, 288-289
searching
    DNS (Domain Name System), 201
    Registry entries, 306
security
    disks, 108, 152
        NTFS permissions, 156
        protecting, 461
        share permissions, 152

fault tolerance, 2
    sector sparing, 27
files, auditing, 162
hosts, Remote Access Service (RAS), 464
logons, auditing, 163
multidomain environments, 277
NTFS permissions, disk resources, 461
permissions, potential problems, 277
Remote Access Service (RAS), 212
    auditing, 464
    callback security, 464
    encryption, 464
    PPTP (Point-to-Point Tunneling) filtering, 464
    security hosts, 464
share permissions, 461
tokens, 123
user accounts, passwords, 115
Security Event Log, 277
Select Network Service dialog box, 206
selecting
    computers, role of, 282
    protocols, 2, 34, 39
        AppleTalk, 48
        NetBEUI, 40, 47
        NWLink, 39, 43, 47
        TCP/IP (Transmission Control Protocol/Internet Protocol), 47
Serial Line Interface Protocol (SLIP), 215
Server dialog box, 70
Server Manager, 101, 143
server operators in local groups, trust relationships, 19
Server Resource Kit, 145
Server service, core services, 456
Server Sessions counter (Performance Monitor), 239
Server Work Queues counter (Performance Monitor), 263
server-to-server traffic (Network Monitor), 255
servers
    DHCP Server Service, 184
    IIS (Internet Information Server)
        Gopher service, 192
        installing, 190
        Internet Service Manager, 193

installations
    BDC (Backup Domain Controller), 59
    member servers, 59
    PDC (Primary Domain Controller), 58
Logon (Network Monitor), 247
roles
    Backup Domain Controller (BDC), 452
    member server, 452
    Primary Domain Controller (PDC), 452
    Windows NT Server, installing, 452-453
Service for NetWare Directory Services (NDS), 454
services
    classifying (Network Monitor), 252
    Computer Browser service, 74
    DHCP Server Service, 184
    Directory Replication
        accounts, 77
        configurations, 77
        export server, 76
        import server, 79
    DNS, configuring, 200
    RAS
        DUN (dial-up networking) application, 210
        security, 212
    Workstation service configurations, 73
Services for Macintosh, 101
    client configurations, 103, 106
    Mac clients on NT printers, 318-319
Services Property page (WWW services), 198
Session Statistics window (Network Monitor), 249
setting up trust relationships, 8, 449
SETUPMGR.EXE utility, 288
share-level access control, 451
share permissions, 152
    automating, 136
    disk resource protection, 461
    troubleshooting, 471
SIDs (security identifiers) on user accounts, 352
simulation questions, answering, 427-430
single domain models, 12, 19
SLIP (Serial Line Interface Protocol), 215
standard error, adaptive form exams, 426

Start command (Capture menu), 248
startup disks, creating (WINNT/OX command), 299
Station Statistics window (Network Monitor), 249
statistics, adaptive form exams
    item characteristic curve, 426
    standard error, 426
    test information, 426
Stop command (Capture menu), 248
STOP errors
    CRASHDUMP utility, 372-373
    Event Viewer, 376-378
    fields, 277-278
    kernel debugging, 372
    troubleshooting, 298
stripe set with parity
    hard disks, configuring, 84-85, 457
    regenerating, 471
    troubleshooting, 471
study strategies (exams)
    active learning, 423
    common sense, 424
    outlines, 423
    pre-tests, 424
subnet masks, 453
Summary pane (Network Monitor), 250
supervisor accounts (Migration Tool for NetWare), 176
SYSDIFF utility, 286-287
system analysis (Performance Monitor)
    application servers, 240, 244
    domain servers, 244
    file servers, 239, 244
    print servers, 239, 244
System Event Log, 277
System object (Performance Monitor), 237
system policies, 128, 460
    check box options, 450
    computer policies, 135-136
    creating, 134
    default file locations, 451
    group policies, 138
    logon process, 138
    planning summary, 449-453

System Policy Editor, 133
types review, 450
Windows 95, configuring, 139
System Policy Editor, 101

T

Take Ownership right, 123, 163
tape backups, troubleshooting, 471
Task Scheduler, monitoring/optimization summary, 464
TCP/IP (Transmission Control Protocol/Internet Protocol), 47
    advantages of, 451
    configurations, 455
        DHCP relay agents, 66
        routing, 63
    connectivity, 46
    DHCP relay agent, 454
    DNS, configuring, 453
    IP Address, configuring, 453
    RAS installation, 208
    routing, configuring, 454
    services, 43
    TRACERT command, troubleshooting, 340
    WINS Address, configuring, 454
TCP/IP Printing service, UNIX clients on NT printers, 316
templates, user accounts, 114
tests, *see* exams
Thread object (Performance Monitor), 236-237
tips for taking exams, 425-430
token rings (Performance Monitor), 244
tools
    Administrative
        DHCP Manager, 184
        DNS Manager application, 200
        Network Client Administrator, 50
    clients on Windows Workstation, 101
    Event Viewer, 472
    Internet Service Manager, 193

Migration Tool for NetWare, 174
    accounts, 175
    passwords, 175
Remote Administration Tools
    Windows 95, 143
    Windows NT, 144
Services for Macintosh, client configurations, 103, 106
Total Statistics window (Network Monitor), 249
Total/sec counter (Performance Monitor), 266
TRACERT command, troubleshooting function, 340, 465
traffic
    Network Monitor, 252
        classifying services, 252
        client-to-server, 255
        server-to-server, 255
    networks, performance optimization, 271
Transmission Control Protocol/Internet Protocol, *see* **TCP/IP**
troubleshooting
    BDC installation, 282
    blue screen STOP errors, 298
    boot failures, 467-468
    combining NTFS and share permissions, 471
    communication failures between BDC and PDC, 283
    computer installation, role of, 282
    connectivity problems, 469
    disk failures, disk striping with parity, 362-363
    disk mirroring, 471
    fault-tolerance failures, 469-471
    installation failures, 467
    permissions, 469
    printer problems, 468
    Registry, 468
    Remote Access Service (RAS), 468-469
    resource access, 469
    share permissions, 471
    stripe set with parity, 471
    tape backups, 471
    tools (Event Viewer), 472
    video driver installation, 283

trust relationships
  complete trust domain models, 16
  directory services, 449
  domains, 450
  groups, 123, 459
  multiple master domain models, 14
  non-transitive, 352
  permissions, 7
  setting up, 8, 449
  single domain models, 12
  single master domain models, 6, 15
  trusted/trusting comparison, 10
Trust Relationships dialog box, 8
tunnels (PPTP protocol), 327
two-way trust relationships, 18

U - V

uninstallation summary, 452
UNIX clients on NT printer (TCP/IP Printing service), 316
user accounts, 112
  database, auditing, 124
  emergency repair process, 301-302
  logons, 247
  multiple master domain models, 6, 14
  names, 115
  passwords, 115
  profiles
    comparing, 129
    roaming, 130
  properties of users, 115
  rights, 121
  SIDs, 352
  templates, 114
User and Group Options dialog box, 175
User Manager for Domains, 143
  global groups, creating, 119
  profiles, roaming, 130
  user account templates, 114

User menu commands
  Copy, 114
  New Global Group, 119
user policies, 136
User Properties dialog box, 115
utilities
  CRASHDUMP, 372-373
  DUMPCHK, 471
  DUMPEXAM, 373-374, 471
  DUMPFLOP, 374, 472
  SETUPMGR.EXE, 288
  SYSDIFF, 286-287

video drivers, installation of, 283
Virtual Private Networks (VPNs), 216, 327
volume sets, configuring, 83, 457

W - Z

wallpaper, default settings, 137
WANs (wide area networks), 47
Web Administration tools, 145, 460
Web sites, Microsoft Certified Training, 421-422
windows (Network Monitor), 248
Windows 95
  client configurations, 105
  Remote Administration Tools, 143, 460
  roaming profiles, 131
  system policies, configuring, 139
Windows Internet Name Service (WINS), 43, 454
  Network Monitor, 219
  WINS Address, 454
  WINS Manager, 101
Windows NT
  core services, 455-457
  Domain Controller, 133
  Multilink, 213
  RAS (Remote Access Service)
    configuring, 209
    DUN (dial-up networking) application, 210
    installation, 206
    security, 212

Remote Administration Tools, 144-145, 460
security model, 161
server roles, installing, 452-453
utilities
    DUMPCHK, 471
    DUMPEXAM, 471
    DUMPFLOP, 472

Windows NT 3.51, Microsoft Certified Systems Engineer (MCSE) certification requirements, 417-418

Windows NT 4.0, Microsoft Certified Systems Engineer (MCSE) certification requirements, 417-418

Windows NT Resource Kit, unknown Registry entries, 306

WinIPCfg utility, troubleshooting summary, 465

WINNT/OX command, startup disk creation, 299

wizards, Add Printer Wizard, 95

workgroups
    benefits, 449
    planning summary, 449

workload characterizations (Performance Monitor), 244

workstations
    client configurations, 105
    Network Monitor, 219
    service configurations, 73

write event, file auditing, 163

X.25, RAS connections, 211, 464

New Riders Certification Titles

Training Guides

Complete, Innovative, Accurate, Thorough

Our next generation *Training Guides* have been developed to help you study and retain the essential knowledge that you need to pass the MCSE exams. We know your study time is valuable, and we have made every effort to make the most of it by presenting clear, accurate, and thorough information.

In creating this series, our goal was to raise the bar on how MCSE content is written, developed, and presented. From the two-color design that gives you easy access to content, to the new software simulator that allows you to perform tasks in a simulated operating system environment, we are confident that you will be well-prepared for exam success.

Our New Riders Top Score Software Suite is a custom-developed set of full-functioning software applications that work in conjunction with the Training Guide by providing you with the following:

Exam Simulator tests your hands-on knowledge with over 150 fact-based and situational-based questions.
Electronic Study Cards really test your knowledge with explanations that are linked to an electronic version of the Training Guide.
Electronic Flash Cards help you retain the facts in a time-tested method.
An Electronic Version of the Book provides quick searches and compact, mobile study.
Customizable Software adapts to the way you want to learn.

MCSE Training Guide: Networking Essentials, Second Edition
1-56205-919-X, $49.99, 9/98

MCSE Training Guide: TCP/IP, Second Edition
1-56205-920-3, $49.99, 10/98

MCSE Training Guide: Windows NT Server 4, Second Edition
1-56205-916-5, $49.99, 9/98

MCSE Training Guide: SQL Server 7 Administration
0-7357-0003-6, $49.99, Q1/99

MCSE Training Guide: Windows NT Server 4 Enterprise, Second Edition
1-56205-917-3, $49.99, 9/98

MCSE Training Guide: SQL Server 7 Design and Implementation
0-7357-0004-4, $49.99, Q1/99

MCSE Training Guide: Windows NT Workstation 4, Second Edition
1-56205-918-1, $49.99, 9/98

MCSD Training Guide: Solution Architectures
0-7357-0026-5, $49.99, Q1/99

MCSE Training Guide: Windows 98
1-56205-890-8, $49.99, Q4/98

MCSD Training Guide: Visual Basic 6, Exam 70-175
0-7357-0002-8, $49.99, Q1/99

NEW RIDERS CERTIFICATION TITLES

 MCSD Training Guide: Microsoft Visual Basic 6, Exam 70-176

0-7357-0031-1, $49.99, Q1/99

TRAINING GUIDES
FIRST EDITIONS

Your Quality Elective Solution

MCSE Training Guide: Systems Management Server 1.2, 1-56205-748-0

MCSE Training Guide: SQL Server 6.5 Administration, 1-56205-726-X

MCSE Training Guide: SQL Server 6.5 Design and Implementation, 1-56205-830-4

MCSE Training Guide: Windows 95, 70-064 Exam, 1-56205-880-0

MCSE Training Guide: Exchange Server 5, 1-56205-824-X

MCSE Training Guide: Internet Explorer 4, 1-56205-889-4

MCSE Training Guide: Microsoft Exchange Server 5.5, 1-56205-899-1

MCSE Training Guide: IIS 4, 1-56205-823-1

MCSD Training Guide: Visual Basic 5, 1-56205-850-9

MCSD Training Guide: Microsoft Access, 1-56205-771-5

TESTPREPS

 MCSE TestPrep: Networking Essentials, Second Edition

0-7357-0010-9, $19.99, 11/98

 MCSE TestPrep: Windows 95, Second Edition

0-7357-0011-7, $19.99, 11/98

 MCSE TestPrep: Windows NT Server 4, Second Edition

0-7357-0012-5, $19.99, 12/98

 MCSE TestPrep: Windows NT Server 4 Enterprise, Second Edition

0-7357-0009-5, $19.99, 11/98

 MCSE TestPrep: Windows NT Workstation 4, Second Edition

0-7357-0008-7, $19.99, 11/98

 MCSE TestPrep: TCP/IP, Second Edition

0-7357-0025-7, $19.99, 12/98

 MCSE TestPrep: Windows 98

1-56205-922-X, $19.99, Q4/98

TESTPREPS
FIRST EDITIONS

Your Quality Elective Solution

MCSE TestPrep: SQL Server 6.5 Administration, 0-7897-1597-X

MCSE TestPrep: SQL Server 6.5 Design and Implementation, 1-56205-915-7

MCSE TestPrep: Windows 95 70-64 Exam, 0-7897-1609-7

MCSE TestPrep: Internet Explorer 4, 0-7897-1654-2

MCSE TestPrep: Exchange Server 5.5, 0-7897-1611-9

MCSE TestPrep: IIS 4.0, 0-7897-1610-0

NEW RIDERS CERTIFICATION TITLES

FAST TRACK SERIES

The Accelerated Path to Certification Success

Fast Tracks provide an easy way to review the key elements of each certification technology without being bogged down with elementary-level information.

These guides are perfect for when you already have real-world, hands-on experience. They're the ideal enhancement to training courses, test simulators, and comprehensive training guides. *No fluff, simply what you really need to pass the exam!*

LEARN IT FAST

Part I contains only the essential information you need to pass the test. With over 200 pages of information, it is a concise review for the more experienced MCSE candidate.

REVIEW IT EVEN FASTER

Part II averages 50–75 pages, and takes you through the test and into the real-world use of the technology, with chapters on:

1) Fast Facts Review Section
2) The Insider's Spin (on taking the exam)
3) Sample Test Questions
4) Hotlists of Exam-Critical Concepts
5) Did You Know? (real-world applications for the technology covered in the exam)

MCSE Fast Track: Networking Essentials
1-56205-939-4, $19.99, 9/98

MCSE Fast Track: TCP/IP
1-56205-937-8, $19.99, 9/98

MCSE Fast Track: Windows 98
0-7357-0016-8, $19.99, Q4/98

MCSE Fast Track: Internet Information Server 4
1-56205-936-X, $19.99, 9/98

MCSE Fast Track: Windows NT Server 4
1-56205-935-1, $19.99, 9/98

MCSD Fast Track: Solution Architectures
0-7357-0029-X, $19.99, Q1/99

MCSE Fast Track: Windows NT Server 4 Enterprise
1-56205-940-8, $19.99, 9/98

MCSD Fast Track: Visual Basic 6, Exam 70-175
0-7357-0018-4, $19.99, Q4/98

MCSE Fast Track: Windows NT Workstation 4
1-56205-938-6, $19.99, 9/98

MCSD Fast Track: Visual Basic 6, Exam 70-176
0-7357-0019-2, $19.99, Q4/98

How to Contact Us

IF YOU NEED THE LATEST UPDATES ON A TITLE THAT YOU'VE PURCHASED:

1) Visit our Web site at www.newriders.com.

2) Click on the DOWNLOADS link, and enter your book's ISBN number, which is located on the back cover in the bottom right-hand corner.

3) In the DOWNLOADS section, you'll find available updates that are linked to the book page.

IF YOU ARE HAVING TECHNICAL PROBLEMS WITH THE BOOK OR THE CD THAT IS INCLUDED:

1) Check the book's information page on our Web site according to the instructions listed above, or

2) Email us at support@mcp.com, or

3) Fax us at (317) 817-7488 attn: Tech Support.

IF YOU HAVE COMMENTS ABOUT ANY OF OUR CERTIFICATION PRODUCTS THAT ARE NON-SUPPORT RELATED:

1) Email us at certification@mcp.com, or

2) Write to us at New Riders, 201 W. 103rd St., Indianapolis, IN 46290-1097, or

3) Fax us at (317) 581-4663.

IF YOU ARE OUTSIDE THE UNITED STATES AND NEED TO FIND A DISTRIBUTOR IN YOUR AREA:

Please contact our international department at international@mcp.com.

IF YOU WISH TO PREVIEW ANY OF OUR CERTIFICATION BOOKS FOR CLASSROOM USE:

Email us at pr@mcp.com. Your message should include your name, title, training company or school, department, address, phone number, office days/hours, text in use, and enrollment. Send these details along with your request for desk/examination copies and/or additional information.

WE WANT TO KNOW WHAT YOU THINK

To better serve you, we would like your opinion on the content and quality of this book. Please complete this card and mail it to us or fax it to 317-581-4663.

Name _____

Address _____

City _____ State _____ Zip _____

Phone _____ Email Address _____

Occupation _____

Which certification exams have you already passed? _____
_____
_____
_____

Which certification exams do you plan to take? _____
_____
_____
_____

What influenced your purchase of this book?
❏ Recommendation ❏ Cover Design
❏ Table of Contents ❏ Index
❏ Magazine Review ❏ Advertisement
❏ Reputation of New Riders ❏ Author Name

How would you rate the contents of this book?
❏ Excellent ❏ Very Good
❏ Good ❏ Fair
❏ Below Average ❏ Poor

What other types of certification products will you buy/have you bought to help you prepare for the exam?
❏ Quick reference books ❏ Testing software
❏ Study guides ❏ Other

What do you like most about this book? Check all that apply.
❏ Content ❏ Writing Style
❏ Accuracy ❏ Examples
❏ Listings ❏ Design
❏ Index ❏ Page Count
❏ Price ❏ Illustrations

What do you like least about this book? Check all that apply.
❏ Content ❏ Writing Style
❏ Accuracy ❏ Examples
❏ Listings ❏ Design
❏ Index ❏ Page Count
❏ Price ❏ Illustrations

What would be a useful follow-up book to this one for you? _____
Where did you purchase this book? _____
Can you name a similar book that you like better than this one, or one that is as good? Why? _____
_____

How many New Riders books do you own? _____
What are your favorite certification or general computer book titles? _____

What other titles would you like to see New Riders develop? _____

Any comments? _____
_____
_____

Fold here and Scotch tape to mail

Place
Stamp
Here

New Riders
201 W. 103rd St.
Indianapolis, IN 46290